D0710424

Environmental *Renaissance*

Environmental *Renaissance*

EMERSON, THOREAU & THE SYSTEMS OF NATURE

by Andrew McMurry

The University of Georgia Press Athens and London

© 2003 by the University of Georgia Press

Athens, Georgia 30602

All rights reserved

Designed by Sandra Hudson and Stephen Johnson

Set in Bulmer with Edwardian display by Bookcomp, Inc.

Printed and bound by Thomson-Shore, Inc.

The paper in this book meets the guidelines for permanence
and durability of the Committee on Production Guidelines
for Book Longevity of the Council on Library Resources.

Printed in the United States of America

07 06 05 04 03 c 5 4 3 2 1

Library of Congress Cataloging-in-Publication Data

McMurry, Andrew.

Environmental renaissance : Emerson, Thoreau,
and the systems of nature / by Andrew McMurry.

p. cm.

Includes bibliograhical references and index.

ISBN 0-8203-2530-9 (alk. paper)

1. Environmentalism—United States—Philosophy.

2. System theory.   I. Title.

GE197 .M36 2003

179'.1—dc21   2003001800

British Library Cataloging-in-Publication Data available

Contents

Preface

During my undergraduate years as a biology major, to my disgust and fascination I spent a good deal of time killing small animals. While preserved supply-house monkeys, rats, and frogs were the laboratory staples, limnology, entomology, fish biology, invertebrate physiology, and field studies all required ample fresh sacrifices. I have especially choice memories of the collection expeditions: sifting through the muddy contents of dredges for crayfish, snails, and insect larvae; baiting vole traps in a big meadow we dubbed the killing fields; and tramping along creek beds indiscriminately electroshocking hundreds of minnows, creek chubs, mud puppies, and lampreys. My classmates and I identified, bottled, and labeled them, then took them back to the basement of the Biology Museum, an old house the department owned near campus. I vividly recall the first time I walked into that storeroom with an armful of minnow jars: I was astonished to discover that it already contained shelf upon shelf of jars of the same species. It suddenly occurred to me that each year there would have to be a new harvest of specimens, produced by a new class of students learning the essence of the discipline from their study of tiny corpses. My father, grandfather, and great-grandfather were all geographers specializing in what today would be called environmental studies, but I think it was at that moment the family business began to wind down.

It would not be true to say that it was the faunal body count alone that eventually led me to switch tracks and move into the humanities. That sort of sensitivity had little disciplinary capital. You quickly developed the detachment of the technician that most students in such programs went on to become. Even as you learned to appreciate its endless stock of beautiful solutions to the problem of survival, you became reckless with life. That is because each individual instance of life is, from the technical perspective, superfluous. In an odd way, life becomes its own example, with the population or genome you imagine standing behind a given animal more tangible than the animal itself. Species count, not specimens. No, I think it was more the repetitiveness and even banality of trying to understand life by fixing it, of swapping the rich context of the living for the pared down context of the lab, that soured me on the whole program. I am quite sure that much of my disenchantment stemmed from my own desultory engagement with the discipline, and I know that many of its practices have had to change in the last twenty years, but at the time the life science felt to me like a branch of archaeology. It was as if I were studying a fantastically vital civilization that collapsed and petrified whenever I put a hand toward it.

Nevertheless, I completed the degree. Afterward, when I was contemplating graduate studies in English, I asked a professor from whom I had taken a course in American literature, a man who thirty years earlier had launched his impressive career with an important book on Robert Frost, about the purpose of advanced scholarship in English. I wanted a signal from him that his discipline could be consequential in the way that I still understood biology to be. Perhaps—and I learned later how tired this idea was—I wanted to hear something that would convince me that humanistic scholarship could act to brake or counterbalance the chilly arrogance of science. He seemed to sputter before he answered, though it may have been an indication of his impatience with the question. The purpose of literary studies? "Why, for dialogue!" he exclaimed.

That response has stayed with me, and sometimes I think it wonderfully suggestive and other times breathtakingly inane. If you are like me and you cannot bear the charge that scholarly work in literature and language is one of the least consequential activities in the modern university, then you might understand why I find his answer so vexing. If we imagine the many ways dialogue can serve to raise consciousness, and thereby transform the person and by extension the culture she inhabits, then the answer serves: dialogue in literary studies is simply a roundabout way of taking on the "real world," with the discipline fully open to its larger social environment, quite capable of stimulating and changing it, if only at a snail's pace. But if we admit how infrequently dialogue in literary studies is truly productive of anything but more dialogue in literary studies, then we must ask ourselves whether or not its conversations are generally too closed, too self-referential, and too academic to affect the discipline's environment in any significant way. Is it enough to put on the harness of pedagogy, take up the bit of scholarship, and mumble "Dialogue!" for the rest of your career in response to the legitimate question, "So what exactly does a literary critic *do?*" For my part, what I have decided "for dialogue!" has to mean is this: my professor was right, the study of literature is about the dialogue, but we are obliged to always think about what the dialogue is doing. And whether it seems to be doing something or doing nothing, we should want to know how and why.

This book began with a hunch that we could use a more interesting dialogue about the inability of human societies to *not* destroy their environments. I want to think that the dialogue introduced in this book is indeed interesting. But I know that *interesting* is a rather weak descriptor, and especially so when rubbing shoulders with a strong concept like environmental destruction. Yet any word more muscular—say, a word like *better*—would raise hackles and smack of immodest pretensions. More important, *better* would signal that I believe dialogue in literary studies can be transformative and not conservative, open to its environment and not closed off from it, talking to the world and not simply talking to itself. I would be signaling, too, that I think the dialogue I hope to prompt with this book would be of that type: transformative, open, and consequential. However, my certitude about these matters is precarious, my goal much more modest, and this book no manifesto or call to arms. Its central thrust is simply that we must think through more rigorously the effects of dialogue (or communication) in general and, more to the point, the effects of ecocritical dialogue on the thing—the *oikos*—that ecocriticism is nominally about. In a nutshell: What does ecocriticism *do?* What can dialogue about nature, from the vantage of literary studies, make happen? Whether something or nothing, we want to know how and why. So this is finally a book that addresses ecocritical theory, not ecocritical practice, even though it is precisely the question of *practice* that I think is in the end most crucial.

On that score, our current environmental vocabulary seems to exude a confidence in environmental praxis we have never—I repeat, never—earned: *sustainability, conservation, renewability, cleanup* are the high-toned markers in this lexicon. Words like these might prompt one to suppose that a regime of positive environmental health actually exists or is on the horizon. But despite what we may hear about the improving state of the environment, on the scale that counts (the planetary one), nothing is truly sustained, conserved, renewed, or cleaned up. Even so, the prestige words of the environmental vocabulary have currency not just with those corporations or governments that want to greenwash their nongreen activities: they are the coin of the realm, too, among environmentalists—in other words, among those who should know better. The rhetoric of nature, even now at nature's end time, draws strength from its embeddedness in the can-do culture of American enterprise. The future security of the American economy, Al Gore argued in his unsuccessful presidential bid of 2000, lies in the high-tech environmental technologies of the twenty-first century. Predictably, he also argued that the future of the American environment lies in a robust and healthy economy. Perhaps he was right; perhaps the "low-impact" drilling practices that inevitably will extract oil from the Arctic National Wildlife Reserve are the sort of win-win proposition he had in mind (though, of course, I am well aware he was specifically against opening up ANWR). But my point is this: when they become vital to the continuation of the human project, even the last remnants of wild nature can be made to look like stakeholders in that project. To save the environment we must creatively destroy it. Emboldened by our pressing needs, having satisfied ourselves we have done all we can to safeguard the planet's interests without seriously exposing our own, we blast and pump away. And fortified by our customary confidence in *technē* and that smiling-in-the-face-of-danger American optimism that says, "in the end most things have a way of working themselves out," well, who knows? Caribou might indeed learn to love pipelines.

The reader may detect a note of sarcasm. Actually, I have no objection to describing our environmental situation, as the pioneering ecocritic Joseph Meeker advocated, in a comic narrative frame, wherein we tell the story of a glass half full—and trust that more water is on the way. But temperamentally I cannot help thinking that the glass is really half empty, like the Ogallala aquifer, and that to no one's amusement it continues to drain. (Some platitude here about the realist being made to look like a pessimist by the optimist.) My gut says that our moment on earth is a thoroughly tragic one, and my impulse at the outset of this project was to pick up the glass and angrily dash whatever water was left on as many hopes as I could. My impression was that ecocritics were far too pleased with their invention of a field, with the elation that justifiably comes when one finds a way to express personal convictions in professional work. I, too, was initially buoyed by ecocriticism's recovery of the "environmental real" in literature. But I became concerned that ecocriticism seemed content to create yet another specialized, genteel conversation about literary history, aesthetics, or reception that belied the absolute centrality of environmental decline to those of us living in the here and now, and to our children who will follow. I wanted ecocriticism to do more than study the four types of engagement that Lawrence Buell says works of environmental imagination provide: vicarious connection with others, including nonhumans; reconnection with places; direction for alternative futures; and inspiration to cherish the physical world (*Writing*, 2). All are laudatory foci for a new school of criticism, to be sure, but I wanted to remind ecocritics that this was not just *any* school of criticism. The point should not have been simply to show that literature was saturated with the *oikos* more deeply than had hitherto been understood; the point was that our species was outstripping the planet's capacity to support life, and what were we literary intellectuals going to do about it.

I found, however, that the tragic frame cannot be inhabited for long. It is a frame that is finally impatient with theory and criticism, finding them inert and ultimately moribund, and thus it is not a frame a theorist or critic can adopt and still believe in the value of his sort of labor. Fortunately, experience tells us that the line between describing the world and changing it, between putting up with it and struggling with it, is, contra Marx, tantalizingly if uncertainly porous. So no matter that the "environmental renaissance" of this book's title began as a cynical homage to F. O.

Matthiessen's *American Renaissance* (in particular the quite true but nevertheless
infuriating little observation, "what drew man out in Concord, what constituted a
major resource unknown to cities, was the beauty of his surroundings" [157], which
manages, in one breath, to condescend to nature, minimize Emerson and Thoreau's
understanding of it, and pit it against the rest of the world); no matter that I still
believe firmly that the world will be unrecognizable in a few decades; no matter
that I know the dialogue the world needs most is nothing like the one found in
these pages or anywhere else in ecocriticism: I have learned that one simply cannot
write a book of this sort without some faith in better things to come, along with the
concomitant faith that one's lucubrations are not wholly sterile and productive of
nothing. Yes, the Earth we are making saddens me to my core. But, for better and
for worse, our species seems constitutionally incapable of dwelling forever on its
abjection. We are all Panglossians at some level. Call it a survival advantage. If the
short term looks grim, take the long view. If the long view appears dire, live in the
moment. As Emerson says, "Up again, old heart!" Humans, intellectuals included,
persevere. And that is not to make any great claim for perseverance: it is simply an
observation about something we do as we go about our day, along with getting out
of bed and thinking about dinner.

   In any event, the practical problem for me was how to write a book that could
grapple with the literary apprehension of the end of nature in neither tiresomely
apocalyptic tones nor aridly academic ones; that could track the precariousness
of our environmental condition from its earlier glimmerings in the century and
literature that most interested me to its likely ruin in the not-too-distant future
(which is really right now); yet that was intellectually satisfying to work on, did
not feel too much like self-induced trauma, and avoided the pitfall of thinking it
replaced the work of culture that it described. I did not want to feign a hope I do
not feel, but neither did I want to reject hope entirely as the condition of possibility
of survival itself, and something without which intellectual endeavor is merely ten-
fingered exercise. Frankly, we do not need any more books that blame humanity
for being human; even environmentalists are all too willing to insist that the cause
of our brutishness is not in the stars but in us. Recognition, guilt, self-loathing,
and atonement can presumably follow, the implication being that we are repairable,
albeit after an enormous amount of soul-searching. But for reasons I discuss many
times in this book, a corrective idealism based on reawakened human powers and
potentials for self-improvement is a conceit we can ill afford. The moral education
of the human species is ongoing, but I am not holding my breath for the kind of
ethical bootstrapping it would take to undo thousands of years of near-hardwired
anthropocentrism.

   I would rather we did focus on the stars, as remote as they seem. How do you stop a cat from killing birds? You do not do it by remonstrating with her or tampering with her brain with a view to altering her character. You do it by changing her environment or the way she can operate in it: move the birdfeeder, put a bell around her neck, allow her outside only at night. If ever in our mode of engagement with the natural world we are to become posthumanist—and I think that is as good a name as any for the orientation we must aspire to—let us apply ourselves to those things we might actually be able to put right: not our genes or psyches or souls but rather the constellations of social communication that enable and disable all our actions, for these are the environments within which human beings operate. In systems theory we find a language that may help.

This book was not meant to be an open-ended project, but it often seemed like one. In the course of its completion it was finished several times. I thank the circle of friends, colleagues, and family who helped me bring it around to its current state of closure. From them I received much support and feedback, including critical comments and insights, awkward silences, knee-jerk responses, useful misreadings, gauntlet throw downs, perturbations, approbations, and inspirations, most of which managed to penetrate the boundary and were more or less absorbed. Some will have no idea how they helped; others know very well: Katherine Acheson, Catherine Boeckmann, Karen Boersma, Beth Cooperman, Robert Cooperman, Courtney Denney, Patrick Gonder, Nathan Houser, Edgar Landgraf, William Major, Cameron McMurry, Charles McMurry, James McMurry, Rebecca Merrens, Michael Merrill, Lewis Miller, Alexander Reid, Lee Sterrenburg, and Glenn Stillar. I thank especially Daryl Ogden for his work on my and others' behalf as Brittain Fellow Coordinator at Georgia Tech. He is the best and the brightest, and it is a great loss for today's academy that it could not hold him. I also thank two anonymous readers for the University of Georgia Press for their observant, detailed responses to the manuscript.

I thank Cary Wolfe for his generosity and for his example. Anyone who knows his work will see that mine was already measured out by his compass.

Lastly, I thank my inner circle: John and Mary McMurry for drawing the circle, Ellen Koehler for filling it in, and Jack for the other side of the distinction.

Abbreviations

Ralph Waldo Emerson

CW: *The Collected Works of Ralph Waldo Emerson.* Ed. Robert Spiller et al.
4 vols. Cambridge, Mass.: Harvard University Press, 1971–.

W: *The Complete Works of Ralph Waldo Emerson.* Ed. Edward Emerson.
Centenary Edition. 12 vols. Boston: Houghton Mifflin, 1903–1904.

Niklas Luhmann

ES: *Essays on Self-reference.* New York: Columbia University Press, 1990.

SS: *Social Systems.* Trans. John Bednarz with Dirk Baecker. Stanford: Stanford
University Press, 1995.

Henry David Thoreau

T: *Henry David Thoreau.* Ed. Robert Sayre. New York: The Library of
America, 1985.

NH: *Natural History Essays.* Salt Lake City: Peregrine Smith, 1980.

Environmental *Renaissance*

The Problem of Nature

I am sure you remember the plain citizen Jourdain in Molière's Bourgeois
Gentilhomme *who, nouveau riche, travels in the sophisticated circles of the
French aristocracy, and who is eager to learn. On one occasion with his new
friends they speak about poetry and prose, and Jourdain discovers to his
amazement and great delight that whenever he speaks, he speaks prose. He is
overwhelmed by this discovery: "I am speaking Prose! I have always spoken
Prose! I have spoken Prose throughout my whole life!"*

*A similar discovery has been made not so long ago, but it was neither poetry
nor prose—it was the environment that was discovered. I remember when,
perhaps ten or fifteen years ago, some of my American friends came running
to me with the delight and amazement of having just made a great discovery:
"I am living in an Environment! I have always lived in an Environment! I
have lived in an Environment throughout my whole life!"*

*However, neither M. Jourdain nor my friends have as yet made another
discovery, and that is when M. Jourdain speaks, may it be prose or poetry,
it is he who invents it, and likewise when we perceive our environment, it is
we who invent it.*

Heinz von Foerster, "On Constructing a Reality"

In the most uncompromising circles of environmentalism, the contemporary global
economy is rhetorically constructed as a ruthless, greed-driven, self-defeating assault
on nature. Anthropomorphisms of this sort are understandable, *cris du coeur* that
have their uses. Nature is registered by the economy in only two ways: as *externality*
or *resource*—outside the economy, in other words, or inside it. Neither side of the
line is preferable: if outside, nature is simply not part of the economy and therefore
irrelevant; if inside, nature is little more than fodder for the ongoing operations
of the economy. From the perspective of nature, it is safe to say, the economy is a
problem with no upside.

Some argue, then, for the adoption of a "natural" perspective, a perspective they
believe would provide some relief, some solution to the problem of the economy.
"Nature is always right," Goethe said. If only we knew the question! Unfortunately,

as participants and coproducers of the economy, humans necessarily speak from the inside of the distinction described above. No matter the use to which nature is put—good, bad, indifferent—nature remains for humans a resource for further thought or action, but never an external standpoint from which to launch a critique against the inside of the distinction. To speak out of nature against the economy would require a subject position that cannot be occupied because by definition it does not exist.

So what might happen if, in a counterintuitive move, we reversed the terms in our problem/solution equation? Our postulates then would be as follows: Let the economy be a solution to the problem of nature. Let the latter pose a complex and thereby threatening set of possibilities for human society. Let the economy be a social evolutionary response to this threat. Let the economy deal with the threat by absorbing natural uncertainty, by effectively rendering it into more easily metabolized quantities, say, money.

On first blush, I think most of us would find this reformulation disturbing and unpalatable, politically and ethically disabling, no more than an up-to-date version of the primal fear that transfixed early *Homo sapiens* as he sat staring out beyond the protective ring of firelight. Nature a threat? Not since the invention of the steam engine, the chainsaw, penicillin, sunscreen. . . . In any case, not for a long time. Extreme weather excepted, nature—for now, defined capaciously as whatever comes to mind when we hear that word—has by and large been rendered quite amiable. But the threat here is really just a function of the economy's observation that it lies at the shallow end of a gradient of complexity; as a system (a set of interrelated elements that controls its own inputs and outputs through a boundary) it lacks the requisite variety to confront its environment (the external correlate to the system, or whatever is not the system, in other words) on even terms. It cannot map the territory point-to-point, cannot take account of its environment's possibilities; hence it is at perpetual risk of being overwhelmed by uncertainty. An environment always contains many more possibilities than does any given system, especially if the elements that compose that system—as is the case with social systems—are evanescent things like words, coins, pieces of paper, or other tokens of communication. The environment of the economy, for example, contains not only nature with all its various organisms, forces, and processes, but people too, along with their art, politics, cars, soda pop, chalk and cheese, and on and on. The economy by contrast consists only of the communication programs and operations that produce decisions about whether money is paid or not paid. The fact that the economy is so limited in its vision of the world is what makes the threat to it so palpable: the economy cannot even begin to entertain the radical contingency that environmental complexity presents. To stabilize its relationship with the environment, to ensure the environment does not inundate it with innumerable choices and stimuli that would require time- and energy-sapping responses, the economy must close itself off to most of those possibilities, allowing only the meager coupling that furthers its continued operations and reaffirms its single-minded vision. What would happen to the economy, for example, if it had to determine not simply whether or not a vein of coal was worth mining but whether or not the coal was beautiful, sacred, or, in what to the economy is the most outrageous non sequitor, whether mining was morally good or bad? The economy would founder on the limitations of its own basic presuppositions, which seek only to produce a decision as to whether or not the mine will pay. Any costs external to that decision simply do not concern the economy. Only if morality came with a price tag could it penetrate the fog—but then pricelessness is what morality must preserve to be moral.

So upon reflection the advantages of our reformulation become clear: just as we do not seek the roots of racism among the victimized or the treatment for psychopathy in the psychopath's prey, we should not look to nature for a corrective to the economy. The perverse logic of the economy emerges from its own internally motivated struggles for organizational coherence and stability. The casualties cannot be held accountable—or called on to explain, propitiate, and otherwise mediate—the contours of that logic, for they are not truly problems except in the worldview of the racist, the psychopath, or in the operations of the economy. Casualties at best provide evidence of pattern, of a consistent appetite for and method of destruction. True, in the absence of potential victims, the destruction could not occur. But no one can believe that the origin of the malignancy lies in the substrate in which it manifests itself. The malignancy, in the case of the economy, is nothing more than the banality of the economy's own vision of things. The scorpion is not evil, says an old fable, though its nature is to sting.

In other words, we should not expect to comprehend the solution that is the economy by looking beyond the economy, toward some ground of appeal just waiting to be brought to the inner side of the distinction where it would instantly clarify the poverty of the economy's operations and reveal a solution to what is in fact already a solution. We—humans in the environment of the economy who are paying attention, that is—know all too well that nature is a problem only in the economy's own self-fashioning. Certainly, while any one of us may look beyond the economy to locate in nature that which makes *individual* understanding urgent and necessary (loss of biodiversity and lifeways, pollution, global warming, animal cruelty, ugliness), an understanding of the economic system in no way depends on a prior understanding of nature (as the economy itself knows all too well). Nature, as part of the broader environment of the economy, is in fact that horizon of unactualized pluripotentiality that is meaningless in the eyes of the economy until the operations of the economy itself make it meaningful. And then, as I have already said, as money and money alone.

But renouncing the right to speak on behalf of nature, this part of the economy's environment that has always been crammed with meaning, is something ecocritics are not likely to do. Nature is the crucial topos, the object of desire and the resource for their own self-fashioning. So ecocritics continue to seek the solution to the solution by reference to nature. They steer with nature as their compass.

And the economy? It sails on: oblivious to nature, its compass itself, destruction its wake.

So who is really blind?

This book is meant to be a contribution to ecocriticism, an anxious genre in which the stuff of language, literature, culture, and nature are combined to express the fears, hopes, insights, and values of ecocritics. Like all literary criticism aimed at worldly concerns, this book would appear to outsiders as an extraordinary mishmash of arrogance, naivety, and faith: arrogance, because at some level I presume that a study of literature can have worthwhile things to say to the world; naivety, because at some level I trust that the world might be willing to listen; and faith, because at some very deep level I believe, to paraphrase Foucault, that people know what they do, they know why they do it, and if only they knew what *what they do does* they would stop doing it.

More to the point: this book is a work of criticism informed by recent developments in biology, cognitive science, critical theory, environmental philosophy, and most centrally, systems theory, the integrative discipline that studies patterned complexity. I take as my starting point nineteenth-century American thinking about nature, and I follow that thinking into the present time. This book, however, is not a paean to nature, nor even a lament to its loss. I consider nature to be a multi-faceted blockage that social systems like the economy seek to ignore, incorporate, or perhaps most politely, handle. In what will be a constantly unsettling approach, I write about nature largely from the perspective of these social systems, attributing to them motivations and interests they clearly do not possess; and when I write about the nature-perspective of conscious systems (i.e., people) I do so only insofar as their perspectives coincide or conflict with those of the social systems, as if people's motives could ever be so simple. A precondition for entering the space of this book is the willingness to imagine that systems use humans to accomplish system-related chores. (For a generation of critics schooled in structuralism and poststructuralism, this should not too much to ask.) By the end of this book, *system* will have been reified to a degree that the point I make now may seem unconvincing: systems really do exist as items in the world, but equally they are abstractions drawn for the purposes of an observer. This ambiguity will be understood as a positive feature of the theory.[1] I say little about nature itself as a system, or as a set of many overlapping systems. Rather, nature exists as something either systematized by society (becoming the focus of internally significant communications) or externalized by society as uncommunicative environment.

These are all necessary theoretical moves, and I do not make them because I dislike *nature* and prefer the shapeless notion of *environment*. Instead, I want to think about how primary, nonhumanized nature—which holds for many of us incomparable power and beauty but evidently none for social systems like the economy—has been *systematically* expunged from the world, to be replaced by what Marx called "second nature," a human-centered, technoecology that overwrites the preexisting one. Even in its most nature-considerate, forward-looking iterations (those I later call the neopastoral, a term that gestures not only to a reduction and rearrangement of wild nature but to the creation of new, unheard of natures from scratch), this technoecology may have only the briefest future: its instabilities are real, its stabilities merely hypothetical.

My discussion, focusing as it does on literary and cultural prefigurations of this systematic replacement of nature, is itself only hypothetically stable; I offer little more in this book beyond a certain self-limited and temporally bounded insight. This is because notwithstanding the moral, aesthetic, and practical reasons one might offer as to why this replacement is dangerous, it is clear that the replacement is a fait accompli, so that "insight" can no longer pretend to survey the problem from a favored, inside-looking, exterior vantage point. In-sight is out; or rather, it is internally deported into the welter of competing, crosscutting, and often mutually exclusive observations. As Ulrich Beck notes, the "remoulded nature devoid of nature is the socially internalized furniture of the civilized world: work, production, government and science at once reconstruct it and furnish it with the norms by whose yardsticks it is to be judged to be endangered and damaged" (*Ecological*, 37). This self-referring nature is now just the world as we find it; we cannot go back to what we had before, whatever we think that was, no matter that you and I believe it was better. We are engaged today in projects of triage, salvage, and restoration, and nothing about even these motley operations is in any way assured. What we would like to do as ecocritics is to find the means by which the resources of culture—at least that part of culture that admits of some stake, however defined, in the creation of a nature-affirming society—could be activated, mobilized, and deployed against what we think we are up against (and defining *what* we are up against will be one of the goals of this book). In this million-fronted war, ecocritics should be content to rhapsodize about nature unreservedly only when a number of things have come to pass: smog no longer chokes babies in their cribs and elders in their sick beds;

organs rife with toxin-inspired tumors are not routinely excised and disposed of as hazardous waste; no incentive exists to dynamite ocean reefs to stun potential aquarium fish; spraying lawns or forests to weed out "trash species" is viewed with the opprobrium it merits; birds and creatures of the land and sea do not die in their billions by coming into contact with skyscrapers, power lines, lead shot, oil slicks, settling ponds, poisoned baits, bolt guns, lab technicians, our feces, their own feces, our tastes, our conveniences, our amusements, our whims; waste disposal is not the primary growth industry in certain African countries and on American Indian reservations; any child can catch and hold a frog in the palm of her hand if she wants to; cars run on sunlight or something even more benign and not a single new road is built because, at last, we realize we do not have to disrupt every quiet corner of this world; everybody knows which direction is north and where the water in their drain is going. Each of these items in this by no means exhaustive list has its own constituency and ongoing relief effort, and the ones that feature sympathetic human players will likely be dealt with first. But nothing is really sure except that in the short and middle terms things will get worse.

A book of this sort invites its writer to reclaim his genre in some new way, to offer a note of hope, or to claim that if only readers will see the problem in the manner outlined or adopt the stance here modeled, somewhere down the road good things will happen. The work of theory, in this view, is to describe problems and situations in ways that might lead to improved practice. But the theory espoused here cannot possibly aim at improving practice for the reasons sketched out above. The best it can aim at is a *prodding* of other theory: I argue that ecocritics must take account of the obstacles to theory *before* they can go about their good work of not just describing the world but changing it. To put the task of this book less obliquely: ecocriticism in its nascent stages has tended to focus on the cultural resources available for critique (literature and other writings about nature, important authors and figures, environmental history and philosophy, ecocritics' own feelings about nature), and it has worked to develop claims about how these resources can be of value to further environmental perception and action. Customarily, the materials to which ecocriticism is applied are held up for aesthetic or psychic inspection or, more radically, probed for relations of power and authority. As with all literary criticism the stakes can be low and high, restricted to issues of interest mostly to other critics or, in what is often the case, framed as vital questions for cultural and identity politics. In ecocriticism, of course, those politics are framed in the context of the cultural discourse of nature. And, as always, it is difficult to say what the critical activity actually *does* (and trying to determine what it does is often part of the critical activity too) because no one knows precisely how the critique of cultural artifacts leads to change in culture and, even more searchingly, change in the structures and processes of society. On the one hand, some argue that all of this is beside the point: the proper study of theory is theory, and praxis can look after itself. On the other, some entertain a far too grandiose vision of what theory can do, a "typical illusion of the lector," Pierre Bourdieu explains, "who can regard an academic commentary as a political act or the critique of texts as a feat of resistance, and experience revolutions in the order of words as radical revolutions in the order of things" (*Pascalian*, 2). It is always difficult to know where to locate ourselves on any continuum (especially, to paraphrase Emerson, on one where we know not the extremes and often believe there are none), but I think it incumbent on ecocriticism to consider how it wants to connect its radiant focus, nature, to the mechanisms of society that are crushing nature.

In short, there is great need for reflection on the *systemic* constraints to perception and action: how do you actually move from the cultural discourse of nature to the social, political, and economic action you would like to see undertaken? That move is doubly difficult for ecocritics because unlike cultural studies of race, gender, class, or nation, ecocriticism has the enormously daunting challenge of making a case for something that lies outside, communicatively speaking, human society itself. Nature, unlike even the most muffled human constituency, does not talk back. With no *thing* able to step forward and testify, ecocriticism typically reverts to its underlying idealism, its tacit moral mission to promulgate what it believes would be good not only for nature but for humans too: society's adoption of an ecocentric perspective. But to the extent that it succeeds in convincing itself that a pinched, speciesist morality (or lack of morality) is the root issue, ecocriticism cannot examine its *own* limitations by holding itself up to the inspection of other, amoral visions.

In other words, ecocriticism does the work of moral interpretation and suasion in the cultural sphere but does not theorize culture's integration into the encompassing social system, which has many other functional modes by no means amenable to morality.[2] In this sense, ecocriticism is not so different from those environmentalist perspectives that lambaste the economy for its "stupidity" and "greediness," appellations that fall implicitly on those people who facilitate its actions (and that can, depending on the emphasis, include every person save environmentalists or be restricted to corporate chiefs and politicians). Given the language game in which such terms are used, these sorts of descriptions hold. But where is the provision for galvanizing the economy—or people, if the economy is figured as the product of their collective will—to behave otherwise? Cursing the fox for entering the henhouse will not get him to stop. So I argue that moralizing is not the game for ecocriticism—no matter how much it interlards that moralizing with the language of critique. What has been missing, I believe, is the social theory that would give ecocriticism some measure of outreach to the world beyond the domain of the moral code—a code that, despite its power, expressivity, and status as the first refuge of the earnest and the well-meaning, is only one of the codes that society uses to observe not just nature but itself. I do not mean to argue for the exchange of a principled moralism for a utilitarian consequentialism; we all know that analyses of consequences implicitly draw on ethical frames anyway. But I am suggesting that morality, as a coding of the world into right and wrong actions, is only applicable to a narrow range of social phenomena; and thus it is code no less narrow-minded than the code of profit and loss.

This book is not critical theory in the sense of aiming to puncture the fabrications that hide a truer relationship to a truer nature. Ideology, says the old adage, turns culture into nature (and, incidentally, I would argue it turns nature into nature too). But I take the various ideologies of nature to be on display for all to see, no unmasking necessary. Nature, as a theme of communication, is just those masks, and critique itself must bring its own mask to the ball—and does so even when it wants to appear only as ideology's unmasker. This is not to say that behind all these masks there is not something that, according to an exhausted nomenclature, is "as real as it gets." But for a host of reasons I need not discuss here we have become convinced that we will never get past the masks and should not speak as if we can. Of course, one cannot discuss nature without acknowledging that it is a master trope used to confer power on certain groups in society. In this pejorative sense of ideology it is clear that some masks are uglier than others. So I stipulate to the ideological as constructions that bear constant monitoring and a rearguard action of deconstruction. But I am weary of critiques that reveal nature's constructedness only to leave us strangely enervated and let down, as if all along the game had been merely to remain critical. This book is not intended for those who cannot recognize ugly ideology when they see it.

Instead I want to cut through to something that offers a little more resistance: not to nature—human or otherwise, for both are dangerous, shaky grounds on which to build theoretical edifices—but to social systems, these consensual hallucinations that seem vaporous until you try to circumvent them. Social systems, of course, are themselves constructions; their boundaries appear and reappear each time we conform to them. But they are constructed very densely, and—unlike with ideology— scales will never fall from our eyes once we see them for what they are. Social systems are like balloons and ideologies are like gases: it does not matter what gas you put in the balloon so long as you fill it. Social systems, then, are not the product of ideology but rather presume the existence of ideology to keep them inflated. They are the hardest-wearing parts of modern existence, sturdy containers for communication that are far less brittle than inflexible, brute matter. You can more easily fell a forest with a handsaw than stop the economy from eying trees.

To put a finer point on this problematic, what I find compelling is the hypothesis that *the ideological construction of nature has no appreciable effect on the problem of nature from the perspective of a social system.* Any ideology is fine from that perspective so long as the nature thus constructed does not conflict with the organizational unity of the given system, which runs its basic programs independently of what we say about them. (In that sense, a system such as the economy is like a force of nature: describe it any way you must so as to navigate it, give it the shape and meaning that gratifies you, but it will still crush you if you get in its way.) The operations of the economy can preserve that organization with equal facility under the dogmas that produce "Love Your Mother [Earth]" or "Save a Logging Family, Shoot a Spotted Owl." In fact, both orientations can and do exist simultaneously. But do those who espouse the former and place the bumper sticker on a Volvo produce a different species of economic transaction than those who espouse the latter and put the bumper sticker on a logging truck? Does the fact that one buys steak and the other tofu mean that we are observing different orders of economic being? Ideologically the difference is significant, linked to the assumption that an emergent ethics of soft living will eventually push the system in the direction of tofu. But the best thinking right now says the only way to save nature is to buy it back from those who want to convert it into steak; and every time we do that what gets confirmed is that everything is for sale. As far as the economy is concerned, it is not what you buy that matters but the fact that you buy at all. Green capitalism turns out to be capitalism on a slow burn, sustainable development nothing more than sustained development with a duck pond next to the parking lot. The economy can still only ever buy, sell, or ignore nature. Using its own particular version of the program, even the socialist utopia when not oblivious to nature finds it infinitely fungible.

Let me follow this line of thought a little further. Every president since Richard Nixon has claimed to be an environmentalist (and thanks to the unforeseen, long-range economic implications of the EPA and the ESA, Nixon actually has the strongest claim); every day is Earth Day for George W. Bush (although one wonders if he has confused April 22 with April 1). More meaningful, there *has* been widespread awareness of the degradation of nature over the last forty years or so. When they are not ignoring that degradation, many Americans are wringing their hands over it, gamely waiting for somebody to do something. They do not want to see nature sullied; most hold nature in high regard, love and respect the great outdoors. Radical environmentalists would say that this condescension is in fact counterproductive, evidence of how the very structures of thought that animate our dealings with nature are conditioned by centuries of alienation, hatred, and homocentrism. In claiming to love nature, we give evidence of our psychological separation from it, betraying the fact that we see nature as just one more place to be visited and enjoyed, like Disney World or a mall. We no longer have any sense of our place *in* nature, the fact that we cannot ever be *out* of it, no matter where we imagine we are. Yet we behave toward nature as if we had a choice: "More nature?" "Yes, please!" In any event, this patronizing fondness for nature is said to be but a small glimmer in the overwhelmingly gloomy American relationship to nature, which is powerfully colored by a history of sexism, racism, self-loathing, deafness to the Other, Puritan self-righteousness and/or guilt, humanist arrogance, technophilia, and so on.

Yet most Americans, if they ever did, do not actively espouse a mechanistic notion of nature, or regard the land as a virgin to be raped, or have no sympathy for animals, or are demonstrably under the sway of any of the other bad conceptual regimes that are routinely linked with the decline of nature: instrumental reason, phallogocentrism, Christianity, Western civilization as whole. To buy into the bad worldview theory we would have to believe, in other words, that Americans' unconscious adherence to these hazardous thought regimes outweighs their conscious concern for and fascination with nature: their patronage of national parks, their membership in environmental organizations, their fondness for gardening, their horror when pets are abused or when whales are stranded. Trivial and banal expressions, to be sure, but one admires them popping up nevertheless—that is, given the heavy press of phallogocentrism and whatnot. In fact, all the ecophobic theory amounts to is the notion that Americans cannot stop hurting the thing they only pretend to love. I think this sort of harrowing of the national psyche is needlessly elaborate—even as it downgrades the nature problem to a case of unhealthful ideology. But where is the society that has ever produced a healthful one? When has humankind demonstrated anything other than a profound commitment to its own needs purchased at the cost of whatever gets in the way?

When one considers that virtually every culture on this planet has begun its descent into disharmony with nature at about the same moment that it invented agriculture, or perhaps just came into possession of a burning splint, one must conclude that such notions as the Cartesian split or the Protestant work ethic cannot be the critical loci of our disenchantment. This is not to say that these epochal paradigms are unconnected to the issue; they clearly have effects around the edges of the nature problem, in the sense that every civilization has pursued its own idiosyncratic path toward ecodisaster. To be sure, what people believe has an impact on what they do on and to this fragile earth. But we must disabuse ourselves of the notion that the history of big ideas can be strongly correlated with ecological history. To deem worldviews the proximate causes of environmental degradation is a category error, as counterfactual as saying that pollen gathering by bees is caused by the ideology of honey. Our collective incursions into the natural order are better described—just as with other species—in terms of carrying capacity, niche, or adaptive radiation. China without communism still would have a billion peasants trying to feed themselves from the land; an America never discovered by Europe would have gotten around to extinguishing the buffalo too, just as it had already killed off the mammoth, the mastodon, and the giant sloth; and a West deprived of Greek rationalism would have grounded its reckless disregard of nature on something else—say, irrationalism. In fact, the real "arrogance of humanism" (to borrow David Ehrenfeld's catchy phrase) lies not in humanism's failure to think through the terrible earthly results of its anthropocentric program, but rather in its failure to notice that *all* human programs end with the same result: humans up, nature down. We have developed—or more properly, evolved—a social system that works to fulfill certain functional goals; to assume that this system is regulated by our cultural precepts and that it could be reoriented by new imaginings is a huge oversimplification, akin to thinking that calling the beehive a commune will change the way the bees go about their business. I anticipate the objection that the human social order is not the same as an insect's, and that to compare them is reductive. I agree wholeheartedly, and hasten to add that the comparison is not humanistic either. But that is precisely my point.

Pinning the blame on the flawed cultural constructs of a flawed humanism, in other words, misses the mark or, worse, aims at an all too easy mark. The steady decline in biotic integrity on Earth means that something more profound than the semantics of nature is affecting environmental quality. We must keep in mind that the human species has assumed what rightly can be called a geologic-scale role on this planet; the enormity of our impact should be understood in terms of that scale, not in terms of relatively puny cultural peccadilloes—which too often swell far beyond their importance in the minds of cultural theorists and critics, who would like to think their bailiwick covers the whole territory. Well, if they want to approach that territory, their own must necessarily recede. On this vaster scale, cultural attitudes toward nature look to be merely the local inflections and vernaculars that array themselves within a general process of social system enlargement and complexification that inevitably tears away at the natural environment. To reiterate: a belief system might determine that a society cannot devour cows, or that cannibalism is acceptable, or that eating meat is wrong altogether. But it will not stop people from requiring protein, or their social systems from striving to secure it by decomplexifying the natural order, one way or another.[3] The rationalization for the reduction might be called Hinduism or McDonald's; it might push the social system well beyond servicing nutritional needs and into the business of spiritual hygiene or gluttony enablement; and doubtlessly it will have ramifications for the lifeways of the society that hews to it—as well as the natural environment in which that society is embedded.

But the myth conforms to the systemic imperative and does not precede it, so that rewriting the myth is, to use the overworked but apt cliché, rearranging the deck chairs on the *Titanic.*

Obdurate, purblind, and dumb as dirt, a leading social system like the economy does not take kindly to overt cultural pressures; it openly defies them, or twists them into new opportunities to assert its logic, often producing bizarre, capricious outcomes. Accordingly we have dolphin-safe tuna and a collapse in the tuna population, protected wilderness areas with traffic and smog problems, natural foods to remind us that the rest of the food is killing us. Every solution is another problem elsewhere in the life web. Ban whale meat and instead vacuum up the krill on which the whale feeds: it is all the same to the economic system, which does not care what you eat but only that money has changed hands. The economy actually uses the paradoxes of modern life to create new, more invasive pathways for its operations. For example, *organically grown* equates to *not unnatural,* and so casts doubt on the other side of the line, the formerly normal, which once covered everything and so could remain unthought as the total horizon of the edible. Here then is a distinction that responds to justified fears by opening up fresh categories of compensatory consumption, new frontiers for the money system to stake out and lay claim.

It might be useful to resurrect in a slightly modified form the antiquated formula whereby ideology is an inversion of our real relationship to material: the ideology of nature is an inversion of our real relationship to complexity. In other words, we have gone too far in thinking ideology determines the way we act toward nature when in fact ideology is largely an allergic conceptual reaction to the increasing internal complexity of social systems. Humans have always invented myths to cope with that which does not respond to myths. But over the last two centuries we have fashioned a social world in which any myth is thinkable but none is adequate to this world's complexity. Against massive complexity all the old Weltanschauungs are clumsy and limited. So we adapt by replacing inconvenient, binding convictions with convictions of temporary convenience. When inevitably they too fail to be good in the way of belief we cut them loose and move on. Few of us, for example, care to believe that spirits inhabit the great forest trees now that most have been cut down to make toilet paper; better to think of them as renewable sources of fiber. The old beliefs are swept up into the flow of money, just as Jesus Christ is now a laissez-faire Republican. On the other hand, if one continues to worship in the ancient groves, one surely knows (and probably most clearly in the moment of supposed transcendence) that one is engaging not in sacred rite but in performance art.

The uncontrolled cupidity of economic realism and the sin-free spirituality of New Age religions make easy targets. Yet none of this hyperrelativism should be

understood cynically, for these newest mythologies are simply self-reflexive responses to modernity's untotalizable complexity; their shamelessness is revolting
but perfectly comprehensible. Situational knowledges, situational ethics, situational
practices: classic liberal causes rub elbows with resurgent, retrograde ideologies of
blood, ground, and god. The only common denominator to be found among these
varied regimes is that they all help the social system stabilize itself by keeping
differences in play rather than resolving them out of existence. Ecumenism and pluralism, in this view, should not be attributed to a willed widening of the franchise
or a flowering of human empathy but to the fact that the system prefers to keep
the lid on outright violence (i.e., systemic *impedance*) by opening up ideological
terrain for everybody. On the frontier of complexity anyone can homestead. Cultural
busywork, of whatever stripe, performs system work.

We pray that this is not a one-way street: it would be nice to think that the
positions the system prepares for us in advance are mutable, that culture is not all
hot air. Without some potential for human-led change, ecocritical theory would be
impotent, mere description of a process over which *no control is possible.* In fact, I
come up just short of saying precisely that, preferring to phrase the dilemma thus:
*attempting control under conditions of radical uncertainty may be as risky as doing
nothing.* (One would be tempted to seize the stick if the pilot collapsed, even if one
had no idea how to fly a plane.) Uncertain, then, of the reciprocal relation between
cultural praxis and system maintenance, and skeptical that switching cultural lenses
on nature would make much difference, I cannot identify the conceptual levers that
might readjust our precarious environmental balance. I have little insight into which
improved myths of nature—upon their improbable adoption by society—would get
that colossal job done most expeditiously. The theory I propound here, as I have
noted above, is not particularly good at recommending improved practices. We will
have to be content with diagnosis; prescriptions are for others to make.

Gary Snyder writes, "If the lad or lass is among us who knows where the secret
heart of this Growth-Monster is hidden, let them please tell us where to shoot the
arrow that will slow it down" (5). Well, the heart of the matter is that there is no
heart: no single organ pumps this beast's lifeblood. Still, we would like to know the
general direction in which to shoot some arrows, however ineffectually.[4] So the short
answer is that solutions cannot be found by switching ideological bait at the level
of human consciousness; solutions have to be approached at the level of systems'
interactions. Suffice it to say, then, that the political system must find a way to
restrain the economic system (and its handmaiden, technoscience) by transmuting
progressive ideas into electable propositions that can then be programmed into
appropriate and binding laws via the legal system. Ecotopia will soon follow! The
need for mainstream green politics is so great that the pursuit of them should occupy

the best minds of our time. How to create those politics, therefore, cannot be the goal of the writer of this book.

Instead, I must be content to explore how the grim situation in which we find ourselves arose and is maintained, despite the most strenuous efforts of many well-intentioned people and groups, ecocritics and nature writers included, and despite the fact that *things did not have to be this way*. Most of the problems that fall under the rubric of social systems theory (and, by the way, literary and cultural studies) are neither impossible nor necessary: they lie in the vast middle ground of the contingent. I take the nature problem to be of this type, which means that it is not theoretically insoluble—though practically it might well be. So while some (Freud, for example) have argued that the ultimate drive of conscious systems is to facilitate their own demise—and by extension that the final goal of our viral civilization is self-digestion—I assume that it is possible for people to *not* want to destroy themselves but still manage to do so as a result of the social systems they unleash. (Obvious examples here are the oversensitive systems of self-defense that triggered World War I and have yet to trigger World War III, the cult of statuary on Easter Island, almost every desert civilization that premised itself on irrigation, and various science fiction scenarios in which self-aware machines turn violently on their human masters.) At the most sweeping level, then, the questions are: How does a system become so good at preserving structural arrangements that may well be suicidal? Why does it insist on maintaining its ignorance of obvious environmental hazards? What are its normative horizons? Is there any way to get its attention? Prior to improvements in the status quo, then, we should know why what would seem to be a very disadvantageous state of affairs—the current destructive stance of our social system toward nature and hence itself—has been so magnificently successful.

At bottom, this book might be called a risk analysis that uses literary and cultural themes as its raw data. Not on the firm footing of morally riveting though as yet unrealizable notions of human and nonhuman liberation, but mired deep in the muck of contingency itself, which always unsettles (and usually gives the lie to) analyses of causality and predictions of future directions—that is where I want to locate this book. I want to examine that muck, even if it turns out to be quicksand.

The above concerns form the broad impetus behind this book. But to gain any kind of purchase on those concerns I must restrict my reach to a narrower cluster of written texts. I read, comment upon, and reconfigure these texts, many of which are themselves simply commentary on other texts. I situate this book, then, at a far remove from the primary text, nature, and I have only a slender hope that out of my intervention some definitive answers to the above questions will emerge—and an even slimmer hope that they will be of any interest beyond the academic audience for whom this book has been written. But I do have enough confidence in my intervention to be satisfied that the problem of nature will not be dissolved by those who refuse to consider nature as a problem for social systems in the first place. Wendell Berry, noting that the newer, scientific discourses of nature have helped render it mere mechanism, writes, "it is impossible to prefigure the salvation of the world in the same language by which the world has been dismembered and defaced" (*Life,* 8). So although Berry would heartily condemn the language I use (it is precisely the sort he objects to), I think in the realm of theory there is room to explore new vocabularies and indeed some obligation to do so.

My approach draws heavily on and provides an introduction to theories of *self-organizing, self-referential, complex social systems,* and in particular to the work of the sociologist Niklas Luhmann, who in turns draws on the cognitive biologists Francisco Varela and Humberto Maturana, the originators of the enormously influential concept *autopoiesis.* I also draw on Bruno Latour, whose theory of modernity provides a valuable counterweight to the above thinkers and a point of comparison between their work and other postclassical theories. (I say postclassical instead of postmodern because one of the issues here is whether the latter deserves its distinction as the successor to modernity—whether, in other words, we are relentlessly and in varying degrees always and only modern.) General systems theory and the related science of cybernetics once aimed at describing where we stood so that better control could be exercised over what we stood on; complex systems theory tells us that where we stand depends on where we stand, and control over the ground below is illusory or at best temporary. I develop the foundations of systems theory and cybernetics in chapter 2, and each subsequent chapter builds on and refines the theory. In particular, I pay very close attention to systems-theoretical accounts of epistemology. Indeed, the basic explanation for the modern nature problem is derived by observing the way that social subsystems, particularly the economy, establish their knowledge of self and environment. Much hinges on the idea that a system's ways of knowing its environment are not just constitutive of the environment, but that the system itself is constituted by its ways of knowing. The *formal constraints* that bear on these knowledges are the main generative principles of this book, with the implications for ecocriticism emerging from them.[5]

But I do not hew precisely to these theorists' frameworks in all matters. First, at bottom my work is not radically posthermeneutic in the way I imagine a true Luhmannian literary criticism would be. That is to say, I do not minimize the particular meanings that my exemplars, Ralph Waldo Emerson and Henry David Thoreau, thought they were making by emphasizing instead a broader communications archive that would better reveal the social systems' environmental program as it emerged in the nineteenth century. I adopt a more unadventurous stance: I take seriously what they say and assume others did too. In effect, Emerson and Thoreau are treated as privileged observers and creators, capable of both registering and redirecting certain currents of discourse; they are not merely nodes in the social program. I make no apologies for this approach: while another sort of book would evacuate their agency altogether, I confess I am still attached to the notion that the differences they defined made and still make a difference. They stand in my mind as the two central, indispensable voices of American literature—perhaps even more so today, given the delicacy of our environmental moment, than in their own time. They exerted a disproportionate and lasting impression on the American ideological landscape in general, and the American system of nature specifically. Their modes of observing nature redounded for generations, and we do well to examine those modes as we try to retool ours.

Second, I balk at systems theory's unappetizing ethical and political dimensions. As the reader will discover, systems theories have always sought totalizing frameworks for understanding social and natural phenomena. In my treatment of Luhmann, for example, it may be bad faith to embrace his systems analysis of modernity without also adopting his disempowering conclusions about ethics and politics vis-à-vis systems—in for a penny, in for a pound, as it were. But while I have already admitted I have no clear sense of the royal road from cultural critique to praxis to social system changes (as Luhmann calls it, "the issue of steering"), I do hold out hope that after the systems diagnosis there may still be, to borrow a term from Emerson's discourse on nature, "prospects." What those prospects may be I have only the barest inkling, but to that inkling I hold fast. (And here I suppose I am indulging in my own version of ecocritical idealism, which I roundly denounced earlier but without which the writing of any book about nature at this moment in history would be no more than self-flagellation.)

The book stages, then, the nature problem with the help of these two familiar literary/cultural figures, Emerson and Thoreau. The choice of these two may seem odd, even counterproductive, given that in the last analysis I am concerned more with the present and future of nature than its past. But they were indeed the public intellectuals of their time, and in a way that we, in our globalized, depersonalized, and fractionated epoch, can barely imagine (and, as I argue, can no longer expect to repeat), what they said did have broad and lasting consequences for the observation of nature. Thoreau's influence is well known and, given the activities undertaken in his name (e.g., the Walden Woods project), the T-shirts displaying his most quotable quotes, and the figures who point to him as an inspiration (e.g., Gandhi, virtually any environmental activist of note), apparently still quite palpable. Emerson's role has been less remarked. One goal of this book, then, is to study what Christopher Newfield calls in the context of politics "the Emerson effect" but here now with reference to his environmental legacy. Other obstacles to this study may be less obvious. The canonical status of these two and the critical heritage they entrain could easily make my use of them an uphill struggle, especially since in my conclusions I suggest that ecocriticism should *not* give any special priority to those writers whose work is, as theirs is, so obviously informed by the problem of nature. Additionally, I admit that it would have been impossible to produce a more unoriginal pairing of nature-friendly authors than Emerson and Thoreau. There is nothing fresh about my choices and, once again, I inveigh *against* firming up the green canon later in the book.

But there are very good reasons why these two figures must form the core of this study, even beyond the basic claim of influence (which is always difficult to quantify anyway). One is that their protoenvironmentalism helps me historicize the nature problem during a critical period in the North American context that particularly interests me. But it must be understood that *protoenvironmentalism* here refers to a systems theoretical view of environment, not an ecological one: it is *the way they process their observations of nature, and not the observations themselves,* that will be my focus. Accordingly, another reason for choosing them is that they write with a suggestiveness that resonates well with the themes of complexity, autonomy, and differentiation that are associated with contemporary theories of self-organizing systems; in effect, their protoenvironmentalism expresses the basic paradoxes that will always humble anyone who seeks to solve this problem from the side of nature. A final attraction is that because so much of contemporary ecocritical thought is brought to bear on writers of this period (and particularly Thoreau but to some extent Emerson), I am able to use these touchstone authors to help locate my differences with other ecocritics. So far ahead of their time in 1850, they rehearse the main schisms in environmental philosophy today—indeed, as I argue, they helped shape those schisms. The nineteenth century drew up the blueprint for our environmental house of cards, the twentieth century built the structure, and the twenty-first century will tear it down and rebuild it properly. Or it will not. In any case, revisiting some of this project's early observers will, I believe, repay the effort.[6]

Out of these attractions and obstacles I distill two central claims about the value of Emerson and Thoreau for the analysis of the nature problem, and my discussions of systems theory are developed around those claims.[7] I unfold them in greater detail in subsequent chapters, but I would like to preview them in the rest of this introduction.

The first claim is that we can lay a lot of what we understand today as American environmentalism at the feet of Thoreau and Emerson. Thoreau, who claimed that "in Wildness is the preservation of the world" (NH 112), is the forebear of the radical line of American nature-thought, the conviction that the nonhuman world ought to be accorded standing, and that naked anthropocentrism will lead only to our doom. This unabashedly moral vision, symbolized by the voice in the wilderness or the monkey wrench, persists in one form or another despite its ongoing failure to gain acceptance in the culture at large. But to the extent that Americans can continue to romanticize nature this vision will never be absent, and at certain moments of global and local crisis those who espouse it will come forward to blockade a logging road or ram a whaling ship—or perhaps merely write a check to those who do. Emerson, by contrast, is great-grandfather to the reformist vision, the pragmatic line that says though nature is indeed our "beautiful mother" (cw 1:36) it is in the last analysis meant "to serve. It receives the dominion of man as meekly as the ass on which the Saviour rode" (cw 1:25). The Emersonian line leads directly to the rational choice and risk assessment theories that bureaucratize our imaginative relationship with nature in the attempt to manage it wisely. When we hear of true cost pricing, the polluter pay principle, and natural capitalism, we know the good offices of the Emersonian line are being faithfully, if insipidly, discharged. Thoreau the preservationist (hands off nature!), Emerson the conservationist (use her prudently!): both nature lovers, to be sure, but one who felt it on the pulse, the other in the brain; Thoreau wishing to bury himself up to the neck in the actual earth, Emerson content to put his head in the clouds and look back at nature from on high. Still, both the radical and reformist strains symbolized by these two thinkers share the basic goal of reconciling competing *human* interests and perspectives—economic, aesthetic, political, and so on—through physical and intellectual fusion with nature, a bringing together of body, brains, and earth into productive harmony. (The real-world counterpart of this triangulation is, I argue, the pastoral, and I have much to say about the pastoralisms of the past, present, and future in this book.)

Now, nothing has been so common in the history of philosophy than to underwrite one's political and social vision with an argument from nature. Thoreauvian environmentalists, for example, hope that by giving nonhuman entities a hand up the ethical ladder, arrogant humans will be simultaneously brought back down to earth as equal partners in a re-enchanted, reanimated, properly ecological version of nature—with the net result, so to speak, that the lamb of fellow feeling will lie down with the lion of self-interest. In this tradition of radical ecology, we can find such dedicated antinomians as John Muir, Aldo Leopold, Gary Snyder, and David Brower. By contrast, Emersonian conservationists are content to manage competing human interests and scarce resources in the service of more or less utilitarian considerations: namely, the long-term mental and material well-being of humans themselves, who had best safeguard their environmental base if they know what is good for them. Theodore Roosevelt, Gifford Pinchot, Ernest Hemingway, Bruce Babbitt, and Al Gore are among the figures in the reformist tradition. In an imagined dialogue between the two traditions, we hear them squaring off during a walk through Concord and its pastoral environs: Say the Henrys: "Let us preserve nature for nature's sake alone. It is only right and good, and we ourselves would be enlarged by our efforts." "A childish fantasy," reply the Ralphs. "Understand that nature has always been about you. Save that part of nature that in doing so provides the greatest good for the greatest part of mankind."

A seemingly intractable argument, as old as philosophy itself, one that touches in at least some respect on any cleavage we could care to invoke: subject and object, self and other, human and animal, I and Thou. But—no surprise here—this neat distinction between a radical Thoreau and reformist Emerson is less real than imagined. Although it is certainly useful to play the two off each other (just as in the ecopolitical sphere the civilly disobedient organization Earth First! makes a good stalking horse for, say, the Sierra Club), in fact the distinction is wholly problematic. I say this not simply because Emerson was Thoreau's intellectual guru but because their versions of radical and reform environmentalism were actually two sides of the same coin: both were looking for correctives to bad *human* behavior, and one simply was willing to damn us more heartily through a vigorous praising of nature. So, to be sure, while there has been a great emphasis placed on the extent to which deep and shallow environmentalisms are prepared to decenter mankind—namely, the radicals a lot and the reformers not much at all—for me it all amounts to much the same. Deep ecologists, for example, proffer Aldo Leopold's still-revolutionary maxim that man must think of himself not as "conqueror . . . but plain member and citizen" of the natural community (240). Reform-minded conservationists, meanwhile, are content to invoke the concept of Christian good stewardship, a concept that keeps humankind very much at the hub of the universe while encouraging us to do right by creation through noblesse oblige. But note that in both cases, nature's rectitude is held up like a cudgel to compel humans to act properly: either as humble ecological egalitarians or reliable prelapsarian Adams.

I do not mean to say that there are not significant *practical* and *rhetorical* dimensions to ensuring that the role we cast ourselves in plays fair with nature. It does indeed make a big difference whether we are plain members or good stewards—and either is far better than the master-of-the-universe role that obtains in the hegemonic strain of environmental thinking, which is to say, the economically aligned vision I described earlier. But how radicals and reformers variously bear up under the anthropocentric burden does not seem to me a *theoretically* interesting problem. More interesting, I think, is the idea that they *both* bear this burden and, in point of fact, cannot *not* bear it. As I hope to demonstrate in this book, it is their common separation from an inaccessible, uncommunicative, environmental Other that tasks and troubles reformers and radicals alike. Human-centeredness, then, as one of the obligations of self-reference: this shared condition will finally signify much more for American environmentalisms—of whatever stripe and whatever degree of commitment—than anything that distinguishes them. I argue, then, that anthropocentrism cannot be defined in terms of varying degrees of speciesism or human chauvinism, or of unwillingness to grant the nonhuman ethical status (although a myopic disregard for nature is certainly a perennial feature of the condition I want to describe). I argue that the price of being a human is participation and cocreation of structures of meaning founded irreducibly on autonomy from environment. One observes a distinction between the human and environmental Others for reasons that are inherent to the operation of observation itself. As a consequence, I claim that any future politics of the environment must embed the problem of observation in its self-description and develop theory that does not demand that we relinquish that which we are required as observers to possess: a sense of *separation* from nature, from each other, and indeed from the society we have created. Such theory—theory comfortable with its failure to overcome differences that allow for no overcoming— would instead shelve stale arguments against anthropocentrism because the concept of human-centeredness is not something we can ever get beyond. Inwardness and self-reference are here to stay, a blessing and a curse. Humans and their societies are *systems*, and all systems use differences to maintain their autonomy and navigate their environments. But I acknowledge in advance that it will take a lot of work to show that turning humans into systems does not create more problems than it leaves behind.

Related to the above issues is the second central claim in this book: that Emerson and Thoreau both launch their protoenvironmentalisms within a sociopolitical framework that was very much unwilling to acknowledge its own blind spot, or even to recognize that it had one. This means that I read Emerson and Thoreau's reports from society about nature as quite discouraging despite their general, if not always specific, tone of ebullience. Preoccupied as we are in the twenty-first century with problems Emerson and Thoreau could never have imagined, any reports from them may seem to have arrived so late in the game as to be of little use. But, again, I want to make the argument about their work in a way that emphasizes their continuity with contemporary environmental thought and demonstrates the advantages a systems theoretical perspective can provide for ecocriticism.

United in their common separation from the nature they want to touch imaginatively, the Emersonian and Thoreauvian visions are, I claim, from a certain angle deeply tragic ones. By this I mean that these visions are undone by the spirit of can-do rationality in which they were conceived, namely, the logic of liberal humanism that made American environmentalism possible and continues to nurture it. That logic is defined by an economic drive to maintain one's self-possession and a political drive to acknowledge the self-possession of others. Liberalism is precisely about perfecting this state of affairs. Self-interest and democracy, in other words, can be made to coexist quite happily when the ratio of individual to social imperatives is at an optimum. Both Emerson and Thoreau sought this formula, wherein individualism would be maximized for the maximum number of individuals. Both triangulated self and society with nature. Thoreau did so by *grounding* self and society in wildness (nature knows best), and Emerson did so by proposing a self capable of *transcending* nature and society alike. For radical environmentalists, of course, Thoreau's strategy is appealing because it embodies what will become the first principle of ecocentrism, that all natural entities (from rocks to rivers to ravens) have rightful membership in the fraternity of being. For reform-minded conservationists, Emerson's transparent eyeballism means that they can stand proudly committed to nature in principle, all the while freeing its materiality in measured amounts for earthier projects of self-realization. Once more, we will find there is not a lot to choose between these visions, for in both lies the contradiction that renders the two branches of environmentalism inadequate to the nature problem they quite admirably wish to resolve.

Two examples to illustrate the identity of the difference. Compare Emerson on cranberries in a lecture version of "Resources" to Thoreau on them in his unfinished manuscript, *Wild Fruits*. [8] Emerson begins by opining that "all material wealth is in the hands of a people who have the facility of invention and practical usefulness" (*Uncollected*, 24).

> [An instance in point was found in the cranberry meadows of the regions of Cape Cod. Every acre of soil would bear a precious harvest, but how should it be transported? A hundred miles of jolting and rubbing would make the fruit worthless.] Can we then enclose each separate berry in an envelope to preserve it tenderly, as we do an orange? Yes, we will; and the inventor fills his barrel only partially with berries and then pumps water in it, and so every berry floated secure in its perfect liquid envelope across the Atlantic to a market. (*Uncollected*, 25)

Anticipating Clarence Birdseye, the one-time field naturalist and father of flash freezing, Emerson imagines the "precious harvest" as part of the "material wealth" of America, ripe for export once ingenuity has determined a way to satisfy the insatiable tastes of remote markets. More to the point, we see how Emerson uses the natural trope as a way to expound on the practical genius of the man, whereby nature is controlled through action, the mind concomitantly elevated, and a tidy profit made to boot. In another version of this lecture, Emerson exclaims, "We like to see the inexhaustible riches of Nature, and the access of every soul to her magazines" (w 8:137). But, he cautions, "The healthy, the civil, the industrious, the learned, the moral race,—Nature herself only yields her secret to these. And the resources of America and its future will be immense only to wise and virtuous men" (w 8:154). In the virtuous cycle of material and men, then, nature offers up its riches willingly to those of character while only those of character can extract nature's riches. The market itself, with inherent incentives to unlock the practical wisdom of men, becomes a moral enterprise, which nature yields to quite willingly.

Thoreau, in so many passages (and on so many different kinds of fruits!), would seem to hold the opposite view, that in taking berries to market we lose their natural taste and they become mere tokens of the market's tastelessness, and by extension, the practical ignorance of men. But it is not that he has no use for the market—indeed, he almost speculated in cranberries himself (*Wild,* 105)—it is rather that what he wants to get from nature is antipractical and antimarket at its root. And what that is, we might say, is the getting away from culture, the curative/corrective that nature provides. Writing of some of the remote cranberry grounds he has visited, he notes:

> I enjoyed this cranberrying very much, notwithstanding the wet and cold, and the swamp seemed to be yielding its crop to me alone, for there are none else to pluck it or to value it. I told the proprietor once that they grew here, but he, learning that they were not abundant enough to be gathered for the market, has probably never thought of them since. I am the only person in the township who regards them or knows of them, and I do not regard them in the light of their pecuniary value. I have no doubt I felt richer wading there with my two pockets full, treading on wonders at every step, than any farmer going to market with a hundred bushels he has raked, or hired to be raked. . . . I would gladly share my gains, take one or twenty into partnership and get this swamp with them, but I do not know an individual whom this berry cheers and nourishes as it does me. When I exhibit it to them I perceive that they take but a momentary interest in it and commonly dismiss it from their thoughts with the consideration that it cannot be profitably cultivated. (167–68)

Anyone who has read even minimally in Thoreau knows that his work is replete with these sorts of observations. Nature yields up so much more to us when left in its wild state, uncollected into bushels but rather stuffed into individual pockets; the exquisite moral flavor of wild fruits is only available straight off the vine; the gift of fruit is found mainly in the picking. Any number of similar maxims have been formulated by Thoreau's imitators to propose that nature is better when encountered and imbibed outside of market conditions and pressures.

So the debate between Thoreau and Emerson as represented here could not be more plain: is the world ample enough for us as it discloses itself, or is it incomplete until we work it into something new? But what should be obvious by now is that this is not a difference that makes a difference. Both positions—the deep and the shallow—arrive at the same critical juncture, with the observer simply trying to carve off more or less of nature by effacing more or less of himself. Thoreau guards his berries closely but would be willing to share them with the right sort of people; Emerson says the right sort of people are already on their way. Thoreau tells us to go get the berries ourselves; Emerson says some practical genius will bring them to you. But note that neither says we should stay away from berries altogether, forget them and never speak of them again. Neither could do so even if he wanted to. That is because berries are finally, in both cases, *about us*. Without us, berries might go forever unobserved; but once we see them, berries are *in play*—they are in the system. All that remains is either to preserve them so you and people like you can savor them privately (Thoreau), or to share them out with everybody else once you can figure a way to do so (Emerson). The real problem is not in picking berries but in dealing with your fellow berry pickers. So in the end, the choice of deep or shallow merely amounts to forcing the substance of liberalism to one end of the tube or the other, to searching for a balance between the individual's quest for meaning with the quests of his or her fellows. Unfortunately, nature gets caught in the squeeze. There seems no way to get around ourselves, no way to put us out of the picture.

Thus do the shallow and deep branches of American environmentalism both run up on the shoals of their own desire to get right with nature. They debate politics and disguise it as a debate about morality. But neither the political program nor the ethical framework has anything new to tell us. In fact, they are like the friend who insists on talking you through a personal crisis even though it is precisely the talking that keeps you from moving on. So I think it is high time to abandon this liberal environmentalism, both strains of it. I think it no longer serves us well, if it ever did. Practically, the liberal formula, hearkening always ahead to the age of postscarcity, requires an ever-expanding natural substrate (as Emerson recognized in his arguments against Malthus in "Farming"). Conceptually, the liberal formula makes unreasonable demands of radicals and reformers alike. Thoreauvians imagine a world in which human self-realization is tempered by an ethic of ecocentric equality; they still maintain that in wildness is the preservation of the world. If that is true, we are surely doomed, for wildness as such no longer exists. The world is already a domesticate, through and through (a garden or a gravesite, depending on your outlook), with each subsequent instance of human self-realization a further subtraction from nature's share of the pie. The healing corrective that is nature is reduced even by our efforts to preserve it, in that wilderness protected from the market makes the unprotected remnants accrue in value. Emersonians, on the other hand, like to imagine we can save nature precisely by marketing it, under the theory that prosperity predicated on creative destruction can better purchase more nature later, and that true-cost pricing will reveal that nature is indeed—as many radical environmentalists would argue anyway—priceless. Yet ecological history has put paid to that argument, as every day we gather more evidence that the earth can no longer restore the substance and pattern that humankind has degraded via an economic system that can place no limits on its own invasive logic. Thus, the manifest limitations of both radical, moralizing preservationism and reformist, amoral conservationism indicate that liberal environmentalism as a whole will end with no nature left to defend or manage. The flaw here is emphatically not in the practical goals of preservation and conservation: we clearly need more of both. Instead, the flaw lies in the way that Emerson, Thoreau, and their associated traditions observe this silent Other we are pleased to call nature. I believe that we might better grasp the extent of this flaw when we understand that Thoreau's vision was more liberal than radicals think, Emerson's less liberal than the reformers think, and that both were more sanguine about nature's chances than they had any right to be. I compare those visions, not with the goal of recuperating Emerson or downgrading Thoreau, but simply to gain some insight into the development of the environmental tradition in America as it was presaged in their respective oeuvres.

Finally—and here is the tiny note of hope—this book also proposes that these writers model other, suggestive modes of observing the world. They rehearse the transformation of culture and nature into systems and environments that is helpful in moving us from the ontological to the epistemological, from asking "What can nature tell us?" to "What can we do to compensate for an economy that observes nature merely as fodder when it is observing it at all?" This key point bears reiteration: the way that they saw, not what they saw, is what interests me. To preview the model I flesh out in subsequent chapters: communication systems (the only kind of systems that concern us here) may be either social or conscious; environments are everything about which the system does not or cannot communicate. In keeping with the sight/sound tropology I am compelled to use throughout this book, it may be said that we use communications to observe the environment, to create connectivity between system elements, and to maintain boundaries between systems and environments. The particular communication regimes that various systems have evolved to foster and remember become their sole modes of knowing. And there is much about the world that they have never learned how to know. In effect, it is communication's silent, unknowable Other that remains environment for all of our various systems, unobserved and unspoken. One could say that the environmental problem is at bottom a failure to communicate about something that cannot communicate for itself.

Thoreau, who if he were alive today could easily be imagined standing beside Earth First!ers shouting "No compromise in defense of Mother Earth!" might seem the most congenial of my two exemplars to the kind of revision I have in mind.

Yet according to the systems-based environmentalism I employ to interpret their visions, Emerson may be of more use to us today: if ever there is to be an environmental renaissance, any at all, we need a better theory of observation, and Emerson was a keener observer of observation than Thoreau, the keener observer of nature. As Holmes Rolston III has noted, "There are similarities [in Emerson's work] to recent thought about the spontaneous generation of integrated order in decentralized systems, as happens in society with language and markets, or in nature with ecosystems. Such decentralized order is not low quality; to the contrary, it is richer and more diverse than centralized order" (97–98). Though it is by no means the mainline of his thought, there is an Emerson who held an *illiberal* view of systems and environments: a view that acknowledged the fundamental incommensurability of decentralized systems pursuing their unique routes to order and stability. It is not a progressive view, in the sense that it models social systems that at best can only ponder each other's self-revealing ignorances and, perhaps, learn to make use of them in ways that we, ignorant ourselves, cannot predict in advance. As for curing our environmental woes—well, the most optimistic scenario may be that under this view we might finally, fully come to terms with the fact that our social system has evolved to do its best when it is doing its worst. To paraphrase Molière, systems die not because they are sick but because they are alive. Self-absorption and insularity are the price of efficiency and stability if only until the time when the world intrudes with a vengeance on delusions of invulnerability. Then all is lost in a moment of terrific yet unusable clarity.

Emerson presaged that we rarely grasp the limitations of this, our brutally successful mode of vision; we still act on the basis of what we can see and have not yet learned that vision is purchased at the cost of its own blindness. *"Nature is hard to observe,"* he wrote (CW 3:29). This book will not make it any easier.

CHAPTER

1

Observing Nature

"Wildflowers of the Asphalt"

In 1902, William Dean Howells published a collection of his essays under the title *Literature and Life*. Several of the pieces fall into the genre of nature writing, including one short review of "Mrs. Caroline A. Creevey's charming looking book on the *Flowers of Field, Hill, and Swamp*" (89). Howells had been unable to get out of New York that spring as was his habit, and in reviewing the book he "was very forcibly reminded of the number of these pretty, wilding growths which [he] had been finding all the season among the streets of asphalt and the sidewalks of artificial stone." Howells lists many examples, including (on the promenade of the Madison Square Roof Garden) "Celandine, and Dwarf Larkspur, and Squirrel-corn, and Dutchman's-breeches, and Pearlwort, and Wood-sorrel, and Bishop's-cap, and Wintergreen, and Indian-pipe, and Snowberry, and Adder's-tongue, and Wakerobin, and Dragon-rott, and Adam-and-Eve, and twenty more, which must have got their names from some fairy tongue" (91). The tone of this essay is a mixture of delight and surprise: delight in the beauty of these flowers, surprise that so many could be found in the city.

This evocation of a clandestine urban nature reaches a climax in the following passage:

> As one turns the leaves of Mrs. Creevey's magic book—perhaps one ought to say turns its petals—the forests and the fields come and make themselves at home in the city everywhere. By virtue of it I have been more in the country in a half-hour than if I had lived all June there. When I lift my eyes from its pictures on its letter-press my vision fronts the image of the sun against the air after dwelling on his brightness. The rose-mallow flaunts along Fifth Avenue and the golden threads of the dodder embroider the house fronts on the principal cross-streets; and I might think at times that it was all mere fancy, it has so much the quality of a pleasing illusion. (91–92)

There are a number of ways to interpret Howells's vision. One could (and strictly speaking should) pass it off as a flowery bit of prose typical of the genre of garden writing. One might, on the other hand, read it as a striking revision of a motif that had dominated nineteenth-century writing about the relationship between nature and culture: I speak of the so-called "machine in the garden" trope. So lucidly explored by Leo Marx and epitomized for him in Hawthorne's description of a locomotive intruding on the calm of the Sleepy Hollow Cemetery in Concord, that trope is here inverted with the garden flaunting itself in the midst of the greatest machine of them all, the urban leviathan of Manhattan. Under that reading Howells is saying something about the ineradicability of nature, that the cultural supplanting of the natural is mitigated by the persistence of nature to manifest itself in the interstices of the metropolis, the very pinnacle of the built environment.

Perhaps. Yet the fact that this flowery vision is inspired by a book—and a book that, as he admits, possesses the power to put him in mind of nature more than nature itself—makes for an ironic counterpoint to his metropastoral idyll. Not the persistence of nature, then, but the indirect, *mediated* character of our encounter with it. This casual textualization of undomesticated and spontaneous nature in "Wildflowers of the Asphalt" is why it stands as a fitting symbol for fin de siècle environmental perception. For by the time Howells wrote it, the frontier, according to Frederick Jackson Turner, had been closed for ten years, and the wildest territory still extant between New York and San Francisco lay in Yellowstone National Park, created by an act of Congress in 1872 as a sort of open-air museum of natural history. The struggle to wrest a nation from the wilderness was essentially over, leaving Americans in total control of their part of the continent; now and forever, the exploitability of its natural treasures was assured. Howells's "pretty, wilding growths" among the New York pavements represent in miniature the trajectory of the formerly "howling wilderness": from vast, intractable obstacle to human progress to that which ekes out a diminished existence in the gaps and waste spaces of a fully humanized earth. (And, to remind us of the extent to which even these little eruptions of wildflowers are just an effect of the human movement across the planet, I simply point out that several of these "wildflowers" are Old World in origin, not native American species at all.)

If we can agree that perceptions of nature must have changed in tandem with these biophysical changes, then we could say that in his discussion of Creevey's book Howells is dealing with, loosely speaking, problems of observation—the observation of what remains of nature, to be precise. The first, trivial, problem of observation: the general observational ignorance of urbanites, which Howells intends to remedy by referring them to Creevey's book. By bringing to his readers' attention these wildflowers, which many city dwellers pass by without noticing, he shows them that nature is not confined to the country. Howells asks them to revise their mental picture of New York's concrete cityscape, to see that even the "artificial stone" is not completely sterile. It is as if he is saying, "look here, New Yorkers, do not blind yourself to the natural beauty yet available to you in these man-made canyons."

A second problem of observation, more complex and interesting, and one that better foregrounds the topic of this book, is Howells's own observational blind spot. This latter is a function of his reliance on a crucial American opposition, the one between the city and the country, which originates in the distinction between nature and culture or, even more fundamentally, between wilderness and civilization. If we think of *wilderness and civilization* as sighting/siting a crucial dualism in American development, we might be tempted to say that Howells is deconstructing that opposition by playfully crossing the boundary between them (exemplified here in the "illusion" of the flowers projecting across the "house fronts").

We might be tempted to say that. But I think we could find a better way to describe the situation. Let me suggest that wilderness/civilization as a distinction or code that provides some organizing clarity within a certain field of discourse (which is to say, a field that encompasses the rhetoric and mythos of progress, sustainability, conservation, resource exploitation, nature worship—in short, the sum total of American environmental perception) is in Howells's trope revealed as a code that is no longer up to the environmental challenge. Simply put, when nature has become something to project across the face of cultural forms, when wilderness itself exists only at the discretion of humans, we can safely infer (although there was never really any doubt) that the opposition put into play here has become vacuous. Thus *wilderness* and *civilization* as a way of calling the difference between what is cultural, artifactual, and human, and what is wild, unbounded, and noncultured has lost its hold if not on our active imaginations and vocabularies than at least on our subconscious ones. The distinction, in other words, *does* nothing; it does not describe our actions in the world; perhaps it can only remind us of a time when a distinction of this sort did. In Howells, then, what stands revealed is a culturally saturated view of nature: he has effectively taken the wildness out of nature and inserted the remaining "pretty, wilding growths" into a scene wholly planned and constructed by humans.

This is not to say that Howells himself was aware of the collapse of the wilderness/civilization code, its failure to any longer enunciate a difference that makes a difference. If in 1900 people still wrote about wilderness as if it actually existed, wilderness as the countervalue to the humanized world made no more sense then than socialism as the countervalue to liberal democracy today: while there may be something that opposes the latter, whatever it is cannot be imagined as lying on liberal democracy's "outside." In both cases, the putative outside is an option that has disappeared, leaving only its trace in the form of nostalgia and linguistic inertia. We twenty-first-century observers of Howells's observation, however, can notice what he does not: that a code better attuned to the fact that "wilderness" is no longer so massive, frightening, and incomprehensible as it once was—that indeed it exists only inasmuch as it can find a place within what has become a largely cultural landscape—we notice that this code is gradually coming into view in the periphery of Howells's vision.

For the relationship of society to the natural world, the formerly howling wilderness, something akin to the paradigm shift ushered in by Copernicus is in the offing. Only this time, instead of it dawning on humankind that the earth is only a peripheral part of the cosmos, the new shift suggests that humans will no longer be able to think of nature as beyond them, as if they had been standing against it, confronting it as an Other. They now begin to realize that they have always been embedded in nature and, in fact, have had much to do with molding the forms nature has taken. And perhaps, as boundaries dissolve, it might be possible to think about the ways that nature is itself embedded in society. The central biological developments of the nineteenth century—the work of Darwin and the rise of evolutionary science— would only serve to reinforce this profound entanglement of humans with their environments.

Strangely enough, the fact that nature is no longer in opposition to society does not seem to have settled any of the problems humankind has always had with nature: for the most part, nature remains something to be consumed—that is, when it does not escape notice altogether. As a result, it does little good, intellectually or practically, for those who wish to theorize this entanglement to build on the truism that "we are now one with nature," as if this realization alone would somehow invalidate the old rules of the game, wherein every claim of identity also identified a difference. The human brain works with contrasts, not unities, and the abolition of distinctions is only a prelude to their reassertion elsewhere. As Kate Soper points out, "Whether . . . it is claimed that 'nature' and 'culture' are clearly differentiated realms or that no hard and fast delineation can be made between them, all such thinking is tacitly reliant on the humanity-nature antithesis itself and would have no purchase on our understanding without it" (15). So given our incapacity to relieve ourselves of the burden of difference-making, what might be a more workable code by which we could describe the sorts of differences that still obtain between the human project and this nonhuman "nature" that persists and demands our attention? How can we reorganize our thinking to deal with the shift in the nature of nature?

I take the, on first blush, underwhelming position that in order to think through the problems created by this shift we must subsume nature under a broader, more supple rubric, namely, that of *environment*. This term has long been used interchangeably with nature, but in the sense I intend it environment includes nature as only one part of a horizon of possibilities that might be defined as "that which does not engage in communication." Environment, in other words, is what lies outside a system of communication. (Because every system presupposes an environment against which it distinguishes itself, the domain of system theory is also by definition equally an environment theory.) Some will protest that if we abandon *nature* from the outset in a favor of this even more generalized concept of a noncommunicating environment we are on a path that may lead to yet greater marginalization of that which we want to preserve—animals, plants, ecosystems, and so on. We will not hear the cries of nature if we relegate it to the noncommunicating environment *tout court.* There is no question that this is a legitimate risk; there is certainly a tendency in systems theory to move toward ecological rationality and away from pathetic fallacy. I cannot decide which option is more dreary: to turn nature into a communication problem or into a gazing pool. The former, as Emerson would say, seems to leave nature all out of us, while the latter puts us too much into it. But in any event, my goal is to show that the systems approach provides us with intriguing alternatives to the shopworn perspectives we currently adopt, alternatives that permit us to reframe the old questions and, maybe, arrive at some different answers. The real danger may lie in *not* challenging the received versions of nature, which, however reformulated, merely encourage variations on the same conversations about nature that we have had to endure for far too long already.

But before we explore how we might best negotiate this shift from nature to environment—and what role Emerson and Thoreau might have played in observing it, perhaps even prompting it—we must establish more clearly what has occurred, and why our current terms of reference are ineffectual and debilitating.

The Reconfiguration of North American Nature

What Howells tells us only backhandedly environmental historians can confirm empirically: by the end of the nineteenth century the reconfiguration of the American natural environment was well underway in all but the most remote areas. With the rise of industrialism, the expansion of transportation networks, the capitalization of resource extraction, and the incursion of Euroamericans into every nook and cranny of the continent, the young nation was able to achieve in a century what in Europe had taken many hundreds, if not thousands, of years: the near-total transformation of a wilderness into a landscape prioritized for human use. This transformation entailed the extermination or decimation of the aboriginal peoples, the bison, assorted large predators, and many plant species across much of their ranges; the introduction of exotic organisms such as weeds, rats, sheep, and cattle; and the application of intensive agricultural, forestry, and hydraulic technologies to the soil and water. Perhaps the single most important factor in speeding the reconfiguration of the environment was the riotous proliferation of major urban centers, from which the transformation of hinterlands was directed and for whose growth the transformation was expedited. William Cronon calls Chicago "nature's metropolis," not because the city was graced by bucolic splendor (the name itself refers to the strong odor of wild garlic that abounded in the swampy region), but because Chicago so dominated the upper-Midwest bioregion. "Those who sought to explain its unmatched expansion often saw it as compelled by deep forces within nature itself, gathering the resources and energies of the Great West—the region stretching from the Appalachians and Great Lakes to the Rockies and the Pacific— and concentrating them in a single favored spot at the southwestern corner of Lake Michigan" (*Nature's Metropolis,* 9). That explanation is not far off: the resources were indeed gathered and concentrated, though the compulsion came not from natural but social forces. Chicago, like the New York of Howells, stands in stark contrast to the natural environment it displaces—yet at the same time the city's very existence depends on a variety of ecosystemic and biotic components that it reorganizes for its own uses. Even the subsequent protection of pre-European nature was often simply a strategy in the furtherance of urban growth, as was the case in the creation of the great Adirondack forest preserve in 1885, which assured New York's water supply (Nash, *Wilderness,* 118).

The extent to which the human impact was metamorphosing nature in America, and globally as well, was famously explored by George Perkins Marsh in *Man and Nature,* published in 1864. Subtitled *Physical Geography as Modified by Human Action,* the book was not even the first American document to note the changes humans created in their wake; William Bartram, Crèvecoeur, even Jefferson himself in *Notes on the State of Virginia* had cited humans' capacity to modify nature. But Perkins was the first to painstakingly catalog the negative effects of such modifications, in the process challenging the myth of natural superabundance and attacking those wasteful practices that threatened the long-term security of resources and natural (and human) health. Marsh writes:

> But man is everywhere a disturbing agent. Wherever he plants his foot, the harmonies of nature are turned to discords. The proportions and accommodations which insured the stability of existing arrangements are overthrown. Indigenous vegetable and animal species are extirpated and supplanted by others of foreign origin, spontaneous production is forbidden or restricted, and the face of the earth is either laid bare or covered with a new and reluctant growth of vegetable forms, and with alien tribes of animal life. These intentional changes and substitutions constitute, indeed, great

revolutions; but vast as is their magnitude and importance, they are, as we shall see, insignificant in comparison with the contingent and unsought results which have flowed from them. (36)

Auguring the words of later environmentalists, Marsh portrays man as an agent of ecological chaos, and his warnings to his contemporaries can be boiled down to a single idea: in the rush to remake the world more amenable to our species we remain blithely unconcerned with the kinds and scales of hazards we cause. As Tocqueville wrote in 1831, "Man gets accustomed to everything. . . . [He] fells the forest and drains the marshes. . . . The wilds become villages, the villages towns. The American, the daily witness of such wonders, does not see anything astonishing in all this. This incredible destruction, this even more surprising growth, seem to him the usual progress of things in this world. He gets accustomed to it as to the unalterable order of nature" (quoted in Williams, 5). With typical incisiveness, Tocqueville reminds us that our continual renovation of static nature can itself be viewed as a natural process. *Nature* is one of those polysemic words that, improbably, can become its exact opposite, depending on how it is deployed and by whom. (Thus, for example, bovine growth hormone, a cloned and manufactured milk additive, can be marketed as "natural"; and endangered species displaced by humans can be classified as "nonadaptive," as if their extinction were sanctioned by nature itself.) Americans had, in effect, beaten back the wilderness, and it might have seemed unlikely they could ever again think about the remaining bits of nature in quite the same way: how could the *landschaft* they had created, endowed now with cultural signs to the same magnitude that pure, untrammeled wilderness had lacked them, still be considered nature? The short answer is that it could be, and was. For most people, even as nature was transformed physically it remained conceptually intact: something apart, first to be fretted over, then conquered, used, and remade. Yet could the scale, rapidity, and success of the transformations have been unaccompanied by *no* profound alterations in the perception of nature by those whose collective efforts had authored the transformations? Did they not notice that the victory was well in hand, that nature was actually on the run and had nowhere left to hide?

A brief look at the part of New England in which Emerson and Thoreau lived and wrote will help illustrate the point that some observers were registering a different set of concerns. This portion of the continent, long and intensively settled by the Europeans, had changed much from the time of William Wood. His memoir, *New England's Prospect,* allowed Thoreau to compare the Concord of 1855 to its counterpart in 1633, when Wood had traveled from Britain to southern New England (Cronon, *Changes,* 3). Wood documents an almost pre-Columbian profusion of animal types while Thoreau, by contrast, finds it more compelling to list the animals no longer extant in the Concord area: bear, deer, moose, wildcat, wolf, beaver, and marten (NH 15). As for flora, Wood notes that "the timber of the country grows straight and tall, some trees being twenty, thirty foot high, before spreading forth their branches" (quoted in Cronon, *Changes*, 25). In Thoreau's time the original forests and their parklike openings were long gone, survived by second- and third-growth woodlots with dense understories of brush and coppice. Thoreau, in "The Succession of Forest Trees" (published in 1860), mentions in passing "a small but very dense and handsome white pine grove, about fifteen rods square, in the east part of this town. The trees are large for Concord, being from ten to twenty inches in diameter" (NH 79). Pines of this size are barely middle-aged, and probably dated only to the beginning of the century, giving us some sense of the relatively well-used condition of local forests. Summarizing his feelings on this decline of diversity in the natural milieu, he writes in his journal in 1856, "Is it not a maimed and imperfect nature I am conversant with?" (quoted in Cronon, *Changes,* 4). (This is a theme that crops up again and again in Thoreau and is a significant feature of his neopastoral cum ecological understanding of nature.)

The difference between the New England ecosystems of Wood's and Thoreau's or Emerson's time is the difference, as Carolyn Merchant puts it, between a colonial and industrial economy. The colonial economy had retained some of the pre-Columbian agricultural practices of the Amerindians by drawing only from nature's "surplus," whereas by the mid-nineteenth century, as Emerson aptly notes, "out of doors all seems a market" (CW 2:39). Merchant describes the shift as follows:

> No longer was it necessary to let fields lie fallow to be restored as the Sabbath restored humans. No longer must forests be left to the activity of plant succession, but species needed for human use could be planned, planted, and harvested by foresters and agronomists. The colonial mercantile exchange of commodities was transformed into a system of production units that employed wage labor on farms, in forests, and in factories. The capitalist ecological revolution was characterized by the efficient organization of land, labor, and capital, competition in the marketplace, and the emergence of large-scale control over resources. (*Ecological,* 198)

Merchant's thesis is that changes in economic modes of production (and thus of the ecological core, which provides raw material and energy) lead to changes in domestic and political reproduction (everyday personal, familial, and social practices), which in turn cause important shifts in the culture's representation of nature in science, religion, art, myth, and language itself (6). These new representations filter back through the levels via behavioral modifications and effect further transformations of the ecological core. Thus when we change nature physically we change the way we think about it, and when we change the way we think about nature we change the way we act on it.

While I am, of course, far less convinced than Merchant about the importance of representations of nature to the integrity of the ecological core over time, this cyclical view can help explain why the concept of nature is constantly in flux and can change as the society develops over time. Nature is not the same thing to a pre-Columbian Haida Indian who needed six months' worth of carefully placed burns to bring down a western red cedar and a modern logger working for Weyerhaeuser who can cut the same tree down with a chainsaw in half an hour. Such a tree is not the same tree in fact or in myth: it has been displaced from the center of a totemic culture to the periphery of a patio furniture culture. Similarly, the nature in the New England of William Wood was not the same place in matter and in mind as the New England of Henry David Thoreau: where the former saw the dissidents and outcasts of England bravely struggling to carve out a civilization in a rugged and unforgiving yet bountiful New World, Thoreau could comfortably lament in one of his not infrequent bourgeois aperçus, "Let us try to keep the new world new, and while we make wary use of the city, preserve as far as possible the advantages of living in the country" (NH 254).

The Pastoral Tradition

The systemic approach embraced by Merchant is an attempt to provide a more coherent understanding of the actual interpenetrations of society and its environment; the model implicitly acknowledges that such interpenetrations must be far more complex than is suggested by rubrics like worldview or organizing metaphor. Indeed, no single mythic frame has ever made much sense when applied to Americans, who have always esteemed nature even as they prepared to overrun and subdue it; moreover, the actual biophysical relations between society and ecology that Merchant describes have generally been nonconsiderations for the critics and historians who have wanted to explain the role of nature on the American cultural scene. One important lens that, at least in theory, touches on those relations and the sorts of changes described in the section above, is the pastoral. The pastoral is one of several exceptionalist scripts that attempt to articulate a defining myth of America by condensing into a single trope the forces that quickened the nation. (Others would include, for example, the errand into the wilderness and the frontier hypothesis.) But I think the pastoral subsumes the others, in that the pastoral represents the liminal zone between *civilization* (the Old World, the city, the established New England colonies) and *wilderness* (the fertile ground of possibility), that generative dyad to which so many other tropes are mere epigones. The pastoral has long formed the connective tissue of that primal dichotomy; in its American variant, what society has in store for its environment takes on a distinctly teleological character, with the end point a return to the beginning: a repacified garden of the sort God had in mind for Adam and Eve.

By latching onto the pastoral as a focal metaphor for American aspirations in the West, many critics unwittingly promulgate an ecologically stunted version of American history, in the sense that the environmental conditioning of society by nature takes a backseat to the technological and ideological determination of nature by humans. Nature is seen as the practico-inert, which through the inspired manipulations of humans is found to be perfectly labile after all. Thus, even in decisive moments when human overreaching, environmentally speaking, is identified, the critical narrative tracks back to the human-made solution or adaptation that is usually just preamble to the next instance of overreaching. *Plus ça change, plus c'est la même chose.* No one ever learns anything, and American history appears as a perpetual series of outrages against nature, which all end in a impoverished version of the pastoral: the friendly natives killed, the natural abundance squandered, the commons fenced in, the lessons of nature ignored.

Perhaps, then, the critical descriptions are quite rightly focused on the moral failures of Americans, the folly of their guiding visions, their inability to measure up to the land. But as I have suggested, I think we must place this cycle of failure in a broader frame: ecocritics must always historicize, but they should do so on an ecological timeline and not merely a cultural/textual one. What happened in America in the nineteenth century was no different in kind than what had already happened in Europe or parts of Asia, or indeed had happened in North America itself ten thousand years earlier: the reduction of environmental complexity by human societies. The scale and speed were different, of course, but without manifest destiny or even the lure of free land, I think we can be sure that the west still would have been won. Myths may retrospectively justify or explain, may provide incentive and texture to the experience of going West, but myth itself is not the engine of human dispersal and domination.

Perhaps the only way out of this human history of failure is to push straight on through to the other side. That does not mean abandoning our mythic frames altogether; we could not do so even if we tried. But it does mean we must revisit them with a view to locating their blind spots and to observing what they do not. Let us begin by reviewing some of the key blind spots of the pastoral project. Pastoralism as a literary mode has a long and rich tradition, stretching far back to the origins of Western literature, perhaps finding its most famous expression in Virgil's *Eclogues*. His idealization of the lives of shepherds guarding their flocks seems to have struck a chord that has rung down through the ages, right into the backyard of the typical

American home today. The sheep are gone, but surveys do report that people are most contented while tending their flower beds.

More to the point, the pursuit of a pastoral life in the recent history of ideas has come to entail forging a via media between a Rousseauian state of nature and the pressures and cacophony of modern life, a bucolic existence close to the earth, with minimal technology and relative independence from the outside world. In the American tradition, Thoreau's Walden Pond venture is probably the locus classicus, but Hawthorne's brief flirtation with the Brook Farm experiment (satirized in *The Blithedale Romance*) is also firmly within the pastoralist tradition. Emerson was intrigued by the pastoral commune as well. Although he was by no means an uncritical exponent of his century's back-to-nature crowd, he was sympathetic to the cause, especially where it jived with his valorization of farmers as primary figures in the human economy and his general sense that climate ("The highest civility has never loved the hot zones" [W 7:25]) and landscape were major determinants of culture: "In this country, where land is cheap, and the disposition of the people pacific, every thing invites to the arts of agriculture, of gardening, and domestic architecture" (CW 1:227). "How much better" he continued, "when the whole land is a garden, and the people have grown up in the bowers of paradise. Without looking, then, to those extraordinary social influences which are now acting in precisely this direction, but only at what is inevitably doing around us, I think we must regard the *land* as a commanding and increasing power on the American citizen, the sanative and Americanizing influence, which promises to disclose new virtues for ages to come" (CW 1:229). Pastoralism, broadly defined as the cure for what ails modern life, was thus a persistent theme for Emerson, just as it has been for many social critics in the twentieth century: from the neo-Luddite texts of Kirkpatrick Sale and the ecoanarchism of Murray Bookchin (not to mention the Unabomber),[1] to the conservatism of southern agrarians like John Crowe Ransom and Allen Tate, and, more recently, to the Christian environmentalism of Wendell Berry. Not surprisingly, the pastoral ideal attracts adherents from both ends of the political spectrum. In fact, the political ambiguity of pastoralism allows it to be deployed equally, as with so many other crucial American topoi, by both left and right. Thus, in rare examples of cooperation, western ranchers find themselves allied with environmentalists in opposition to developments that encroach on traditional herding and subsistence economies; while small business owners and the Amish work with social activists and organized labor to prevent incursions of Wal-Mart into rural Pennsylvania. The mobilizing metaphors for both sides hearken back almost invariably to small-town and country values versus the city values of technology, free markets, and progress at any cost. Those value systems, of course, have a centrist appeal as well: they were certainly in play in the rise of suburbia after World War II, which was an attempt to split the difference between urban compaction and country living. Here pastoralism played out largely as an exercise in the semiotics of marketing—witness the profusion of Beechwood Estates, Villages on the Green, and Colonial Acres, those bastions of urban out-migration styled after the trees cut down during construction and the mushiest versions of American history.

The pastoral ideal was never more aptly or ironically concretized than in Henry Ford's rose-colored, museum-piece version of his childhood, Greenfield Village. Located on what was then the edge of Detroit, the new capital of the industrial age, Greenfield Village was perhaps the first example of techno- or neopastoralism, which I would define as a sort of industrial neoteny. (Neoteny indicates the retention of juvenile characteristics of the organism into the adult form.) The neopastoral preserves the agricultural past into the industrial present, and in its most cutting-edge forms may be the template for the postindustrial future. Alexander Wilson, in *The Culture of Nature,* notes that "rural nostalgia has become an industry, with its own product lines and tourist destinations." The commodified nostalgia of neo-nineteenth-century Main Street or Seaside type towns and theme parks seems only the current manifestation of an elusive pastoral ideal against which even Emerson's and Thoreau's Concord (precisely the sort of community Disney's Celebration or Heritage USA is meant to evoke) would not have measured up. Historical theme parks like these, says Wilson, "construct the idealized past of an organic community in harmony with nature, in the belief this harmony is something we cannot look forward to again" (205). I think there is a rising expectation, however, that this harmony is something we can look forward to in a more widespread way; at the very least, the market is ready to capitalize on such an expectations. (Again, I am agnostic on the chances of this happening, but it is a central theme I return to in chapter 5.)

That the pursuit of this ideal harmony was a long-standing project is proved by the protopastoralist or agrarian history of Henry Nash Smith's *Virgin Land,* in which we learn that the trans-Appalachian West was figured as the garden of the world even before Independence by writers such as Crèvecoeur and Jefferson. In *Notes on Virginia,* for example, Jefferson makes clear that he prefers to see America develop as an agrarian nation, with the vast lands of the West providing the ground on which the yeoman farmer may realize the pastoral life. Even though foregoing industrial development would put the country in a dependent relationship with Europe in terms of machined products, the moral development of the people, thought Jefferson, was better served by agrarian policies. (It should be pointed out that Jefferson knew his vision of a nation of independent yeomanry was unlikely to materialize, and that he offered it up mainly as the kind of politically useful platitude that it still is.)

In the nineteenth century, the myth of the garden continues to be a compelling touchstone, which reveals itself in a variety of genres: dime novels, political speeches, popular pamphlets. Smith charts the sundry ways in which political and social forces configured the West and shows that it is as much due to the internal dynamics of the industrial East as the notion of free land that impelled settlement. By expanding west, the nation could forge a connection with the Orient and turn its back on the moldering countries of Europe. But the agrarian cum pastoral ideal is variously evoked for often contrary purposes. Merchants and industrialists use it to push unemployed immigrants West and defuse potential civil unrest in the East (the safety-valve theory). On the other hand, union activists invoke it as a way to keep wages high in those same cities by bleeding off excess labor. The South wants to be the nexus for westward settlement in order to maintain its power balance with the industrializing northeast; but New England abolitionists advocate settling the garden from the North in order to keep slavery out.

In *The Machine in the Garden,* Leo Marx more precisely configures the Jeffersonian vision as the pastoral. According to Marx, Jefferson did not draw upon French physiocrat theory (which considers an agriculture-based economy to be the most prosperous mode of life) in his call for an independent yeomanry; rather, he drew upon a literary tradition, beginning with Virgil and leading right up to *The Tempest,* that had prepared America as a site for the realization of the pastoral life. Marx integrates the classic American texts into this tradition, seeing each as working out a resolution between the pastoral and the rapidly encroaching forces of industrial capital. The key figure for this collision is, as I have suggested above, the locomotive intruding on the scene of a rural reverie—the "interrupted idyll" of Hawthorne at Sleepy Hollow, or Thoreau at Walden Pond with the Fitchburg Railway in the near distance. Such machine/garden collisions are typical of American literature and can be refigured in different but structurally identical ways: Ahab against the whale, Adams's Virgin and the dynamo, Jay Gatsby in the industrial wasteland near West Egg, Long Island. These are examples of complex pastoralism, in which authors attempt virtual resolutions—private, often futile reconciliations that typically end in tragedy—between a more harmonious and peaceful pastoral past and an industrialized future with all the implications for psychological dislocations such a future implies.

But there are some problems with the pastoral histories assembled by Smith and Marx, both of which have come under fire by critics writing in the wake of the green consciousness movement that emerged in the late sixties and early seventies. The revisionist efforts of Richard Slotkin in *Regeneration through Violence* and *The Fatal Environment* are instructive. Slotkin questions, for example, the triumphalist notions of progress that Smith left largely unchallenged in his own book. Smith did not want to repeat what he saw as a mistake in Frederick Jackson Turner's frontier hypothesis—the idea that the lure of free land to the West is responsible for the development of the nation—by ignoring the extent to which the settlement was galvanized by the myths and symbols created expressly for the particular social and political goals of the East. But according to Slotkin, Smith writes out an absolutely crucial fact: that the previous occupants of the "virgin land" were violently displaced. Thus, in eliding the role of the American Indian, Smith exchanges the tragic dimension of American history for what is finally a progressive one. Slotkin will rewrite this history, so to speak, in blood. The two authors' readings of the Leatherstocking tales show the difference. For Smith, Leatherstocking is a liminal figure: he exists on the divide between wilderness and civilization, always trying to keep one step ahead of the settlements. Leatherstocking is white, yet he embodies the attractive features of the American Indian: he is, in a sense, himself a "noble savage." Smith rightly recognizes in Cooper the conservative, class-based rhetoric that informs his vision: he manages to place everyone on a scale of civilization, with the lowest people—bad Indians and bad whites—at the bottom. But while Indians could be good and whites could be bad, the point is that this is always explained in Cooper as a matter of individual character. Smith's error is that he seems to accept this sort of evaluation at face value. A good Indian is thus one who allies himself with the good whites, and an Indian who allies himself with his own people during wars against the encroaching whites is by definition bad. Slotkin instead wants to see this typology of character as the culturally specific bigotry that it is, evidence of the race warfare that is the real plot of the Leatherstocking tales and, by extension, the real history of the American garden.

Leo Marx suffers from the same amnesia when it comes to the social circumstances in which the pastoral subject arises. For Russell Reising, Marx's version of the pastoral turns a blind eye to the social and political spaces in which the pastoral idylls were written; just as Smith obliterates racism by focusing on character, Marx obliterates history itself by seeing these texts as the private ruminations of solitary artists. As a result, says Reising, the machine/garden dichotomy remains undialectical, with the conflict between progress and tradition largely static from Hawthorne through to Faulkner. Indeed, Marx's conclusion says precisely this: complex pastoralism is not the place to resolve the real world issues of machine/garden disruptions; that terrain is better left to politics. But for Reising, Marx's conclusion reflects a critical heritage that has its own political motives for denying to literature a relevant political context and a role to play therein. Thus, for example, Marx sees Hawthorne's "Ethan Brand" as a story about a Faustian bargain gone sour rather than recognizing in it a historically accurate portrayal of American community being socially and ecologically disassembled by technological innovation. The tale's odd cast of variously displaced characters (about whom Marx is strangely silent) incarnate for Reising the devastating effects of these changing technologies on human life. But Marx must ignore such complications if he is to maintain his position that classic literature comments solely on private, psychological dislocations, and on the moral character of specific individuals rather than the social conditions in which they are formed.

Another revision of the pastoral tradition is provided by Annette Kolodny in *The Lay of the Land*. Again, the Leatherstocking tales form a critical locus: Kolodny detects in the novels a consistent pattern of casting the land as female. This "gyneotropic" pattern provides a good deal of insight into the way we structure our experience of the natural world. As Kolodny points out in *The Land before Her*, the use of gendered terms is not exclusively the conceptual tic of male writers: though she had hoped otherwise, female writers do the same thing. But in the works of pioneer women writers she does at least find an alternate myth to the male penchant for domination, exploitation, and restlessness. This feminine myth is based on the farm garden, which is conceived as a figure for domestic rootedness, stability, and harmony with nature. Through the garden image, writers such as Caroline Kirkland and Willa Cather tried to fashion a myth of "at-homeness" in the harsh, primitive conditions of the frontier, which contrasted sharply to the cut-and-move-on ideology imbibed by most of their male counterparts.

A final theoretical matrix in which to reimagine the pastoral is developed in Myra Jehlen's *American Incarnation*. In Jehlen's view, the central problem with Marx and Smith is that, despite their attempts to update the classic pastoral tradition, they simply reify America as a "blessed land," the "garden of the world." America is a "heroic geography," uniquely suited to human occupation; it becomes a land risen out of nature, not history. Even in Slotkin, says Jehlen, there is the implication that the real failure of the pioneering American is that he was not adequate to the land *itself*, that he could have done better by it. Emerson himself had helped establish this brand of exceptionalism, the notion that "the land is the appointed remedy for whatever is false and fantastic in our culture" (cw 1:226). So rather than representing the tragedies of the extermination of aboriginals, the crushing of local communities who could not coexist with industrialization, the contamination of land and water as failures of a social organization, Jehlen's predecessors merely displace the causes on to individuals' feckless relations to the land (and thus these critics reinscribe the logic of ravenous individualism Jehlen wishes to challenge).

The revisionists thus bring to bear on the pastoral genre a variety of contextual factors that in the case of Smith were elided because of the progressivist notions of expansion he inadvertently espouses; and in the case of Marx were never even considered, blocked as they were by his notion of literature as the freestanding product of individual geniuses romantically set apart from the economic and political milieus in which they are immersed. The marginal details—social conditions, natives, women, the otherwise excluded Others—are effectively brought back into the equation by the revisionists. Amending these oversights is clearly a necessary precondition for an updated pastoralism, and the work of revision is surely valuable too, in that bit by bit we build up a thicker understanding of the ideas informing the expansion. We might look forward, for example, to cultural analyses of meat consumption (especially beef) as a propellant of the expansion, a gustatory mark of distinction in America that still has enormous ramifications for the imperilment of nature. That sort of study would bring to light the neopastoralism in the heart of even modern factory agriculture, where beef is thematized as an enduring American value that provides strength through the consumption of nature.

But to my mind no specific, ideologically sensitive reading of the pastoral can fully encompass what pastoralism really presents as a possibility for ecocriticism, which I explain in various ways throughout this book and in detail in the final chapter. My argument is that the pastoral is best understood as a topos (both a real place and a rhetorical commonplace) where the social system itself may be observed working out its problematic relationship with its environment. The pastoral bodies forth both the externalization of nature and its social internalization; it is the liminal zone where the social system finds acceptable modes of coupling with the natural environment and where nature can make its last, best stand against those systems. The pastoral is one place where, just maybe, the resources of culture may actually have some say in precisely how the social system decomplexifies nature.

As a preview of that discussion, let me focus for a moment on the actual environmental conditions that constituted the garden. I shall use by way of example a passage from Thoreau: in a description of the passage of certain railcars on the Fitchburg Railway, Thoreau writes,

> And hark! Here comes the cattle-train bearing the cattle of a thousand hills, sheepcots, stables, and cow-yards in the air, drovers with their sticks, and shepherd boys in the midst of their flocks, all but the mountain pastures. . . . The air is filled with the bleating of calves and sheep, and the hustling of oxen, as if a pastoral valley were going by. . . . A car-load of drovers, too, in the midst, on a level with their droves now, their vocation gone, but still clinging to their useless sticks as their badge of office. . . . But the dogs, where are they? . . . Their vocation, too, is gone. Their fidelity and sagacity are below par now. They will slink back to their kennels in disgrace, or perchance run wild and strike a league with the wolf and the fox. So is your pastoral life whirled past and away. (T 419)

Leo Marx would see this as the typical collision between a traditional past and an industrial future, for which the production of *Walden* itself is Thoreau's sole anodyne: a literary treatment of the collision is about all the author can carry off, for a real resolution is not in the cards. But what if, instead of reading the image as a virtual synthesis, we read it as accurately registering—through its fanciful but altogether apt descriptions—the complexity and ambiguity of the relationship between nature and society as it stood in the 1840s? As we have seen above, the kinds of ecological revolutions occurring in Boston's hinterland were signaling not just the end of certain modes of material production but were part of a massive reorganization of the social relationship humans had maintained with each other and, by extension, their natural environment for hundreds if not thousands of years.

So rather than simply a whimsical farewell to a dying past (the pain of which is somehow assuaged in the act of writing about it), could Thoreau's description of mobile pastures and degenerating dogs act as a signpost to the critical task ahead, the task of rethinking the boundaries of the human and the nonhuman, of locating where one begins and the other ends: in short, the crucial problem of nineteenth-century (and, indeed, twenty-first-century) environmental thought? Might this nostalgic image, in which the garden is essentially loaded up onto the machine, indicate a truly problematic feature of the machine in the garden theory, namely, that the garden and its bred, cultured, hybridized contents are no less products of industrial society and capitalist modes of production than locomotives or textile mills? While it is true that Thoreau's image vividly records the end of a particular conception of the pastoral, he also knows that his own beloved Concord had not been pastoral in the Virgilian sense for some time, as evidenced by its entanglement with all the vagaries of market economies and agricultural technologies, which Thoreau himself documented bitterly in journal and essay.[2] When we bear in mind that the historical environmental context in which this version of the pastoral appeared was a highly modified landscape already, we understand that Thoreau's resolution, virtual or otherwise, would have been compromised from the outset: there is no getting back to nature because nature is always already acculturated. We might therefore say that what Thoreau's pastoral figure marks is not the clash between the machine and the garden but his registration of the hybrid origins of the nature/culture entities that confronted him wherever he looked—even in the wilds of Maine, as I discuss in chapter 4.

To some extent, this contradictory impulse of Thoreau—the hankering for an antiquated pastoralism while surreptitiously acknowledging its always already transitional state as unspecified future-possible—is part of the ideological grammar of the American pastoral, which according to Lawrence Buell requires that we

> must . . . recognize the crosscurrents that keep any example pure: on the one hand, the centripetal pull of consensualism that threatens to draw the radical text over into

the sleepy safe domain of nature's nationalism, the ho-hum pieties of American civil religion; and, on the other hand, the centrifugal impulse always incipient, though usually contained within modest limits, for pastoral to form itself in opposition to social institutions of whatever sort. This duality was built into Euro-American pastoral thinking from the start, for it was conceived as both a dream hostile to the standing order of civilization (decadent Europe, later hypercivilizing America) and at the same time a model for the civilization in the process of being built. (*Environmental*, 50)

As Buell adds, "It is hard to keep one's eye on a target moving in two directions at once. But if, as Fitzgerald said, the test of a first-rate intelligence is the ability to hold contradictory ideas in the mind and still maintain the ability to function, serious readers ought to be equal to the task" (50)—and, needless to say, serious writers should too. In Thoreau's case, in his production of hybrid tropes—tropes which rehearse the contradictory nature of the nineteenth-century American pastoral milieu by *not* eliding the facts of the always already entangled and problematic relation of nature and culture that the pastoral traditionally attempted to pass over in silence—we may be seeing the outlines of an emergent perspective. In it, the wilderness/civilization split is not resolved at all, but is instead shaping up to become a different sort of dichotomy altogether, one which reflects the expansion of the human sphere into its environment without implying that the pastoral idyll was *ever* anything like a "safe domain." If the pastoral marks, *pace* Buell, a point of struggle between the reaffirmation and denunciation of cultural traditions, then perhaps it may also mark a point of struggle between old and new conceptions of nature, between nature, static and singular, and environment, multiple, variable, and hybrid. In effect, the pastoral and its successor are the sites where we observe the problem of nature being worked out. Here I review the old (if still dominant) discourse of nature and then end the chapter by pointing the way toward the successor vocabulary: the discourse of systems and environments (introduced in chapter 2).

The End of Nature

Most recent attempts to build fresh and compelling conceptions of nature unsurprisingly have as their impetus the inarguable fact that we must come to grips with the degradation and exhaustion of the biosphere. The physical reconfiguration of nature described above has become not merely a matter for environmental historians or nostalgic neopastoralists but a source of anxiety and even panic for everyone. Most of us are already benumbed by the statistical evidence that points to our gross long-term mismanagement of the earth's resources, biota, atmosphere, soil, and water. The *State of the World* reports from the Worldwatch Institute in Washington, for example, provide disturbing yearly roundups of the various obstacles the planet faces in its "progress toward a sustainable society," as the reports' subtitle judiciously puts it. Yet that "progress" toward sustainability still awaits confirmation. World Watch director Lester Brown and his associates lament in one typical foreword, "One of these years we would like to write an upbeat *State of the World*, one reporting that some of the trends of global degradation have been reversed. Unfortunately, not enough people are working yet to reverse the trends of decline for us to write such a report. We are falling far short in our efforts" (xviii). Another judicious use of rhetoric, because as a sequential reading of the reports quickly shows, not only are we "falling far short" but the decline becomes ever more precipitous with each passing year. Typical articles try to put a brave face on unmitigated disaster: "Conserving Biological Diversity" discusses the earth's declining biological diversity; "Confronting Nuclear Waste" explores the technical incapacity of humans to deal with the residues of fission; "Reforming Forestry" documents the annihilation of the earth's forests; "Reviving Coral Reefs" describes their worldwide decline.

The discourse of environmental destruction has taken on apocalyptic overtones, yet all the anxiety in the world seems to do very little to diminish the magnitude and rapidity of what has been termed planetary overload. Biological meltdown, not nuclear annihilation, appears to be the main threat to the continued presence of humans on the planet.[3] Just as smokers or alcoholics do not perceive the ongoing catastrophe in their cells and tissues and hence can project the day of reckoning far into the future, so too does our steady environmental decline become a problem of perception. Despite the clear evidence that humans are no different than other organisms in their total reliance on relatively stable environmental conditions, our social system has not evolved the robustness to recognize environmental hazards in a timely and amelioratory manner; in fact, it is constructed on the basis of ignoring such problems. It attempts to constitute itself as if its environment does not exist. The clear necessity of a radically altered perspective may be obvious to many people, but the competency of society to absorb nature's lessons and react appropriately remains a question mark. Can society and its discrete discourse communities (such as business, science, or politics) muster themselves to respond to an environment that does not "speak" at all, but that can only stimulate these social discourses to produce more of their own communications? We come up against the common situation whereby environmental problems are endlessly recontextualized, analyzed, moralized, debated, and circulated through bureaucracies to the point where environmental protection consists largely in changing the definition of *wetlands, wilderness,* or *clean water* to conform with the state of what already exists. Indeed, from some postmodern perspectives, it is questionable that society any longer operates on the basis of a difference between cultural sign and environmental referent. So heavily entangled are our cultural superstructures with the natural environment that we are powerless to precipitate out a real nature as the benchmark against which to measure correct environmental practice. As Jean Baudrillard notes of Death Valley, "It is useless to strip the desert of its cinematic aspects in order to restore its original essence; those features are thoroughly superimposed upon it and will not go away. The cinema has absorbed everything—Indians, *mesas,* canyons, skies" (69). What goes for the already stark desert goes double for everything else.

In a tone less apocalyptic than Baudrillard's but no less unsettling, Bill McKibben suggests that our technological and conceptual prostheses have brought us to the "end of nature" itself. But his is more than a declaration of simple closure. In fact, McKibben's thesis is not that nature (as in the environment or the earth's biosphere) is strictly speaking dead; rather, his point is that it no longer makes any sense at all to think of nature as a realm existing independently, immutably, and imperviously beyond the human sphere of influence. Humans have so insinuated themselves and their various *technē* within the natural world that it is simply not natural anymore. In a semiotic sense, nowhere on the earth's surface can one avoid the signs of humankind's handiwork; for example, the entire globe is linked via airborne toxin trails that lead back to factories in New Jersey or hydrogen bomb explosions on Pacific atolls.

The theoretical implications of the end of nature are not always thoroughly worked out in McKibben. As powerful as his end of nature thesis was when he declared it in the late eighties, what might have been more powerful and searching would have been a declaration of the end of the very *idea* of nature. But then nature has always been an especially difficult category for critical reflection: at once a social artifact, a fractured, amorphous placeholder filled with the detritus of history, nature is also the concrete *Ding an sich,* the fixed field of all existence. The concept of nature is in constant crisis and impossible to pin down, for as Raymond Williams points out it redounds with so very many of the central themes in human thought and experience (224). From the vantage of twentieth-century critical theory, nature has long been an anachronism, for to speak of a nature at all is to refer to something so overstamped by human actions and conceptualizations that it no longer properly exists. Fredric Jameson, for example, holds that nature "has systematically been eclipsed from the object world and the social relations of a society whose tendential domination over its Other (the nonhuman or the formerly natural) is more complete than at any other moment in human history" (170). Still, nature as ultimate biological horizon poses a practical challenge to the theoretical posture of total constructivism: if nature is always ideological, it is not only ideology. As the material limits of the world assert themselves in the form of global warming, changes in weather patterns, etc., we are reminded that nature does not dissolve into discourse. As Soper reminds us "it is not language that has a hole in its ozone" (151). It must be understood, then, that when we speak of nature we are talking about real limits, forces, and entities—but ones that are always mediated through culture.

In *The Dialectic of Enlightenment,* Max Horkheimer and Theodor Adorno identify the Enlightenment project—the very terms of which Bacon defined as the conquest of nature by action—as the problematic source of the eclipse of nature in man's schema. The "enlightened" world is a disenchanted one, in which all nonhuman life is instrumentalized. In *Biosphere Politics,* Jeremy Rifkin notes, "The past several centuries have been dominated by the mechanistic thinking of the En-lightenment, with its emphasis on the privatization and commodification of nature and man; detachment and isolation from the natural world; and a near pathological obsession with creating a secure, autonomous existence, independent of the forces of nature" (2). Assertions by Bacon right through to Gifford Pinchot, one of the first American professional conservationists and Theodore Roosevelt's handpicked chief of the nascent Forestry Service, give support to Rifkin's assessment. Echoing Descartes's dichotomy of cogito and objects (not to mention Emerson's "Me" and "Not Me"), Pinchot averred that "There are just two things on this material earth—people and natural resources" (325).[4] Michel Serres notes that "social systems, which are self-compensating and self-enclosed, press down with their new weight, that of their relations, object-worlds, and activities, on self-compensated natural systems, just as in the past natural systems put social systems at risk, in the age when necessity triumphed over reason's means" ("Natural Contract," 37). He summarizes the dichotomy between humans and the object world as follows:

> Mastery and possession: these are the master words launched by Descartes at the dawn of the scientific and technological age, when our Western reason went off to conquer the universe. We dominate and appropriate it: such is the shared philosophy underlying industrial enterprise as well as so-called disinterested science, which are indistinguishable in this respect. Cartesian mastery brings science's objective violence into line, making it a well-controlled strategy. Our fundamental relationship with objects comes down to war and property. (32)

Philosophy has long addressed itself to the repair of just this sort of schism, which appears to have its origin in our basic mental architecture: for whatever evolutionary advantage, we are programmed to be a self-discommoding creature, ready at a moment's notice to launch new actions that imply previous ones were insufficient. Restless malcontents that we are, it is no surprise that toward the object world we envision ourselves unhappily separated, always already east of Eden. The prescription has taken any and all forms: moral or spiritual transport to the extramundane; return to the primal unity by a forgetting of modern disunity;

recognition and reconstruction of the role of language, culture, and consciousness as they pertain to the alienation; readjustment of the perverse social relations that put us at odds with each other and nature; some other therapeutic holism that radically amputates the dualistic legacy. Serres's solution is the "natural contract," an extension of the Declaration of the Rights of Man:

> Back to nature, then! That means we must add to the exclusively social contract a natural contract of symbiosis and reciprocity in which our relationship to things would set aside mastery and possession in favor of admiring attention, reciprocity, contemplation, and respect; where knowledge would no longer imply property, nor action mastery, nor would property and mastery imply their excremental results and origins. An armistice contract in the objective war, a contract symbiosis, for a symbiont recognizes the host's rights, whereas a parasite—which is what we are now—condemns to death the one he pillages and inhabits, not realizing that in the long run he's condemning himself to death too. (38)

On the face of it, there can be little debate that Serres's tropes of synthesis (contract, symbiosis, armistice) are preferable to those of antagonism and division (war, mastery, parasitism, and so forth). The humane impulse is to overcome the very rifts we cannot stop generating. But perhaps it is time we accepted that such dualisms are not merely obstacles to a progressive unfolding of human consciousness but instead mark the constitutive and constituting feature of modern society in its relationships with its environments. Dualisms, no matter how they have been denigrated, deconstructed, and deracinated are simply ways of *making distinctions*—perhaps the most elementary means we have of distinguishing and grasping the world cognitively. It then follows that distinctions as such can only be replaced with other distinctions, never done away with altogether. The challenge will lie in imagining how to incorporate, deploy, distribute, and rework our distinctions in ways that do not bring along with them debilitating hierarchies and rigid structures that block flexible (and reflexive) thinking. Thus, we may need less rhetoric of "bad dualisms" and more inquiry into the way that distinctions actually distinguish. On this score the work of such thinkers as Niklas Luhmann, Pierre Bourdieu, Anthony Giddens, and Ulrich Beck (sociology), Chantal Mouffe, Ernesto Laclau, and Slavoj Zizek (political philosophy), Humberto Maturana and Francisco Varela (biology and cognitive science), and Donna Haraway and Bruno Latour (science studies) prove salutary.[5] Each of these thinkers, engaging the issues outlined above from different disciplinary perspectives, gives support to the notion that any serious attempt to grapple with the nature problem can only begin by moving from questions of continuity (between nature and culture) to questions of difference (between systems and their environments). Ecosophic concepts such as *interconnectedness, holism,* and *worldview,* which play down difference, must be replaced by *subject position, situational knowledge, partial perspective,* and *functional differentiation,* concepts that keep difference very much in play.

In the work of Bruno Latour and Donna Haraway, for example, the nature/culture dualism is viewed as an Enlightenment effort to "purify" the hitherto culturally/naturally admixed and ambiguous entities that Latour calls "hybrids" and Haraway figures as "material-semiotic actors." Nature emerges as a discrete entity—to be by turns reviled, sanctified, ignored—only when it can be disengaged irrevocably from the human sphere. Latour argues that this compulsion to separate the world into two parts actually promotes the potential for mixing, engendering the proliferation of ever more hybrid "nature-cultures." And what is odd is that these hybrids of social and natural processes have to be denied as such because, along with such correlates as objectivity and subjectivity or human and nonhuman, the idea of nature versus culture helps sanction the various ideological, scientific, and bureaucratic ways we break the world into manageable chunks. Policing the segregation of the cultural and the natural is therefore essential, because to acknowledge that something could straddle both categories would complicate determinations of jurisdiction, slowing or halting our progressive rationalization of the world. So there is much at stake in keeping these distinctions alive, helping to explain, for example, why those who oppose the use of bovine growth hormone in cattle call it unnatural while those who market it claim it is perfectly natural. Is BGH an artifact, or as natural as milk itself? The answer depends on how you define *natural.* But more significant, the invocation of the natural/cultural distinction rewards foes and friends of the product alike, for rhetorically it helps them locate BGH in prepurified categories that instantly clarify the chemical's ontological pedigree.

In chapter 3 I argue that Niklas Luhmann's social systems approach can help explain why such distinctions are efficacious not only in terms of socioeconomic goals, but are in fact structurally unavoidable. For Luhmann, the historical development of society has produced a situation in which the various zones of social communication (the legal, the political, the economic, etc.) have differentiated into self-referential subsystems, which are organizationally closed but structurally open to their environment. The internal dynamic of each is a programming structure that reduces environmental stimuli into a binary code of the form $x/not-x$, by means of which the system can carry out its operations (e.g., any communication to be processed by the legal system must be reducible to a decision about legality or illegality); only stimuli that can be coded in this fashion can be processed and incorporated into the system's unity. Thus, each system can only see what it can see—it is effectively blind to stimuli that exceed its functionally specific encoding capacity. *Nature* under this scheme is necessarily plural, just one more item in a system's total environment, so that the challenge lies in pressing each of the systems to develop more capacity to observe nature according to its own unique predilections, rather than seeking to limit its understanding of nature to the same predefined category of meaning (presumably submitted and monitored from elsewhere).

What would perspectival shifts such as these—away from discovering objects' essences or their continuity with the human, and toward the mapping of differential relations or disjunctions between various modes of observation—require of criticism, particularly for those wishing to revise the pastoral tradition of American literature? How could the critical notions of system, environment, and hybrid be deployed to reinterpret or redirect the ideological uses to which Emerson and Thoreau have been put? As we have seen, after Leo Marx the pastoral literary text is said to connect nature and civilization by a process of mediation: because the author cannot find the pastoral synthesis in life (due to the constant acceleration of industry and technology), he is left to create a "virtual resolution" on paper. By contrast, my aim is to offer a replacement of the so-called nature/culture split with a system/environment distinction, rather than proposing the former's resolution (or, as is now actually the more orthodox position, its deconstruction). When the nature/culture split is superceded by a system/environment distinction, traditional philosophical approaches are largely beside the point, for the difference between a system and an environment draws more on biology or cognitive science than phenomenology or dialectics. Indeed, much of what I propose in subsequent chapters is rooted in the idea that we can sidestep many of these metaphysical impasses when we recast them in the terms and concepts provided by theories of self-organization and autonomy.

Along those lines, I argue in chapter 3 that what Emerson and Thoreau are confronted with is not nature per se but a hypercomplex, heterogeneous environment. In that view, we read them *not* to see how they resolve the disharmonies and contradictions presented by that environment (which, of course, I acknowledge freely is the strong reading of what they are trying to do) but rather to see how they catalog, codify, and specify environmental hypercomplexity. That is, I am interested in their raw observations, not their dialectics, and in the moments when irresolution is still in play, not when all loose ends are safely tidied up. If we attend to the passages when environmental uncertainty is most pronounced, we may find ourselves asking new questions about the roles of Emerson and Thoreau in the American tradition of environmental conservation. Can, for example, Emerson's theory of nature serve as a social theory if read through the lens of autopoiesis? Could Emerson, who is now seen essentially as a spokesperson for the utilitarian view of nature, be more valuable as a diagnostician (and, at times, victim) of the systemic blindnesses and observational limitations inherent in the functional differentiation of society? In some of his essays, for example, he replicates the programmatic work of the social system itself, whose self-referentiality is constructed and maintained on the basis of an insurmountable difference with an external environment. In the case of Thoreau, his unabashed allegiance to the wild over the tame casts him as the prototypical American ecosoph, concerned with finding and grounding morally correct action in pure nature. But in his coding of environmental complexity along a moral axis (as opposed to Emerson's "sharing-out" of environmental complexity among several different coding regimes) does Thoreau still adequately model our current system-environment predicament?

Emerson and Thoreau bookend the span of American environmentalism: On the one hand, in Emerson we see a source for the anthropocentric, shallow ecological paradigm advocated by Roosevelt, Pinchot, and the early Leopold, which seeks to conserve nature by touting its multiple uses to humankind; on the other hand, in Thoreau we see the stirrings of the more ecocentric vision, an uncompromising, morally charged commitment to the nonhuman world also expressed in the writings of Muir, the later Leopold, Carson, and present-day deep ecologists and ecofeminists. However, if these traditions of conservation/environmental thought that Emerson and Thoreau helped shape follow trajectories rooted in systemically conditioned options rather than in totalizing ethical principles (as the members of those traditions would have us believe), we may better understand their tenacious hold on the American imagination. What is more, by bearing in mind that both Emerson and Thoreau are constrained in their visions by the same observational strictures that all systems must obey when regarding their environments, we may be surprised to discover that what is pertinent about these authors for ecological thought today does *not* arise from their most lapidary, quotable observations about the value, beauty, and sanctity of nature. Instead, what may be most crucial is precisely that which Emerson and Thoreau *did not say, did not see,* and *could not know* about those environments that they lived in, wrote about, and which they so obviously loved. As we explore the significant features of systems and environments, what crystallizes is the paradoxical proposition championed by Luhmann that fits well my exemplars' predicament: reality is what you do not see when you see it.

Systems Theory, Cybernetics, and Self-organization

The Dream of a Systems Theory

I begin this chapter by conceding that it is quite beyond the scope of this book—and me—to provide a thorough background discussion of systems theory and the related strains of contemporary thought that contribute to the critical approach I unpack in subsequent chapters. Fortunately, such a discussion would be unnecessary to the book's main arguments, since the particular systems approaches of Varela, Maturana, and Luhmann represent a decisive enough break with previous theory that they can be presented without lengthy prologue in the context of their application to the target texts by Emerson and Thoreau. Thus, I can safely and happily leave the history of systems theory and its congeners to others.[1] But as a general introduction to the style of thinking involved here, it may be helpful to delineate briefly some of the key issues in systems theory, cybernetics, and self-organization. The concepts that have emerged from these fields are thrown around quite casually; I am as guilty as anyone. But this looseness is intrinsic to the discourse of systems theory, and in part this chapter explains why. (For readers reasonably familiar with the discourse of systems theory and cybernetics, this chapter can be safely skipped.)

First, I must define *system* more precisely than I did in the introduction. There I said that a system was an interrelated set of elements that controlled its inputs and outputs through a boundary. More precisely, a system can be defined as "a set of *components* interacting with each other and a *boundary* which possesses the property of filtering both the kind and rate of flow of *inputs* and *outputs* to and from the system" (Berrien, 14–15). The components act in a mutually beneficial fashion; that is, the interrelation of components produces an organization of such type that the organization in turn facilitates the continued interrelation of the components. Implied in the very concept of the system is its complement, the environment, with the boundary of the system serving to demarcate the two. Inputs and outputs flow across the boundary in the form of matter, energy, and/or information; the boundary might be as discrete as a cell wall or as amorphous as the semiotic gradient that exists between different dialects or discourse communities. The distinction between closed and open systems is also crucial. Closed systems control their boundaries so tightly that there is no traffic with the environment; open systems permit the passage of matter, energy, and information. Closed systems are highly improbable, so much so that total closure to the environment is only theoretical (or approximated within a laboratory setting); even among machine systems (for example, clocks or computers) designed to be closed, periodic inputs of energy or information are required. Moreover, in nature, systems never exist in isolation and so, to varying degrees, all are open. When I speak of systems in this book—and especially social systems, the systems I am most concerned with—I am always referring to open ones (no matter that their structural openness may be predicated on other kinds of closure).

The foregoing definition, however, still has not established what sorts of things can be understood as systems—or, to put it another way, what sorts of things *cannot* be understood as systems. In fact, almost anything can be defined as a system: from atoms to organisms, from soap bubbles to conversations. Ervin Laszlo claims

> we can discern systems of organized complexity wherever we look. Man is one such system, and so are his societies and his environment. Nature itself, as it manifests itself on this earth, is a giant system maintaining itself, although eventually all its individual parts get sifted out and replaced, some more quickly than others. Setting our sights even higher in terms of size, we can see that the solar system and the galaxy of which it is a part are also systems, and so is the astronomical universe of which our galaxy is a component. (12)

Systems, evidently, are just the familiar contents of the world redescribed as systems. "The term [system]," writes Frederick Bates in a more obviously constructivist vein, "refers to a complex cognitive apparatus that organizes or orders an image of empirical phenomena in the mind of an observer according to a structural strategy. . . . It operates in the mind as a kind of artificial 'thinking' machine that imposes an order on the mind's transactions within itself and between itself and a world encountered through the senses" (69). It goes without saying that such impositions can take innumerable forms, as many as can be imagined.

Due in part to the undiscriminating nature of its central concept, the story of systems theory (or "system theory" in its earliest incarnations) is one marked by breathtaking promise and underwhelming fulfillment. A theory with such broad sweep is quite attractive in principle but extremely unwieldy in application, and its history indeed shows that we invoke systems theory less and less even as we draw implicitly on systems concepts more and more. Effectively, the systems approach has been routinized within traditional disciplines, while many of its lofty integrative goals have gone by the boards. Thus, on the one hand, systems theory's central preoccupation—to regard the whole instead of the part, patterns of concerted behavior instead of atomized units acting mechanistically—has become a given in a great many fields, from business management to environmental studies. Politicians speak of infrastructures as effortlessly as biologists of ecosystems, and medical doctors want to treat the whole person just as educators want to teach the whole child. On the other hand, the failure of systems theory to find the logicomathematical formulae that would correlate, say, ecosystems to human communities through invariant patterns of organization means that systems theory has produced very little in the way of a grand, unifying paradigm that its early pioneers had promised.

Even so, whenever there is a need to emphasize the nondiscreteness of selected phenomena the language of systems invariably is invoked. Like structuralism—an approach to which it bears more than a passing resemblance—systems theory promises integration of the world's flux on the basis of formal relationships, and for a host of reasons such an approach is more attractive than classic analytical modes. Writing in 1972, Laszlo noted, "Whereas traditional reductionism sought to find the commonality underlying diversity in reference to a shared *substance*, such as material atoms, contemporary general systems theory seeks to find common features in terms of shared aspects of *organization*" (19-20). Today, few wish to be characterized as atomistic, so even admittedly reductionist projects like E. O. Wilson's attempt to unify all disciplinary agendas and the knowledges they produce take on systems theory's less provocative vocabulary and holistic style of thinking. In Wilson's case, the "strong form [of reductionism] is consilience, which holds that nature is organized by simple universal laws of physics to which all other laws and principles can eventually be reduced" (55). But that reduction is complemented by broad synthesis, with the result the holistic "jumping together" of knowledge that the term *consilience* is in fact meant to evoke. Such a stance is meant to take some of the edge off Wilson's more outré statements about ethics, religion, or literary criticism, especially claims that these domains may be best understood by reference to the "biologically evolved epigenetic rules that guided them" (213). (I concede to a certain attraction to Wilson's basic passion, the notion of finding a small number of factors capable of producing vast complexity. But as I suggest below, there is a big difference between his confident reductionism and contemporary systems approaches, which, though undeniably reductive on the one hand, are thoroughly aleatory on the other.)

Perhaps, then, a latent desire for holism (which some critics argue is merely a recent version of an age-old organicism) explains the systems approach's continuing

allure. Perhaps, too, uncovering hitherto unnoticed resemblances is inherently appealing, like finding hidden faces in a drawing. But the early systems theorists had
more pragmatic impulses as well, much more in line with science's long-standing
aspirations and self-conceptions. According to A. Bogdanov, a pioneering but largely
overlooked system theorist of the early Soviet era, an "organizational science" should
begin with a very clear understanding: "Dominion is a relationship of the organizer to
the organized. Step by step, mankind acquires control over and conquers nature; this
means that step by step [mankind] *organizes the universe;* it organizes the universe
for itself and its own interests. . . . Mankind has no other activity except organizational activity, there being no other problems except organization problems" (1–3).
A systems science would apply itself to those problems, producing instruments and
methods to exert superior control. Only a bit less grandly, Ludwig von Bertalanffy,
systems theory's first great synthesist, called on researchers to seek out and formalize
isomorphisms through a general theory of systems, which would be valid for any
and all phenomena that obeyed the basic system criteria. It is important to point
out that Bertalanffy never argued that diverse systems would not require further,
specific explanations and local laws. But he did claim that "the existence of laws
of similar structure in different fields makes possible the use of models which are
simpler or better known, for more complicated and less manageable phenomena"
(80). A general system theory would be "an important means of controlling and
instigating the transfer of principles from one field to another [so that] it will be
no longer necessary to duplicate or triplicate the discovery of the same principles
in different fields isolated from each other" (80–81). In other words, Bertalanffy
wanted a theory of isomorphisms that not only would save science time and effort,
but whose success in doing so would prove that "the structure of reality is such
as to permit the application of our conceptual constructs . . . in the sense that a
certain conceptual construct is unequivocally related to certain *features of order*
in reality" (83; my emphasis). Those features of order, he explained, would be
found in far different fields, from language development to evolutionary biology
and geomorphology. They include principles "such as those of wholeness and
sum, mechanization, hierarchic order, approach to steady states, equifinality" (84)
as well as principles relating to growth, competition, centralization, and feedback.
Once identified, they would give unparalleled opportunities for implementable solutions to a wide range of problems, not just theoretical ones but those encountered
in the day-to-day operations of particular systems. The work of Stafford Beer in
management science and Kenneth Boulding in economics are cases in point, but
even Talcott Parsons's action-oriented social systems approach had clear normative
implications for education, medicine, and psychology.[2] "Systems," as Bertalanffy
puts it, "at many levels ask for scientific control" (xx).

But while the basic conceptual strategy of focusing on patterns of organized behavior rather than on mechanism has become a central tenet in almost every field of inquiry, Bertalanffy's great dream of integration has been quietly laid to rest. As I have already suggested, a key drawback is the very essence of the general systems approach: that almost anything one wants to call a system meets the definition of system. I, my computer, my community, and the universe are all systems, possessing interrelated sets of components and boundaries that control inputs and outputs. It is true that Bertalanffy addressed the ontological question by classifying systems according to degree of concreteness (e.g., "a galaxy, a dog, a cell and an atom are *real systems*" to be contrasted with "*conceptual systems* such as logic, mathematics . . . which are essentially symbolic constructs" [xxi]), but the overwhelming thrust of his writings is toward broad integration. The dizzying prospect of a true systems multidisciplinarity, which sounds enormously powerful in theory, might be difficult for any researcher to put into practice. As Laszlo puts it,

> The systems approach does not restrict the scientist to one set of relationships as his object of investigation; he can switch levels, corresponding to his shifts in research interests. A systems science can look at a cell or an atom as a system, or it can look at the organ, the organism, the family, the community, the nation, the economy, and the ecology of systems, and it can view even the biosphere as such. A system in one perspective is a subsystem in another. But the systems view always treats systems as the integrated wholes of their subsidiary components and never as the mechanistic aggregate of parts in isolable causal relations. (14–15)

This flexibility must be purchased at the cost of practicability, precision, and verifiability, frequently making the results of systems investigations appear anecdotal; too often they read like redescriptions of old findings rather than new contributions.

Conceptually, the first generation of systems theory was never able to move past *analogy* as the primary figure for relating diverse organized phenomena. The analogic is a weak comparison that suggests resemblance of structure, appearance, or process. While analogy is quite useful in prompting one to look for more specific, formal commonalities after noting the general one—and thus to homologies and true causal explanations—it may just as easily lead one down false trails. For example, the parallel development of isolated language groups with the same root stock is an analogue to the parallel evolution of isolated species with common genetic origins. But the comparison begins and ends there. No formal law connects the two phenomena, though one could waste a lot of time searching for it. Similarly, suppose the rate of industrialization in a country matched its birth rate (in fact, this occasionally happens). Now, even if the curves are mathematically identical we have no reason to suppose that the functions so described are "unequivocally related" to a structure of reality; there are undoubtedly factors relating the functions, but all of them are completely equivocal. It is we who have decided, out of a sea of possible comparisons, to put these two side-by-side and marvel at their congruency. It would be almost as absurd to find a potato that looked like Richard Nixon and blame the resemblance on an underlying law of form. At best we can say that our "conceptual constructs" have constructed a striking isomorphism; we certainly cannot say that they have wrapped themselves around "features of order in reality."

In James Grier Miller's remarkable and in many ways admirable opus, *Living Systems*, one encounters a one thousand–page unpacking of a fascinating, multi-layered analogy between nineteen critical subsystems that make up seven different levels of living systems: cells, organs, organisms, groups, organizations, societies, and "supranational" systems.[3] The analogy plays out across each of the seven levels where, owing to common evolutionary origins and a "shredding out" (essentially, a division of labor) of necessary functions, all nineteen of the critical subsystems can be accounted for by examining the structures each of the seven levels has at its disposal. For example, the "motor" subsystem in a cell consists of flagella, cilia, pseudopods, or other organelles that facilitate movement, while in society the motor includes "Organization in transportation or construction industry, armed forces, space agency; [the motor function] may be downwardly dispersed to groups such as family, work group, or to individual person or domesticated animal; [it may con-sist of] artifacts such as windmill, mill wheel, wagon, sailboat, truck, locomotive, ship, military tank, plane, missile, earthmoving machine" (768). One could add to this list, justifiably I think, *anything:* baby buggy, knapsack, garden hoe. But the addition, like Miller's list itself, must be on the basis of a stretched analogy, of a contortion of fact to fit the model. The principle of locomotion that does define the primary function of motor organelles translates over to social systems in only the most generalized way. If systems theory is rooted in such generalizations, then all poets are systems theorists, for when they use metaphor they are being only slightly less precise than Miller when he identifies an amoeba's pseudopods with bulldozers.

In his conclusion, Miller claims that "the relations among the components of the living systems are not put there by the imagination of the observer, as shepherds idly trace out a crab in the stars or patients find bats in the inkblots. The relations are inherent in the totality of the system and are empirically discovered by the scientist because they are there, patterning the coacting reality" (1051). Thus, the contribution of a general theory is to demonstrate the continuity of living systems via these fundamental relations—and by extension the unity of science. But the demonstration cannot avoid a chief weakness of the first generation of general systems theories: despite Miller's assurances, it is an *observer* who sees the system, and it should come as no surprise that he has defined systems (and concomitantly the principles of their organization) that conform to his penchant for isomorphisms. Again: in the right light, anything can look like anything else, and if you are looking for Jesus, you can expect to find His face on Mars or in a tortilla.

The extraordinary audacity of systems theory did not go unchallenged. In 1978, Robert Lilienfeld's devastating critique, *The Rise of Systems Theory*, charged that systems thinking is an "objectification and reification of the scientist's attempt to control nature, including human and social nature, by seeing nature as controllable, so that the subjective intentions of the scientific intellectual become reified as a set of 'facts' which are treated not as aspirations but as facts" (278). Systems thinking in his account is thoroughly ideological, with three classes of promoters: "(1) the engineers, the cyberneticians, and the operations researchers, located for the most part in the aerospace industry and in the sectors of the academic world that are oriented toward technology; (2) academicians, including economists, political scientists, sociologists and biologists, oriented primarily toward science or 'scientism' in one form or the other; (3) the bureaucrats of the social service world" (268). I do not think it is necessary to expand a great deal on this taxonomy. The ideological predilections of this first generation of systems theorists seem of a piece with the Cold War consensus about the uses of technology, the inherent superiority of Western liberal democracy, and the nature and role of the sciences and scientists within the latter. But I do think it is important to add to Lilienfeld's critique that what we are dealing with here is not simply a problem of ideology—sociopolitical visions masquerading as objective science, authoritarian mindsets lurking behind flexible and fluid methodologies. For there is a serious epistemological problem as well. Even if we wanted to take the advocates of systems theory at their word and accept that systems exist and can be described value-free, today we cannot be satisfied with systems theory's lack of *self-reflexiveness:* unquestionably, the first generation of systems theories was proudly positivist, with a straight, unproblematic line running from phenomena to their observation and description.

Accordingly, a more supple accounting of the crucial role of the observer is a prerequisite for any revived systems approach. In fact, given that even the pioneers of general systems theory acknowledged a certain degree of construction on the part of the systems scientist, we might want to explore that idea further by postulating that construction is precisely what systems themselves do: construct themselves and the world they take themselves to be in. (Systems theory itself, by the way, as a theoretical discourse with components and boundaries will be no exception.) What, then, would be entailed in drawing a distinction between a system and the rest of the world—both for the system, which is trying to distinguish itself from the nonsystem, and for an observer of that system, whose observation also begins by making a distinction between system and nonsystem? And what of another observer, who observes the second observing the first? While we will not wish to take the nominalist route and conclude that all systems are finally in the eye of an observer, we cannot ignore the fact that without *embedding* the observer of systems in the theory itself, systems theory must remain little more than a study of form, and Platonism by any other name.

News of a Difference

Closely allied to systems theory is cybernetics, the science of "control and communication in the animal and the machine," as its founder Norbert Wiener famously defined it in the subtitle of his 1948 book, *Cybernetics*. Drawing explicitly and implicitly on the general systems approach, cyberneticists were also much interested in the organized behavior of complex phenomena. But now the focus became the inputs and outputs of systems across their boundaries and, especially, the circulation of information within and between systems. The activation and control of information circuits was the main issue for cybernetics, and it is quite easy to see how in the Cold War period such a science, with its implications for computing, robotics, rocketry, and advanced weaponry, would attract enormous interest and support. The names associated with cybernetics include some of the twentieth century's most influential thinkers: Wiener, Claude Shannon, Warren Weaver, John von Neumann, Warren McCullough, Margaret Mead, and Gregory Bateson.

The writings of Gregory Bateson provide a useful point of transition between cybernetics, the first generation of systems theory described above, and the second-order approach I introduce in the next section. Bateson, as a true interdisciplinarian with credentials in biology, anthropology, and psychology, was profoundly influenced by the developments in systems, cybernetics, and information theory that were ushering in the computer age. He quickly recognized in this work a style of thought that could potentially undo the Enlightenment mind-body split. He claimed that "cybernetics is the biggest bite out of the fruit of the Tree of Knowledge that mankind has taken in the last 2000 years" (*Steps,* 476). What he meant was that by thinking cybernetically we stop looking at the world as a collection of discrete objects; we perceive it in terms of flows of information, of pattern and form, and complex determination rather than simple causation. A cybernetic perspective would force us to abandon the notion of the object world altogether, Bateson thought. Ultimately, his pursuit was to unify mind and nature through a "pattern that connects," a metapattern capable of linking up contingent phenomena on the basis of a harmonious aggregate of patterns (*Mind,* 8).

The basis for Bateson's optimism begins with the concept of *difference*. Modifying Kant's statement that the *Ding an sich* (for example, a piece of chalk) contains an infinite number of facts, Bateson suggests

> that there are an infinite number of *differences* around and within the piece of chalk. There are differences between the chalk and the rest of the universe, between the chalk and the sun and the moon. And within the piece of chalk, there is for every molecule an infinite number of differences between its location and the locations it *might* have been. Of this infinitude, we select a very limited number, which become information. In fact, what we mean by information—the elementary unit of information—is a *difference which makes a difference*. (*Steps*, 453)

In selecting a finite number of differences to represent an object, we are reminded of the map/territory distinction of Korzybski: the map never comes close to representing all the possible differences in the territory. Another way to put this is to say that any representation—whether, say, an actual map or mental map—always contains far less information and complexity than the thing itself. Bateson describes the situation as follows: "I receive various sorts of mappings which I call data or information. Upon receipt of these I act. But my actions, my muscular contractions, are transforms of differences in the input material. And I receive again data which are transforms of my actions. We get thus a picture of the mental world which has somehow jumped loose from our conventional picture of the physical world" (*Steps*, 455).

The realization that the world is not so much represented as enacted in a cyclical transformation of inputs and outputs leads Bateson to deduce that the entire flowing circuit of information should be considered a mind. His example of a tree and a woodchopper illustrates the principle. In the Cartesian paradigm, a thinker-subject manipulates an ax in order to fell the tree-object. Simple causal interaction, in other words, between one distinct entity and another—our language (with its subject-verb-object structure) is well designed to describe such interactions. Under Bateson, however, the important interaction is the information circuit, not the matter-energy flow. The person wields the ax, the ax makes the cut, and "news of a difference" is passed through ax to arms and from tree to eye; adjustments are then made by physiochemical processes, a new cut is made, difference is again registered as new information is fed back. There is a constant circulation of information between subject and object. But those two categories have to be reconfigured now because the whole idea of a separate, inviolate mind acting on an object is called into question: Bateson believes that whatever mind is at work here must include the environment, which is part of the cybernetic loop. In Bateson's view, mind =

organism + environment. The nature versus culture antagonism is thus a dangerous illusion, for if you destroy your environment, you are destroying a part of your mind: "You decide you want to get rid of the by-products of human life and that Lake Erie will be a good place to put them. You forget that the eco-mental system called Lake Erie is part of *your* wider eco-mental system—and that if Lake Erie is driven insane, its insanity is incorporated in the larger system of *your* thought and experience" (*Steps,* 484).

The problem, of course, as even Bateson admitted, was that we do not know how to think cybernetically. It is one thing to reason that mind and nature are interlinked; it is quite another to feel that connection in everyday practice. I do not wish to pursue Bateson through his later work on the "pattern that connects," his effort to locate the metapattern that united the rest. Suffice it to say that this is a quest, in my view, that belongs more to religion than systems science. But what I wish to retain from Bateson as I move on to second-order cybernetic paradigms is his particularly compelling notion of *system,* the minimal requirements of which are as follows:

1. The system shall operate within and upon *difference.*
2. The system shall consist of closed loops or networks of pathways along which differences and transforms of differences shall be transmitted. (What is transmitted on a neuron is not an impulse, it is news of a difference.)
3. Many events within the system shall be energized by the respondent part rather that by impact from the triggering part.
4. The system shall show self-correctiveness in the direction of homeostasis and/or in the direction of runaway. Self-correctiveness implies trial and error. (*Steps,* 482)

According to Bateson, a system might be compared to a closed, self-regulating organism that receives and acts upon information in its environment. In reacting to such information, the system *observes* something about its environment, which may or may not have consequences for its own regulatory functions. Like the wood-chopper, such a system is looped in to its environment along a great many more pathways, and "differences" in the environment may enter the system as "transforms of differences."

What is most valuable here for my subsequent discussions of Maturana, Varela, and Luhmann is this issue of information transformation between system and environment. What might it mean, epistemologically speaking, to say that a system processes not information about the environment per se but rather transforms of information? The conceptual limitation we encounter under the Batesonian model is that there seems to be no accounting for this transformation by the organism. Does "news of a difference" simply register as raw stimuli playing over the surface of the organism, system, or mind, which then go on to recreate the sources and processes that must have produced the stimuli? Is there a point-to-point correspondence between the differences in the environment and the system? If the system or mind consists of organism + environment, how shall the system preserve its own pattern of organization in the event of environmental information overload?

Bateson comes closest to answering these questions when he states "many events within the system shall be energized by the respondent part rather than by impact from the triggering part." This may suggest that the system does somehow reorganize incoming information into systemically usable forms, effectively reducing input into more easily cognizable or assimilable codes. What is essential for a model of how, say, human societies interact with their environment is a more precise articulation of how that information or difference is uptaken by the society in a way that the society can act on it or disregard it. If, for example, we wish to understand the stance of nineteenth-century culture to a natural environment that had been significantly transformed, humanized, and otherwise relegated to a subordinate status, we need a model that can better explain how complex and variable environmental data are actually processed by social and conscious systems. We want to model how societies and individuals deal with the flood of stimuli they receive at every moment from their environments. We want to know how they channel this flood, how they organize it, make use of it, internalize it—and, most important, ignore almost all of it by *observing it selectively in the furtherance of their own priorities.* We want, then, a theory of *self-organizing* systems and their environments.

Self-organization

Despite the foregoing critiques, it is obvious that the systems approach has proved extraordinarily valuable in moving us away from object-oriented, atomistic modes of reduction and compartmentalization. While a general theory of the sort Bertalanffy imagined never emerged, a second-generation of systems approaches is flourishing, aided and abetted by a second-order cybernetics. Building on advances in such fields as nonlinear dynamics, complexity theory, and evolutionary science, these approaches to *biological* and *physical* systems can help us to better understand the theories of spontaneous *social* and *conscious* (and, as I argue, *textual*) ordering and differentiation that are at issue in Maturana and Varela and in Luhmann. The names associated with these approaches include Stuart Kauffman, John Holland, Ilya Prigogine, Isabel Stengers, Per Bak, Hermann Haken, Lyn Margulis, James Lovelock, Milan Zelany, and Heinz von Foerster. An indispensable concept in the work of all if these thinkers is *self-organization.*

Self-organizing systems are a subset of closed systems, those that maintain their organization on the basis of increasing self-involvement and concomitant indifference to the environment. There are a number of ways to define self-organization, and I cannot pretend to be exhaustive. John Mingers, for example, recognizes six self-organizing system types: self-influencing, self-regulating, self-sustaining, self-producing, self-referential, and self-conscious (83). As noted, all are closed systems, but each pursues its boundary maintenance and component interrelation in different ways and with varying degrees of insularity. What I want to emphasize is the idea that all such systems are constantly engaged in a struggle to maintain their overall organization against a countervailing tendency for their structures to dissipate, owing to the second law of thermodynamics. (I use *organization* to refer to the pattern in which real structures are put together, in the same way that *house* is the organizing pattern I apply to a certain assemblage of wood, bricks, and shingles.) Instead of becoming more open and responsive to their environments, self-organizing systems take the opposite tack. It is quite accurate to say that such systems remain self-organized by staking all on remaining self-organized. They do so by obeying a relatively small set of rules, "preadapting" to environmental insults, and, most significant, generating all of the processes, operations, and products that maintain their structures from moment to moment. In classic Marxian terms, they reproduce the conditions of their reproduction, but with the addendum that they refer only to themselves as they fashion and refashion their structures (including in the case of neural systems, thoughts) exclusively from within themselves, regardless of environmental provocation or penalty. Their key features are thus *circularity, self-production,* and *autonomy* (i.e., they take their own measure, they do for themselves, and they listen to no one).

When it comes to the systems I am primarily concerned with here—conscious and social—these key features must be kept in mind, because they indicate that the way such systems arrange themselves is inseparable from the way that they know the world. Their structures for observing and processing their environments cannot be detached from the pattern of their organization. In other words, only what the structures are capable of recognizing as relevant enters the system; and what enters serves to reaffirm the pattern of organization that enables the structural capacities in the first place.

This idea—that the structure and organization of the system are indivisible from the way the system knows its world—conveniently solves the problem of the observer I mentioned earlier. Returning to those earlier concerns of general systems theory, we ask, "Are systems real or merely diagrams? Are systems merely the impositions of order on the unmediated flux of experience?" We might choose to argue that these questions are in a sense false ones—or, in the Rortian sense, bad questions we might do well to stop asking. We cannot provide a satisfactory answer to them any more than we can to the question "Do objects exist?" If we are prepared to say that, yes, objects do exist, then we can equally argue that systems (i.e., patterns of organization that determine the structural coherence of objects) also exist. But when we are talking about self-organizing systems, we can provide another, more interesting—and I think satisfying—response to such questions: I can reasonably make the claim that what I describe in the following chapters are systems that actually do exist, in that my system description identifies the form that a *solution* takes in response to a *problem*. In other words, I am identifying phenomena that for my purposes behave like systems, and that for the purposes of the phenomena behave like systems too. They are my impositions—but they are not merely my impositions. We have moved from a question of ontology to a question of function.

What self-organization allows us to do that goes beyond the general systems approach is to say that instead of abstracting principles of organization that can apply to any phenomena, we choose to look at phenomena that seem to abstract themselves to achieve certain goals. This version of systems theory will describe phenomena that work systematically to solve environmental problems that threaten to erode the capacity of the phenomena to maintain their particular concatenation of structures. As a crude example, a house resists its degradation by striving to maintain its house organization, which is simply the overall pattern of its structures. But clearly, a house does not actually strive to do anything; its resistance to degradation is a function of the soundness of its construction. The organization of *house* is imposed entirely from outside—by the builder or repairer of the structures who wishes to maintain the house in a livable condition. So a house is precisely the sort of system we do *not* find compelling because it does not engage in self-organization; its organization is never its own concern. Thus, there is no particular value from a conceptual point of view to look at it as a system: it is well described under traditional modes of analysis.

Then what sorts of systems are compelling? Such systems would likely be complex (contrasted with simple, rule-governed systems like machines, including even computers), with indecomposable patterns of organization; they might be multileveled, nonlinear, capable of spontaneous change, possessed of emergent properties. Along these lines, there is one category of phenomena preeminently compelling: life. Life resists the imposition of external organization; in fact, life tries to preserve its internally set pattern of organization at any cost. In a book that ranges far from living systems before responding to the implicit challenge posed by its title, *Life Itself,* Robert Rosen concludes that *"a material system is an organism if, and only if, it is closed to efficient causation.* That is, if f is any component of such a system, the question 'why f?' has an answer within the system, which corresponds to the category of efficient cause of f" (244). In other words, the purpose of the structures of an organism can be found only in the organism. Rosen notes that under this regime, "Biology becomes identified with *the class of material realizations* of a certain kind of relational organization, and hence, to that extent divorced from the structural details of any particular kind of realization" (245). Rosen, a theoretical biologist much interested in a formal, mathematical definition of life that could help biology become a "*creative* endeavor,"[4] comes very close here to what in the next chapter I call the autopoietic definition of a living system: it is a concrete realization of structures according to a particular organization that, so long as this organization remains intact, is unconcerned with how its structures are concretely realized.

This definition seems on the surface to be no more insightful than Popeye's declaration "I yam what I yam." It is one thing to define a house tautologically since the purpose for its organization can be supplied from outside, but for living systems a tautological self-definition smacks of an evasion or displacement of the problem of purpose: where is the explanatory power of "life is life"? A number of other questions arise, too. If we assume that living organisms are self-organizing, self-referential systems along these lines, precisely what sort of systemic principles do they share? Are there fruitful distinctions to be made between simple, brainless organisms, those with sophisticated neural and immune subsystems, and those that share complex symbol systems (i.e., language) across a number of brains (i.e., a society)? Even more daring, might those nonliving symbol systems that are extruded by living ones also operate according to the principles of self-organization?

It will take a good part of the rest of this book to address this last series of questions. But I want to try to give a sense of the stakes of the answers right now using an extended analogy. In particular, this analogy is meant to preview the relevance of self-organization to environmental perception, a topic I take up again in earnest in the next chapter. Let us imagine a man has raised a cat in a windowless apartment. This man had some sort of traumatic experience involving a train during his childhood, and every time he hears a train whistling from the track a few blocks a way, he must vent his anger. He does so by squirting the cat thoroughly with a water pistol. The cat learns very early on to behave appropriately: to flee, in other words, when it hears the train coming. But usually the man can track the cat down before his anger abates and give it a good soaking. From the point of view of the cat, this ritual is fairly routine and always unpleasant; from the point of view of the man, it is necessary and justified. Now, from the point of view of an outside observer— say a friend who visits the man one evening—the ritual appears as something else entirely: bizarre, perverse, aberrant, and so on. I will ask an odd question now: epistemologically, what is happening here?

The answer must take into account how each character in this drama knows the grounds, limits, and validity of its experience of the world around it. In other words, what constitutes a belief for each of the participants? From the perspective of the man, he is observing in his mind's eye the figure of his childhood angst, the train; as he sees it, he is properly releasing his anger on the nearest being with which he can share and thus assuage his suffering. His knowledge of the events that produce the unpleasant result for the cat is complete and well grounded; that is, he knows why the audible sign of the train produces the chain of events that lead to a soggy cat and his temporary mollification. A reasonable observer of the man, of course, understands the episode in an entirely different way: a man spontaneously behaving thusly is surely unhinged.

The most interesting perspective is the cat's. The cat knows what a train whistle means, and like many things in its life, accepts it without too much reflection, if any; reality for a cat is mostly action and reaction, instinct and reflex. It has no understanding of the relationship of the sound, the train, the man's state of mind, or of anything at all, in fact, that exists outside the apartment. It knows as its environment only the apartment itself. In that world, its goal is to preserve itself in its favored state: satiated, comfortable, and dry. Whatever events occur to cause the man to spray it every time a certain noise is heard are beyond the ken of the cat. It reacts only to the observation that a certain sound proceeds a certain, well-defined threat to its preferred internal state. In other words, the cat knows what it means to be a whole, contented cat: it knows the items in its environment that go toward maintaining that catfulness (such as its food dish, its litter box, etc.) and those that do not (the squirt gun, the man's rage). Its world, for all intents and purposes, is just the world that it perceives in its attempt to maintain its catfulness. The world beyond the apartment is completely irrelevant to that maintenance, as are even many of the items found within the apartment. In fact, the whole notion of the cat being raised in an apartment with no knowledge of a larger world was a red herring: even if the man showed the cat the train and explained why he was doing what he was doing, the cat would not understand. From the cat's perspective, the items in the world outside the apartment are irrelevant (even the tins of cat food at the grocery store or the factory that produces its cat litter) to the cat's catfulness.

What is more, this example has not been an analogy: I have in fact delineated at least four discrete, very real, self-organized neural systems: those of the cat, the man, the observer, and our own (which is, of course, really a conflation of three others: mine, an implied reader, and an actual reader). What I have described here, then, epistemologically speaking, is a system (the cat) that specifies its environment; an observer (the man, who himself is a system) whose environment includes the cat; and an observer of the observer (again, also a system), whose environment includes the first man, the cat, and the troubling relationship between the two. We ourselves, as observers fully removed from the interaction, understand the whole drama completely differently: it is an example that records a certain relationship to evidence, proof, textuality, and so on. Each of these systems, in other words, sees things from a different angle. This is not simply to say, in a casual way, that everybody sees things differently; rather, it is to say, in a foundational way, that for every observer a different environment is specified, and this environment is specified on the basis of certain knowledges (defined simply as perceptual activity that permits responses to the environment, whether automatic or consciously monitored) that allow the system to cohere as a system. The cat knows what it is to be a happy cat, the man knows what he knows about the horror of trains and its assuagement, the friend knows what he knows about reasonable behavior, and we know something about how analogies are constructed to explain otherwise obscure phenomena or ideas. Knowledge in this sense is not about representing the world but about assembling what counts as a world to conform with what counts as (for want of a better word) self. The only validation for the correctness of the construction is that what counts as self is maintained. In other words, each system is organized around a particular version of self, and it maintains that self-organization by constantly checking to see if its current activity and interaction with its world reaffirms or threatens that organization. It will try to maintain that organization through whatever means it has at its disposal (e.g., the cat will run away; the man will make sure that his water pistol is always full; the observer will try to persuade the latter to seek therapy; "we" will decide if this example adds up to what we think of as explanation). With more precision in the subsequent chapters, I suggest that "knowledge of the world" and "self-organization" are two ways of talking about the same thing: that to come to know the world is to come to know yourself, that what you are is what you observe. The key to unlocking a form of awareness that we can rightly call common knowledge is to perform what I have alluded to already: a second-order observation, or the observation of observation. We will no longer seek an underlying ground by which to square these varied observations (of a cat, a man, and a friend) but rather stand outside of the whole zone of interaction, survey it, determine what the observers see and do not see based on their own unique and mutually exclusive angles of vision, and as best we can, expose our own critical angle that would presume to encompass and arrange all the rest.

Before I end this chapter, I want to anticipate what I know may be an objection to the sorts of readings I am going to undertake using a version of the systems theoretical approach I have outlined above. In the following chapters, I bring together literature, environmental philosophy, and systems theory in what I take to be a productive confluence. Yet I am fully aware that interdisciplinarity of this sort can often look like the scientization of literary studies. As Bruce Clarke notes, "scientism is preeminently a rhetorical device, one that often succeeds in cloaking both its rhetorical nature and its desire for cultural authority behind a borrowed façade of 'scientific objectivity' " ("Science," 152). Clarke argues that second-order systems theory imported for literary critical purposes avoids scientism because of the constructivist, self-reflexive nature of systems theory's epistemological frame, which this chapter has gone some way toward outlining. But I do want to make one final comment about the difference between the first generation of systems thinking and the second-order systems approach I adopt in this book, with the hope that some of those fears of scientization may be allayed.

Ironically, I begin with a claim that may at first seem to do nothing of the kind: when it comes to systems, most of the explanations for why things proceed as they do indeed can be boiled down to fitness. The rhetorically charged nature of this word does not escape me, and I know that any invocation of it carries great risks. In the old systems theories, fitness meant systems had to adapt to conditions to survive. In the West, the progressive march into modernization was taken to mean that Western systems—scientific, economic, social, political, psychological— were the fittest systems around, in that they were able to structure themselves in accordance with the environmental complexity both they themselves and the other non-Western social systems introduced. Indeed, the fact that the larger Western social system managed to cohere meant that for whatever problems were being introduced, the system was providing its own solutions. The Western social system's trajectory would produce the best of all possible worlds; Soviet critiques of the West's inevitable self-immolation were merely the imprecations of a closed, involuted system that had in fact mistaken its own reductions of social, political, and economic complexity for proper homeostatic self-regulation. It is hardly surprising, then, that in the wake of fascism, at the height of the Cold War, before Vietnam, and perhaps just a decade or two away from utopia, systems theory and cybernetics wanted to bolster—rather than be content to describe—the West's adaptive adequacy to the future's conditions of fitness.

But this sort of evolutionary paradigm got evolution itself wrong: *adaptation to conditions* now sounds vaguely Lamarckian; *preadaptation* is a better way to think about what we now more clearly understand as the nondirected—indeed, nonevolutionary—nature of evolution. What happens in evolution is that a mutation succeeds by dint of a lucky correspondence of structural expression to environmental conditions. It is more accurate, for example, to say that giraffes possess long necks because they have not yet been harmed by possessing them than to say giraffes have adapted to treetop eating. The latter formulation implies that evolution is a progressive, teleological process, which makes no more sense than calling "progressive" someone who happened to be on vacation when her house was leveled by a tornado. Chance mutations work, maybe not too well but enough to get by, and their bearers stay around. Or they do not and their bearers go away.

There is no doubt that even this nugatory version can sound reductive, in that negative progress is simply teleology turned on its head. As well, it has become clear recently that there must be more to evolution than an orthodox theory of selection can explain; orders emerge that seem to stake less on chance than on the main chance. When handling these concepts we are wise to be cautious; if the humanities scholar cannot be sure of getting everything right he must at least be sure he does not get the big things wrong, and nothing could be more wrong than reducing literature and culture to throws of the dice. However, in addition to these well-known risks, reduction does have the benefit of parsimony—for both systems and scholars who would like to make their environments a little less threatening and slightly more manageable. If we are honest, it is no more reductive to claim the evolution of social systems (including the literary system, which I argue for in the next chapter) proceeds on the basis of fitness to certain conditions than on the basis of adherence to, say, beauty, truth, or rationality. It might even be the case that beauty, truth, or rationality form the conditions of fitness for some systems.

The distaste for reduction to fitness—even as metaphor—lies in the fact that the reducers usually reduce in order to declare that there is nothing to be done: you cannot get away from biology, and therefore you cannot get away from x social arrangement or y economic organization, which are induced from that biology. With systems theory, however, we have to keep in mind that what is selected and works could always have been selected otherwise. And we have no way of knowing what might work until it is proved out. In this sense, the law of natural selection takes second place to a law of radical contingency. Any attempt to find a teleology of systems is foiled by this law. There is no long-term goal with systems, only a continual fumbling around for solutions to immediate problems. With systems, it is better to be lucky than good, stolid than smart. Crocodiles and cockroaches have been around tens of millions of years though none have won a Nobel prize.

So in the end, the reduction of complexity—by systems and scholars—is really about making virtues out of accidents or, said another way, mining risk for stability. To return this discussion back to the unwelcome scientization of literature and culture: what we are talking about here is viewing systems (of whatever stripe: social, conscious, literary, etc.) as solutions to particular environmental exigencies, no more, no less. But a systems approach can finally say absolutely nothing about the efficacy of those solutions beyond the environmental conditions in which they appear to have emerged; for there may be many other ways to handle the problems that elicited them. Systems may always be otherwise. In that we may take some comfort.

Emerson's Environments

The Crisis of Vision

For Emerson, the critical choice always lay between mob or monad, copy or original, disciple or demiurge. The difference between a man and a great man is determined by the latter's capacity to recognize and activate the inner genius that resides in all but slumbers in most. Yet in the following passage from "Experience" (from the subsection Emerson called "Subjectiveness"), he seems undecided whether this reflexive awareness is blessing or curse:

> It is very unhappy, but too late to be helped, the discovery we have made, that we exist. That discovery is called the Fall of Man. Ever afterwards, we suspect our instruments. We have learned that we do not see directly, but mediately, and that we have no means of correcting these colored and distorting lenses which we are, or of computing the amount of their errors. Perhaps these subject-lenses have a creative power; perhaps there are no objects. Once we lived in what we saw; now, the rapaciousness of this new power, which threatens to absorb all things, engages us. Nature, art, persons, letters, religions, objects, successively tumble in, and God is but one of its ideas. (CW 3:43–44)

The euphoric egoism of "Self-Reliance" is replaced by the world-weary tones of one who has lost much and found little comfort within the perimeter of his own being—into which, granted, flows the entire world, but which, on the other hand, distorts that world in such ways that he may no longer be sure what is "world" and what is "him." At one time, Emerson's brush with solipsism was but a step on the virtuous path to transcendence; now he wonders if idealistic free play has not been a curse all along. That transition—from a self-reliant supereyeball, which operates on the basis of *"Whim"* and hopes off-handedly that "it is somewhat better than whim at last, but . . . cannot spend the day in explanation" (CW 2:30), to a self-deceiving "subject-lens," which perceives obliquely and with an unknown degree of astigmatism—seems like a move from activity to reactivity, from vision as creation to resignation to the visual. There is in "Experience" the not very veiled sense that many things turn out to be beyond our view and beyond our control, that "men seemed to have learned of the horizon the art of perpetual retreating and reference" (CW 3:28), while "forget[ting] that it is the eye that makes the horizon" (CW 3:44). Where does Emerson find himself? In "Self-Reliance" his location is irrelevant for, as he says, "my giant goes with me wherever I go" (CW 2:46); by "Experience," stalled in "a series of which we do not know the extremes, and believe it has none," the giant is visibly absent (CW 3:27).

What brought on the change in emphasis? We can be sure that the death of his young son Waldo contributed greatly to Emerson's funk; so too did the economic crises of the late 1830s test the faith—in the advancing cause of America, humanity, the universe, and, in particular, the self—of even the most resolute individuals, Emerson most definitely included. But whatever the specific sources of the rather constricted optics of "Experience" (as contrasted with the mostly ecstatic earlier essays), I would like to suggest that this trend toward a more limited, fragmentary, and partial vision of "vision" simply transposes onto a literary canvas what the modernization of the country was bringing about on the socioeconomic scene in general. For those sensitive enough to apprehend the broadest implications of that modernization, a certain anxiety, even pessimism might have been the most human response, given that no language, philosophy, or historical precedent existed that could have smoothly integrated these incipient transformations into some safe and comfortable frame of reference. Hegel had said that if history teaches us anything, it is that history has taught us nothing; and, indeed, what analysis of history *could* have produced a vision adequate to this modernity still under construction, a modernity that was to shatter the long-standing hierarchical sedimentation of the social, economic, and sacral orders, and replace it with an agglomeration of mutually antagonistic communication domains, whose unity from now on lay only in their common drive to insulate themselves from the environmental influence of each other and of nature itself? The effects of such parcelization and discontinuity would have been more felt than comprehended, more sensed as generalized incoherence and upheaval than coolly rationalized as the functional adjustment of a society confronted with growing internal complexity. The easiest way for us to imagine what Emerson and his contemporaries faced (or refused to face) is to picture that old and durable "great chain of being," which for centuries had imaginatively connected the earth and its continuum of life-forms, plant, animal, woman, man, king, on up to the angels and God himself—picture that chain snapped and scattered. In its place envision a honeycomb of enclosed fields or pastures, each with its own specific and voluble contents (somber-toned religion in here, the clamorous market in here, and stentorian politics over there); each shielded from its neighbors by a low wall that obstructs sight lines and muffles voices; and around them all a thorny, if not impenetrable, hedgerow, on the other side of which is everything that cannot speak for itself, wild nature included. The vertical now horizontal, the gaze up and down a glance over the shoulder, and the vision of "One" a profusion of divisions.

Although Emerson never precisely comes to terms with this new arrangement (how could he have?), it is not his problem alone. Even today we do not have an answer to the challenges posed by multiple frames of reference and, indeed, are troubled by the thought of a world without "One," some reliable principle of certainty that remains true across time, space, culture, faith, and so on. No one seems particularly comfortable with radical relativism. In fact, the difficulty of narrating in joyful voice the relativity of all observations has created a vacuum into which some sly observers have been able to substitute practical power for the lost position of unity, and hence presumed themselves to be in possession of the one crucial perspective on the total environment. From that position of presumptive centrality they interpret, for example, environmental degradation as the unintended backslap of the economy's invisible hand, the same hand, which given time and more capital, will caress the environment back to health. The crisis of "One" has meant, in effect, not the end of metanarratives but their transmogrification into a kind of perverse commitment to the "way things are," which simply means that the problems associated with extreme environmental contingency, complexity, and risk are viewed only from the perspectives of growth economics and technocratic pragmatism, those "mature" perspectives that thrive on the analysis of such problems but that have so much to do with the problems in the first place.

That the crisis announced in "Experience," too, would be dealt with by Emerson's later, more sober, more "experienced" reformulations of the ecstatic positions taken in earlier essays is a point made well and frequently by others before me. This is not to say that there was no bright thread connecting Emerson's thought from start to finish; rather, in a sense his entire career was a continual reweaving of the same basic set of issues and ideas. As Carolyn Porter notes in a discussion of the later essay "Fate," "It is easy to regard Emerson's declining optimism as a belated ascent to maturity. But we will fail to appreciate Emerson's rhetorical power or understand the sources of his limitations if we do not see that they are both grounded in contradictions inherent in his critical position from the outset of his career" (112). Those contradictions, to my mind, are most apparent in the short period between *Nature* and "Experience"; and they map well onto the contradictions that existed between the emerging social and natural orders in industrializing America. There were many discourses—most of them already obsolete—that were attempting to describe that new order and respond to it (e.g., Luddism, Fourierism, Hegelianism, and soon, Marxism). But of those discourses, perhaps Emerson's (unsystematic, contradictory, and impressionistic as it may have been) was more attuned to the zeitgeist than almost any other. "Experience" shows that "From the mountain you can see the mountain" (CW 3:30), a synoptical narrowing tantamount to sightlessness alongside the "I am nothing; I see all" exultations of *Nature* (CW 1:10). Yet "Experience" shows, too, that some rescaling of self before the unfolding challenges posed by an increasingly multivalent and multiplex social system was appropriate.

What form those challenges took, how Emerson sought in his own way to articulate them, and why they have a bearing on the concept of nature as it developed in the nineteenth century, is the subject of this chapter. I propose that certain developments in systems theory open up not only new ways of thinking about these challenges but new ways of asking old questions: about Emerson, about his understanding of nature, about his hopes for nature's leavening of the excesses of society. I show that Emerson's epistemological trajectory as he moves from *Nature* to "Experience" reveals a growing awareness of what will become one of the key implications of systems theory: that our insights into specific workings of the world depend precisely on a kind of general blindness to insight's "outside." Said another way, the price we pay for remaining who we are from moment to moment is that we can never have what Emerson says we most want, "an original relation to the universe," which I gloss as an unceasing openness to the total horizon of environmental possibility. For Emerson, ironically, it is exactly his relentless rooting out of the original, the new, the distinctive possibility, that brings him face-to-face with this crucial insight of a self-observing/self-conscious system: that it is upon one's closure to the world that all openness is predicated.

Autopoietic Systems

Humberto Maturana and Francisco Varela begin their essay "Autopoiesis: The Organization of the Living" by noting, "A universe comes into being when a space is severed into two. A unity is defined. The description, invention and manipulation of unities is at the base of all scientific inquiry" (*Autopoiesis*, 73). The cut creates two entities, and separating out one instantly identifies the other. In making such distinctions, scientific inquiry—any inquiry, really—finds purchase on the world. Emerson might have agreed. He says in the introduction to *Nature*, "All science has one aim, namely, to find a theory of nature," and goes on to claim that "Philosophically considered, the universe is composed of Nature and the Soul" (CW 1:8). Emerson makes his opening move by finding what he perceives as a crack in the smooth eggshell of the world, which he uses to establish two identities: his own soul/mind/self, and everything else—"Nature" or, as he will also say, the "Not Me" (what is often called elsewhere the mind/body or the subject/object dualism). While Emerson's goal in the rest of *Nature* is to repair this crack (and he fails, of course, to do any more than displace it), his founding gesture replicates the strategy that Maturana and Varela view as critical for autonomous, self-organizing systems: establishing an impermeable, organizational boundary between the system and its environment.

Like many other theorists in the life and cognitive sciences, Maturana and Varela wondered how complex biological systems can maintain their coherence in the face of even more complex environments, retaining their formal integrity even as their internal components adapt and change over time. How, too, they asked, can such systems develop greater complexity than their constituent components and structures taken separately might suggest? In other words, as the question was once framed, why is the sum of an organism so much more than its parts? The term *autopoiesis* was coined by Maturana to draw attention to what he decided were the defining features of living systems: their circular, self-referential organization, or *autonomy;* and their continual creation *(poiesis)* of the components that structure and sustain that autonomy (*Autopoiesis,* xvii). Maturana and Varela imagine a living system as an "autopoietic machine," organized "as a network of processes of production, transformation and destruction of components that produces the components which: (i) through their interactions and transformations regenerate and realize the network or processes (relations) that produced them; and (ii) constitute it as a concrete unity in the space in which they exist by specifying the topological domain of its realization as such a network" (*Autopoiesis,* 135). Autopoietic systems thus maintain their organization (a defining relationship among the various components and processes of a unity) even as their *structure* (the actual assemblage of components and processes that make up the unity) may change as a result of perturbations in the environment. The example of a toilet can demonstrate the difference between organization and structure: the toilet mechanism is organized as "an apparatus capable of detecting the water level and another apparatus capable of stopping the inflow of water. The toilet unit embodies a mixed system of plastic and metal comprising a float and a by-pass valve. This specific structure, however, could be modified by replacing the plastic with wood, without changing the fact that there would still be a toilet organization" (*Tree,* 47).[1]

To say that a toilet is organized on the basis of its water-regulating capability may not strike all of us as obvious. We tend to think that a toilet is organized on the basis of its function in human waste disposal, which is certainly its primary function both as it is used and as it was conceived, and as far as the toilet bears on these human goals, the water-regulating function appears as a necessary but certainly not sufficient feature in the toilet's definition. However, as Maturana and Varela explain, that we can create a "purpose" for an autopoietic machine, or simply place it within a larger context of organization, are notions "intrinsic to the domain of observation, and cannot be used to characterize any particular type of machine organization"

(*Autopoiesis,* 78). It is thus a matter of convenience, of nomenclature, to ascribe any purpose at all to an autopoietic entity. Varela puts it this way:

> It is important to realize that we are not using the term organization in the defini-
> tion of an autopoietic machine in a transcendental sense, pretending that it has an
> explanatory value of its own. We are using it only to refer to the specific relations that
> define an autopoietic system. Thus, autopoietic organization simply means processes
> concatenated in a specific form: a form that constitutes and specifies the system as a
> unity. It is for this reason that we can say that if any time this organization is actually
> realized as a concrete system in a given space, then the domain of the deformations that
> the system can withstand without loss of identity (that is, maintain its organization)
> is the domain of changes in which it exists as a unity. (*Principles,* 13)

If this passage sounds like a tautology, it is: a system is organized as it is organized, and if its organization changes then it is no longer organized in the way that it was originally. But we must remember that *autopoiesis* is conceived precisely to provide a definition of system based only on its organizational unity and the reproduction of that unity. Recalling the founding role of "making a distinction," we can say that the system is what it is, and is not what it is not: there is the toilet itself, and there is the rest of the world. The reference of the system only to its own immanent self-regulating, self-organizing autonomous structural processes is what simultaneously allows it to distinguish itself from its environment and constitute its unity. If a system can continue to meet the demands of its own organization, despite structural changes, then it maintains its identity (the toilet stays a toilet); if changes in structure force a change in organization, the system loses its identity, either by disintegrating, or by creating a new identity with a new organization (the toilet becomes, say, a water pump). When an observer ascribes purpose or use to an autopoietic machine he places it outside of its own autopoietic space, within which the only "purpose" is always simply to preserve autopoiesis. A corollary is that self-conscious systems (i.e., humans) may observe their own behavior and place it in contexts the consciousness-system does not properly have at the fundamental level of its organization. We stand outside ourselves and observe our actions and behaviors; only rarely do we attribute them to the simple fact of pursuing the goalless "goal" of preserving organizational coherence. In general, according to the theory of autopoiesis, though we consciously grant ourselves and others all sorts of motivations and purposes, at the level of our autopoietic functions there is no teleonomy at all. Marjorie Levinson says, "this amounts to a question of representation as survival," such that "The ghost in the rationalist and materialist machine is shown to be nothing but the survival of a form of organization in the real world as perceived by another system in that world, a system perforce specified by that organization and thus included in it" (122).

I have more to say about the role of self-observation below, but it may be useful here to note that what is interesting about Emerson in this regard is that he, so influentially among his American peers, grounded his entire philosophy in principles of autonomy, self-organization, and, in general, a concept of the individual that required no teleonomy other than what was already inherent in the individual's own organization. Emerson was unambiguous about this, insisting throughout his career on the need to follow the dictates revealed by the interior gaze: "It is simpler to be self-dependent. The height, the deity of man is to be self-sustained, to need no gift, no foreign force. . . . Everything real is self-existent. . . . I make my circumstance" (CW 1:203–4). The use of the reflexive form here and elsewhere reads almost like a tic: self-reliance, self-trust, self-sufficiency—we have heard the list. Emerson asks, "What is the aboriginal Self, on which a universal reliance may be grounded?" His answer: "The inquiry leads us to that source, at once the essence of genius, of virtue, and of life, which we call Spontaneity or Instinct. We denote this primary wisdom as Intuition. . . . In that deep force, the last fact behind which analysis cannot go, all things find their common origin" (CW 2:37). But what is all that interior vision supposed to produce? Emerson replies, "In the hour of vision there is nothing that can be called gratitude, nor properly joy. The soul raised over passion beholds identity and eternal causation, perceives the self-existence of Truth and Right, and calms itself with knowing that all things go well. Vast spaces of nature, the Atlantic Ocean, the South Sea; long intervals of time, years, centuries, are of no account" (CW 2:39–40). It seems that when we peel away all our various encrustations and look directly upon the generator of self, we can dispense with the idea of purpose or motivation altogether, for the purpose of the self, across time and space, is simply to remain identical with itself. To paraphrase God's tautological self-definition, we are what we are.[2]

If an autopoietic system works exclusively to reproduce its autopoiesis, how does it interact with its environment? Would it not be blind to that environment and likely to stumble inevitably in self-defeating directions, perhaps to the point of destroying its environment? In fact, this is always possible, so that just as with the evolution of species, only the successfully adapted systems persist.[3] By definition, an environment is always more complex than the system; the system's challenge is to continuously respond to those environmental factors that have a bearing on it—and screen out the rest. It does this through *structural coupling*, which Varela defines as "the continued interactions of a structurally plastic system in an environment with recurrent perturbations [which] will produce a continual selection of the system's structure" (*Principles*, 33). In effect, the environment may trigger changes in the system because the system is structurally open, but because the system is also *operationally closed* what forms those changes take are determined solely by the system itself as it strives to maintain its organization. Only the system can determine its structural changes, and only if further autopoiesis is secured can the changes to environmental pressures be considered appropriate.[4] The environment, in other words, can initiate changes but cannot determine how they play out in the system. For example, a nervous system will react to various sensory stimuli (touch, image, etc.) by reconjugating the order and arrangement of neural firings, which in turn may lead to particular motor responses. But considered at the level of its organization, the nervous system is simply attempting to maintain the already existing organization of its components, which has been perturbed by the environmental stimuli. Richard Lewontin, a geneticist whose work has been informed by dialectical materialism, confirms that "organisms actually change the basic physical nature of signals that come to them from the external world. As the temperature in a room rises, my liver detects that change, not as a rise in temperature, but as a change in the concentration of sugar in my blood and the concentration of certain hormones" (90). In a passage that should resonate well with the readers of Maturana and Varela, Lewontin says "The last rule of the relation between organism and environment is that the very physical nature of the environment as it is relevant to organisms is determined by the organisms themselves" (91).

Perhaps what is most interesting here is that the operational closure of the nervous system suggests some far-reaching epistemological consequences for systems in general and cognitive ones in particular. When we define the nervous system as closed to its environment, we seem to be saying that it is essentially solipsistic, in that its operations are self-referential and directed solely toward the maintenance of specific relations between internal structures. Yet at the same time, autopoietic systems do have the ability to structurally couple with environmental elements, and thus in some sense must be able to account for the environment internally. To put a finer point on the ramifications of their work, Maturana and Varela claim that the brain

is not solipsistic, because . . . it participates in the interactions of the nervous system in its environment. These interactions continuously trigger in it the structural changes that modulate its dynamics of states . . . This is so despite the fact that, for the operation of the nervous system, there is no inside or outside, but only the maintenance of correlations that continuously change. . . . Nor is it representational, for in each interaction it is the nervous system's structural state that specifies what perturbations are possible and what changes trigger them. . . . it brings forth a world by specifying what patterns of the environment are perturbations and what changes trigger them in the organism. (*Tree*, 169)

Ultimately, "Anything said is said by an observer" (*Autopoiesis*, 8), a crucial point made over and over again by Maturana and Varela to emphasize that communications are always made from within an observational domain and so are distinct from system-specific operations. We can dispense with debates about representationalism and solipsism if we simply remember that while systems do adjust themselves as they attempt to maintain their organization in a complex environment, it is observers who attribute those adjustments to specific system/environment interactions (i.e., behavior).

We have arrived now at the point of the traditional clash between realism and idealism: is the real world grasped by the nervous system according to some sort of empirical mapping procedure, or is the real word produced by a priori categories of perception hardwired into the brain? In what is Maturana and Varela's crucial insight, this question can be set aside when we realize that the operational closure/structural openness of systems under the autopoietic paradigm allows us "to maintain a clear *logical accounting*" (*Tree*, 135) between the domains under consideration. The authors offer the analogy of a person who has (improbably) lived all his life in a submarine and been trained to keep dials and gauges within certain parameters by correctly manipulating levers and knobs to compensate for fluctuations. This pilot is a metaphor for the autopoietic process itself. When the submarine arrives near a shore, an observer congratulates him for his ability to handle the craft, for successfully negotiating the reefs and surfacing the submarine at its destination. The pilot replies, " 'What's this about reefs and surfacing? All I did was push some levers and turn knobs and make certain relationships between indicators as I operated the levers and knobs. It was all done in a prescribed sequence which I'm used to. I didn't do any special maneuvering, and on top of that, you talk to me about a submarine. You must be kidding!' " (*Tree*, 136–37). The outside observer assumes the pilot is representing the situation in the same way he is, that is, as if the pilot is trying to guide the submarine through the sea and toward a destination. The outside observer thinks the pilot sees what the observer sees because the pilot is assumed to reconstruct through his instruments the same picture of the world the observer constructs through visual sampling. But the pilot is simply observing the internal dynamics of system-specific operations; he believes he is carrying out certain procedures and corrections in order to maintain the correct organization of the system. In other words, the pilot does not even know he is a pilot. But "logical accounting" tells us that the two perspectives are both correct within their particular domains. The observer is correct because from a system-external viewpoint the submarine has displayed purposive action in an environment; he sees the submarine's movements as the pilot's way of dealing with particular environmental stimuli. The pilot is correct too, because he is speaking from within the domain of the system itself, in which the only pertinent goal is the maintenance of the system's organization, and in which environmental stimuli appear not as representations of an outside world but as perturbations of structures (i.e., dials and gauges) that, by reference to prior states of stability, the pilot attempts to correct.

Social Systems and Their Environments

Here it might be pointed out that autopoietic theory seems to flirt with the relativistic paradox familiar to anyone with even a passing knowledge of postmodernism and contemporary debates on epistemology. If Maturana and Varela are suggesting that different observational perspectives produce different observations, and that observations could always be otherwise, then we appear to be traveling down a well-worn path. Furthermore, if they are heard to say that autopoietic theory provides a metaobservation, an "observation of observation," whereby we take a perspective that includes all other partial ones, in what way do they depart from Bateson's concept of a "pattern that connects"? In fact, however, they reject *tout court* the possibility of an extramundane perspective from which diverse observations could be bound together; nor do they obey the traditional pragmatic or Russelian injunction simply to ignore nettlesome logical paradoxes by retreating to the next level of logic. They refuse as well to make the deconstructive gesture of fixating on the contingency of observation—the fact that it is "observation all the way down"—and so do not reinscribe "reflexivity" itself as kind of privileged signifier. In fact, they are not interested in probing how we may evade epistemological relativism at all, but would rather ask, to paraphrase Richard Rorty, relative to what do we think we are being relative? The crucial move here is a reinterpretation of what epistemology is supposed to ground in the first place, namely, the subject's *knowledge* of the world. Varela proposes that "the proper units of knowledge are primarily *concrete*, embodied, incorporated, lived. This unique, concrete knowledge, its historicity and context, is not 'noise' that occludes the brighter pattern to be captured in its true essence, an abstraction, nor is it a step toward something else." Rather, it is "how we arrive and where we stay" ("Reenchantment," 320). The issue of relativism becomes a moot point because knowledge is always embodied knowledge, situated by the observational cut that defines the system/observer. Relativism is not something we need to solve; it is rather just the condition of possibility of observing the world. When I want to look at what is in front of me, I do not lament that I can no longer see what is in back of me. The sacrifice I make to see where I am going is that I do not see what I have left behind.

"Knowing" under this regime is not to be understood as a representation of a pregiven reality but as a kind of mental coping activity—cognition that is better described as Darwinian than Cartesian. We move from philosophy to biology, simply leaving behind the dilemmas that cognition (through philosophy) has presented to itself. Cognition becomes a function of the "fast dynamics" (rapid emergence and selection) of cognitive structures or "microstates," the myriad neural ensembles that give rise to thoughts and actions by drawing from the history of structural coupling between organism and environment as embodied in previous cognitive microstates. We learn by doing and by doing we learn: "perception and action are embodied in self-organizing sensorimotor processes; . . . cognitive structures *emerge* from recurrent patterns of sensorimotor activity" (335). Purposive thoughts and actions are quickly assembled from available cognitive structures, often jerry-built to meet the demands of new and unfamiliar situations from "ready-to-use," habitual patterns of behavior. Varela summarizes as follows:

> First, knowledge appears more and more as built from small domains, that is, microworlds and microidentities. . . . What all living beings seem to have in common . . . is knowledge that is always constituted on the basis of the concrete; what we call the "general" and the "abstract" are aggregates of readiness-for-action. Second, such microworlds are not coherent or integrated into some enormous totality regulating the veracity of the smaller parts. It is more like an unruly conversational interaction: the very presence of this unruliness allows a cognitive moment to come into being according to the system's constitution and history. The very heart of this autonomy, the rapidity of the agent's behavior selection, is forever lost to the cognitive system itself. Thus, what we traditionally call the "irrational" and the "nonconscious" does not contradict what appears as rational and purposeful: it is its very underpinning. (336)[5]

At the social systems level, the jostling of observational domains mimics the action of the brain itself, resulting in an ungrounded epistemology that allows the acquisition and validation of knowledge to proceed not by referring statements to some transcendent checklist but rather via continuous self-observations combined with the constant reference of one domain to another. In fact, any particular observational domain is actually blind to its own categories of selection, the distinctions it uses to navigate the world; it simply cannot see what it uses to see. What counts as common knowledge (though a better term might be common ignorance) is the sum of many observational domains pointing out the blind spots of one another. Each social domain privileges its own view and slights those of its peers, and out of all the crisscrossing something like integration emerges. Knowledge looks over its shoulder to avoid tripping over its feet. When we try to ground knowledge in one domain to the exclusion of others, then it can be said that knowledge as such ceases to exist. Just as a brain restricted to one channel of interaction is autistic, a society focused on one mode of observation, and therefore one kind of knowledge, is likely dysfunctional.

Indeed, the implications of closed/open systems with multiple observational domains have not gone unnoticed by social theorists. As an extension of the cognitive science work of Varela and Maturana to problems in social, political, and economic organization and development, the work of the German sociologist Niklas Luhmann is exemplary. Luhmann has attempted no less than a complete reappraisal of human society from the perspective of autopoietic systems theory. Recognizing that Varela and Maturana's autopoietic theory could include social and psychic in addition to living systems, and building on Talcott Parsons's structural-functional sociological approach, Shannon and Weaver's information theory, Husserl's transcendental phenomenology, and the formal logic of George Spencer Brown, Luhmann redescribes society as a supraself-organizing system capable of producing and reproducing its own constitutive components and fashioning new ones to maintain its unity. The social system is defined as the total domain of communication, outside of which is the noncommunicating environment; as opposed to action-based systems theories of society, communication is *the* crucial factor that allows social systems to organize themselves. That organization may be described from the ground up as consisting of elements (communications), concepts (meaning), events (actions), processes (sequences of events over time), structures (programs for processing communications), functional subsystems (e.g., the legal subsystem, the economic, the scientific), and the social system in its entirety. The crucial insight allowing autopoiesis to be applied to societies is Luhmann's hypothesis that the fundamental system/environment distinction "re-enters" at all levels of the society, so that each of society's subsystems becomes organized around self-reference, and everything becomes an environment for everything else. It is important to bear in mind that individuals, although obviously crucial to social system formation, maintenance, and the production of communications that feed systems, are actually part of the social system's environment and are therefore not the system's center or subject, or, for that matter, even the normal object of systems analysis.

This consignment of persons to the environment of the social system is perhaps Luhmann's most provocative insight, the leap that takes him beyond Parsons and other theorists who use systems theory for sociological analysis. By making communication—not persons, their behaviors, or their social roles—the elemental, undecomposable unit of system formation, Luhmann's theory is radically and thoroughly posthumanist. As well, it does not allow recourse to a center or governing "decider" subsystem; indeed, there is no promise in Luhmann that agreement about the system state can emerge, or that taking a rational approach to overall system control could anywhere find purchase (to the distaste of social theorists like Habermas still committed to some version of the project of reason). As Cary Wolfe puts it, "Luhmann insists that the distribution of the problem of paradoxicality and the circulation of latent possibilities can take place only if we do *not* opt for the quintessentially modernist and Enlightenment strategy of the hoped-for *reduction* of complexity via social consensus" (*Critical*, 71). That is the upside of the theory; but the downside, as Wolfe explains, is that Luhmann "levels [the social field] by refusing to complicate his epistemological pluralism—that we are all alike in the formal homology of our observational difference—with an account of how in the material, social world in which those observations take place some observers enjoy more resources of observation than others" (76). It is this incommensurability between the theoretically balanced observational "orthoganality" of social and conscious systems and their practical ability to unbalance, out-observe, or otherwise occlude one another (whether, for example, through an economic or moral overdetermination) that is the particular concern of my final chapter.

In its broadest definition, a social system consists of all meaningful communication elements, which are constituted as tripartite "signs" decomposable—if only by other elements in the communication system, according to Luhmann—into the functions of information, utterance, and understanding (ES 3). (It is important to bear in mind, by the way, that for Luhmann to unshackle social systems from the conscious determination by human beings, no persons are attached to these communications; though clearly persons produce them, communications are to be understood as communicating with communications, and so the metaphor of transmission—sending and receiving—I use below is misleading but unavoidable.) Roughly, *information* is the referential content of the communication (the *representation* function in Karl Bühler's pragmatic language model, which Luhmann appears to adapt); *utterance* is the communication considered as the self-indicating product of a sender (the *expression* function); and *understanding* is the receiver-based decision about which side of the inner/outer, information/utterance dichotomy will be pursued (the *appeal*). In other words, communication elements are processed through the system as either communication about communication or communication about the environment. So in that communication is simultaneously about something else *and* about its own production, a receiving element will have to show interest in the "hetero-reference" or the "self-reference" of the communication (ES 3). If the communication is "Today it will rain," a receiver could focus on the informational content of the statement (e.g., how much rain) or it could question the context of the utterance (e.g., but this sender is usually wrong). The oscillation between information and utterance means that the unity of the two is always problematic, but at the same time, it is precisely the reason why further communication can take place. Continued communication in the system depends on the possibility of previous communications being continually processed as a distinction between informational content (heteroreference) and autopoietic (self-referential) functions, thus keeping alive the possibility that receivers can ask for more information about the environment or probe the conditions of the utterance. Either way, there is an "interpenetration" of communication from sender to receiver, and receivers can use the communication to further their own autopoiesis as, on the one hand, information is selected and the difference between the system/receiver and its environment is reinforced, or, on the other hand, utterance is selected and the receiver's self-reference becomes the focus.

The inevitable question: what role does meaning have in this scheme? Luhmann follows Husserl here, defining meaning as that selection that emerges from a horizon of possible references, if only momentarily and with the proviso that all the nonselected references remain in play as the backdrop of available alternatives. In meaning-producing systems in general (social and psychic systems), this capacity to discern alternatives is crucial: according to Hans Ulrich Gumbrecht, "Observations are operations that imply an 'awareness' of other operations that *might* have taken place instead of those that actually occur—and it is this awareness of a selectivity that Luhmann calls 'meaning' " (399). As Derrida, perhaps more forcefully than anyone else, has made abundantly clear, what we call meaning is restless, and the attempt to shut down the play of meaning in a given context can happen only because meaning is never fully and transparently present to begin with. In Derrida's terminology, meaning is a function of *différance,* the difference of significr and signified and the indefinite deferral of the moment of their unity. Without *différance,* the sign would never emerge from pure presence, the total horizon of possible reference. Luhmann's information theory–based schema says something quite similar: information increases with "noise"—in fact, the more "disordered" the communication, the more are its possibilities for meaning. In the case of completely ordered information (in other words, information that is identical with utterance), there can be no communication of meaning at all. As Luhmann notes, "without the basic distinction of information and utterance as different kinds of selection, the understanding would not be an aspect of communication, it would be a simple perception" (ES 12).

Understanding allows the system that uses this form to structurally couple with its environment (via the selections of information) while simultaneously maintaining the closed organization of society (via the utterance). "In other words: communication is an evolutionary potential for building up systems that are able to maintain closure under the condition of openness" (ES 13). Furthermore, when a communication "means" something, we can think of it as an action, an action that both sender and receiver can respond to with more action, through further communication or the production of events (e.g., if rain is indeed imminent, get the umbrella). Action allows communication, which is ambiguous and reversible, to be mapped irreversibly into the system. But actions do not play out in totally unexpected ways, because there are well-defined regulatory structures that limit novelty and maintain order. Thus, when the communication is "It looks like rain," a receiver does not reply, "What looks like rain?" or shout for the nearest policeman. In a sense, by translating communications into actions, and regulating actions according to recurrent patterns or traditions of behavior, systems are able to reduce the complexity of information into assimilable packets by which the closure of the system (i.e., its continued autopoiesis) can be maintained. Communication under Luhmann is highly improbable, and the challenge for systems is to develop ways to keep it going: "The process of sociocultural evolution can therefore be viewed as the transformation and expansion of the conditions for effective communication on which society constructs its social systems; this is clearly not just a process of growth but one of selection and of determining what kinds of social system are feasible and what kinds have to be rejected as too improbable" (ES 89). One can imagine any number of genre and discourse regimes that enforce programmatic, conservative communications while yet allowing the play that makes innovation and change always possible, and at times even desirable.

At this point, it may be useful to consider the purpose of Luhmann's use of a communication-based model. If a society is integrated through time by communication—the full range of written, oral, and gestural languages—with action as the extruded result, we need only imagine what would happen if language suddenly disappeared to understand that for social systems, communications are the bricks. Meaning, now understood as a selection from a field of possibilities (rather than a nugget of truth possessed by some transcendental ego) is the mortar of communication and of social systems' autopoiesis. (Bricks and mortar are, again, metaphors Luhmann would disapprove of, but I find them helpful.) Action mapped onto meaningful selection allows the system to build up the material structures that both constrain and augment the potential for further selections (no instant communication at a distance without radios or telephones). For Luhmann, the whole process of social system evolution occurs without the need of guiding subjects or a deus ex machina. In effect, system building produces structures of meaning without an internal or external designer. Humans produce the communications, of course, but they are no more responsible for social system self-organization than individual polyps are responsible for the shape of the Great Barrier Reef.

Thus, unlike previous social system approaches that did take action or even the individual as the elemental unit, Luhmann's approach radically dehumanizes the system. Removing things like subjects and consciousnesses and their various motivated actions from the system description may be disconcerting, but the point is that it is an evolutionary advantage achieved by complex social systems. When we recall that autopoiesis explains how organisms conserve their organization in the face of a complex environment, we can see that communications in social systems also conserve organization by allowing the system to reintroduce the distinction with its environment into its quotidian operations: by repeating that distinction to structure and carry out its operations, the system is engaged in autopoiesis at every level. Communication allows the system to increase its own complexity in order to act more effectively in an environment that is by definition always more complex than the system.[6] A social system is analogous to a species of freshwater fish confronted with an increasingly saline environment: to avoid succumbing to the osmotic differential between themselves and their medium, such fish must evolve structures to allow them to withstand the ambient conditions. This requires them to increase their own internal salinity and develop more effective renal organs to decrease salt retention. For social systems and their various subsystems to deal with an environment that they themselves make more complex for one another, each subsystem must generate the structural sophistication to attenuate the pressure of that external complexity. Because systems cannot couple point to point with the infinite number of environmental factors, they must create structures that can determine which of those factors are most pressing: "Only complexity can reduce complexity" (ss 26). In effect, systems become both more complex and less complex at the same time, in that their selective possibilities increase precisely so that their responses to the environment can be made more predictable.

Luhmann postulates that the evolution of the modern social system began in earnest in the eighteenth century, when a hitherto stratified, hierarchical arrangement based on territory, rank, and kinship began to differentiate into an arrangement whose unity could no longer be attributed to the presence of a king, aristocracy, or some other principle that embodied and regulated the whole of society. Instead Luhmann says,

> Modern society has realized a quite different pattern of subsystem differentiation, using specific *functions* as the focus for the differentiation of subsystems. Starting from special conditions in medieval Europe, where there existed a relatively high degree of differentiation of religion, politics, and economy, European society has evolved into a functionally differentiated system. This means that function, not rank, is the dominant principle of system building. Modern society [which in Luhmann's view is now as well a worldwide society] is differentiated into the political subsystem and its environment, the economic subsystem and its environment, the scientific subsystem and its environment, the educational subsystem and its environment, and

so on. Each of these subsystems accentuates, for its own communicative processes, the primacy of its own function. All of the other subsystems belong to its environment and vice versa. (ES 178)

In a significant departure from other approaches to the differentiation of society (Durkheim, Weber, or Parsons himself), Luhmann contends that these subsystems marshal themselves around basal structures called "codes," function-specific binary oppositions that act as the systems' steering pivots. The simple, bivalent nature of the code allows subsystems to evolve the programs needed to deal with environmental complexity by focusing only on communications that ultimately can be guided toward the code. The relation between system complexity and the simplifying procedure that a binary code represents is explained as follows:

> System differentiation necessarily increases the complexity of the overall system. The converse is equally true: system differentiation is possible only if the overall system can constitute more elements of different kinds and link them in stricter selective relations. In system differentiation, not only are smaller units formed within the system, but the system differentiation repeats the formation of the overall system within itself. The overall system is reconstructed as the internal difference between a subsystem and the subsystem's environment, and this reconstruction is different for each subsystem. Following these internal cutting lines, the overall system is contained within itself many times over. It multiplies its own reality. . . . Differentiation not only *increases* complexity; it also enables new forms for *reducing* complexity. Every subsystem takes on, so to speak, a part of the overall complexity in that it simultaneously orients itself to its own system/environment difference. . . . The subsystem relieves the strain on itself by assuming that many reproductive requirements needed in the overall system are fulfilled elsewhere by other subsystems. (SS 191–92)

In other words, systems repeat and multiply the system/environment distinction right down to the level of codes, thereby making possible more pathways through which to process communications and allowing fewer chances for pertinent communications to go awry or unnoticed. An increase in overall system complexity thus registers as an apparent decrease in the complexity of the environment of the given system.

At the same time that complexity is being generated, a paradox is put in play that is not—and must not be—acknowledged internally: "[The system] can oscillate within [the code], and develop programs that regulate the coordination of the operations to the positions and counter-positions of the code *without ever raising the question of the unity of the code itself*" (*Ecological*, 37). Why the insistence on the value of *not* observing the binary nature of the code? Because, as noted in the earlier discussion of Varela, any knowledge is grounded in the capacity of an observing system to exclude everything but what it is prepared by its particular observational "cut" to receive. For example, in the legal system, illegality is defined as what is not legal, and vice versa. There is no correspondence between those values and anything else: the system is "systematic" only so long as it can continue to process communications toward either value, the sole object being to determine which value applies. If the system paused to consider that the legal/illegal values make sense only in relation to each other, that they are untethered from any ground or transcendent referent and are simply "gates" that allow certain communications to proceed or not proceed, the system could no longer function as a system, for it is the code and only the code that marks the system's systematicity. So it must remain blind to its enabling paradox because it evolves all of its various programs and operations around that distinction: at bottom, it is *nothing but* that distinction. Luhmann writes: "Such a paradox is not simply a logical contradiction (A is non-A) but a foundational statement: The world is observable because it is unobservable" ("Paradoxy," 47). (And as he is quick to add, "Obviously this makes no sense. It makes meaning.") Just as in Varela's formulation, the system cannot see what it uses to see—only *another* observational domain can do that. Second-order observation—the observation of another system's observation—therefore becomes the typical *critical* move because the paradox of the code cannot be "deparadoxized" by the system itself if the system is to continue to function.[7] Moreover, knowledge itself can no longer be traced back to an objective reality; knowledge is located in the observation of the distinctions made by observers.

This discussion of Luhmann's theory has been restricted so far to his own central focus, which is the development of a general *social systems* theory. But what of the systems of consciousness that he has deemphasized? How does his theory deal with the necessary role of humans as the producers of the elemental units of social system autopoiesis (i.e., communications)? I do not wish to evade this question, but the interpenetration of conscious and social systems is not the focus of my own investigation, and so an extensive review of Luhmann's thinking on this phenomenon is not necessary. A more pertinent and related question, however, is how does the paradox of observation apply to humans? As self-conscious systems, humans are not restricted to one particular media code; they can and do deploy an infinite number of observational distinctions. We decide to say this, not that; we look at this object, not the other; we walk over here, not over there. Each of these are "observations," in the sense that they simultaneously indicate one side of the distinction and implicitly indicate the other by exclusion. More plainly, they select one possibility after another out of the horizon of all possibilities. And each of these observations obeys the same formal logic as the social function systems: draw a distinction; say x and thus not-x.

But unlike social systems, conscious systems continuously shuffle through many different distinctions, never settling on one code for long—except, I argue, when a conscious system leans heavily toward reduplicating in its own operations the media code of a specific function system. Thus we call someone "officious" when he looks at everything legalistically, or someone else "money grubbing" when she is consumed by issues of gain. (Incidentally, the repertoire of schemes available for justifying the particular paradoxical distinction in use is commonly known as "culture.")[8]

Much more can be said about the logic of function systems, codes, and programs, but we are now prepared to do so in the context of our discussion of Emerson, someone who for the most part aligned himself with no particular media code but, more useful for my purposes, seemed to register their emergence. In the following analysis of several of his key essays, I show that Emerson's work is implicitly marked with a system/environment distinction, and that in his observation of environmental complexity he identifies several codes that circumscribe those aspects of the environment he finds significant. The "Not Me" at this stage is already crisscrossed by a variety of system/environment distinctions, each of which serves different functional requirements of the "Me." In other words, the dehiscence of stratified society along the lines suggested by Luhmann is congruent with Emerson's own anatomy of nature in, for example, *Nature* itself.

Unlike the Kantian form of idealism Emerson is frequently associated with, the categories of observation he explores in his first major work are drawn from what might be termed a rather trivial reading of the way nature was delineated in his contemporary milieu. But it is precisely this superficiality that makes his reading so acute: by dividing nature into "Commodity," "Beauty," "Discipline," and "Language," Emerson emphasizes the roles of, respectively, the economy, aesthetics, science, and conscious systems. When Emerson explains how nature can be observed from different perspectives and for different purposes, he is closer than he knows to describing the process of the functional differentiation of society, whose emerging subsystems use each other for the raw data of experience. Nature, crucially, becomes for Emerson part of a complex environment that simply cannot be circumscribed by one code alone, and even the initial attempt to reunify all of these codes under the sign of the "transparent eyeball"—the religious code—does not negate the validity of the partial perspectives he has already established. After the discussion of *Nature,* I demonstrate that his apprehension of partiality through the "observation of observation" (in "Circles") opens up possibilities the transcendent move is at pains to resolve. The panoramic vista spread before the euphoric individual residing in a realm where "all mean egoism vanishes" (CW 1:10) is a difficult perspective to sustain, especially when in the everyday world the individual's observations are constantly occluded—by politics, by economy, by biology (for example, death), and by the individual himself, who is seldom as unified in vision as at that moment of "crossing a bare common" (CW 1:10). In most waking hours "every man is a partialist," as Emerson admits in "Nominalist and Realist" (CW 3:144). Indeed, in "Experience," the futility of maintaining a transcendental perspective in the face of overwhelming environmental complexity finds its clearest, and most poignant, articulation. The problem for Emerson—and it is a problem that remains for us today—is whether environmental indeterminacy and what I call "self-referential fatigue" (Emerson's version of the perils of relativism) will lead to a kind of pragmatic interdiction to raise one code over all the others or, alternatively, to an acceptance of the fact that there are many ways of knowing nature and that, paradoxically, nature is known only insofar as one does not know it.

History shows that the former move is more powerful—or rather, power accrues when force is directed with consistency and unity of vision or purpose. Nevertheless, it is the latter, weaker, move that I seek to elicit in this chapter and indeed in the rest of this book. But I must acknowledge in advance that Emerson's systemslike approach to the perils of relativism described above is hardly his last word. There are many Emersons. They exist alongside one another and have beggared generations of critics. Recently critics have begun to see that Emerson's incoherence as a philosopher of the nineteenth century (when system building was still the rage) is what makes him interesting as a philosopher of the present. The challenge, as Porter and others have suggested, lies not in tracing an evolving, maturing perspective but in keeping account of the same suite of perspectives undergoing constant renovation. To whit: one perspective I am *not* trying to trace is the one in which after "Experience" (and even before it) Emerson channels environmental/natural communications to the economic system (coded, roughly, profit/loss) by way of the liberal self, which that same system authorizes. When this happens, even the religious code seems to take on secondary importance in his imagination. The promise of mobile subjects with multiple observational domains under functional differentiation is suppressed by the emphatic resonance of the economic, which recontains partiality and submits the subject to the continued stratification of aesthetic, material, and spiritual resources. Arran Gare puts it this way: "One does not have to be a Marxist to recognize that it is the dynamism of the economy which has the most power to determine the direction of modern societies and the economy is the system to which all the other function systems are constrained to adapt, and it is what is defined as an economic problem which comes closest to defining what are taken to be the problems and goals of society as a whole" (74). One also did not have to be a mouthpiece for capital—and Emerson did not think of himself as one—to have believed that the best response to modernity, with its challenges to certainty, God, its melting of "all that is solid" into air, might be a reaffirmation of the singular vision and unlimited power of the individual in full possession of himself, at peace with a universe that always puts him properly in his place. This is the Emerson who provides aid and comfort to the man of practical genius who can somehow juggle the notions that he is both self-fashioning *and* marked out for greatness by God. The self becomes "imperial," to borrow from the title of Quentin Anderson's book on American individualism; it is a self that views everything in its environment as a division between what belongs to it and what does not, between what is a resource and what is not, between what it can use (Power) and what it cannot (Fate)—the familiar ontological problem of difference and identity taken now as a basis for possessive individualism.[9] In short, if there is an Emerson of partial vision and partial subjectivity, there is also an Emerson who asserts the unity of the imperial self with a vengeance, turning a system of multiple perspectives with multiple ways of observing environments into what looks very much like a marketplace of multiple use.

However, I caution that this last statement is not meant to diminish the nuanced treatment of individual power in the later Emerson (of, for example, *The Conduct of Life*). Again, Emerson was not the sort of thinker who poured his drinks neat. The tendency always is to assume that classic texts are saturated and overdetermined by the ideology of their period. While I think this is generally a safe bet (though I am tempted to say that what is really at issue are the ideologies of the present as projected on the past), I wish to resist the assumption here. For part of Emerson's continuing appeal is that he tried to think outside the box at every turn, to anticipate and defy expectations—his own, those of the times, and, as best he could, those of the times to follow. (In fact it is this feature, his relentless quest for originality, that I make a key concept in this discussion.) Thus, the specific historical exigencies of his moment that made what I have loosely characterized above as a reactionary retrenchment of individual power may be glossed, in another sense, as a progressive response to social destratification, whereby the liberal self must become the repository of all that resists "fate" or the "hurrah of masses" (w 6:249). As Robert Milder puts it, "the recent argument that all individualisms are ultimately expressions of the capitalist ethos is deeply ahistorical so far as it minimizes bitter mid-nineteenth-century contentions for power in favor of a late-twentieth-century ideological Manichaeanism in which the only alternative to entrepreneurialism is some form of collectivism—all rival individualisms, however antimaterialist, amounting finally to capitalist fellow travelers" (53). Along those lines, one could easily show that Emerson was a bigot, a misogynist, and utterly bourgeois. But it is profitless to measure the past with the yardstick of the present. It would be more helpful to note simply that Emerson's mainline solution to functional differentiation—neither to embrace or denounce but to demand that the individual rise above the unfolding social system's worst excrescences by tapping into the unity that abides beyond the mundane—was in its own way thoroughly radical and consistent with its author's earliest struggle (i.e., his revolt against Unitarianism's evacuation of agency). We have to remember that the same Emerson who believes whole peoples will come up cosmic snake eyes ("The German and Irish millions, like the Negro, have a great deal of guano in their destiny" [w 6:16]) also believes their luck can be made to change ("if the Universe have these savage accidents, our atoms are as savage in resistance" [w 6:24]). Though tempered by the passing of twenty-five years, the faith in human power correctly applied hearkens back to the most epiphanic moments in *Nature*. So I do not want to suggest that Emerson lost his nerve and backslid into unitary vision during his mature phase; rather, I acknowledge that refining that unitary vision via the test of experience is what Emerson was always about.

But sometimes his misses are more illuminating than his hits. In a sense, then, it is not the mainline, affirmative Emerson who is interestingly off the mark: it is the Emerson that Emerson himself wants to supercede whom I want to examine.

Emerson and the System of Literature

There are undoubtedly many ways one could go about employing autopoietic and systems theory to illuminate our understanding of literary texts. However, I want to begin with the following proposition: we do not invent literary history, nor do we discover it, but instead we select the particular facts we are already prepared by our own autopoietic, programmatic distinctions to perceive. Such distinctions arise in the circular process of checking and rechecking observations, so that they are not a priori categories of perception but, in a functional sense, have developed to serve the maintenance of our own autopoiesis. As observers we do not represent history so much as allow its traces to trigger our own constructions of a usable past. "Reality," writes Varela in a similar vein, "is not cast as a given: it is perceiver dependent, not because the perceiver 'constructs' it at whim, but because what counts as a relevant world is inseparable from the structure of the perceiver" ("Reenchantment," 330). All of this goes toward saying that by attempting to discern in Emerson's writings a protosystemic style of thinking, I concede that my own distinctions have worked to divide his writings between what goes toward making my case and what does not. This admission should not appear scandalous; what is scandalous is when one acts as if one is not deploying distinctions at all but is only empirically sorting through the past with no favored angle of vision.

I make two other assumptions I think necessary before the theory of autopoietic social systems—with all the epistemological implications—can be applied usefully to the discussion of literary texts, Emerson's in particular, or indeed, those of any literary figure. The first and most crucial is this: literature, broadly defined, is itself a self-organizing, autopoietic system. The particular literature we designate under the name of, say, "Emerson" persists only so long as his work is still resonant within this system, which I henceforth identify as the literary system. Now, it is not altogether clear that Emerson was engaged strictly speaking in a literary enterprise, as opposed to a philosophical or even a political one (although if we listen to Emerson himself we would certainly be led to think he thought of himself primarily as a litterateur); nor is it even clear that the literary system is a fully differentiated *function* system as such, because its development of a specific "media" code remains a question mark. But for the purposes of discussion, my own observational "cut" is to assume that he was and it is.

In effect, then, I am suggesting that literature forms a social system that is closed at the level of organization, open at the level of structure, and fully self-referential in that it processes communications (works of literature) according to its own particular codes and programs. Contrary to Luhmann, however, who has suggested beautiful/ugly may be the code of a general system of art, the code I am proposing for the literary function system is original/derivative, for which the synonyms new/old can form a shorthand. [10] Although observations like beautiful/ugly, high/low, etc. can, of course, continue to be accommodated within the function system at programmatic levels, the defining moment of a literary communication now comes to hinge on whether it marks a new distinction (and literary criticism, incidentally, is therefore an exercise in determining what distinctions were worth making). Because making a new distinction (or as Emerson might say, drawing another circle) is the defining gesture of the literary text, *the functional differentiation of the literary system is based on the code of distinction itself.* "Is what you say distinct?": this is the pertinent question, and the system is set in motion in the pursuit of an answer. Like the Russian formalists who prized defamiliarization as the signature strategy of works of literature, or Wallace Stevens, who demanded in "Notes to a Supreme Fiction" "It must change" (389), the literary system oscillates between what is original, what breaks with the past, what says something in ways never before heard or thought, and what is archaic, what is derivative, what says nothing new and may as well have said nothing at all.

Emerson was fully aware of the compelling nature of the new (although his level of awareness matters little to my argument). His essays are rife with paeans to the value of the new, but I enumerate only a few examples. In the initial lines of "Art," Emerson, while not surprisingly attributing the drive toward the new as a function of the soul rather than to the organization of the art system, nonetheless identifies the existence of such an aesthetic code: "Because the soul is progressive, it never quite repeats itself, but in every act attempts the production of a new and fairer whole. . . . Thus in our fine arts, not imitation but creation is the aim" (CW 2:209). This jives with his observation in "Experience" that "In the thought of the genius there is always a surprise; and the moral sentiment is well-called 'the newness,' for it is never other; as new to the oldest intelligence as to the young child,—'the kingdom that cometh without observation' " (CW 3:39–40). Furthermore, in "Quotation and Originality," Emerson claims that in literature, "Quotation confesses inferiority. In opening a new book we often discover, from the unguarded devotion with which the writer gives his motto or text, all we have to expect from him. If Lord Bacon appears already in the preface, I go and read the 'Instauration' instead of the new book" (W 8:188). Later he observes that "The divine resides in the new. The divine never quotes, but is, and creates" (W 8:201). Moreover, "vast memory is only raw material. The divine gift is the instant life, which receives and uses and creates, and can well bury the old omnipotency with which Nature decomposes all her harvest for recomposition" (W 8:204). Thus, it is not even that old works cannot be made new: *new* is simply a comparative value that works with its code countervalue, *old*. As we will see in a moment, it is precisely his attraction to the new/old distinction (entangled as it obviously is in morality and divinity) that marks the relevance of Emerson to the differentiation and orientation of the literary function system in America.

For the unconvinced, it may help to recall that the attribution of a code should be understood in the following context: a code is simply a way for the system to reintroduce the system/environment distinction into its operations. In a sense, all codes are effectively yes/no distinctions: yes—the meaning of the communication succeeds in terms of the function system; no—the meaning of the communication fails. The system either recognizes the communication as part of its domain and accepts it, or the system does not and rejects it. Thus, in the literary system, *new* is a way of saying "yes" and *old* is a way of saying "no." But this is not to say that everything original is embraced and everything derivative is rejected; in fact, quite the reverse can happen, as the history of literature shows. The code belongs to the system, not the literary object, and the code is merely the closed contrast set used by the system to decide whether or not further communication about the text is warranted—and depending upon other criteria and programming the actual degree of novelty can be very small, or even mean that the inferior value of the code is to be accepted preferentially. For example, in certain genres of fiction, the repetition of stock themes and situations with little variation may be precisely the source of the texts' value, their currency in the system. In other words, although observers may think that there is some particular truth about the system embodied in the code, in fact the code is simply a kind of switch that allows stimuli to either enter or not enter the system so as to maintain autopoiesis. The system does not care what value any particular stimulus takes on, only that not every stimulus enters and overwhelms systemic autonomy.

It may help, then, to consider how such codes can help or inhibit the autopoiesis of specific systems. Consider a case in which the code of science was dialectical/nondialectical: we might then see, for example, the development of a biological science that devastates a nation's agricultural infrastructure and casts doubt on its own integrity because it rejects Darwin in favor of Lamarck, as indeed happened during the Lysenko period in the Soviet Union. Or imagine instead that the code of literature was patriotic/unpatriotic: we can easily suppose that the best works were in fact the *least* patriotic—but the point is, we might never *see* them because texts would always be in the service of a political function system, with little autonomous existence of their own. In both examples, the autopoietic differentiation of the system is undermined because the code itself works against system autonomy and self-organization; the code is not the system's own, but imposed from somewhere else. On the other hand, a system self-coded for new/old can privilege the first term, favor innovation, originality, and distinctiveness, maintain its autopoiesis, and continue oscillating with the second term (which it needs in order to keep marking the difference), precisely because the code is determined in the function system itself—not from some other location in the environment. One could say that the code is simply a way for the system to continue to recognize *itself* as an independent, self-referential function system.[11]

Now granted, the proposed new/old dichotomy is a relatively modern as opposed to classical notion of literary production and reception—but classical/modern is simply another way of framing the code. As Gianni Vattimo points out, both Walter Benjamin and Martin Heidegger were interested in the concept of *shock* as it pertains to modern art; they both redefined aesthetic experience in the modern context as "an experience of estrangement" (51). Formerly, says Vattimo, "From the Aristotelian doctrine of catharsis to the free play of the Kantian faculties, to the beautiful as the perfect correspondence of inside and outside in Hegel, aesthetic experience seems always to have been described in terms of *Geborgenheit*—security, 'orientation' or 'reorientation.'" But Heidegger and Benjamin (particularly in "The Origin of the Work of Art" and "The Work of Art in the Age of Mechanical Reproduction" respectively) recognized that "the state of disorientation . . . is constitutive and not provisional. This is precisely what is most radically new about these aesthetic positions compared with both traditional reflections on the beautiful and the survival of this tradition in the aesthetic theories of this century" (52). If, as I am suggesting, the newly autonomous literary system did not cohere around the beautiful/ugly distinction but instead a code that privileged a constant production of new distinctions, the line between classical and modern, at least in terms of literary aesthetics, may be viewed as a preferential shift from order to disorder (in the informational sense), which allowed a concomitant jump in the possibilities for legitimate literary communication—which in turn meant greater system autonomy. In other words, the nascent aesthetic systems could only distinguish themselves from the religious and political systems that they had historically been enlisted to support when they managed to expand their observational cut to include more of their environments and, in the process, to reorient their operations to produce objects and communications that explicitly demoted the concepts of harmony, beauty, and orderliness. Shock, newness, rupture, distinction, originality become the cruxes of a system that must constantly break with its past in order to keep ahead of the rival systems, which always threaten its autonomy. The new/old distinction and its role in system differentiation helps explain why in modernity "aesthetic experience is *directed towards keeping the disorientation alive*" (51) rather than simply toward identifying the presence of a perpetually *re-presentable* arrangement of textual components called "the beautiful."[12]

Also granted is the fact that this formula tells us only about literature that evokes communications, and there are economic, political, and even religious reasons why some writings never have. But what remains relevant, what is communicated about, what survives, is that which is usable, broadly speaking (and always with an eye turned to those economic, political, and religious function systems that seek to insert themselves here and have their say) to those engaged in literary communications and productions in the present. But a work of literature is not timeless, not in the sense that it tells the eternal truths over and over again; in fact, it has only the future those in the present are able to arrange for it, because the future will know nothing of it if the present defeats it. (Under this regime, literary critics are not the preservers of the literature's past but instead the preparers of its future.) The role of time, then, is to aid in the distinguishing of new from old, not in the diachronic sense but rather in the synchronic assessment of the relevance of works to the current moment. Shakespeare does not belong to a realm of permanent human truth but is instead very much in time—and will be so long as he can be made new for each particular present. Similarly, what gets forgotten, what drops out over time, is that which has no life beyond its own time and cannot be made new—or must wait until a time when it can be made new again. *Originality* is the synonym we should always bear in mind, because it expresses the reversibility of time in the functioning of the new/old code: an original work may have an effect on the present, but it also forces us to reassess the past in new ways. As T. S. Eliot noted, "the difference between the present and the past is that the conscious present is an awareness of the past in a way and to an extent which the past's awareness of itself cannot show" (39).[13] It is in this sense that we understand every communication involving the literary system to be potentially both new and old, progressive and conservative, hearkening back to traditions and at the same time breaking with them. The correlate is that we can see that the code itself does not determine whether something is actually new or old, just as a fork in the road does not determine whether you will take the road less traveled by: there are other factors that program the decision long before it must be made, with the bifurcation providing only the opportunity and impetus to choose and so clarify.

To reiterate: what is marked in the ongoing autopoietic differentiation of the literary system is that which is new, original, and distinctive. But where does this leave notions of excellence, taste, and so on? Literature, art, music, cultural communications in general, are frequently linked together under the rubric "aesthetic," but the new/old code does not imply an aesthetic orientation, as does the beautiful/ugly dichotomy. Indeed, as I am defining the literary system, it cannot foreground the idea of beautiful writing, for popular forms of writing have as much to do with a literary system as does high modernist poetry: re-issues of a Stephen King novel are immeasurably more frequent than print runs of *Four Quartets*. Yet the new/old code cannot tell us which is of greater literary merit. Those to whom merit is the preeminent consideration need only remember that new/old is not a determination of literary value. Values are invoked and defined at a different level in the function system. The code, rather, is simply a way to see things—and a way to keep the communication going. Having nothing whatever to do with aesthetics as such, codes are nevertheless essential to the ongoing autopoiesis of the literary aesthetic system. Without a code, the system cannot differentiate itself from the general swirl of communication around it. Thus, the purpose of the code of the literary system is to process texts in a way that allows the conversation to continue and the autonomy of the system to be maintained.

To digress only slightly, it might be pointed out that current debates on the status and ambit of literary studies—or, more broadly, cultural studies—often result in the impression that there is no autonomous system of literature, that indeed, rather than increasing its autonomy, the system of literature, such as it is, risks dissipating into an undifferentiated field of communication forms. There are many who suggest literature (and its attendant producers, critics, and consumers) is in the process of losing whatever coherence and independence from the other systems that it formerly had, interdisciplinarity and multimodal forms of expression leading to the end of an autonomous literary sphere rather than its renewal. Implicit here is the idea that some sort of specifically literary value is erased in the breakdown of the boundary between literary and nonliterary writing. Thus, the autopoietically pugnacious sphere of literature (which in America was shaped in no small part by Emerson's espousal of doctrines of self-reliance, exceptionalism, and a historically savvy ahistoricism) may be on its way out. As one critic laments, "if literature is no longer to designate a set of objects distinct from those in, say, anthropology, or even anything as loose as a perspective distinguishable from history or sociology, what is left as the professional contribution that justifies our continuing existence?" (Sabin, 14). It is a good question, but one that assumes literature is simply the totality of what people say it is (and now they are saying it is too many things) rather than an autonomous system with its own agenda independent of our own.

For his part, Luhmann has insisted that his is a theory to explain "the normal as improbable," to create "problem formulations that make it possible to represent the normal experiential contents of the life-world as an already-successful solution to the problem, but one that could also, perhaps, be otherwise" (ss 114). Therefore, we could look at the current crisis of the literary function system as a particular solution in progress to a variety of environmental conditions (gender issues, questions of race, class, power, and so on) that the system is responding to by increasing its own complexity and selectivity of information. What some perceive as the disintegration of literature may instead be a way for the system to continue autopoiesis by generating a greater capacity to structurally couple with its environment, an evolution of programs and criteria that will better accommodate the concerns and challenges issuing from other function systems, and even from within the literary system itself. *Autonomy* in the sense that I have been using it never presumes a closed system, but rather an open system closed only at the level of organization. As for the imminent (and perpetual) crisis of Literature, I would simply echo the sentiment of a former editor of PMLA who asked, "isn't the notion that there ever was a consensual definition of what distinguishes the literary from the nonliterary a constitutive myth of literature, and haven't the meanings of literature and its boundaries been contested and negotiated since the concept [of literature] gained legitimacy and cultural capital?" (Stanton, 359).[14]

In part, it is just this complexification of the literary system and its environment that provokes me to suggest that the beautiful/ugly code does not adequately define the communicational axiology of the literary system, which takes as its mandate not simply traditional literary genres such as novels and poetry but a variety of textual forms and approaches that are more effectively processed through the system on the basis of their distinctiveness rather than their beauty. It is quite true that the new/old code may seem to be a reflection less of literariness than of something like fashion, but then that dichotomy too may simply serve to remind us of the system's tendency to discriminate between the trendsetting originals and merely trendy copies. In a related sense, postmodernism agrees with the new/old code—the restless search for new distinctions, articulations, connections and reconnections in a rhizomatic environment of signifiers untethered from signifieds, with a tendency to embrace the play of difference—these are singularly important features of communications in the literary sphere today, and tell us something about the way such a system must code itself if it is to handle the ramified and superabundant flow of textuality. In fact, if we press the coding of the literary system, we can understand it to be coding for a difference between difference and identity, in which case the system is *already* self-thematized with problems of second-order observation, indeed, may even be the function system that strives to organize itself on the basis of a constant reflection on the paradoxical unity of society (and this is a point that is explored more fully later in the chapter). Another way to think through this problem is to suppose that the enlargement of the scope of the literary system signals the formation of a completely new subsystem, one circumscribed by what we call literary theory or just theory. According to William Rasch and Eva Knodt, the new system analyzes self-reflective codes and second-order observations in not just literary but a variety of domains: "We find it helpful," they write, "to assume that the various intellectual initiatives we tend to subsume under this name [theory] constitute what Luhmann calls a 'function specific reflection theory,' a scientific subsystem in its own right that deals specifically with problems arising at the level of self-observation, not only in literary studies, but in a great number of related disciplines as well." Because this particular "subsubsystem" takes a third-order perspective on "problems of an interdisciplinary nature, literature no longer occupies a privileged position (i.e., as the defining object of a discipline), but functions merely as one focal point among others where such problems crystallize and can be studied paradigmatically" (4). While this view seems promising, my own intervention still assumes itself to be engaged in a specifically literary, not scientific, brand of theoretical activity, and therefore is situated in the system of literature and susceptible precisely to the blind spots implicit in that system (notably, to being derivative and, programmatically speaking, ugly, but not, as in science, either true or false!).

But to return to the main line of our discussion: my second assumption is that within this system of literary communications, certain relatively stable observational perspectives have developed that serve to reduce communications toward recurrent and repeatable touchstones. Criteria and programs develop to guide behaviors, actions, and communications in expected directions, to allow systems, in effect, to maintain the status quo (as much as this is possible and desirable) and, hence, their autopoietic stability. I think it is fair to say that what we are talking about here is, in all its fullness, *culture.* For any social system, cultural regularities form the memory functions, the storage mechanisms that ensure continuity from one iteration of the system to the next. But I do not mean to suggest by this that systems—and, in particular, the literary system—are inherently opposed to producing new elements (such as texts) spontaneously or only after a great deal of struggle. Of course, we know the literary system is entirely predicated on constant innovation. Luhmann explains the memory function this way:

> Maintenance is not simply a question of replication, of cultural transmission, of re-producing the *same patterns* under similar circumstances, e.g., using forks and knives while eating and only while eating, but the primary process is the production of *next elements* in the actual situation, *and these have to be different from the previous one* to be recognizable as events. This does not exclude the relevance of preservable patterns; it even requires them for a sufficient quick recognition of next possibilities. However, the system maintains itself not by storing patterns but by producing elements, not by transmitting *memes* (units of cultural transmission analogue [*sic*] to *genes*) but by recursively using events for producing events. Its stability is based on instability. This built-in requirement of discontinuity and newness amounts to a *necessity to handle and process information.* (ES 10)

All social systems, in other words, generate newness to unfold through time, in that processing information is what systems *do,* and by definition only "news of a difference" counts as information. (But we should keep in mind that the self-maintenance of a system is not the same as its function code, which is used to determine what *sort* of information is to be processed.)

Beyond programs and criteria there is another type of structure that reduces disorder: "On the highest level of establishing expectations, one must . . . renounce all claim to establishing the correctness of specific actions. One works only with—or talks only about—*values*" (ss 317). Examples of values might include self-reliance, nature, freedom, equality, and so on, which, as part of the cultural semantics of America, become central themes in American literature. (Again, communications about such things are not exclusively aesthetic communications—they also exist within the political system, for example—but the literary system does use them as conventional topoi of aesthetic reflection.) Each of these values is, of course, a distinction—a form that assumes the existence of an outside. Values can be renewed simply by adjusting the boundary between the inside and outside term, but values are rarely questioned *as such,* either by primary or second-order observers: "the concept of value denotes preferences the validity of which can safely be assumed in social communication without having to face disagreement" (ES 134). Everyone, for example, will claim to be for "freedom," whether they are calling for more freedom for themselves (and less for others) or simply critiquing someone who calls for a different sort of freedom. Even the most repressive regimes justify themselves by appealing to such commonly held values. What is significant here is that each time an attempt is made to bring the value up-to-date, some part of it is negated so that something else can be made new. A break with the past is thus inherent in every redefinition of the value (although of late, the neoconservative voices that perfuse the political system seek renewal by exhuming from the past a set of values presumed to be found there whole and intact).

The role of *style* as a means of establishing continuity between distinct, individual aesthetic objects is also crucial here, Luhmann says, so as "to organize the contribution of the work of art to the autopoiesis of art, and in fact in a certain sense against the intention of the work of art, which aims for self-containment. Style corresponds to and contradicts the autonomy of the individual work of art. . . . It leaves the uniqueness of the work of art untouched and yet establishes lines of connection to other works of art" (ES 197). Again, Emerson seems to agree: "the artist must employ the symbols in use in his day and nation, to convey his enlarged sense to his fellow-men. Thus the new in art is always formed out of the old" (CW 2:210). Style, in other words, is one way to distinguish new distinctions from old ones, distinctions that might remain too indistinct without the manipulation and recombination of stylistic conventions. This notion of style, along with other programs, values, and criteria, becomes a way by which the literary system channels its communications toward the fork in the road, that is, the new/old code.

These two propositions—that there *is* a literary system and that it *has* evolved an assortment of programs, criteria, and values—are certainly disputable and worth more consideration than I can accommodate here. But what is fascinating and distinctive about Emerson when we reflect on his own observational distinctions, values, systematizations, and the way these play out in his treatment of latent aesthetic structures, is that the code of the literary system as I have defined it appears to have coincided with his own customary angle of aesthetic vision, his own writerly cut into the surface of the world. That is to say, for Emerson the only distinction worth making was the original one, and the only value worth pursuing was the one that allowed a break with received values. Though not always Emerson's most observant reader, George Santayana did rightly note, "A happy instinct made him always prefer a fresh statement on a fresh subject, and deterred him from repeating or defending his trains of thought" (260–61). Emerson made it his mission to point at the future in everything he wrote, and in doing so he seems to have set the terms for much of American literature that followed him: the literary system, in its relentless quest for the original distinction, is distinctively Emersonian. Emerson asked, "Why should not we also enjoy an original relation to the universe? . . . why should we grope among the dry bones of the past, or put the living generation into masquerade out of its faded wardrobe? . . . There are new lands, new men, new thoughts. Let us demand our own works and laws and worship" (CW 1:7).

My interest in Emerson as an exemplary early observer of the relationship of systems to environments is cemented by this apparent homology between the observational code of the literary *social* system, Emerson's own preferred *psychic* orientation, and, only dimly perceivable to him, the increasing differentiation and autonomy of the various function systems of society. In Emerson's anatomy of nature we can see the new literary code taking form as it intersects and interacts with the codes of the other nascent systems, which are designated approximately by *commodity* (the economic, with its code of profit and loss); *discipline* (with its true/false scientific code still yoked uncomfortably to the sacred code of religion); *beauty* (the aesthetic, yet coded as beautiful/ugly, and still relatively undifferentiated as a nonautonomous component of a stratified social and sacral order); and *language* (the system/environment distinction itself). This "interpenetration" of codes means that we always have to keep *three* levels of distinctions in mind when we observe Emerson observing the observing systems: our systems theoretical approach, Emerson's quest for originality, and his society's functional differentiation according to binary codes. *We* can therefore observe that for each of the subsystems Emerson identifies, the demand for the new, for the difference that will make a difference, is guided as much by his literary effort to leave behind "the sepulchres of the fathers" (CW 1:7) for the "new yet unapproachable America" (CW 3:41) as it is by his observation of how these new economies, sciences, churches, arts, and polities actually function. In terms of Emerson's self-observation, it must have been one thing to say Americans needed "an original relation with the universe"; but it must have been quite another to imagine a society that would crave the shock of the new in all its various parts. Emerson's goal was no less grand than that: to make the American pulse pound to the beat of a perennially new drum. In his reinterpretation of the old hierarchies of nature, he takes the first tentative step toward moving the literary system—and by resonance, other social values as embodied in other subsystems— in this unceasingly progressive direction. As Emerson describes this movement in "The Method of Nature," it seems even the sphere of the literary scholar—the observer of observations—will be autocatalyzed by the innovative forces it unleashes:

> Here, a new set of distinctions, a new order of ideas, prevail. Here, we set a bound to the respectability of wealth, and a bound to the pretensions of the law and the church. The bigot must cease to be a bigot to-day. Into our charmed circle, power cannot enter; and the sturdiest defender of existing institutions feels the terrific inflammability of this air which condenses heat in every corner that may restore to the elements the fabrics of ages. Nothing solid is secure; every thing tilts and rocks. Even the scholar is not safe; he too is searched and revised. (CW 1:121)

But what should be born in mind as we consider *Nature* is that Emerson's demand for the new—required by his premise that there exists an original, unique, and correct relation for all men that awaits discovery or invention—has precisely the effect of *unsettling* every attempt to lapse into a single, permanent, and unchanging relationship with one's environment. The price of being an "original," as Harold Bloom has noted, is to feel constantly the pressure and anxiety of being merely a copy, a derivation; it is to be continually reminded that there have been and will be many ways, historically speaking, to view the world. The paradox of finding the original relationship begins and ends, as Emerson writes in "Experience," with the idea that "Nature does not like to be observed, and likes that we should be her fools and playmates" (cw 3:29). I want to tease out this duality in Emerson, the fact that the same writer who speaks of our proximity to the divine through our rediscovery of nature also admits that the environment we confront every day is largely inscrutable and always keeps its distance, an idea he signals as early as *Nature* itself:

> We are as much strangers in nature as we are aliens from God. We do not understand the notes of birds. The fox and the deer run away from us; the bear and the tiger rend us. We do not know the uses of more than a few plants, as corn and the apple, the potato and the vine. Is not the landscape, every glimpse of which hath a grandeur, a face of him? *Yet this may show us what discord is between man and nature, for you cannot freely admire a noble landscape if laborers are digging hard by. The poet finds something ridiculous in his delight until he is out of the sight of men.* (cw 1:39; my emphasis)

I stress these last sentences to identify what for me is a crucial point: it is only when nature is understood as distinct from the human that the attempt to subsume it becomes an issue. Epistemological doubt—this can of worms that Descartes opened up and many thinkers, including Emerson, tried to close—seems from a systems perspective not so much an obstacle to knowledge as its precondition. We depend on our prior alienation from nature (i.e., the subject/object opposition that I want to rewrite as a system/environment difference) for systems of thought and knowledge to form. We require a complex environment that cannot be encompassed by one static mode of observation: we may crave with Emerson "an original relation with the universe," but we do not have one—we are forced to have many. As if to acknowledge the necessity of the system/environment difference, Emerson's commitment to originality in essays like *Nature* and "Self-Reliance" evolves by the time he writes "Circles" and "Experience" into a kind of full-blown second-order observational perspective, which tacitly repudiates his previous transcendental attempts to observe all the complexity of the environment from a single perspective, a perspective that would be available to the subject no matter in what domain—scientific, moral, economic, aesthetic—it might find itself.

We should also bear in mind something else, something that may help connect more directly my invocation of systems in what follows to the Emersonian mode as it has been discussed recently by those such as Stanley Cavell, who want to

take Emerson seriously as a legitimate philosopher of language, not simply as a
Romantic who sought to break with older forms of literary aesthetics. Emerson's
fascination with the original distinction indeed goes toward a very basic feature of
autopoietic systems—whether conscious or social—that links their functionality to
Cavell's particular philosophic interest in Emerson. As we have seen, autopoietic
systems operate on the basis of screening out a great deal of their environment.
They have to, in fact, because they would grind quickly to a halt if every input,
every stimulus, every communication had to be traced down and preserved, always
kept in the foreground, like a lifetime of conversations saved up and repeated in
the same instant and every succeeding instant. So systems find a way to deal with
this problem of saturation: they learn to forget. Systems are built to persist—but
not necessarily to retain: "Memory [in self-organizing systems] . . . is impossible
without some form of selective forgetting" (Cilliers, 92). And as Emerson might say,
this feature of systems—of life itself—appears to be the "most unhandsome part of
our condition," for it means that even the pain of a dead son can fade over time,
perhaps even the *memory* of that pain: "something which I fancied was a part of me,
which could not be torn away without tearing me, nor enlarged without enlarging
me, falls from me and leaves no scar. It was caducous" (cw 3:29). As Cavell puts it,

> The feeling as if we have to penetrate phenomena is evidently produced by a feeling
> of some barrier to or resistance of phenomena (as if the conditions of a thing's ap-
> pearance were limitations in approaching it; as if skepticism accurately registers the
> world's withdrawal from us, say its shrinking); as if language has difficulty in *reaching*
> phenomena, let alone grasping them. Then all our words are of grief, and therefore of
> grievance and violence, counting losses, especially then when we ask them to clutch
> these lost, shrinking objects, forgetting or denying the rightful draw of our attraction,
> our capacity to receive the world, but instead sealing off the return of the world, as
> if punishing ourselves for having pain.—The feature I am trying to place intuitively
> within the overlapping of the regions of Kant and Emerson and Wittgenstein lies, I
> might say, not in their deflections of skepticism but in their respect for it, as for a
> worthy other; I think of it as their recognition not of the uncertainty or failure of our
> knowledge but of our disappointment with its success. (*This New*, 88)

What Cavell from the skeptic's perspective admires as Emerson's capacity to
simultaneously grieve for the closure of the world while still appreciating its limited
openness, I wish to rewrite as Emerson's anticipation of the paradox of observing
systems—that the reason they can see anything is because they cannot see everything, partial vision turning out to be not tragic but absolutely indispensable. In
my rewriting, those works that are often taken up as Emerson's meditation on the
subject/object problem become instead a record of his grapplings with this more

basic, biological predicament: the handsome/unhandsome condition of being a self-conscious, living system, a condition that requires us to come to grips with an environment that is knowable only in that it remains fundamentally unknowable, available to us at one level only by remaining closed at another. In the case of Emerson's commitment to the new/old code, then, what we are seeing is a technique by which he confronts imaginatively this problem of perennial loss and limited gain. My insistence on the centrality of this code to Emerson stems directly from my sense that the drive to seek out the original or the new simply marks a displacement of the desire for contact and clarity, this hopeless *hope* of "reaching phenomena" that must somehow survive our every failure to overcome the world's implacable and so far as we know permanent resistance. For Emerson, the code of the nascent literary aesthetic turns out to embody much more than just a quest for new and original means of American literary expression: the quest for the original disguises the quest for the *origin*, the quest for the new the quest for *renewal*. This new secular aesthetic is therefore still an ontotheologically tinged aesthetic, haunted by the underlying desire to know whatever it is that would bring us rest, to know what we imagine God himself would know. In systems terms, then, the desire for the new is the drive to grasp an environment that must remain out of reach, a drive that depends on its certain failure to deliver precisely that which it makes one long for.[15] (I have more to say about the cognitive roots of this drive in chapter 4.)

But how could anyone, anyone at all, deal with hope's continual dashing? Clearly, different survival strategies would have to emerge. No wonder, for example, that so much of memory is "caducous," for a conscious system could not function if it remembered all its history—if every debacle, every failure, every wound remained agonizingly open. A system *needs* the lacunae provided by the loss of memory, spaces in which to respond to environmental stimuli in new, still hopeful ways, whereby expectations can continually form and different responses tried out, failing and succeeding to materialize as may be the case. The system retains what is useful and forgets the rest, because otherwise it would not persist in an environment that is itself constantly changing, throwing up new and often threatening challenges. So as we trace the vagaries of Emerson's use of this nascent literary code—a code which may be understood as a manifestation of the basic tension of being a conscious, individual system, a system that may hope to observe clearly but by design never can—we might want to take him at his word when he says, "Life is a series of surprises, and would not be worth taking or keeping if it were not. . . . The results of life are uncalculated and uncalculable. The years teach much which the days never know. . . . The individual is always mistaken" (CW 3:39–40). *Experience*— the residues of memory, to put it one way—is knowing that, as Cavell might say, when it comes to living, we must always and necessarily remain *inexperienced*.

Let us now test the hypothesis that the code of the developing literary system— newness, originality, distinction itself—is indeed Emerson's favored angle of vision, and that it is through this particular lens that he makes his most important observations. I begin with *Nature* because it is where Emerson begins, and conclude with "Experience" because it is where, it seems to me, his deployment of this new code reaches a zenith. In what follows, then, I observe Emerson as a second-order observer; I focus on how he uses his favored code to point up the shortcomings and note the strengths of the various domains (systems) of thought and communication that appear to parcel up his world. What I find as I move through these essays is that Emerson always ascends up a hierarchy toward those codes (in particular, the religious code), which for him take the widest view of things. In each case, the challenge he has set for himself is to reconcile his commitment to the new with his allegiance to what—at the top of the ladder—awaits as Truth, God, the One. In each case, he believes he has literally saved his soul by subsuming all codes into the code of transcendence, which he assumes is the master code that contains the rest— and which will bring welcome peace to those who, like himself, are irremediably original. Yet by "Experience," with the weariness of constantly renovating *everything* wearing hard, Emerson comes face-to-face with what he fears most: the possibility that even God himself cannot heal the rift between self and world, this necessary difference that permits autopoiesis to proceed, this blindness that makes possible all our insights. My conclusion will be that by aligning himself so intimately with originality, in applying this incipient new code of the literary aesthetic to everything he encounters, Emerson now finds himself, too, "searched and revised" by the very forces he has unleashed. In a sense, his reliance on this new literary code forces him to reflect on his own status as code—as a distinction in a perpetual hunt for new distinctions, no longer a "transparent eyeball" who sees all, but a "subject lens" who sees what he does precisely because he does *not* see all. As Luhmann puts it, "When observers . . . continue to look for an ultimate reality, a concluding formula, a final identity, they will find [this] paradox. Such a paradox is not simply a logical contradiction (A is non-A) but a foundational statement: The world is observable *because* it is unobservable" ("Paradoxy," 46). And to *know* this, we might add, would represent *the* crucial insight for any observer, for it is no less than the self-knowledge of one's own status as a self-organizing system.

The Codes of Nature

Emerson begins his anatomy of nature by isolating the class of use he calls commodity, which he takes to mean "all those advantages which our senses owe to nature" (CW 1:11). Commodity is understood to mark the material value of nature, the "only use of nature which all men apprehend." He approves of the "useful arts" but there is no question the material use of nature is a "mercenary benefit" at best (CW 1:12). When Emerson criticizes the mercenary aspect of commodities, he is actually unpacking the functioning of the modern economic system as it oscillates within its particular code. The reason he is able to do this is because he is making his observations via the new aesthetic code. He says, in other words, what only a second-order observer using another code would see about the functioning of the market, namely, that it is nothing more than "penny-wisdom" (CW 1:43)—that it sees only what it sees (the movement of money) and no more. What is lacking is precisely the wisdom part of the equation: what good is the mere exchange of pennies, when one can strive for so much more, nothing less than an *original* relationship with the universe and all the things in it? For commodities to help us work toward this end, we must come to know that our current relationship with nature as commodity is static, that such commodities are only useful if we realize their original value is not as mere exchange matter but as symbols of the deeper laws. Emerson thus deparadoxizes the economic code by revealing its limited scope, effectively showing that when looked at rightly one sees that the economic code only describes part of the material value of nature.

This process of deparadoxization is Emerson's basic strategy here and in the other sections of *Nature.* It is an unfolding of the fact that these incipient function systems dumbly go about registering an event or stimulus in their environment through one or the other of their code values. But this fact does not mean that the stimuli cannot *mean* something else. Just because matter registers in the economic system as a matter of debt or credit only means that we have not bothered to look at the larger picture. What Emerson does, then, is to deploy his favored code of the old/new to show that debt and credit together compose only *one* side of a *broader* distinction, the distinction between crude market considerations of nature and something that, as he say, smacks of "profounder laws" (CW 1:24). This technique is not the same as a deconstruction of the binary code in that there is no overturning of the code; it is rather simply a demonstration of the fact that the code sees only what it sees and nothing else.

Emerson begins this demonstration by describing how nature "ministers" to man, "[a]ll the parts incessantly work into each other's hands for the profit of man" (CW 1:11). Nature gives itself over to our use, exorbitantly, seemingly without preconditions, yet as Emerson says in his conclusion to the section (which I quote now in full), "this mercenary benefit is one which has respect to a farther good. A man is fed, not that he may be fed, but that he may work" (CW 1:12). The wealth of material nature thus cannot be considered apart from the economic system it is meant to maintain, and the progressive, constantly regenerative direction toward which he believes the system should point. Emerson, descended from stern Calvinist stock, did not want to give the impression that nature was so bountiful a New Englander could "ramble all day at will" eating wild dates like "his fellow who enjoys the fixed smile of the tropics" (CW 2:134). When he dissects nature as discipline—which, as he says, "includes the preceding uses, as parts of itself" (CW 1:23)—that impression, if it was given, is corrected, by a careful delineation of what the economic system at bottom is meant to produce:

> The same good office [nature as a disciplining force on the "Understanding," i.e., practical reason] is performed by Property and its filial systems of debt and credit. Debt, grinding debt, whose iron face the widow, the orphan, and the sons of genius fear and hate;—debt, which consumes so much time, which so cripples and disheartens a great spirit with cares that seem so base, is a preceptor whose lessons cannot be foregone, and is needed most by those who suffer from it most. Moreover, property, which has been well compared to snow,—"if it fall level to-day, it will be blown into drifts to-morrow,"—is the surface action of internal machinery, like the index on the face of a clock. Whilst now it is the gymnastics of the understanding, it is hiving, in the foresight of the spirit, experience in profounder laws. (CW 1:24)

Clearly, the economic system is designed to facilitate the exchange of money and property, to handle questions of credit and debt. But for Emerson credit and debt are old, tired ways of observing the material value of nature—penny-wisdom to be sure. What lies beyond them is what those with an eye for the new should seek: the profounder laws that serve to build character. Those laws exist in the "unmarked space" that the code of credit and debt cannot discern with their particular brand of blindness.

Less clear, however, to Emerson (or any one else of his epoch) would have been the idea that in stratified societies, "Property and its filial system of debt and credit" were all linked to social standing and heredity, but that as modern society began to take shape, with the rise of a mobile bourgeoisie and the decline of a fixed correlation between class and means, "debt and credit" became untethered from less mobile property—or rather, property became simply another form of capital. One could have capital without property, and one could have property without capital, but the trick was to avoid debt in either case. "Property" in its material manifestation as goods or land increasingly comes under the auspices of the system of laws as a legal entity, while debt and credit, loss and profit (or more fundamentally, according to Luhmann, "payment or non-payment" [*Ecological*, 52]) were "hiving" out to constitute the code of a rapidly self-organizing economic function system, which in turn came to circumscribe all monetary transactions, regardless of class and property. The differentiation of the economic sphere meant that all were subject to its "iron face"; there was no longer a custodial guarantee for the peasantry from their former lords, nor was there reprieve for the debt-ridden members of the aristocracy, despite their exalted lineages and historical privileges. Both groups had to deal with the market. As Emerson avers in the early address "The Young American," "the uprise and culmination of the new and anti-feudal power of Commerce, is the political fact of most significance to the American at this hour" (CW 1:229). In America, the notion that one was judged on the basis of the ability to make payments became constitutionally entrenched, since most other traditional categories of discrimination were expressly forbidden, in theory at least, if not always in practice. The African slaves, as chattels of a southern ruling class that was effectively one of the last pockets of feudalism in North America and Europe, were possibly the only ones that could still rely, perversely, on the care and keeping of an overlord, who sheltered them from the code of the economic system (although, to be sure, after Reconstruction, those same slaves, now free to incur debt and, theoretically at least, to extend credit, saw how easily the power relations that obtained under the feudal system could be replicated under the economic code).

For the Emerson of *Nature,* these implications of the debt/credit code were not pursued to any great degree. In later essays, by contrast, the code will reappear in many different guises, all of which will serve to map the territory *Nature* merely stakes out. (Notable examples include the doctrine of self-reliance with its code based on self-possession and "Wealth," in which Emerson declares "Every man is a consumer, and ought to be a producer" [W 6:85]). Here, however, Emerson was emphasizing in fact the contempt he felt for the raw code of the market: "the use of commodity," he cautions "regarded by itself, is mean and squalid" (CW 1:26). Nature as a commodity was but the first and most common use of nature, and in this ranking it becomes a yardstick for what, at this point in his career, he believed the economic code should mean to his readers—which is to say, it would hold a value exactly in inverse proportion to the worth of the person. When man sees nature merely as a commodity, "He lives in it and masters it by a penny-wisdom; and he that works most in it, is but half-man, and whilst his arms are strong and his digestion good, his mind is imbruted, and he is a selfish savage. His relation to nature, his power over it, is through the understanding; as by manure; the economic use of fire, wind, water, and the mariner's needle; steam, coal, chemical agriculture; the repairs of the human body by the dentist and the surgeon" (CW 1:43). The problem identified above in the "Prospects" section but already introduced in "Commodity" is that purely economic uses of nature are, so to speak, half-measures. Emerson proposes that instead of applying ourselves so weakly to nature we must rather restore it, literally re-new it; and just as in most of his subsequent work, the thrust here is that the fallen, old world of commodity fetishism may be fine for Europeans, but it is not fit for Americans, this new race of potential giants.

Strange, then, that the attempt to inject the vision of newness into the material domain of nature should follow with what appears to be a rather pedestrian version of the natural aesthetic in "Beauty." The question could rightly be asked of beauty: is there anything in nature that is not beautiful? In the right light, says Emerson, "even the corpse hath its own beauty" (CW 1:13). Actually, as with most questions involving the supersensible functions of reason, both the highest and lowest points on the continuum of beauty are left to be considered in later sections, such as "Spirit" and "Prospects." Still, even while focusing on the more mundane perceptual domain of the understanding, in "Beauty" Emerson tends to view his topics as a contest between the progressive and the merely constant, between beauty that is original and beauty that has become conventional. Again, we can think of this as a process of deparadoxization: the old code of beautiful and ugly is encompassed by a more expansive code that sees the former aesthetic as tired and narrow. For example, he tells us there is a threefold appeal of beauty: "simple delight," a "spiritual element," and the "object of the intellect." Firstly, the most delightful things are always the newest, and we must be alert to their evanescence: "To the attentive eye, each moment of the year has its own beauty, and in the same field, it beholds, every hour, a picture which was never seen before, and which shall never be seen again. The heavens change every moment, and reflect their glory or gloom on the plains beneath" (CW 1:14). Secondly, the infusion of spirit in beauty comes in the form of "the mark God sets upon virtue," and the virtuous are usually those who break the bounds of convention, such as explorers like Columbus: "Does not the New World clothe his form with her palm-groves and savannahs as fit drapery?" (CW 1:15). Thirdly, the intellectual apprehension of beauty is reciprocally related to the "active powers," in that "the beauty of nature re-forms itself in the mind, and not for barren contemplation, but for new creation" (CW 1:16). Indeed, it is the intellectual response to beauty that is responsible for taste and, relatedly, artists, who "have the same love in such excess, that, not content with admiring, they seem to embody it in new forms. The creation of beauty is Art" (CW 1:16) (and we note that art is not beauty but the creation of beauty). In each of the three examples, what Emerson suggests is that it is toward the new we must direct our attention, for there lies real beauty.

Although the demand for innovation is omnipresent in his discussion of "Beauty," the code, as I have suggested, of the aesthetic system Emerson inherits remains beautiful/ugly. Although Emerson wants to push the limits of this system, to make it see beyond its stale marking of inherited notions of aesthetic value, the system's restrictive optics ensure that the system is still largely entrained with other systems (especially religious, political, economic systems), which determine the sorts of subjects and qualities suitable for aesthetic contemplation. He is, as it were, half in and half out of this system, bound to look for beauty and ugliness—but increasingly unsure that these terms are still useful (recall that even corpses can be beautiful for Emerson). Aesthetic systems were only beginning to differentiate themselves, perhaps around the time the Romantics began to speak of "art for art's sake." Harro Müller states, "If one applies Luhmann's suppositions regarding evolutionary theory to art, one may surmise that in segmentary societies, art is seamlessly bound up with the mechanism of reproduction in the form of rituals" (47). Segmentary societies (such as those of pre-Columbian North America or Neolithic Europe) gave way to stratified societies, in which a limited "differentiation ensues, but art is still closely bound up with religion and politics" (47). Functional differentiation is fully underway by Emerson's time, but many of the new social subsystems have yet to detach themselves from their segmentary linkages with other subsystems (e.g., science, which still retains close programmatic ties with theology). In *Nature,* Emerson is still clearly conflating the apprehension and construction of beauty with the scientific, moral, and, ultimately, religious sentiment: "Truth, and goodness, and beauty, are but different faces of the same All" (CW 1:17). It should come as no surprise, then, that his notion of art was inextricably tied to his notion of nature and a fortiori God; he had yet to make explicit (although, as I am saying, it was already implicit) the move whereby the artist became an independent creator, if not on par with the Creator himself then one whose work was evidence of the god in all. As for the differentiation of art and/or literature according to the code new/old we can only say that by introducing nature as the artist's perceptible benchmark—"the standard of beauty is the entire circuit of natural forms" (CW 1:17)—Emerson was at least furthering the Romantics' attempt to carve out the secular aesthetic, one which was accessible to everybody, especially to those like him who opposed the doctrinaire fables of religion, not to mention politics.

The work of Pierre Bourdieu, if not already understood to be in important ways consonant with Luhmann's theory, should come to mind here most especially. Bourdieu supposes that the integrity of the artistic "field" is constantly at stake in the struggle between advocates of the autonomous principle of "art for art's sake" and advocates of "the heteronomous principle, favourable to those who dominate the field economically and politically (e.g. 'bourgeois art')" (*Field,* 40). Romanticism's privileging of a "pure aesthetic gaze" focusing on and deriving force from the natural spectacle is a crucial link in the development of a functionally specific aesthetic system or series of interrelated systems. As Bourdieu notes, "From the angle of phlyogenesis, the pure gaze, capable of apprehending the work of art as it demands to be apprehended (i.e., in itself and for itself, as form and not as function), is inseparable from the appearance of producers of art motivated by a pure artistic intention, which is itself inseparable from the emergence of an autonomous artistic field capable of formulating and imposing its own ends against external demands" (*Field*, 256). What we can add here, vis-à-vis Emerson, is that the idea of the "new" as the code of this emerging field (or system) is lent credence by the notion that such a code cuts precisely against the grain of the established patterns of bourgeois art. Art that has become art for its own sake owes no allegiance to established cultural protocols, cares not for patrons or consuming publics (at least within the process of an unfolding system self-definition!). It is art valued and retained only because it is like nothing that has ever been seen before. It does not conform to what has already been expressed but rather challenges every settled and comfortable truth we hold, and by doing so disengages itself from those systems (such as the economic and political) that have long constrained it.

The foregoing uses of nature condition the understanding (although we will skip the section "Language" for the moment, which would also be included therein). By contrast, when Emerson speaks of discipline he is talking about reason, which is that which "transfers all these lessons [of understanding] into its own world of thought, by perceiving the analogy that marries Matter and Mind" (CW 1:23). For philosophers, scholars, scientists, and thoughtful people in general, nature disciplines both the intellect and the conscience: "Whilst thus the poet delights us by animating nature with his own thoughts, he differs from the philosopher only herein, that one proposes Beauty as his main end; the other Truth" (CW 1:33). Nature demands observance of a code of logic and a code of transcendence—it accounts for the role of science and religion. For the former, nature "pardons no mistakes. Her yea is yea, and her nay, nay" (CW 1:27). The differentiation of specific branches of science are the result of this unequivocal true/false code: "The first steps in Agriculture, Astronomy, Zoölogy . . . teach that Nature's dice are always loaded; that in her heaps and rubbish are concealed sure and useful results" (CW 1:27). Reason educates, and unlike beauty and commodity, discipline serves reason by conveying the steadfastness of natural objects and processes, not their variability. Yet even so, Emerson's attachment to the new leads him to exclaim, "Here again we are impressed and even daunted by the immense Universe to be explored. 'What we know is a point to what we do not know.' Open any recent journal of science and weigh the problems suggested concerning Light, Heat, Electricity, Magnetism, Physiology, Geology, and judge whether the interest of natural science is likely to be soon exhausted" (CW 1:28).

The procedures of science, the testing of theories against nature's yea or nay, are the result of an abiding human desire to bisect unknown nature by new and different means in order to multiply ways of knowing the world. (Emerson will return to the question of why we are drawn to the unknown in "Circles.") Luhmann notes that "the scientific code of truth and falsity is directed specifically towards the *acquisition* of new scientific knowledge" (*Ecological,* 78). "What is new," writes Luhmann, "has to be freed from the suspicion of being an exception or being false. This occurs through an improbable, culturally historical preference for innovation, indeed for curiosity *(curiositas),* that has to be tested and standardized itself, i.e., find its boundaries within itself (resonance) and not its objects. Similarly, scientific analysis does not serve to solve problems but to multiply them" (78). [16]

In essence, Emerson deparadoxizes science by noting that yea and nay (true and false) see only what they see—and that if they are to lead us toward the truth of things we must keep in mind as well how they "point to what we do not know." There is a transcendent space beyond the narrow confines of science's yea and nay; indeed, yea and nay serve only to determine how material nature functions so that we can in turn discover the profounder laws that point to science's "beyond."

If discipline aligns the intellect in accordance with nature's laws, then, it does so to educate the understanding to the higher functions of reason: "nature is ever the ally of Religion: lends all her pomp and riches to the religious sentiment" (CW 1:26). As a reflection of the reasoning conscience, nature is again a disciplining force, dividing itself between the immanent and transcendent code of religion, which Emerson here conflates with the moral code of good and bad, although later he will reject the moral code as too much the product of history and social convenience to be indicative of the higher laws toward which the soul must bend. As he will note in "Self-Reliance," "Good and bad are but names very readily transferable to that or this; the only right is what is after my constitution; the only wrong what is against it" (CW 2:30). Luhmann affirms that "religion could not stake everything on the difference of good and bad behavior" because the code of morality is often patently paradoxical and therefore causes problems for religious observance (*Ecological,* 95). Instead, religious systems posit a difference between the world as it appears and "a complete, all-encompassing second version of the world where self-reference has meaning only as other-reference, complexity has meaning only as implexity (Valéry) and transcendence has meaning as what cannot be transcended" (95). Although earlier he espoused processes of deparadoxization, Emerson now does not want to suggest that the religious code leaves anything out, for to him this is the code that sums up all the rest. It includes every possible configuration of the world—and for every configuration it points to a transcendent world beyond. There are true and false things in the world, and good and bad ones, but they are only components of the fallen world in which we live. The religious code includes all of this world— and all the ways of limning it—in the inferior term of *immanence,* which stands for whatever is part of this shrunken world of matter that now "fits [us] colossally" (CW 1:42). By contrast, the superior value of the code, transcendence, is not even *of* this world. It refers to the realm that is beyond us and so we will never find anything in this world that actually takes on its value. If transcendence is the yes to immanence's no, all most of us ever hear is a chorus of no's (although, Emerson tells us, an occasional whiff of the transcendental is possible, if not likely). Yet because the superior value is ineffable and indefinable, it makes the paradox of the religious code seem to disappear. In other words, the religious code serves to invoke the unity of God that transcendence promises by referring all questions of ultimate meaning out of the immanent realm where such questions are asked but can never be answered. In effect, the *absence* of God in the world is explained by the separation of a transcendent from an immanent realm that the code itself serves to enforce.

In a widely quoted journal passage from 1837, Emerson reflects on the question of the unity of the religious code:

> Who shall define to me an Individual? I behold with awe & delight many illustrations of the One Universal Mind. I see my being imbedded in it. As a plant in the earth so I grow in God. I am only a form of him. He is the soul of me. . . . Yet why not always so? How come the Individual thus armed & impassioned to parricide, thus murderously inclined ever to traverse & kill the divine life? Ah, wicked Manichee! Into that dim problem I cannot enter. A believer in Unity, a seer of Unity, I yet behold two. (*Journals*, 164)

The problem for Emerson is that when the paradoxical unity of the immanence/ transcendence code (or, as in this passage, its congener, individual/God) is probed too deeply, one arrives finally at the point where the Pascalian wager between reaffirmation (faith) or dismissal (skepticism) must be taken: either accept the code and its elusive promise of transcendence or simply refuse to participate any longer. Yet perhaps Emerson was heroically trying, as Stephen Whicher suggests, to juggle the two kinds of truth that resulted, "the intuitions of faith, and the other facts of experience," and become a "Plotinus-Montaigne" figure, a dual self composed of one "who sees through to the mystical perfection of things, and the detached observer . . . who gives their due to facts" (32). One way to synthesize the two positions, and the one Emerson appears to choose, is to subsume the difference and to ignore the paradox on the basis of one's own authority. In other words, one assumes as one's own the position of unity (God). The rise of a different sort of subject during the functional differentiation of society in the seventeenth and eighteenth centuries allows this position to become increasingly imaginable. Luhmann says that "After Kant, a new kind of subjective individualism became possible; given the turn to the 'transcendental,' the facts of consciousness had to be evaluated by a kind of double standard: empirical and transcendental." As a result, "the individual (not only the Cartesian mind) emerged as the subject, as subject of the world. Experiencing the world, the individual could claim to have a transcendental source of certainty within himself. He could set out to realize himself by realizing the world within himself" (ES 111).

This self-referential transcendental authority—the radical newness of which we should always bear in mind—would seem to explain Emerson's moves in the rest of *Nature*. When we consider the later sections we see that the basic function system types with their observational criteria are still inscribed in the margins: "It appears that motion, poetry, physical and intellectual science, and religion, all tend to affect our convictions of the reality of the eternal world" (CW 1:35). So too is Emerson's penchant to privilege that within those systems which responds to the principle of originality. But now Emerson explicitly seeks to integrate all of these observational perspectives on nature into a single standpoint. The fundamental paradox of the religious master code is ignored, immanence and transcendence bundled together, so that Emerson can say "all the uses of nature admit of being summed in one, which yields the activity of man an infinite scope. Through all its kingdoms, to the suburbs and outskirts of things, it is faithful to the cause whence it had its origins. It always speaks of Spirit" (CW 1:37). Again Emerson catches sight of the various function systems already identified, but now with a view to marking the distinction between observer and the observed and emphasizing the observer's capacity to make a visionary reconstruction of nature. Rather than simply noting and responding to what appears novel in nature, the ideal observer is one who can bear the observer/nature distinction in mind so that material nature can be seen for what in the last analysis it is: a product of the "senses and the unrenewed understanding" (CW 1:30). To the *renewed* understanding (i.e., reason) nature becomes something else, that which the transparent eyeball signified, and which Emerson now explicates in "Idealism" as follows:

> Until this higher agency [reason] intervened, the animal eye sees, with wonderful accuracy, sharp outlines and colored surfaces. When the eye of Reason opens, to outline and surface are at once added grace and expression. . . . If the Reason be stimulated to more earnest vision, outlines and surfaces become transparent, and are no longer seen; causes and spirits are seen through them. The best moments of life are these delicious awakenings of higher powers, and the reverential withdrawing of nature before its God. (CW 1:30)

The result is that the ideal observer, unlike the first-order animal eye, can observe his own observation of nature; he sees himself seeing "the difference between the observer and the spectacle—between man and nature," and he reasons that "whilst the world is a spectacle, something in himself is stable" (CW 1:31). The poet "unfixes the land and the sea, makes them revolve around the axis of his primary thought, and disposes them anew. . . . To him, the refractory world is ductile and flexible" (CW 1:31), while "the astronomer, the geometer, rely on their irrefragable analysis, and disdain the results of observation" (CW 1:34). The poet uses the aesthetic code to make of nature what he will, and the scientist sees past brute matter with his true/false code to find the higher law that, following Euler, is " 'contrary to all experience, yet is true' " (CW 1:34). Idealism raises the stakes of observation: it "is a watcher more than doer, and it is a doer, only that it may better watch" (CW 1:36).

Of course, and to repeat, Emerson wishes to reconnect these domains of observation under spirit, and so render partial into singular perspective. Because both ideal observers, poet and scientist, engage in second-order observation, it is not what they see with (the aesthetic and scientific codes respectively) but what they see *past* (the quotidian function system codings of the world) and what they see *to* (the master code immanent/transcendent) that is significant. "Culture," as Emerson calls what I have been calling functionally differentiated society, "inverts the vulgar views of nature, and brings the mind to call that apparent which it uses to call real, and that real, which it uses to call visionary" (CW 1:46). Partial perspective, then, is for Emerson the result of a fall, not an evolution, into collective organization, which compels us to see, through its various "subject lenses," only the vulgar world of matter, commodity, and simple, not sublime, beauty. But by erecting a ladder of categories of perception, Emerson encourages us to climb up through the intellectual, moral, and religious domains of experience to the domain of spiritual transcendence in which the "real world" is precisely that which is not normally observed: "The problem of restoring to the world original and eternal beauty, is solved by the redemption of the soul. The ruin or blank, that we see when we look at nature, is in our own eye. The axis of vision is not coincident with the axis of the things, and so they appear not transparent but opake" (CW 1:43). Luhmann says that in the transcendent phase, "the individual leaves the world in order to look at it" (ES 113); it is in this phase that Emerson dissolves nature and his own corporeality (which we recall is "Not Me" as well) so he may better "see All." He is participating in the standard attempt to overcome the system/environment distinction and return to some originary, undifferentiated spirit or being position, a "nondistinction" wherein observation is no longer partial but unimpeded, total, and plenipotent.

Is Emerson therefore another in long series of transcendental philosophers? What makes Emerson something more than a cracker-barrel Kant or a watered-down Hegel, both figures to whom he variously bears comparison? The difference (that makes a difference in essays like "Circles" and "Experience") is that he effectively asks us to climb the ladder of transcendence on the basis of nothing more than a commitment to see things with "new eyes" (CW 1:44). He asks us to see things his way, which, at bottom, is guided by a perceptual code that privileges what is original. That he routinely refers us back to a time when man was not "disunited with himself," to the "morning knowledge" we once shared with God (CW 1:43), does not diminish his commitment to newness, whether it lies along an originary or telic vector; in fact, I suspect that for Emerson, referring truth to the misty past rather than to a promised future is more a function of the prelapsarian mythos he inherited than a significant dimension of his epistemology. In any event, in this relentless search for the new he is not as yet troubled by consistency, which as he claimed was the "hobgoblin of little minds" (CW 2:33). Instead, like the confusing and rapidly changing social milieu in which he lived, Emerson's work is charged with a variety of observational perspectives that, despite the predictable moves he makes to repackage them under one code, seem to fluctuate from essay to essay, even within essays.

In other words, his attraction to a universal religious code (and, later, to a certain degree, the economic code as embodied in the liberal self) is dialogically tempered by his subversive allegiance to the literary aesthetic code, and the second-order observational perspective it represents. Both perspectives—the dominant first-order and the subservient second-order—Emerson would have wanted to claim are unified by the presence of God in man, by the transcendent referent that in our moments of "perfect exhilaration" (CW 1:10) we feel we have touched, but it is by no means clear that he was always able to bring these perspectives together, either in his work or in his personal life. Rather, they constantly contend for dominance: "I am existed directly from God, and am, as it were, his organ. . . . Then, secondly, the contradictory fact is familiar, that I am a surprised spectator & learner all of my life. . . . Cannot I conceive the Universe without a contradiction?" (*Journals*, 165).

The answer was no. The second-order observer in Emerson would not allow him to stare at the world from one angle only, much as he wished to be a monist. His insistence on making an original distinction would drive him to cut across all settled ways of seeing; it would undermine his powerful, religious desire to land upon a final code, the one that would end all differences. In this way, the restless vision of Emerson (to be sure, only hinted at here in *Nature*) seems quite familiar— all skeptics suffer (or benefit) from partial perspective, and attempts to harmonize observational distinctions succeed only in displacing them onto new distinctions. So in "The American Scholar," Emerson was almost right when he said,

> there is One Man,—present to all particular men only partially, or through one faculty;
> and . . . you must take the whole society to find the whole man. Man is not a farmer, or

a professor, or an engineer, but he is all. Man is priest, and scholar, and statesman, and producer, and soldier. In the *divided* or social state, these functions are parcelled out to individuals, each of whom aims to do his stint of the joint work, whilst each other performs his. The fable implies that the individual to possess himself, must sometimes return from his own labor to embrace all the other laborers. But unfortunately, this original unit, this fountain of power, has been so distributed to multitudes, has been so minutely subdivided and peddled out, that it is spilled into drops, and cannot be gathered. (CW 1:53)

He was almost right because in the functionally differentiated society that was developing around him, *each* person would have to partake of all the various functions: no longer was one's whole viewpoint determined—politically, economically, intellectually, spiritually—by the stratum in which one entered the world. Yet ironically, the rise of the autonomous individual, the "One Man" who Emerson thinks can reclaim his rightful wholeness from the rapidly differentiating society with its divisive, "parcelling" effect—that "One Man" is made thinkable and desirable precisely as a result of his atomization. To become once again new, an "original unit," is a distinction made possible only by the fact that, as he puts it in "Self-Reliance," "now we are a mob" (CW 2:41).

The Experience of Second-Order Observation

I have suggested that the attempt to subsume all difference under the master code of the religious system requires one to ignore that code's inherent paradox. To assume the burden of that paradox can be a difficult task, even for those well prepared by the religious system's institutional programs to do so. For someone like Emerson, who had already renounced his vocation and divested himself of most of the external forms of his religion, the effect of taking on that paradox meant that he must try continually to reconcile his faith with his skepticism, his first-order status as an observer and his second-order status as an observer of observation. I now want to explore what price this position would extract from Emerson. In considering that price, which manifests itself most fully in "Experience," I begin with the "Language" section of *Nature*.

"Language" describes another one of the lower uses of nature, but it is interesting to note that it is the second longest section, which if nothing else may count as a measure of Emerson's enthusiasm for the topic. "Words," we are told, "are signs of natural facts" and in Emerson's Swedenborgian analysis nature in turn is "the symbol of spirit" (CW 1:17). The trick is to link words to things in their proper sense, and so open the eyes wide to the continuity of visible nature with spirit. A true understanding of the original sense of words allows us to read nature like scripture, to "purge the eyes to understand her text" (CW 1:23). Once we know, for example, that *"right* originally means *straight"* (CW 1:18) as in a straight tree branch, we can begin to see that natural facts encode spiritual facts: "Every appearance in nature corresponds to some state of mind" and so "an enraged man is a lion, a cunning man is a fox, a firm man is a rock, a learned man is a torch" (CW 1:28). From there, it is a short step to know the moral truth of nature, to comprehend that "the axioms of physics translate the law of ethics" (CW 1:21). Emerson summarizes as follows: "A Fact is the end or last issue of spirit. The visible creation is the terminus or the circumference of the invisible world. 'Material objects,' said a French philosopher, 'are necessarily kinds of *scoriae* of the substantial thoughts of the Creator, which must always preserve an exact relation to their first origin; in other words, visible nature must have a spiritual and moral side' " (CW 1:22–23).

Nature corresponds to spirit, but as we have perhaps suspected and as Emerson confirms in "Prospects," man's spirit has long since receded from nature so that where "once it fitted to him, now it corresponds to him from far and on high" (CW 1:42). Freud famously ascribed this loss of the "oceanic" to a process of ego detaching itself from external world: "Our present ego-feeling is, therefore, only a shrunken residue of a much more inclusive—indeed, and all-embracing—feeling which corresponded to a more intimate bond between the ego and the world about it" (5). Nature, as "the terminus or the circumference of the invisible world" seems to mark an outer limit, an ultima Thule of meaning-fullness, which we may once have inhabited but now exists only on a mythic plane. Composed of *"scoriae,"* nature may even be in a sense the waste product of the Creator, so that as Michael Gilmore puts it, "man's relation to an excremental universe turns out to be one not of mastery but of estrangement" (27).

It is easy to discount the "Language" section as an ebullient but highly problematic portion of *Nature,* for as David Van Leer points out, "the axioms of physics have stopped translating ethics in the next chapter . . . and correspondence is defined out of existence by the noble doubt" (43). Yet in the way Emerson constructs the difference between language and nature a pattern is revealed that carries over to later essays. Translating this pattern into systems terminology, it is possible to say that what Emerson describes is a situation in which systems are confronted with a highly complex environment, which cannot be circumscribed by what we say about it—our language is unable to mirror the copious informational content of nature. Diminished as we are, "shrunk to a drop" (CW 1:42), "we know more from nature than we can at will communicate" (CW 1:21). Language no longer connects point-to-point with material objects in the way Emerson imagines it once did, and though we may dimly grasp these connections in our habitual discourse, seldom does it rise "above the ground line of familiar facts" and become "inflamed with passion or exalted by thought" (CW 1:22). Poets, of course, and "wise men" have some ability to "pierce this rotten diction and fasten words again to visible things" (CW 1:22), but in general, *Nature,* as with the rest of "Our American literature and spiritual history," is written in the "optative mood" (CW 1:207).

This inadequacy of words to things is the pattern that connects the themes in "Language" to those in the later essay "Circles." In our linguistically impoverished state, nature (taken as "environment") always appears, borrowing a metaphor, to "out-circle" the present capacity of the self, or what Luhmann calls the psychic or conscious system. As Emerson reminds us, St. Augustine described God as a circle whose center was everywhere and its circumference nowhere; but as we know from *Nature,* our own fallen condition is marked by the expansiveness of a material world against which we do not measure up, so that it might be correctly observed that man in his dwarf state is a circle contained by nature whose center is the individual and its meager circumference the collective. This collective mob is precisely what holds the individual back from his true greatness, as "Self-Reliance" so witheringly explains. Society, therefore, is a restrictive, disciplining system, a circle that confines the individual within certain limits—and it is up to the individual to bypass society and reconnect to nature through the "original" use of language. By drawing new circles we can limn more deeply the natural world or, in other words, generate system complexity so that our selective capacity vis-à-vis the environment is enlarged.

But as Emerson discloses in "Circles," the horizon of knowledge seems to be in constant retreat: "Our life is an apprenticeship to the truth, that around every circle another can be drawn; that there is no end in nature, but every end is a beginning" (CW 2:179). In language that surely strikes a chord with us even today, he writes, "Every ultimate fact is only the first of a new series. Every general law only a particular fact of some more general law presently to disclose itself. There is no outside, no inclosing wall, no circumference to us. The man finishes his story,—how good! how final! how it puts a new face on all things! He fills the sky. Lo! on the other side rises also a man and draws a circle around the circle we had just pronounced the outline of the sphere. His only redress is to forthwith draw a circle outside of his antagonist. And so men do by themselves" (CW 2:181). Not only is the issue that of being worsted by others but by oneself.

Having opened this Pandora's box of partiality and second-order observation by appropriating so much authority to the individual, Emerson must find a way to explain unremitting environmental complexity—or, put another way, our ability to keep making new circles—because it seems to confound idealism. At some point we must come to rest, to a point of observational stability where, to paraphrase Emerson, the axis of our individual vision is aligned with the axis of things. The way to recontain the paradox of a subject who is his own authority, who can always draw another circle out into the environment, is achieved, again as in *Nature* (and as in all of his essays) by cross-coding back to the religious domain where the transcendent code itself cancels the apparent distinction between "Me" and "Not Me," or psychic system and environment: for if I am divine, nature is in me, and the difference between nature and me simply dissolves. Circularity, one might say, is precisely what "Circles" seeks to avoid. Emerson writes, "Whilst the eternal generation of circles proceeds, the eternal generator abides" (CW 2:188). It is no cause for alarm that we can forever increase the radius of our circle because its center is always there to anchor and coordinate all new observations.

But while in *Nature* the efficacy of the transcendent move was never really in doubt, "Circles" so effectively demonstrates the complexity of our environment (or, said another way, the fact that our system can always be enlarged) that by the end of the essay it is not at all clear that Emerson has successfully arrived (or rather, returned) to the ultimate distinction, the one that puts an end to the play of circles. In his lecture series "The Present Age," delivered during the same period in which he was writing "Circles," Emerson, says Robert Richardson, "now proposes a complex, many-sided subjectivity, no longer a simple affirmation of the self: 'What is man but a congress of nations?' The multifaceted, fractionated self is now a given, a starting point, though the goal of thought and perception remains the same" (333). But to reiterate, while the goal may have been the same, Emerson's game-saving invocation of the "One" seems to come too little too late for this "fractionated self": the bulk of the energy of "Circles" has already gone toward proving that "every action admits to being outdone" (CW 2:179), and very little is left to impress us that "the eternal generator" is a principle of stability—or rather, that if there is a center to all these circles its goal is stability and not constant surprise or shock. The only constant appears to be the drive for the new: "Why should we import rags and relics into the new hour? Nature abhors the old, and old age seems the only disease; all others run into this one. We call it by many names,—fever, intemperance, insanity, stupidity, and crime; they are all forms of old age; they are rest, conservatism, appropriation, inertia, not newness, not the way onward" (CW 2:189).

Moreover, in Emerson's view the "eternal generator" or "central life" is paradoxically also the "circumference" that we can never reach: "That central life is somewhat superior to creation, superior to knowledge and thought, and contains all its circles. Forever it labors to create a life and thought as large and excellent as itself, but in vain, for that which is made instructs how to make a better" (CW 2:188). The center or system is what generates more system around itself, yet at the same time in Emerson's conception it is presumed to escape the play of the system. Like St. Augustine, Emerson imagines as the center of his circles a point that exists everywhere and thus nowhere, a center that masters the entire circumference of which it is/is not a part. In other words, whether he knows it or not, Emerson is caught in a double bind: the principle of stability, this "eternal generator" is a center that causes us to generate the very circles that remind us that our understanding of the world is never complete, never "one." The difficulty for Emerson, as for postmoderns today, is that once you embrace this *mise en abyme* you cannot turn around and substitute its "conditions of possibility" (i.e., something like *différance*—or the "eternal generator") as its ground, because you have already revealed that the unity of the system is based on a paradox: the center is the center because it is not the circumference—or the system is the system because it is not the environment. Similarly, the self (system) stands in contradistinction to nature (environment), the "Me" and "Not Me" of *Nature*. The point here, however, is not that Emerson is wrong to invoke this distinction; in fact his project is only possible on the basis of him remaining blind to it as an enabling paradox. That difference is what allows Emerson to construct his reality—it is the blind spot of insight. Luhmann puts it in this typically paradoxical way: "Cognitively all reality must be constructed by means of distinctions and, as a result, remains construction. The constructed reality is, therefore, not the reality referred to" ("Cognitive," 76). The system is erected on differences, and the quickest way to eliminate the integrity of the system is to erase its distinction from its environment. Therefore, to the extent that Emerson actually imagines the self subsuming or transcending its Other (the system completely filling its environment), his insight must necessarily become undifferentiated, incognizable, information without order, white noise—what he likes to call "One" and what Derrida might call "pure presence." And nothing more can be observed. What would one say *after* one has become a "transparent eyeball"? As the metaphors of "One" are introduced and multiplied, the simple fact of their production means that the "One" Emerson seeks has not yet arrived.

For Emerson, this means that once again the question is: can the desire to end difference (which can only be produced by uncritical faith) and experience (which produces doubt) coexist harmoniously in the same mind? Reason and understanding—these two kinds of intelligence, one directed at the transcendent and the singular, the other at the quotidian and the complex—live in an uneasy relationship, the disembodied eyeball versus the embodied but myopic writer. I take the anxiety produced by this "two-mindedness" to be the underlying sentiment of the following passage:

> Our moods do not believe in each other. To-day, I am full of thoughts, and can write what I please. I see no reason why I should not have the same thought, the same power of expression to-morrow. What I write, whilst I write it, seems the most natural thing

in the world: but, yesterday, I saw a dreary vacuity in this direction in which now I
see so much; and a month hence, I doubt not, I shall wonder who he was that wrote
so many continuous pages. Alas for this infirm faith, this will not strenuous, this vast
ebb of a vast flow! I am God in nature; I am a weed by the wall. (cw 2:182)

The hyperbolic ambivalence of that last sentence goes to the heart of what I
believe this essay finally achieves: in a manner of speaking, what *Nature* sought to
decisively confirm—that an anatomy of nature reveals a necessary unity—"Circles"
undermines. The essay suggests that our apprehension of the world is always partial,
observation never total, subjectivity a transient phenomenon. As in *Nature,* his
allegiance to the literary distinction of new/old as the catalyzing force behind these
recognitions is clear, but now the power of the code to unsettle is ratcheted up.
Because making new circles is underpinned by the desire to encompass a reality that
always remains unknown, the fact that one can always draw a new circle is, for him,
unbearable. Emerson's inability to contain relativism in "Circles" foreshadows the
self-referential fatigue that such a posture must eventually produce. That fatigue is
engendered by his commitment to a literary aesthetic code that requires the constant
solicitation of new distinctions; that code is the second-order observational stance
par excellence. Whereas in *Nature* the interpenetration of the literary code with the
various function codes settles on the transcendent/immanent distinction as the key
to stabilizing our relation to nature or environment, in "Circles" Emerson describes
a self-perpetuating optics that seeks to enlarge its field of view by ceaselessly drawing
a new distinction. What is the purpose of all these circles? The frankest evaluation of
his motives comes at the end of the essay, when he writes, "The one thing which we
seek with insatiable desire is to forget ourselves, to be surprised out of our propriety,
to lose our sempiternal memory, and to do something without knowing how or why;
in short to draw a new circle. Nothing great was ever achieved without enthusiasm.
The way of life is wonderful; it is by abandonment" (cw 2:190).

This is truly Emerson at his giddiest. In opposition to his transcendentalist's
desire to contain all circles, Emerson's incentive in drawing a new circle stems
from a need for more circles, for surprise, for a fresh way of looking at things, for
the incipient unknown. And why is this? Simply because the last circle did not
produce the closure, the clarity, and the knowledge he had hoped, in his perennial
and hopeless optimism, it might. This underlying hope outweighs the desire to
concede to the comforts of blind faith, to stop circling and cut his losses; thus, "there
is no sleep, no pause, no preservation, but all things renew, germinate and spring"
(cw 2:188). The "eternal generator," a metaphor meant to reflect both permanence
and change, seems a center that, literally, cannot hold, if we take Emerson at his
word in these concluding passages. Circles can be said to be centered only if we

allow as the center an effect of permanent decentering—if we say, in other words, that the only universal is that everything is relative. In the final analysis, I believe Emerson concludes that the only way to deal with circles is, as Luhmann might say, to create more circles. Still, in its exuberant disregard of the circularity of its argument, "Circles" seems like Emerson's way of making a silk purse from a sow's ear: in ignoring paradox and abandoning ourselves to circles, we can defer the self-referential fatigue that a constant generation of circles would seem to bode as its most tangible, if never final, result.

But that fatigue is not denied in "Experience"; indeed, fatigue seems to infuse the essay from its disoriented beginning to the rallying "up again, old heart!" at the finish (CW 3:49). The most obvious impetus for this essay stems from the psychological wounding Emerson received upon the death of Waldo, but along with that biographical fact we must consider, from the systems viewpoint, the implications of the nascent second-order observational perspective developed in "Circles." The functional differentiation of society means that no single way of looking at the world can coordinate multiple observations (albeit, that fact will never stop Emerson, however unconvincingly, from trying). When Emerson looks at any particular domain, he sees incommensurable divisions: the world by one account seems divided into words and things; by another into beauty and ugliness; by still another into profit and loss. In systems parlance, not one of these perspectives can cover the whole field of existence; they all observe only by excluding their peers. Yet Emerson had figuratively "staked his soul" on the chance that each of these distinctions could be abstracted as a difference between mind and matter, or the "Me" and "Not Me." That primary difference would then in turn re-enter the superior side of the difference ("Me") so that the distinction becomes simply spirit and nature, two sides of the same transcendent option. In this way, all the various divisions in the world "climb the ladder" and finally admit to being summed up by "One." Nature equals God equals soul in a grand sublation of difference.

By the time of "Experience," however (and over and against his avowed holism), the undeniable problem for Emerson is that even as he attempts to coordinate these distinctions together into "One," he has never had more incentive to see "Two." My contention is that now his preference for originality has become so profound—even desperate—that it obliges him to discriminate between, simply put, unity (one) and difference (two), even though in making the distinction he foils his own attempt to end the unfolding of difference: the "seer of Unity" "yet behold[s] two" (*Journals*, 164). But on the other hand, a system employing such a code sees not only the contingency of other observational distinctions, but that all other distinctions mark two sides of the same coin: ugly things like corpses are beautiful, profit and loss are equally useful teachers, good and bad both depend on whim, and even love and loss cannot carry us "one step into real nature" (CW 3:29). In response to this emptying of experience, the code then tries to identify the unmarked space left over. The code designates this as the space of the necessary, the original, the "real," of that which differs from merely contingent unities. For Emerson, that is the space we need to recover, the site of unactualized possibilities where the "One" can still be imagined. And into that space will be inserted whatever particular entity currently stands in Emerson's mind as the best exemplar of that originary space: the poet, the entrepreneur, the scholar, the young American, the farmer, or, as in "Experience," death (and in particular, the death of Waldo), which becomes the one "reality that will not dodge us" (CW 3:29). The "inclosing wall or circumference," which asymptotically is never reached, signifies the infinitely charged, undifferentiated space that permits its constant differentiation just as every circle admits of being outdone; it is the "perpetually retreating horizon" of the environment Emerson has always wished in vain to bring under the compass of his system.

Another way to describe this situation is to say that because Emerson's preferred observational code sets him to look for the "actual" conditions of possibility of other systems' distinctions, he sets himself up only to fall; wherever he finds unity he reflexively looks for difference. We recall from autopoietic theory that system stability is maintained through a recursive process in which observations of the world are checked against the current state of the system, but because Emerson privileges new observational distinctions, his own psychic system is embroiled in a continuous process of self-transformation and self-revision. Like the developing autonomous literary system, Emerson is in a sense in perpetual reaction against himself as he oscillates between rest and motion, tradition and revolution. To maintain himself in an "original relation with the universe" he must repeatedly undermine his present— already on the verge of "unoriginal"—relation with the universe. Such a stance must eventually become disconcerting, perhaps untenable, engendering as it does a constant dissatisfaction with one's current system-state, those self-descriptions that inevitably seem stale and ineffectual the moment they harden into "truth"; it is a stance of inconsolable skepticism. In "Experience," the following passage registers the ambivalence of a faith always prospective—made so by its unwillingness to confine itself within fixed boundaries: "Life has no memory. That which proceeds in succession might be remembered, but that which is coexistent, or ejaculated from a deeper cause, as yet far from being conscious, knows not its own tendency. So it is with us, now skeptical, or without unity, because immersed in forms and effects all seeming to be of equal yet hostile value, and now religious, whilst in the reception of spiritual law" (CW 3:40–41).

What we know at any given moment, Emerson seems to say, is never sufficient because of our awareness that there is always much more yet to know. As Cavell says, we are always inexperienced: "Loss is *as such* not to be overcome, it is interminable, for every new finding may incur a new loss" (*This New*, 114). The "eternal generator" ensures that the self is overlaid with a complexity that can never be fully appreciated, and so never rejoined with the "deeper cause" at its core. The exhausted, vulnerable Emerson of "Experience" wishes the self could be content in what it is, but the quest for originality means that it never will. Thus his recuperations of the disunified world appear weak and fatalistic: "Bear with these distractions, with this coetaneous growth of the parts; they will one day be *members,* and obey one will. On that one will, on that secret cause, they nail our attention and hope. Life is hereby melted into an expectation or a religion" (CW 3:41).

The difference between these optative sentiments and the grandiloquent spiritual certitudes of his earlier essays should, I think, be clear, but it is illustrated even better in a subsequent passage. About the "vast-flowing vigor," which "the Chinese Mencius" generalizes enigmatically as that which "assists justice and reason, and leaves no hunger," Emerson writes,

> In our more correct writing, we give to this generalization the name of Being, and thereby confess that we arrived as far as we can go. Suffice it for the joy of the universe, that we have not arrived at a wall, but at interminable oceans. Our life seems not present, so much as prospective; not for the affairs on which it is wasted, but as a hint of this vast-flowing vigor. . . . So in accepting the leading of the sentiments, it is not what we believe concerning the immortality of the soul, or the like, but *the universal impulse to believe,* that is the material circumstance, and is the principle fact in the history of the globe. (CW 3:42–43)

In *Nature* Emerson decried our self-imposed limitations and the "penny-wisdom" (CW 1:43) that saw man apply to nature "but half his force" (CW 1:42). But in the passage above he seems resigned to the fact that all we may really possess are such predeterminedly inadequate wisdoms, whose only saving grace is that simply in having them we are expressing the very real (and very Jamesian) "will to believe" in this "vast-flowing vigor." I think, too, that the distinction he makes between a "wall" and "interminable oceans" is particularly significant: this latter figure promises that our approach toward Being is not decisively blocked and the journey can continue, but it also promises that the continent itself is *never reached.* Where Emerson had said, again in *Nature,* to "Build therefore your own world. As fast as you conform your life to the pure idea in your mind, that will unfold in its great proportions" (CW 1:45), now he projects an image of the material unable to catch up to the ideal, a life of understanding spent forever in preparation for a reality and a reason that never arrives—except perhaps in death. Even his attempt to recuperate this image has the quality (like the "Up again, old heart" of the conclusion) of forced levity:

"Thus journeys the mighty Ideal before us," he writes. "It never was known to fall to the rear. No man ever came to an experience which was satiating, but his good is tidings of a better. Onward and onward!" (CW 3:43). A "new picture of life awaits," a "new statement," a "new philosophy" that will gather up the "skepticisms" and the "oldest beliefs" alike (CW 3:43).

Perhaps it is this friction between the desire for closure and the inevitability of receiving new and unsatiating environmental inputs that is at the heart of the following well-known passage (which we can, I think, take as the nonexuberant counterpart to the "abandonment-to-circularity" conclusion of "Circles"): "I take this evanescence and lubricity of all objects, which lets them slip through our fingers then when we clutch hardest, to be the most unhandsome part of our condition. Nature does not like to be observed, and likes that we should be her fools and playmates. We may have the sphere for our cricket-ball, but not a berry for our philosophy. Direct strokes she never gave us the power to make; all our blows glance, all our hits are accidents. Our relations to each other are oblique and casual" (CW 3:29–30). Here Emerson expresses what will become a leitmotif in subsequent modernist writings, whether philosophical, psychological, or literary: the felt sense that we are bound to come up short in our grasp of the world, yet still compelled to make the attempt—or at least to keep announcing our failures. The challenge here, for Emerson or anybody, is, as Cavell puts it, "the stepwise overcoming of skepticism, say of the immeasurable distance from the world, by the process of nearing as indirection, so an instruction in mortality, finitude" (*This New*, 116–17). And one aspect of approaching our finitude indirectly requires that we acknowledge that what we want is what we will never have: "All I know is reception; I am and I have: but I do not get, and when I fancied I had gotten anything, I found I did not" (CW 3:48). What Emerson experiences as spiritual involution and a curtailment of the possibilities for direct contact with the world, and what later writers (for example, Nietzsche or James) will take as a sign of our absolute freedom from metaphysical constraint, in systems terminology may be described as a psychic response to the apprehension of overwhelming environmental complexity—the self-referential fatigue of realizing again and again that our autopoietic closure is made possible only on the basis of openness to an insuperable environment. In other words, Emerson discovers that to maintain a unitary self exacts the price of *not* transcending the difference between that self and its Other: the "Me" of *Nature* is "Me" only because it is not the "Not Me"—and never can be. Again using the oceanic imagery, he writes, "Souls never touch their objects. An innavigable sea washes with silent wave between us and the things we aim at and converse with" (CW 3:29). Far from being the obstacle to "real" self-observation and "true" knowledge, the split between what we take as ourselves and what we take as not ourselves is the paradox that experience tells us is the precondition of knowing not just ourselves but anything at all. You cannot become one with nature, for example, because you need the galvanic draw of an eternally retreating environment of unactualized possibilities to shock you into thinking that you are still who you imagine you are. The environment, so to speak, is what keeps pinching you awake; it keeps you from being a mad brain in a vat. Every attempt to assimilate that environment only reveals that we can never get away from ourselves, and thus does "every object fall successively into the subject itself. The subject exists, the subject enlarges; all things sooner or later fall into place. As I am, so I see; use what language we will, we can never say anything but what we are" (CW 3:45–46). The "transparent eyeball" turns out to be a chimera precisely because it proposed a static relation of self to nature that is not in accord with experience.

I have finally come full circle and can summarize what I think are the main ideas to be retained from the discussion of the Emerson up to and including "Experience" and his relevance to a systems theoretical view of nature and environment. As I noted at the beginning of this chapter, the penchant for originality and newness, combined with the second-order perspective it generates when pushed to the limit, comes at a time in the life of Emerson and America when the old rules of order were breaking down. To reiterate, literature, now delinked from its traditional close association with the religious and socioeconomic order, is free to invent its own code and procedures for determining its field of view and operational closure. The particular code I have proposed suggests that the breakdown of the established rules of the social system's harmony allowed the nascent literary system to develop a reflexive autonomy that could take as an important theme in its problem field the critical consideration of other levels of reality, that is, the rest of the social subsystems and their idiosyncratic environments. Thus, although the idea of "art for art's sake" is clearly one facet of this autopoietically closed system, another is the outward facing, second-order perspective that allows literature to internalize and comment upon the paradoxes it sees in the world; in fact, the literary system becomes a site where society can unfold and play out the paradoxes and disjunctions of its various subsystems. (This closed yet open conception of the literary system, incidentally, might provide a means to reframe the long-standing critical split in American criticism between those who have seen embodied in literature the refusal to participate in social struggles and those who understand literature to be precisely a working out or *intensification* of those struggles, to borrow Larzer Ziff's term.) But simply because the literary system is a specialized, Janus-faced system that is particularly adept at critiquing its fellow systems does not mean it possesses a special insight into the workings of the new social order: though it modeled modernity, it could not see that its own angle of vision was relentlessly modern, new, and "onward." Neither could it see that the fragmentation or parceling of society, people, and nature was a way to maintain overall social system coherence by delegating the problem of dealing with increased internal and external complexity across a number of function systems. The differentiating literary system instead reads this complexity as evidence of social disintegration, chaos, and personal fragmentation, and produces a literature marked by anxiety, dislocation, psychological confusion— in general, a kind of "future shock" we have typically associated with, for example, the writers of the American Renaissance. (Indeed, given these kinds of conditions, it should be no surprise that this period has often been read, probably accurately, as a literature of reaction, which proposes a retreat to a simpler, happier past as the only solution to current woes.) "Experience" was Emerson's closest approach to comprehending that the partial vision beginning to emerge at this time was not merely an aberration, not merely a perspective to be either transcended or refused. He saw, rather, that partiality was a necessary consequence of the increasingly heterogeneous nature of modern society. Thus in "Experience" we find little of the boundless optimism of *Nature* or the self-assured fatalism of later essays; instead there is only a brave, unflinching, occasionally defiant, diagnosis of the condition. He may not have liked what he observed (or did not observe), but he sensed in this essay as nowhere else that, to paraphrase Varela, partiality was where he had arrived and where he had to stay.

To connect that partial vision to the larger point I want to make: chapter 1 established that one of the specific transitions America saw during this period was a rapid reconfiguration of the pastoral milieu that had long served to mark in segmentary societies a point at which the society and its larger environment had met and, so to speak "coupled." As the via media between society and nature, this permeable, pastoral boundary became a site of contestation and uncertainty: the kinds of seamless environmental selections segmentary societies made in coupling with the overarching environment (selections based on, for example, age-old agricultural practices, folk arts, herbal medicine, traditional know-how, all of which were tied closely with a relatively stable religiopolitical organization) were now giving way to multiple modes of knowing and acting on that environment, modes that may have contradicted each other and, indeed, were often mutually exclusive. The rise of science threatened theological interpretations of the meaning of nature; new economic imperatives trumped long-held rights of common usufruct; the aesthetic domains feared technological encroachment into the pastoral was a menace to the imagination; and the new democratic political and legal institutions were expected to mediate between these many variable interests. Country life was becoming more complex, more risky. Therefore, when we consider the many changes in this liminal zone between wilderness and civilization, instead of trying to explain how *one* society reshaped *one* environment according to some principle like capitalism, virgin land, or industrialism, we now must account for the roles played by many function systems, each of which sees and acts upon, for all intents and purposes, a different environment. In this respect, Emerson was quite prescient to propose the anatomy of nature that he did, and more right than he wanted to be when in "Experience" he recognized the elusiveness of the singular perspective that would align nature's many facets.

In the trajectory examined in this chapter—a trajectory that runs from the transcendental idealism of *Nature* to the self-limiting relativism of "Experience"—we have seen in miniature one of the main shifts implied by the functional differentiation of social systems: the shift from the first-order idea of a *"Nature,* in the common sense," which "refers to essences unchanged by man; space, the air, the river, the leaf" (CW 1:8), to the second-order idea of multiple *environments,* which are no longer defined as *essence* but as a *difference* from the various systems—living, conscious, and social. A system must distinguish and channel as environment equally such complexities as "Nature, art, persons, letters, religions"; for all of these "objects successively tumble in, and God is but one of its ideas" (CW 3:284). In other words, an environment cannot be thought of as nature alone, but is composed of other social phenomena and communications as well, all of which are resolved and refigured according to the guiding codes of the observing social and conscious systems. *Environment* becomes an inclusive term that allows us to ponder, with Emerson, the idea that "we animate what we can, and we see only what we animate" (CW 3:30). One could replace *animate* with *distinguish,* and be reminded that nature remains unknowable only in the sense that any other environmental element is also unknowable: in the sense that we distinguish what we can, and we see only what we distinguish. Nature, in the Luhmannian sense, is inscrutable only so long as we do not observe it, talk about it, generate the system complexity and selectivity in order to account for it. If one must translate this notion into the old Cartesian terms, one could say that while nature may be an object, it now has the potential to be a subject too. But better to say simply that the more systems can make distinctions, indications, and selections of their environment, the more they are able to integrate environmental considerations into their internal operations. As a consequence, one can reject the idea "that somewhere in the world there are states of affairs one cannot know, above all not in the old sense of the essence of nature's being secret" (Luhmann, "Cognitive," 76). Though nature forever exceeds us as society's ultimate Other, a book never to be fully translated because environmental knowledge is by definition never exhausted, *nature* is really just the mystifying term granted to that which has not yet been distinguished.

Emerson says near the end of "Experience," "I know that the world I converse with in the city and the farms, is not the world I *think*. I observe that difference, and shall observe it. One day I shall know the value and law of this discrepance" (CW 3:48). The style of knowledge Emerson pined for here, as in *Nature*—a transcendent knowledge drawn from the direct connection of his essence to the essence of nature— was becoming unthinkable. What in "Experience" he feared but suspected was true *was* true: he and the world were necessarily disunited. Ironically, the disunity was the reason why he could observe his environments and gain a knowledge of them in the first place. The system/environment distinction, as the paradigmatic difference that gives us purchase on the world, means that our confidence in the reality of nature is won by its slipping from our grasp—that most unhandsome part of our condition. Thus, the "value and law of this discrepance" between the world of Emerson's thought and the world he conversed with in "the city and the farms" simply boils down to this: had he not observed this difference, he would not have observed anything at all.

Thoreau's Moral Vision

The De-ontologization of Nature

It is almost a cliché to observe that Emerson's *Nature* is about nature in the same way that Melville's *Moby Dick* is about whales. Nature, of course, was simply a means for Emerson to get to his favorite topic: the human spirit. A bit less hackneyed, however, is to wonder if Henry Thoreau's work is meant as an appeal from culture *for* nature, or as a reproach from nature *against* culture. If by now we are inured to the perils and, yes, futility of pursuing an answer to that sort of question, it is still worth noting that the opposition of nature and culture is something that Thoreau, along with much of the tradition he has spawned, seems unable to do without. True, most environmental philosophers claim to reject the nature/culture opposition outright, because a continuity, not a separation, between the two has long seemed more desirable. Bateson strove to articulate a unified "organism-plus-environment" that would expose the distinction between subjects and their surround as little more than a dangerous illusion. But he could not do so without invoking the very terms he wanted to eliminate, for as yet we are incapable of *not* relying on the nature/culture opposition in some form or another, so integral is it to our mode of talking about the world.

The consensus these days is that dualisms like this one are reprehensible. Not only are they understood to be reductive and conventional, but also they serve to perpetuate explicit or implicit hierarchies. We appreciate that the world contains more grayness than binaries allow. The subject/object problem is a particular irritation for philosophers, one condemned, too, by ecocritics as a root cause of the nature problem. Separation from the world, an attendant anthropocentrism, a habitual denigration of other living creatures—these all can be laid at the feet of this archdualism. But try moving past it! In "Subject and Object" Adorno gave voice to the quandary: "The separation of subject and object is both real and illusory. True, because in the cognitive realm it serves to express the real separation, the dichotomy of the human condition, a coercive development. False, because the resulting separation must not be hypostatized, not magically transformed into an invariant. This contradiction in the separation of subject and object is imparted to epistemology" (139). And epistemology instantly serves to fortify ideology. "The mind will then usurp the place of something absolutely independent—which it is not; its claim of independence heralds the claim of dominance" (139). The object is reshaped into the mind's image. In other words, although the subject/object split accurately reflects our perception of our alienated state (whether from nature, each other, the universe in general) we should not allow that alienation to harden into identity under the subject. Rather, the object must remain object, and have a kind of dialectical pride of place, since even subjects are objects to other subjects. Understood correctly (presumably through Adorno's own critical theory), "the relationship of subject and object would lie in the realization of peace among men as well as between men and their Other. Peace is the state of distinctness without domination, with the distinct participating in each other" (140). The collective, not the individual, then, is where to look for resolution to the subject/object problem. At the intersection of many distinctions, we arrive at a state of equilibrium where we are informed by but not re-formed by the distinction that is the Other.

It is an extraordinary formulation of the problem, and I return to it in chapter 5. For now, it is safe to say that dualistic thinking remains quite tenacious and peace does not reign. Adorno's appealing solution has not transformed the world, nor, as far as we can tell, have any of those proffered by others before or since. Why is that? One possibility is simply that because all dualisms are based on distinctions, and because the cognitive operation of distinguishing is very nearly unavoidable, dualisms like "nature and culture" that appear to draw on the subject/object split must have proven themselves quite useful over time. What this suggests is that no matter the dubiousness of their ontological status, the harm they cause by design or accident, dualisms allow us to *do* things. In this light, perhaps we might agree with Heinz von Foerster that it is never a question of rejecting binarisms outright or pacifying their dominant/subordinate structure, but rather of always acting so as to increase the number of choices (308).

In the last chapter I examined Emerson's typology of nature through the lens of systems theory, and I proposed some ways that this paradigm helps explain his responses to complex social and environmental phenomena. I want to continue to explore the critical applications of these concepts of self-reference and autopoiesis, but as my touchstone now the writings of Thoreau, whose work lets me unpack the concepts with a different consideration in mind: the conscious rather than the social system. At the same time, I can broaden the discussion by contrasting the systems approach with another posthumanist theory, that developed by Bruno Latour. Latour goes every bit as far as Luhmann in rejecting the Cartesian isolation of the reasoning *cogito* from the rest of the universe. With Latour, the act of drawing distinctions is once again understood as a contingent operation by which pockets of order are carved out of an undifferentiated flux. But for Latour the "darker" side of the distinguishing process—its repressive power—gets emphasized more often than in Luhmann, whose abstractness does little to conceal a stunning political quietism. According to Latour, modernity (for Latour, what we *erroneously* call our most recent epoch) was made possible by a forced split between nature and society. It is a distinction within which we have ensnared ourselves and one that Latour would very much like to undo, because for him this split is not indicative of a fundamental epistemological system/environment distinction but is simply a choice (and a particularly grievous one) about how to define the terms of the Enlightenment. In systems theory, making a distinction is the primary act of cognition, allowing Luhmann to claim that as society evolves into organized complexity by reinserting that distinction into its many levels, we cannot help but be modern. For Latour, on the other hand, the recollection of a time (indeed, nostalgia for that time) when society was, so to speak, *less* differentiated prompts him to declare, in the title of his most provocative book, that "we have never been modern." Latour, in fact, sees the nature/culture distinction as a *reduction* of social complexity whereas Luhmann, it is safe to say, would see that distinction as a crude formulation of the system/environment distinction, thus marking social systems' tacit acknowledgment of an *increasing* social complexity. For Latour, hard and fast distinctions limit freedom; for Luhmann (to paraphrase Hegel), freedom comes from the recognition of such distinctions.

Despite these important differences, both Latour's theory and the theories of self-organizing systems reflect a desire to move beyond the dialectics and deconstruction of binary oppositions, which appear to have devolved into a tiresome game of postmodern chicken in which each thinker attempts to critically expose the vestigial metaphysic retained by the last. In the case of Latour, oppositions such as nature and culture must instead be rethought in light of a radical historicization that returns us to the premodern, undifferentiated field of hybrids, a "Middle Kingdom" in which objects now defined by the nature/culture opposition are instead seen to be composed of amalgams of social, natural, and discursive forces, and hence are always already characterized by impurity, mixing, and contamination. Everything for Latour becomes part of this middle as oppositions are dissolved and distinctions are seen for what they are: conventional, contingent, and contested. At bottom, Latour's attempt to move beyond—or rather, erase—modernity is part of his broader effort to de-ontologize the natural/social divide in order to knock the pins out from under authoritarian, objectivist science, exposing it as the fully social activity he believes it is. In systems theory, by contrast, the attempt to move beyond deconstruction and dialectics means not the demotion of the role of distinctions but a reassessment of what they actually reveal. When we turn, for example, to Francisco Varela's version of autopoiesis, we see there too the de-ontologization of nature and society, but if for Latour all is middle, for Varela it is rather the concept of the excluded middle—the either/or distinction between system and environment—that is crucial. Like Latour, Varela seeks a path between the poles of subjectivism and realism. But he finds it by theorizing the groundlessness of the autopoietic self and the circular epistemology that characterizes all self-referential systems, rather than by imagining a rough equivalence between all acts of distinguishing.

Latour's value to us in this discussion is that he lets us place Thoreau's problematic and conflicted delineation of the relationship between nature and society in the context of a larger modern project. We can gain a better sense of how he limned the existence of hybrids—and a hybrid existence for himself—as a solution to the nature/culture split. Even so, Latour will not provide much insight into the related issue (explored in the second part of this chapter): the debilitating disconnection that Thoreau still *feels* exists, despite his own hybridity, between his culture and the wild, the body and the mind, himself and the world. While Latour's theory reassures that there are no such animals as nature and society, it does not address why thinkers as astutely hybridizing as Thoreau still agonize so much over an imaginary schism. Thus, the "bad" dualistic work these terms perform will not be the final word on the subject; the systems approach I take will show that there must be more to the distinction of nature/society than meets the eye, that in fact it reveals something very basic and inescapable about the way we structure our commonplace experiences of self and environment.

Thoreau's famous Mount Ktaadn summit revelation will serve as a crucial topos. There, at the moment of his maximum physical immersion in pure, "unhandselled nature," Thoreau feels most divorced from it. Latour's theory will indeed get us up the mountain to the point where this paradoxical modern separation *and* hybridization of nature and culture reaches a peak. In those terms, Thoreau's confusion about the significance of this sublime moment will seem fully justified, because the nature he discovers is not raw at all, but is in fact, as Latour suggests, always already fully inflected by the social. Yet Latour cannot get us back down the mountain and tell us why this feeling of disorientation follows Thoreau into the valley, the everyday, the quotidian. In plain terms, the experience of the sublime is one thing, but why is it that Thoreau, despite his love of nature and his intellectual understanding that he is "one with it," so often feels divorced from it? This is where the theory of autonomous, self-organizing systems can help. The notion of *embodiment*—a kind of middle way that precisely reflects the strange combination of separation and connection Thoreau experiences routinely with respect to nature—will allow us to take Latour's concept of hybridization to another level. The desire for a hybrid existence between nature and culture (perversely dependent, according to Latour, on the simultaneous desire to keep nature and culture in separate boxes) actually masks a deeper desire for a *ground of certainty*, a desire to fold our seemingly incomplete humanity into the environment—to become a transparent eyeball or to achieve, as Thoreau will say, "Contact." Yet that kind of embodiment would actually be *disembodiment,* for *embodiment* according to Varela means that the only guarantee of a stable reality comes from a successful history of structural coupling by a system in a viable environment—a history that itself is made possible only because there is no certain path by which the coupling must occur. In the essay "Walking," it is the apprehension of this kind of ungrounded embodiment—the idea that things could be otherwise, that despite appearances the world could be different—that gnaws at Thoreau wherever he goes, be it mountaintop or city.

In the first section of this chapter, then, I employ Latour's theory to explain the way the nature/society opposition operates in some of Thoreau's key texts. In the second section, I show that the impasse both Latour and Thoreau reach (an impasse because both finally are stuck within the structure they so brilliantly deploy) can be resolved by recasting the nature/society split as a system/environment distinction, so that the hybrid life they imagine is revealed as a kind of poetic/philosophic rapprochement of autopoietic *embodiment*—a state that, sadly perhaps, indicates that rapprochements can only be stopgap measures at best. As a final point, I arrive at a Thoreau that places him subtly, but decisively, at odds with the Emerson of the previous chapter. I have already touched on the idea that there are two main branches of the environmentalist family tree on the American scene, and that Emerson can stand as the exemplar of one while Thoreau stands for the other. From the systems perspective we have seen that Emerson becomes surprisingly relevant in a postmodern context with his epistemologically decentered view of nature. There is with Thoreau something of the reverse situation, for finally his project is disabled, theoretically speaking, by the very moralism that makes his writings so powerful. Nevertheless, I do not conclude that we should withdraw from Thoreau the inspirational status now conferred to him; that would be a facile response, merely a move in the hagiographical game I have avoided throughout this book. But I demonstrate that in what are becoming vitally important considerations of the obstacles to ecological communication Thoreau was demonstrably less modern than Emerson, and that in the deployment of the codes of nature the Thoreauvian moralistic view of *nature* ultimately hinders *environmental* perception.

The Deep Cut and the Hybrids of "Spring"

As an initial foray into the vicissitudes of the nature/culture distinction, let us look briefly at the famous "deep cut" passage in the "Spring" chapter of *Walden.* The passage begins as follows:

Few phenomena gave me more delight than to observe the forms which thawing sand and clay assume in flowing down the sides of a deep cut on the railroad through which I passed on my way to the village, a phenomenon not very common on so large a scale, though the number of freshly exposed banks of the right material must have been greatly multiplied since railroads were invented. The material was sand of every degree of fineness and of various rich colors, commonly mixed with a little clay. When the frost comes out in the spring, and even in a thawing day in the winter, the sand begins to flow down the slopes like lava, sometimes bursting out through the snow and overflowing it where no sand was to be seen before. Innumerable little streams overlap and interlace one with another, exhibiting a sort of hybrid product, which obeys half way the law of currents and half way that of vegetation. As it flows it takes the forms of sappy leaves or vines, making heaps of pulpy sprays a foot or more in depth, and resembling, as you look down on them, the laciniated lobed and inbricated thalluses of some lichens; or you are reminded of coral, of leopards' paws or birds' feet, of brains or lungs or bowels, and excrements of all kinds. (T 565)

One might say that on the surface it is the intermingling of the geologic and biotic components of nature that chiefly engages Thoreau in his consideration of the railroad cut. This "hybrid product," this spectacle of inorganic organicism, makes a strong impression on him, in part owing to its sheer magnitude and the swiftness of its appearance, but mostly because it is yet another instance of the divine force working out its design in matter:

The whole bank, which is from twenty to forty feet high, is sometimes overlaid with a mass of this kind of foliage, or sandy rupture, for a quarter of a mile on one or both sides, the produce of one spring day. What makes this sand foliage remarkable is its springing into existence thus suddenly. When I see on the one side the inert bank,—for the sun acts on one side first,—and on the other this luxuriant foliage, the creation of an hour, I am affected as if in a peculiar sense I stood in the laboratory of the Artist who made the world and me. . . . You find thus in the very sands an anticipation of the vegetable leaf. No wonder that the earth expresses itself outwardly with leaves, it so labors with the idea inwardly. (T 566)

What may get passed over as incidental in Thoreau's elucidation of the *pars pro toto* method of nature, but is the detail of the tableau I wish to point out, is the railroad cut itself, the substrate upon which the sand foliage appears.[1] One wonders if Thoreau grasped a certain irony here: while the sands may well seem to "anticipate the vegetable leaf," the railroad cut, so to speak, anticipates sand and image both. The cut is where the orders of nature and culture meet: the sand foliage, after all, is inscribed on a blank canvas laid bare during the construction of the Fitchburg line. Without the quarter-mile stretch of transfigured earth (provided courtesy of surveyors, engineers, Irish work gangs, the state of Massachusetts and, to press it, James Watt himself, whose steam technology helped inaugurate the age of the railroad) would Thoreau have been deprived of these images—that is to say, the sand images themselves and the tropes they provide? Here we have an instance in which Thoreau discovers a trope "unearthed" by the natural seasonal thawing of a sandy clay, which was itself unearthed by the highly "unnatural" process of rail development. Nature in culture, culture in nature: it is hard to tell in this chicken-or-egg scenario which sequence the observer is observing.

We are used to such paradoxes in our postclassical epoch, when observer is always implicated in observation, but in the Newtonian world of trains and mud we tend to expect, and generally find, the presupposition of strict causality. And, of course, there really is not much worth puzzling over if one wishes to cut to the chase: this paradox is a paradox only if not pursued to its natural conclusion, that is, that even what humans do (make railroads) is ultimately carried out on the earth itself, which is nature writ large. All a railroad cut does is make more easily viewed what is already there. And Thoreau does wish to cut to the chase: the specificity of the rail cut is unimportant, for, like a holograph, every part of the earth manifests the primary forms: "The atoms have already learned the law, and are pregnant by it" (T 566). As the topological tropology of the deep cut is further elaborated, we see in fact that this natural continuity between the earth's inner and outer forms is expressed in the very words needed to describe it:

> The overhanging leaf sees [in the earth] its prototype. *Internally*, whether in the globe or animal body, it is a moist thick *lobe*, a word especially applicable to the liver and lungs and the *leaves* of fat, . . . *externally* a dry thin *leaf*, even as the *f* and *v* are a pressed and dried *b*. The radicals of lobe are *lb*, the soft mass of the *b* (single lobed, or B, double lobed,) with a liquid *l* behind it pressing it forward. In globe, *glb*, the guttural *g* adds to the meaning the capacity of the throat. (T 566–67)

It seems fairly clear, then, that for Thoreau there was really no question about how the natural and cultural continuum was arranged: like the sand images squeezed out of the earth, language and writing are ultimately products of natural laws. In fact, the universality of basic natural forms means that "The whole tree itself is but one leaf, and rivers are still vaster leaves whose pulp is intervening earth, and towns and cites are the ova of insects in their axils" (T 567). If towns and cities obey this fractal-like principle, it is easy to imagine that a railroad cut might mimic, say, the natural process of canyon formation. As Thoreau points out, even the human body obeys the universal pattern of morphogenesis:

What is man but a mass of thawing clay? The ball of the human finger is but a drop congealed. The fingers and toes flow to their extent from the thawing mass of the body. Who knows what the human body would expand and flow out to under a more genial heaven? Is not the hand a spreading *palm* leaf with its lobes and veins? The ear may be regarded, fancifully, as a lichen, *umbilicaria,* on the side of the head, with its lobe or drop. The lip—*labium,* from *labor* (?)—laps or lapses from the sides of the cavernous mouth. The nose is a manifest congealed drop or stalactite. (т 567)

Max Oelschlager claims that in the deep cut passages Thoreau had presaged the "fundamental evolutionary principles" that allowed complex systems to develop out of simpler compounds (164). I think this states the case too strongly. In fact, the word play, the fluid parade of metaphors, and the rather antiquated hylozoic theory Thoreau propounds in these passages combine to signal that in his explication of the sand images he was probably pushing the limits of what he, as a natural historian, actually took to be the case. Any precise parallels between the ontogenesis of sand, plant, human, society, and language must break down eventually, as Thoreau, keen observer of natural history that he was, would have known. I think more consequential than these formal parallels is his idea that even the supposedly inorganic matter of the earth is perfused by a living force, that, "There is nothing inorganic. These foliaceous heaps lie along the bank like the slag of a furnace, showing that Nature is 'in full blast' within" (т 568). The presence of this élan vital indicates that "The earth is not a mere fragment of dead history, stratum upon stratum like the leaves of a book, to be studied by geologists and antiquaries chiefly, but living poetry like the leaves of a tree, which precede flowers and fruit,—not a fossil earth, but a living earth" (т 568). For Thoreau, what counts is the *aliveness* of the whole planet, from the "great central life" expressed by the "molten earth" (upon which, in fact, "all animal and vegetable life is merely parasitic"), on up to the human "institutions upon it, [which] are plastic like clay in the hands of the potter" (т 568). It is typical of Thoreau's rhetorical style to not only reject the conventional view by positing an unbroken continuity between nature and culture, but to go the next step and actually invert the hierarchy; we are left in these passages with the clear sense that humans—in their bodies, languages, institutions, towns and cities, and no doubt, railroads—are but a kind of secondary exudation from this living earth and, as will become apparent, are less pure and perhaps even less worthy because of it.

But I want to return to what I continue to take as the most unsettling feature of the sand image passages. While it is Thoreau's contention that the nature/culture split is resolved by reference to the holistic, cosmological principle that runs through everything, I think he was also cognizant, if not here then certainly elsewhere, of another principle represented by the railroad cut. The cut is the tangible reminder of the "machine in the garden"—the Fitchburg line and all it symbolizes—and in passing over this material fact in these passages (but not elsewhere in *Walden*), Thoreau betrays the dual consciousness that is characteristic of his work. This duality takes the form of an alternating near- and farsightedness: close up, with eyes focused on the minutiae of the world, nature and the built world are continuous; but from a critical distance, culture seems radically distinct from nature. That latter apprehension of *disunity*, deplorable but ubiquitous, is in fact precisely what *Walden* is all about, as Thoreau had explained so forcefully earlier in the book:

> Let us settle ourselves, and work and wedge our feet downward through the mud and slush of opinion, and prejudice, and tradition, and delusion, and appearance, that alluvion which covers the globe, through Paris and London, through New York and Boston and Concord, through church and state, through poetry and philosophy and religion, till we come to a hard bottom and rocks in place, which we call *reality,* and say, This is, and no mistake. (T 400)

The sand images of the deep cut would logically represent the exact antithesis to the "mud and slush" above, and it is precisely because of this that their "hybrid" origins seem so jarring. The railroad cut is just the sort of technological "appearance" that Thoreau cautions us here in this passage to regard with suspicion. But in order to make the point about the continuity of all things—the thread that connects the "alluvion" of the earth with the "alluvion" of culture, railroads presumably included—he must ignore "the big picture" signified by the very tangible collision of wild nature and "railroad culture" in the sides of the deep cut and focus instead on their metaphoric reconciliation in the details of the frost designs, designs made visible by the very technology he generally bemoans. In other words, for Thoreau to dig into his metaphysical dirt he must muddy himself unawares with the mundane process of digging train lines. In a manner of speaking, the "things themselves" not only intrude upon, but in a certain way, facilitate his transcendental project.

Drawing now on the vocabulary provided by Bruno Latour, it might be said that Thoreau is engaging simultaneously in two apparently contradictory but ultimately interdependent projects: on the one hand, he seeks to purify nature from culture by ignoring the mixed origins of the deep cut sand images; on the other hand, by translating these same images across geological and biological domains into the domain of the social, he creates entities of nonhuman and human components (e.g., bodies of clay, towns like insect eggs, and languages that resemble leaves). When he is engaged in purification he ignores the translation, and when he engages in translation, he cannot see he is purifying. We could say that processes of purification and translation divide the world, one pulling things apart, the other putting them together, and while each activity makes sense only in opposition to the other, the challenge for Thoreau is to pretend they are two distinct and unrelated processes. Now, it is true, the entities described above are literary ones, and unlike the railroad cut itself have no independent existence outside the text. But whether we go from text to world or back again the split between processes of purification and processes of translation remains intact, and it is clear that Thoreau's discursive construction of hybrids in *Walden* and blindness to the real ones at Walden Pond go equally straight to the problematic heart of the modern project: in order to make hybrids like railroads, computers, metaphors, or ozone holes, moderns like Thoreau must keep the orders of nature and culture in two entirely separate ontological boxes—all the while that, through the production of hybrids, they are freely mixing them.

Hybridity and Modernity

To explain why Thoreau might be apt to ignore some of the wider significations of the deep cut hybrids (and other hybrids, as we shall see below), we must look more closely at Latour's theory. In *We Have Never Been Modern,* Latour posits an alternative to the familiar story of the Enlightenment—the narrative that tells of scientists, standing on each other's shoulders over centuries of patient attention to the phenomena of nature, gradually peeling away layers of ignorance and superstition, while at the same time political thinkers, philosophers, and visionaries are freeing individuals from the shackles of kings, gods, and a hidebound and repressive sociality. This tale of positive progression has been described differently depending on who was telling it—humanists, Marxists, capitalists, organicists, etc.—but the denouement is usually the same: humankind is brought ever closer to a true understanding of itself and its place in the universe. "Modernity" is the name given to this period of incessant forward motion, arguably now over in some respects, and "moderns" are those who urge it on. In Latour's view, however, the project of modernity is made possible by a number of contradictory "guarantees," which allow it to proceed, in Luhmannian fashion, by remaining blind to its enabling paradoxes. Latour proposes "a speculative exercise imagining that . . . a Constitution has indeed been drafted by conscious agents trying to build from scratch a functional system of checks and balances" (*We,* 30). This heuristic "Constitution" might appear as follows:

FIRST PARADOX

Nature is not our construction; it is transcendent and surpasses us indefinitely.

Society is our free construction; it is immanent to our action.

SECOND PARADOX

Nature is our artificial construction in the laboratory; it is immanent.	Society is not our construction; it is transcendent and surpasses us infinitely.

CONSTITUTION

First guarantee: even though we construct Nature, Nature is as if we did not construct it.	Second guarantee: even though we do not construct Society, Society is as if we did construct it.

Third guarantee: Nature and Society must remain absolutely distinct: the work of purification must remain absolutely distinct from the work of mediation.

(*We*, 32)

Added to these guarantees is what Latour calls the "crossed-out God," who, as in Luhmann's scheme, is both in the world and beyond it, with His "immanence" in the human heart palpable and real only in so far as it keeps us focused on a promised realm of transcendence. The natural world is now ready to be delineated by science, the human world by politics, with society still free to refer borderline questions to "God" whenever deemed necessary. The power of these guarantees overall lies in their potential to allow the code of immanence and transcendence to be deployed as needed, depending on the situation. Nature can be either a construction or something beyond our control; the same is true for society, and God can be invoked to settle disputes. This flexibility becomes a powerful advantage to the moderns because they can have everything both ways. In the ancien régime where alchemy, angels, and supernatural causality lumped together all sorts of natural and artificial elements under one cosmogonic roof, explanations for complex phenomena served to reinforce the seamless imbrication of society and things. But with modernity comes the promise (or threat) of multiple referentiality made unavoidable by increasing internal and environmental complexity.

The blind spot of the modern constitution lies in the simultaneity of the processes of purification and mediation: by always keeping the orders of nature and society distinct through purification, moderns need never reflect upon the hybrid nature of the entities they create. Moderns assume nature and society operate by different laws and are incommensurable. Because they are incommensurable, anything that happens at the boundary between them (such as the production of social/natural hybrids) is merely transitional. Hybrids created through mediation are quickly processed as either nature or culture. In fact, they are thought of not as true mediators but simply as intermediaries between the two poles (variously construed as subject/object, nature/society, etc.), and as such never appear as anything but alloys of the pure elements, always decomposable into their constituent parts. In the philosophy of Kant, for example, the subject/object dichotomy opposed things-in-themselves (inaccessible) to an equally remote transcendental subject. Hybrids of those two basic ontological categories fill the middle ground and are accepted but "only as simple intermediaries, which merely betray or transmit pure forms— the only recognizable ones" (*We*, 56). Hegel attempts to resolve the subject/object dichotomy through dialectics, yet here too "the countless mediations with which it peoples its grandiose history are only intermediaries that transmit pure ontological qualities—either of the spirit, in its right-wing version, or of matter, in its left-wing version" (*We*, 57). Later, phenomenology and the semiotic turn succeed in widening the gulf between purification and separation by, in the first case, transforming the world into a constant tension between a knowing consciousness and a vast array of intentional objects and, in the second case, autonomizing the realm of signs from the realm of reference and ending up with a kind of hyperincommensurability between matter and speaking subject, to be filled by textuality itself. For Latour, then, practitioners of the modern project are damned if they embrace hybrids and damned if they try to get rid of them, because the entire series of subject/object, society/nature, culture/science, and spirit/matter is like a tar baby, which once touched cannot be released. Even if you reject these distinctions you must do so by invoking them.

Latour's central point is that this compulsion to separate the world into two parts actually enhances the potential for mixing, engendering the proliferation of ever more hybrid nature-cultures. His goal is to create instead an alternative history in which the middle ground of hybrids comes to occupy the whole zone of interaction, the place where we begin and stay, not the "fallen world" where we end up after mixing the "real" domains of nature and culture. But what exactly is a hybrid, and how does Latour's conception of it serve to recalibrate these dualisms we have come to find lurking everywhere? Hybrids may be understood as neither human or nonhuman, social or natural, but, following Michel Serres, as "quasi-objects," "luminous tracer[s] of the social bond in the black box" (*Genesis*, 81). Donna Haraway suggests the more awkward term "material-semiotic actor" to describe the new conception of the object, the boundaries of which "materialize in social interaction. Boundaries are drawn by mapping practices; 'objects' do not pre-exist as such. . . . What boundaries provisionally contain remains generative, productive of meanings and bodies. Siting (sighting) boundaries is a risky practice" (200–201). There are visible hybrids (technologies, machines, artifacts) but there are less substantial ones too (processes, discourses, myths, ideas). The difference between "hard" and "soft" hybrids is less relevant than one might initially think, for the common ingredient of all hybrids is *meaning*. Moreover, these hybrids or quasi objects are no longer to be thought of as inert receivers of social categories determined by others, for they are capable of a certain kind of *agency*—which is their ticket to having a seat and a voice in what Latour calls "the Parliament of Things" (*We*, 142–45). The questions multiply, however, for in what sense can hybrids be thought of as agents, and what are the implications of such a move?

To respond to such questions we must look more closely at the recent work in the social studies of science. Much of the thinking of Latour, Haraway, Serres, and others has been focused on artifacts and technology, these nonhumans that nevertheless clearly embody social actions, needs, and ideas. While sociotechnical entities certainly mediate between society and nature, Latour claims that even more important the recruitment of such artifacts allows us to see that the dualist paradigm was wrong from its inception, starting with its definition of humanity as distinct from artifacts: "Even the shape of humans, our very body, is composed in large part of sociotechnical negotiations and artifacts. To conceive humanity and technology as polar is to wish away humanity: we are sociotechnical animals, and each human interaction is sociotechnical. We are never limited to social ties. We are never faced with objects" ("Mediation," 64). But what does it mean to say that humans are composed of "sociotechnical negotiations and artifacts"? The discourse of the cyborg is extensive enough to answer that question in one way, but I want to come at the question from the other side, from the side of the nonhuman that is no longer faced as an object. Latour has written extensively on the different ways in which humans and things mutually penetrate, but one example can illustrate here: a gun. The old dualist paradigm is exemplified by the NRA dictum that "guns don't kill people, people kill people." In other words, only humans are equipped with agency. A gun is nothing but an inert object waiting for a user. But we might be willing to object along with Latour that the gun is actually full of the history of society that made it. We might also object that when a gun is in the hand of a man, the two are transformed into something called a "gunman," a hybrid entity now capable of something that neither the gun nor the man alone were.

Harder to accept, however, will be the crucial idea that the gun itself is an agent, or more properly, an "actant." Latour's idea is that if we think of a gun as simply a reification of social categories, we ignore the fact that the gun itself helps create those categories. In other words, once humans begin enlisting artifacts into their society, they no longer have a purely social arrangement to oppose to things or nature. In what is essentially a Heideggerian move, Latour proposes that the tools start to use the tool users. But he goes farther and claims that we must therefore replace the notion of "society" with something called the "hybrid collective," in which humans and nonhumans multiply in the number and scales of interaction and "swap properties" (i.e., a person imparts something to a gun, but a gun also imparts something to a person). In this collective, humans no longer have the last word. Latour answers the objections that immediately arise in a remarkable passage worth quoting in its entirety:

> But is symmetry between humans and nonhumans really possible? Do not humans always have the initiative? This commonsense objection is not commonsensical, since in most of our activities we do not attribute a causative role to humans. Scientists, for instance, like to claim that they do not speak, that nature speaks (or, more precisely, writes) through the medium of the laboratory and its instruments. It is reality, in other words, that does most of the talking. We find the same conundrum in political theory (Hobbes Sovereign acts, but the People write the script) and also in fiction (novelists like to say they are forced to write by the Muse or by the sheer impulse of their characters), while many historians and critics appeal to still another collective force which novelists play the expressive role of medium, that of society or that of the zeitgeist. A second glance at any activity undermines the easy, commonsense idea that humans speak and act. Every activity implies the principle of symmetry between humans and nonhumans or, at least, offers a contradictory mythology that disputes the unique position of humans. The same uncertainty bedevils techniques, which are human actions that end up being the actions of nonhumans. Responsibility for action must be shared, symmetry restored, and humanity redescribed: not as the sole transcendent cause, but as the mediating mediator. ("Mediation," 53–54)

One does not have to be convinced by the logic of Latour's argument to understand its purpose: the "contradictory mythology" Latour proposes, this hybrid collective or "Parliament of Things," is ultimately an *ethical* and *political* program. By bringing nonhumans into the conversation (granted, through their own mediators, such as scientists), he hopes to make thinkable, for example, what Serres (writing in an environmental jeremiad) has called a "natural contract" between humans and the world, which cannot occur until nonhumans are granted the agency required to sign on. Because we have historically recognized only agents with intention or language, we have not only furthered the gulf between a world and its linguistic reproduction, but also the gulf between those subjects who can re-present and those objects which only present. As Michel Callon and John Law, two theorists sympathetic to Latour's project, remind us, "The bias is in favor of the speakable, or, we might add (*pace* Jacques Derrida), the writable . . . [but] signification is more general than talk. It comes in all kinds of forms" (503). Instead of privileging representation, they suggest "translation" as a broader way of imagining many different sorts of linkages between the members of the hybrid collective. The attribution of agency usually places all the freight of an interaction on a language-deploying, human prime mover, but Callon and Law point out that it need not be that way if we understand linguistic representation as simply one form of translation, which also includes, for example, the embodiment of skills, the use of instruments, the actions, plans, and preferences of animals, or even machinic or "thing" agency "performed in patterns of translation that are foreign to us; forms of agency that are, for instance, nonstrategic, distributed, and decentered," and which we can only imagine or may never even notice (503). [2] But are such translations indicative of a hybrid agency? Because hybrids make themselves known and felt in innumerable ways to the people who are joined with them through such networks and mediations (and who in turn speak on their behalf), Latour and others believe we could certainly think so.

The notion of hybrid agency is an intriguing one, a provocative way of moving toward the nonanthropocentric worldview that environmental philosophers of all stripes have called for. Perhaps a way to bring the discussion back to more familiar territory, and to think more easily about how translation, mediation, or hybridization have taken place even as nature and society have remained conceptually distinct is simply to take a hard look at that which we still refer to as the pastoral milieu. What we see is characterized by impurity and disequilibrium: second- or third-growth forests composed of monoculture pines; abandoned farmers' field reclaimed by nonnative brambles and weeds; canyons and river basins once sculpted by wind and water transformed by engineering projects and riparian reconstruction; freshwater lake ecologies metastasized by exotic flora, fauna, and chemicals into grand-scale limnological experiments; and managed populations of acceptable wild animals accommodated in a range now prioritized for domesticated herds. This second nature is a cross of organic process and human action. Broadly speaking it is *technē*, but more precisely it is a hybrid sign-scape where humankind has violently inscribed its preferred meanings. So when we look at the pastoral milieu today, we are referring to a mixed medium that is no longer aboriginal, no longer Other, no longer not of our making.

Yet even so, for most of us there remains an important difference between, say, the built environment of the city and less-built country. We believe the orders of nature and culture as epitomized by these environments are distinct, and we tend to resist their cross-contamination—if not in *fact* than surely by way of the *myths* we use to construct our world. We need the conceptual anchoring that the unbuilt world provides. In that latter sense we are simply keeping in play, in one form or another, the various philosophical dramas of subject and object common since Descartes; and we are ensuring not just that the hybridized quasi object remains inscrutable, but that the subject (read, "our culture," "our humanity") remains in an *elevated* position vis-à-vis that object.

But once again, in the sheer facticity of the things we have made, including much of this landscape, we cannot deny that we have created countless hybrids of nature and culture. The hinterlands today are full of parks, interstates, farms, golf courses, ski hills, dumps; they are mapped, subdivided, owned, leased, willed; and they are celebrated, memorialized, enjoyed, narrated, and sung. They are *blends* of humans and nonhumans—but no less real or unitary because of it. They cannot be purified unless we are somehow prepared to deem the blending as nothing but a transitional phase, as if hybrids were like unstable chemicals shortly to decompose into their constituent elements. (The modern project, of course, *is* prepared to deem them as just that.)

As a slight digression, for those like Bill McKibben who say that the difference between the natural and cultural components of our world has now completely disappeared (i.e., a loss of purity) and is no longer as significant as the fact of their contamination (mediation), the only conclusion can be that the end of nature is at hand. But under Latour's formulation, one can reply that the end of nature is nothing new: true, while the scale of mediation has changed, the pastoral milieu of the eastern U.S. today is not so hugely different from the rural scene in Thoreau's time. Many of the major changes associated with the advent of industrial culture had already occurred (discussed in chapter 1), and as McKibben himself has noted, in some important respects (forest cover, deer and bear populations) "wild" New England has today made substantial recoveries.[3] In other words, although the number and types of hybrids in this environment have certainly multiplied, the network of translations running between nature and culture is not a recent invention. Furthermore, the end-of-nature school, no less than anyone else, begins by presuming a prior separation of nature and culture, which it now laments as lost only as the hybrids begin, so to speak, to come out of the woodwork and overrun the whole middle ground.

It is tempting to remark that Latour's theory seems driven by a fondness for symmetry and so is possibly too neat by half. Yet the basic notions of hybridity and the separation between processes of purification and mediation can help explain some interesting lacunae in Thoreau's work. What I propose is that the notion of a middle kingdom provides a way of seeing past Thoreau's perennial attempt to find the "hard bottom" of reality to the various places where not only is the hard bottom already compromised but is in fact unthinkable without its prior hybridization with almost everything it seeks to exclude. Like the natural laws to be observed in the sands of the hybrid deep cut, Thoreau's construction of pure nature or wildness is made possible by the omnipresence of that which he would rather overlook: the natural/cultural hybrids from which his pure ontological categories are distilled. In other words, Thoreau proposes a nature/culture distinction to purify a world in which nature and culture are already visibly and overwhelmingly entangled. In fact, he would not have needed this distinction had he not apprehended at some level that indeed hybridization was taking place. We crave a black and white world only when it has become distressingly gray. Nature versus culture, or wildness versus domesticity, is summoned up to clarify an impure world. But their deployment marginalizes the existence of the very hybrids they are intended to purify. This blindness helps explain why Thoreau can engage in purification and then use the purified entities to make *new* hybrids without ever seeing the contradiction, for he believes that the purpose of purification is ultimately to allow a superior sort of hybridization.

Luhmann's work can remind us how we as second-order observers might want to think about the theory of hybrids. We can say that the nature/society distinction, like the difference of system and environment, is a method of observation that, as with any other distinction, cannot see what it sees. In this case, Latour proposes to call hybrid those entities that fall through the cracks of the code, or rather, resist their reduction into either category. How do they resist the code? Latour says that it takes a "non-modern" perspective to unfold the paradoxes of the modern constitution; I gloss him to mean that one must take a second-order perspective to see that the world is composed of hybrids and "non-hybrids"—supposedly "pure" objects, the hard bottom of the real. Using that distinction we can now better observe what Thoreau does not see: again, the problematic relationship between his overt literary quest for the hard bottom of reality and his concomitant lack of attention to the entities (such as the deep cut) that always belie the existence of hard bottoms. When looking for pure nature he must sort any observed objects into the cultural box or the natural box. He looks at Walden Pond (and elsewhere) as a shifting front between an encroaching and vulgar world of humans and a retreating but still potent realm of wildness. But with a second-order observational code of hybrid or nonhybrid we can see that the things he shunts into the category of natural are actually hybrids—including much of the wilderness itself. The pure, unalloyed nonhybrid never appears; it serves only as the other side of a distinction, an unmarked space to the lee of the fallen world where Thoreau and the rest of us actually live.

Now, it is quite true that in a certain way Thoreau did understand that questing after pure nature was a fool's errand from the outset: "It is in vain to dream of a wildness distant from ourselves . . . I shall never find in the wilds of Labrador any greater wildness than in some recess in Concord, i.e., than I import into it" (quoted in Krutch, 8). But that understanding did not stop him from routinely trying to extract the natural and cultural elements out of the hybrids. In *Thoreau's Nature,* Jane Bennett says Thoreau understands "Wildness is . . . partially constituted by a consciously cultivated longing for it, a longing [he] seeks to invoke in himself and his readers and put to ethical effect" (36). But she adds, "That the wilderness is in some sense a domestic product does not mean that there is nothing other or Wild about it" (36). One might conclude, then, that for Thoreau there was a metaphysical quest that was independent of the physical project, in that the revelation of the wildness of pure nature was not reliant upon the actual existence of wilderness.[4] Yet on the other hand, he did believe that the experience of wilderness could facilitate that quest, that its protection was critical to society, and that, literally, in "Wildness is the preservation of the World" (NH 112). Thus, we see the Latourian paradox of nature in play: a determination to find the transcendent natural law beneath all cultural facades combined with the simultaneous desire for an authentic social order that holds merely immanent nature in high esteem. Of course, there is no reason why one cannot think nature has value at both levels, but one must acknowledge there is a certain contradiction: if the natural law underlying all culture is what counts, it does not matter how culturally transfigured nature becomes; but if one wishes to preserve specific parts of nature, then one is saying that the purity of matter, so to speak, matters.

The way Thoreau deals with this contradiction, not surprisingly, is simply by keeping the processes of purification blind to the processes of mediation. He does only what all great artists must: close their eyes to their enabling contradictions, those tensions that spur the imagination onward ahead of the danger of conclusiveness, of having nothing more to say, of becoming old. Keeping the processes straight means Thoreau can be a transcendentalist and a materialist at the same time. He can, for example, separate nature and culture in his writings (e.g., the metaphysical pursuit of the hard bottom) while ignoring the real hybrids all around him (e.g., the mixed origins of the deep cut), and he can also create metaphors to demonstrate the hybridity of nature and culture in his writings (e.g., the sand images that connect earth to humans) even as he sets out to find a pure nature distinct from culture at Walden Pond, in Maine and Canada, and the top of Ktaadn.

What for Thoreau is the world of putatively pure nature or wildness is for us the unmarked space that by definition exceeds the domain of hybrids. This space is what his metaphysical and physical processes of purification seek to delineate; both processes can be thought of as ways of trying to escape the confines of another place, that is, the mundane realm of writing and making hybrids, that impure world where we actually live, think, and act. Therefore, the space of the nonhybrids must always remain inaccessible, an untrammeled wilderness devoid of any cultural significations that dissolves as soon as it is approached—either on foot or in thought. It is a place always just past the horizon or over the next hill, perpetually beyond the limit of life and language. For Thoreau, this space is pregnant with the possibilities of an unmediated encounter with nature—precisely that which he hopes to achieve on top of Ktaadn. There, at the most remote, "inhuman" spot in New England, Thoreau believes the immanence of "unhandselled" wilderness will foster his ascent to an absolute wildness of spirit (T 645). But the only way to keep the potency of that encounter alive is to remain blind to the very hybridity of which that encounter is composed: what Thoreau thinks of as "wildness" (probably his most privileged signifier of all) is the hybrid figure par excellence.

Contact as Separation, Separation as Contact

Before we make that climb with Thoreau, it is worth looking at his earliest long work, *A Week on the Concord and Merrimack Rivers,* in order to gain a clearer sense of how the selfsame hybrid figure can mark both our separation from and closeness to nature. Reacting to the marked contrast between his own travel observations and a historical description of the Concord, New Hampshire, area in the early part of the eighteenth century, Thoreau writes, "But we found that the frontiers were not this way any longer. This generation has come into the world fatally late for some enterprises. Go where we will on the surface of things, men have been there before us. We cannot now have the pleasure of erecting the last house; that was long ago set up in the suburbs of Astoria City, and our boundaries have literally been run to the South Sea, according to the old patents" (T 248–49).

Thoreau, like Emerson before him, laments the belatedness of his entrance onto the scene, and, again like Emerson, he imagines the cure is not merely a matter of making new things (such as here, "houses," or as with Emerson, new "works and laws and worships"). No, Thoreau is more concerned with the problem of inauthenticity, the lack of the "original relation with the universe." As he points out, "the lives of men, though more extended laterally in their range, are still as shallow as ever. Undoubtedly, as a Western orator said, 'Men generally live over about the surface; some live long and narrow, and others live broad and short'; but it is all superficial living" (T 249). The regrettable lack, so to speak, of *profundity* in our dealings with the world means that try as we might to seek new frontiers for exploration and settlement we will fail as miserably out there as we would have if we had simply stayed home.

Fortunately, the solution to this problem of depth (or lack of it) becomes clear once Thoreau more precisely defines what it is we are looking for: "The frontiers are not east or west, north or south, but wherever a man fronts a fact, though that fact be his neighbor, there is an unsettled wilderness between him and Canada, between him and it. Let him build himself a log-house with the bark on where he is, fronting IT, and wage there an Old French war for seven or seventy years, with Indians and Rangers, or whatever else may come between him and reality, and save his scalp if he can" (T 249). We recall that in *Walden* he would say much the same thing: "If you stand right fronting and face to face to a fact, you will see the sun glimmer on both its surfaces, as if it were a cimeter, and feel its sweet edge dividing you through the heart and marrow, and so you will happily conclude your mortal career. Be it life or death we crave only reality" (T 400). This passage echoes the life-and-death stakes involved in "fronting facts," the idea that truth is a blade that kills off comfortable illusions even as it reminds us that we are indeed alive. Like the frontier, which divides civilization from the wilderness, facts *cleave,* and one must decide whether one wants to live as a scalped victim of the facades and shams or as a whole person in a real world.

What about the image of the log house and the *last* house from the passages from *A Week on the Concord and Merrimack Rivers*? Do they also have a parallel in *Walden*? We know that Thoreau spent much of his time during the Walden Pond experiment writing and polishing *A Week on the Concord and Merrimack Rivers,* and in that light the special significance of the "log-house" reference is obvious. Even so, these houses take on an added dimension if we consider how "immaterial" Thoreau thinks they are to the point he is trying to make. The houses, the brute matter that does not matter to the philosophical thrust of the passages, are raised only to be rejected as a real option should one wish to make contact with reality. In other words, one need not travel the Oregon Trail to find the real world, nor for the same end build a log house in the woods; these extravagances are only incidental to the point Thoreau wants to make: reality is anywhere and everywhere for one who cares to look.

However, it seems that Thoreau did believe a log house could *help* us to front the facts. While he rejects as the pivot of reality the last house in Astoria (in favor of the reality available right under his nose), he does go off to build a semiremote cabin in which to write the books that confirm our ever-present proximity to that reality. In doing so he appears to indulge in precisely the sort of superficial frontier-seeking exercise he excoriates in print. We come down to this rather paradoxical pair of imperatives: forget about the frontier, for if you want to separate the facts from the appearances you can and must do so no matter where you may be; at the same time, why not go into the woods and build a log house if you wish to "live deliberately, to front only the essential facts of life" (T 394)?

Clearly, following the logic of Thoreau, a cabin in the local woods should be just as irrelevant to the encounter with reality as the house in Astoria, in that neither by themselves bring us any closer to reality. Both sites are belated insofar as they represent merely a deferral of what is required in the here and now if one is to face up to the poverty of superficial living. It is in this sense that one ought to be as likely to front reality in the middle of downtown Concord, not to mention Boston or New York, as one would at the frontier. But if we consider that the two houses are constructed for two entirely different purposes, we may be able to explain the contradiction. The log house at Walden Pond is built to help Thoreau bring his cultured outlook in contact with the rawness of nature, whereas the house in Astoria is introduced as a metaphor in order to help Thoreau dramatize how distant culture always is from reality. One house is meant to demonstrate our continuity with nature while the other simply exposes our separation. What we can then say from the angle of the second-order code of hybrid and nonhybrid is that *both* houses are situated in the middle ground between the two imaginary poles of existence, so that the reason why some houses are valuable and some are merely superficial is finally not because one is in Concord and one is in Oregon, but simply because when Thoreau wants to show our connection with nature he can only do so by making hybrids, and when he wants to show our disconnection he can only do so by unmaking or purifying them. In this sense, purification simply becomes a form of negative mediation, the point being that whether he makes or unmakes them, the hybrids are where Thoreau, literally and figuratively, lives; they are what he works *on* and works *with*. The last house may signify for Thoreau the proliferation of his bad and duplicitous culture and its disconnection from nature, while the log house in Walden woods may signify his desire to recover a good and real nature beneath that layer of encrusted convention, but from our perspective they are both hybrids, which signify the ultimate futility of keeping separate the two branches of the modern project. Hybrids are natural, social, and discursive all at the same time, and to the extent that Thoreau takes them as signs of contact or signs of separation means only that he remains strategically blind to their common production in the human involvement in a world "not distant from ourselves."

This difficulty in finding a critical distance from which to measure the facades of society (or, said another way, to find the uncontaminated space of nature) is illustrated by his trip to Mount Ktaadn, the record of which is collected in *The Maine Woods,* the volume on wilderness travels published shortly after his death. The "Ktaadn" essay in particular forms a short lesson in the reconfiguring process of the American landscape, which by the mid-1800s was well underway even in the northeast wilderness. As Thoreau proceeds deeper into the woods and finally to the top of Ktaadn itself, we notice that the layers of cultural contamination are peeling away; but the hard truth is we never leave behind the pervasive signs of his culture. Those signs take the form not only of dams, cabins, roads, the ravages of logging—

but also the tools, techniques, and representations Thoreau uses to navigate and comprehend the wilderness. The former are the sorts of hybrids Thoreau, the nature lover, detests; but the latter, in the usual modern myopia, are the hybrids he himself proliferates but will seldom acknowledge.

Critics such as Sherman Paul and James McIntosh have found significant the following early passage from "Ktaadn," in which Thoreau takes some initial bearings on the Maine woods: "This was what you might call a bran-new country; the only roads were of Nature's making, and the few houses were camps. Here, then, one could no longer accuse institutions and society, but must front the true source of evil" (T 603). The question, of course, is what does Thoreau imagine is the "true source of evil"? For Paul, that question is answered at the top of Ktaadn, where the rawness of the wilderness is so to speak, at its peak. With no trace of anything human, on the summit Thoreau must concede that "the Creator of Ktaadn was obviously not the Artist of the railroad cut; for matter here was not fluid and obedient to idea, and even his body, Thoreau felt, had become matter which was strange to him" (361). The radical alterity of the pure wilderness is for Paul what Thoreau views as the "true source of evil," and indeed, that moralistic strain of nature perception had been an enduring one since the time of the Puritans.

But as Ronald Wesley Hoag points out, Paul's reading ignores the seventy-five pages of intervening material in which Thoreau finds everywhere (and seems bewildered, if not repulsed, by) the marks of the *human* presence in the wilderness. As if to emphasize his awareness of this anthroposemiotic incursion, in the paragraph immediately following the "source of evil" passage Thoreau enumerates the "three classes of inhabitants who either frequent or inhabit the country": loggers, settlers, and hunters (T 603). Hoag provides a helpful enumeration of their effects:

> Ringbolts in lakeside rocks, wooden crosses abandoned by long-gone missionaries, handbills plastered to bark-stripped trees, dents left by loggers' spikes in the boulders of streams, lumbermen's brands on forgotten and rotting piles of logs, cedar beds and burned out campfires left by hunters and explorers—the once pristine Maine woods are littered with man's debris and defaced by his scars when Henry Thoreau makes his pilgrimage to Mount Katahdin. (29)

Against Paul, Hoag claims it is "Man [who] is evil because, in Thoreau's view, his constant imperative is to mark the wilderness as his own, an obsession that always leads to the defilement of nature" (23). The journey to the mountaintop is precisely an attempt to get above that defilement, to a place the hand of man has never touched. What is perceived by Paul as transcendental disillusionment or revulsion is instead to be understood as "a religious experience of the sublime, described appropriately in language borrowed from Edmund Burke" (24). For Hoag, the trip toward Ktaadn is a passage through a blasted landscape, with the holy grail a direct and uncontaminated encounter with nature at journey's end. Far from the wellspring of evil, the summit marks the point at which all the human-made veils to reality have dropped away, a place where the map ends and the territory begins. The encounter with reality is so overpowering that in his initial account of the cloudy summit Thoreau can only turn to the mythic to describe it: "It reminded me of the creations of Atlas, Vulcan, the Cyclops, and Prometheus. Such was Caucasus and the rock where Prometheus was bound. Aeschylus had no doubt visited such scenery as this. It was vast, Titanic, and such as man never inhabits. Some part of the beholder, even some vital part, seems to escape through the loose grating of his ribs as he ascends" (T 640).

Hoag's invocation of the sublime seems apt, and it is worth noting that Thoreau's most intense rendering of the mountaintop is appropriately "recollected in tranquillity" as he makes his way back down. That description begins with the following passage:

> Perhaps I most fully realized that this was primeval, untamed, and forever untamable *Nature,* or whatever else men call it, while coming down this part of the mountain. We were passing over "Burnt Lands," burnt by lightning, perchance, though they showed no recent marks of fire, hardly so much as a charred stump, but looked rather like a natural pasture for the moose and deer, exceedingly wild and desolate, with occasional strips of timber crossing them, and low poplars springing up, and patches of blueberries here and there. I found myself traversing them familiarly, like some pasture run to waste, or partially reclaimed by man; but when I reflected what man, what brother or sister or kinsman of our race made it and claimed it, I expected the proprietor to rise up and dispute my passage. It is difficult to conceive of a region uninhabited by man. We habitually presume his presence and influence everywhere. And yet we have not seen pure Nature, unless we have seen her thus vast and drear and inhuman, though in the midst of cities. (T 645)

This passage is notable for a number of reasons. First, it precedes the scene at the summit and its desultory tone serves as a sharp contrast to the apocalyptic note struck there. Second, although the "Burnt Lands" are a "natural pasture," Thoreau immediately reacts to them as a sort of human-made pasture, and feels himself "traversing them familiarly." He acknowledges that it is hard not to think of pastures otherwise, to imagine a pasture or "region uninhabited by man." This leads us to a third point: What does Thoreau mean that we have not seen nature unless "we have seen her thus vast and drear and *inhuman*"? Has he not just remarked that we cannot conceive of "her" apart from man? The admission that we can even see this "inhuman" nature "in the midst of cities" is even more jarring. He seems to be saying that the presence of culture does not undermine the presence of nature in the city, so we must conclude that the *absence* of culture in the mountains does little in fact to increase the purity of nature in the sense that Thoreau considers important. Once again, there seem to be two projects here, a transcendental one and a materialist one, and it is never entirely clear how they relate, whether they can be separated, and why if they can does the summit of Ktaadn hold especial significance. A more daunting challenge, following this logic, might be to arrive at an appreciation of nature's sublimity in Concord or Boston.

The correct response to these objections is simply to observe that while the climb to Ktaadn is quite possibly a sufficient condition for the "peak" experience of pure nature it is not a necessary one. If one has the eyes to see a similar revelation might be possible in any place, perhaps "even in the midst of cities." Yet Ktaadn promotes the experience, makes it more likely. The contrast, then, the shocking difference between wild nature and culture, must be what catalyzes the moment of sublime recognition, and Thoreau is at pains to point out just how profound that contrast is:

> Nature was here something savage and awful, though beautiful. I looked with awe at the ground I trod on, to see what the Powers had made there, the form and fashion and material of their work. This was that Earth of which we have heard, made out of Chaos and Old Night. Here was no man's garden, but the unhandselled globe. It was not lawn, nor pasture, nor mead, nor woodland, nor lea, nor arable, nor waste-land. It was the fresh and natural surface of the planet Earth, as it was made forever and ever,—to be the dwelling of man, we say,—so Nature made it, and man may use it if he can. Man was not to be associated with it. It was Matter, vast, terrific,—not his Mother Earth that we have heard of, not for him to tread on, or be buried in,—no, it were being too familiar even to let his bones lie there, the home of Necessity and Fate. There was there felt the presence of a force not bound to be kind to man. It was a place for heathenism and superstitious rites,—to be inhabited by men nearer of kin to the rocks and to wild animals than we. (T 645)

The moment of maximum separation of nonhuman nature and human culture is actually the moment of maximum hybridization, so that the point at which Thoreau imagines he has reached an absolute division is precisely the moment when he has made his biggest mediation. But Thoreau does not see this. Why? Granted that the sheer rawness of Ktaadn would seem to put society at the farthest remove, but according to Latour the project of purification mobilizes ever more hybrids the more it believes it has penetrated into nature. Think, for example, of how many hybrids are required in order to smash an atom. Think of how many hybrids it takes to get Thoreau on top of Ktaadn to describe its radical alterity, its distance from everything he has ever known before: maps, guides, boats, lumber trails, equipment, geology, poets, deeds of gods and heroes. Think of the literary freight he takes up with him, the memories and metaphors that help him bind the summit experience to known things:

> We walked over it with a certain awe, stopping, from time to time, to pick the blue-berries which grew there, and had a smart and spicy taste. Perchance where *our* wild pines stand, and leaves lie on their forest floor, in Concord, there were once reapers, and husbandmen planted grain; but here not even the surface had been scarred by man, but it was a specimen of what God saw fit to make this world. What is it to be admitted to a museum, to see a myriad of particular things, compared with being shown some star's surface, some hard matter in its home! I stand in awe of my body, this matter to which I am bound has become so strange to me. I fear not spirits, ghosts, of which I am one,—*that* my body might,—but I fear bodies, I tremble to meet them. What is this Titan that has possession of me? Talk of mysteries!—Think of our life in nature,—daily to be shown matter, to come in contact with it,—rocks, trees, wind on our cheeks! The *solid* earth! the *actual* world! the *common sense! Contact! Contact! Who* are we? *where* are we? (T 645–46)

The Emersonian separation between the "Me" and "Not Me" is never greater for Thoreau than right now, as he pronounces himself a spirit or ghost, evanescent and insubstantial in contrast to the "hard matter" of things, including his own body. While this apprehension of nature is felt like a slap, not a gentle caress, just as with Emerson's "bare common" episode, Ktaadn has opened Thoreau's eyes wide to the material world all around him. Is "Contact" a figure for what he *has* or what he *lacks*? (As explained below, the answer may be: "both.") But what Ktaadn has closed his eyes to are all the hybrids that he had noticed in the wilderness below, as well as their continuing importance to the summit experience. We can deconstruct that seen/unseen duality in the following way: if "hard matter" is ontologically pure nature, and if "spirit" is the nonmaterial stuff of the human mind, then the "museum" collection, as a synecdoche for culturally inflected nature, is a kind of "soft matter," a *hybrid* that was ordered, tamed, and organized—once hard matter, now made digestible by its place in the human world. That mixing of nature and culture in museums and even the Maine woods is what Thoreau wants to put behind him decisively at the summit, and this passage is where he believes he has recorded it. But what undermines that effort are the very grounds on which he must stand to produce his account. Thoreau reveals that the ontological purity of nature and culture is highly compromised—compromised in the effort to separate them in the first place. Purification becomes a kind of negative mediation, because it is only by conveying his own culture to Ktaadn that he is able to contrast its wildness with culture's tameness. The myths of savages and ancient reapers, Titans, Mother

Earth, God, Chaos, museums, metaphysics, and Concord itself are the hybrids he needs to understand (and domesticate) absolute wildness. The summit experience must be filtered through these imaginatively in order to make it comprehensible. As a result, he does not so much find pure nature as he *extends the domain of hybridity that much farther.* Thoreau tells us at one point that he "had brought [his] whole pack to the top," and it seems that he was right in more ways than he imagined (87).

The middle ground is thus inescapable. From our second-order perspective, the trip to Ktaadn—either as a journey into cultural evil or away from it—is better described as a prototypically modern extension of the nature/culture code into a new field, an effort that produces hybrids even as it remains blind to them. As Thoreau gets closer to the summit, the number of visible hybrids seems to decrease; there is less of his society to recognize in the wilderness. But even as hybridity diminishes in this respect, even as the overt mixing of nature and culture declines, Thoreau can never quite eliminate the social taint in the objects he discovers. He can never eliminate it because he himself brings it along with him, so to speak, in his backpack. He is an agent of what he wants to transcend, and right behind him is entrained all the baggage he thought he was leaving below. The point, whether Hoag or Paul is right in what precisely constitutes the evil, is that we must, as it were, go beyond Thoreau's moral code of a sublime good or evil if we are to see that his experiences in the Maine woods are never unmediated: he must always affix them to what he already knows. Thoreau supposes that we can say of the pure nature at the summit that "Man was not to be associated with it." But man *is* associated with it, as surely as he is in the cities. Pure nature is everywhere overdetermined by the signs of humans, and perhaps nowhere more pervasively than in the places where we believe we have pushed aside the veils to reality most decisively.

Conscious Systems: From Hybridity to Embodiment

While Ktaadn stands as the clearest example of his apprehension of the absolute alterity of pure nature, it is also fair to say that Thoreau feels a certain dislocation *wherever* he goes and constantly seeks ways to reassure himself (and us) that he is still seeking the hard bottom—even as it is not the hard bottom but the middle ground that he seems ultimately to prize. The itinerary I have traced so far—from Walden to Ktaadn—expresses the proposition to which Thoreau's whole life was dedicated: that one could live a hybrid life between town and wilderness while at the same time keeping a weather eye ever-fixed on the realometer, as if one anticipated that the hard bottom would someday heave into view. But the objections immediately multiply: Why suppose the hard bottom is imminent when your world has always appeared as a mixture of the pregiven (nature) and the constructed (culture)? How, anyway, would you deal with a real that apparently can be approached only through an Emersonian subject lens, or that when encountered directly (as on Ktaadn) is essentially incognizable? And how can you reconcile your aspirations for the harmonious hybridization of nature and culture, body and world, with this relentless desire to contact something unhybridized and absolute? The short answer to this last is: you can try. But it is likely that you will run into the same problem that Thoreau always does, the sense that the ground is always shifting, that the "hard matter in its home" is no place to build *your* home, as the Ktaadn experience so massively reminds him. The middle ground is the place where, by necessity, we must (sometimes reluctantly) stay, for the hard bottom is simply too *unsettling* to occupy.

To make headway with these objections—and with what is finally the blind spot of Latour's hybrid/nonhybrid code—we must shift our terms of reference. I pointed out at the beginning of this chapter that despite its effectiveness in allowing us to think about the conventionality of the nature/culture split and the omnipresence of the middle ground, hybridity would only take us so far in our analysis of Thoreau's relationship with his environments—social or natural. The theory does not answer the question as to why Thoreau seems to *feel* that the middle ground is not always where he is—or even where he wants to be. Recall, for example, (in the "Ktaadn" passage quoted above) that he refers to *himself* as a "ghost" and to his body as "hard matter," as if to say there is an enormous and incommensurable gulf between the two, a Cartesian/Emersonian extraction of mind from corporeality. His discomfort indicates that while the figure of a hybrid, middle ground always has great appeal (exemplified by Walden Pond itself), it cannot eradicate his apprehension of a profound disjunction between self and world (apprehension brought to a head on Ktaadn). Latour's theory provides a powerful framework for analyzing Thoreau's typically modern blindness to processes of translation and processes of purification, but it does not satisfactorily deal with this cognitive oscillation, Thoreau's felt sense that he cannot successfully bridge the distance between self and world, can only, as it were, shuttle back and forth between them.

This question of Thoreau's ungrounded subjectivity can be addressed by revisiting the systems paradigm, in effect rewriting the nature/culture dichotomy as a system/environment distinction. In common conception, "environment" is the outer and "system" is the inner; cognition would then be understood to be very much about the recovery of that outer world. But in autopoietic systems theory the notion of a pregiven world is abandoned: we do not represent in our minds some outer reality but instead enact through various structural (i.e., sensorimotor) linkages what we take as reality. As in the example of the submarine operator who manipulates instruments to keep them within certain parameters, systems deal with stimuli by reconjugating internal states to maintain an invariant organization. Their operational closure means that the results of their various structural processes are the processes themselves, the only goal being the preservation of the overall relations between structures—even as the structures remain open and adaptable to the environmental perturbations. I propose, following a suggestion made by Varela, that one of the consequences of the closed/open mode of autopoiesis in conscious systems (i.e., humans) is precisely the alternating feelings of groundlessness and at-homeness I have attributed to Thoreau.

Before I continue I should point out that Latour would undoubtedly reject the move to a systems perspective from the outset. For him, it is symptomatic of modernity to experience such cognitive dislocations because of a double-mindedness that must be cultivated in order to maintain the separate processes of purification and translation; hence any questions of a conflicted subjectivity need only be referred back to the terms of the modern constitution. As he says, "The notion of system is of no use to us, for a system is the end product of tinkering and not its point of departure. For a system to exist, entities must be clearly defined, whereas in practice this is never the case; functions must be clear, whereas most actors are uncertain whether they want to command or obey; the exchange of equivalents between entities or subsystems must be agreed, whereas everywhere there are disputes about the rate and direction of exchange" (*Pasteurization*, 198). For Latour the middle kingdom has no inside or outside: it is neither system nor environment but a complexity that is formed into networks by actors deploying *"many forces"* (198), who despite their different ways of rendering this complexity are all still dealing with the same reality—which, by the way, will ultimately discipline their construction of it. I propose precisely that systems *are* our point of departure, that they enact different realities, and that our analysis must finally account for those systems. So if we really want to understand what Thoreau is doing with the hybrids he assembles or purifies we must now imagine him as a psychic system pursuing autopoiesis and consider especially the type of subjectivity such a situation might produce.

But what sort of subjectivity would be associated with conscious, autopoietic systems? We can start to address that question by reviewing some recent work on the structure and function of the brain itself. The same cybernetics revolution that informs the social systems approach of Luhmann also gave rise to a new branch of inquiry, namely, cognitive science. Cognitive science's dominant paradigm—the "cognitivist" approach, much indebted to figures like Warren McCulloch, Noam Chomsky, and Marvin Minsky—has contributed mightily to a great many areas outside of brain research itself, most sensationally to the attempt to design artificial intelligence, computers capable of understanding human language and responding appropriately to any input (i.e., to generate their own programs spontaneously).

Such a thinking machine would by definition pass the Turing test, which is to say its responses could not be distinguished logically from a human's in a blind examination.

The assumption has been that our own cognitive flexibility originates in the brain's ability to create—somewhere within its 10^{15} neurons—symbolic representations of the contents of the world (and by *representation* I refer to the strong, epistemological sense of the word as a correspondence between symbol-in-the-mind and pregiven thing, not in the weak, semantic sense as simply the way we use one thing to stand for something else in everyday communication). The AI would be equipped with a similarly comprehensive symbolic catalog; it would be able to turn inputs into appropriate symbols, rearrange them in new patterns based on complicated algorithms, and produce the most effective response to a given stimulus. But while current rule-based programming languages have a remarkable capacity to process routinized information, the cognitivist approach is seen increasingly as fatally flawed: the generative grammar necessary to respond to an infinite number of input contingencies may be impossible to design. In fact, as early as the famous Macy conferences in the mid-fifties, the notion of cognition as a centralized, rule-governed process of information coding, decoding, and routing was being questioned. The connectionist paradigm has been offered as a possible alternative. In this model we find the concept of *emergence*—a view of the brain as a networked system of connections that produces global consequences arising spontaneously from many localized neural firings—beginning to take center stage. Emergence depends not simply on real-time effective response to external stimuli but also on the history of previous neural activity. This means that if particular neurons have in the past participated in local activity, the bond between them and their partners is strengthened and, conversely, diminished when there is less coordinated activity (Hebb's Rule). As Varela puts it, "the system's connectivity becomes inseparable *from its history of transformation,* and related to the kind of task defined for the system" ("Whence," 245). In other words, an intelligent computer designed along these lines would "grow" its pattern-recognizing capacities just as a human does: by learning and shoring up its cognitive capacities over time. A significant implication of the theory of emergence is that the notion of the brain as primarily a symbol-processing organ must be discarded, for cognition arises from patterns of neural activity that occur at a subsymbolic level, meaning that particular symbols are not encoded point to point with the environment but instead are relative to the overall state of the neural system.

But despite this important shift, connectionism as an approach to AI once again awaits the development of some kind of generative grammar, for no matter how fine-grained the grammar may seem, "At the heart of the most volatile pattern-recognition system ('connectionist' or not) lies a von Neumann engine, chugging along, computing a computable function," as Daniel Dennett playfully puts it (269). The connectionist model is in the final analysis still a representational one, because the brain works only insofar as it can replicate within its distributed structures some sort of accurate picture of the world within which it must operate.

To fully leave behind the representationalist approach, Varela has proposed a modified connectionist approach. This *enactive* model looks very much like the logical extension of his and Maturana's general theory of autopoiesis to the study of cognitive systems. According to Varela, enactive cognition can be delineated by answering three basic questions:

> *Question #1:* What is cognition?
> *Answer:* Effective action: History of structural coupling which enacts (brings forth) a world.
> *Question #2:* How does it work?
> *Answer:* Through a network of interconnected elements capable of structural changes undergoing an uninterrupted history.
> *Question # 3:* How do I know when a cognitive system is functioning adequately?
> *Answer:* When it becomes part of an existing ongoing world of meaning (in ontogeny), or shapes a new one (in phylogeny). ("Whence," 256)

Taking these three points together, we understand that the crucial departure from the connectionist view is that now we can dispense completely with the idea of the brain reconstructing internally an external, pregiven world, and instead say simply that cognition and world arise simultaneously. The brain does not merely produce behaviors that accurately register the contours of an outside world but, based on biological, psychological, and social histories, determines for itself what counts as its world. In no way can this process be thought of as representing, because the world brought forth can quite literally vary from brain to brain depending on the history of structural coupling produced during phylogenetic and even ontogenetic development. For example, colors, shapes, and shadings are not out there to be recovered (nor, to anticipate the charge of idealism, in here to be projected) but instead result from specific selections of information, selections that emerge during a history of interaction. The world as seen though the compound eyes of an insect as opposed to the binocular vision of a human is not simply a different view of the same fundamental reality: what is taken as "world" actually coevolves with the sensorimotor apparatuses that have coupled with it. Depending on how those apparatuses have developed, the embodied actions of the organisms produce particular cognitive states, which in turn reproduce the effective actions that guide perception in that world. In other words, the world appears as it does neither because we project our internal states upon it nor because we retrieve from it invariant properties but because we have evolved to see and act on it in specific ways—and, to a very substantial degree, *it has evolved with us.* [5] In *The Embodied Mind,* Varela and coauthors Evan Thompson and Eleanor Rosch write:

> The key point, then, is that the species brings forth and specifies its own domain of problems to be solved by satisficing [solving problems by using whatever works, not what is optimal]; this domain does not exist "out there" in an environment that acts as a landing pad for organisms that somehow drop or parachute into the world. Instead living beings and their environments stand in relation to each other through mutual specification or codetermination. Thus what we describe as environmental regularities are not external features that have been internalized, as representation and adaptationism both assume. Environmental regularities are the result of a conjoint history, a congruence that unfolds from a long history of codetermination. (198)

The point to bear in mind is that the brain does not receive information from the environment as input; it creates its own information on the basis of physiologically opening itself selectively to perturbations in the environment. In reductive terms, it is a kind of adequation-as-survival, a jerry-rigging of perception, cognition, and action to what surrounds us: we see what we see because it works, and until it stops working we will continue to see it that way. "Thus," say Varela, Thompson, and Rosch, "the overall concern of an enactive approach to perception is not to determine how some perceiver-independent world is recovered; it is, rather, to determine the common principles or lawful linkages between sensory and motor systems that explain how action can be perceptually guided in a perceiver-dependent world" (173). [6]

Varela has theorized that conscious human systems (i.e., what we call "minds") operate through this same combination of organizational closure and structural openness discussed many times previously. Once again, a main concern here is to steer a course between, as Maturana and Varela say, the Scylla of realism and the Charybdis of idealism. Thinking machines designed along these lines would, through many receptors and their own associated effectors, respond to various environmental stimuli appropriately—*without* the presence of a central processor with a universal grammar coordinating the total activity through a master representation of the environment. What looks to an observer like a system using an inner map to navigate a territory is rather an ensemble of microresponses, each sensorimotor unit pursuing its own goals with the only proviso being that the various units (structures) must be compatible (i.e., to have evolved in parallel) so that their independent activities do not lead to the interruption or destruction of the totality of activities (the organization).

An apt analogy here is the coordinated movement of a school of fish or a flock of birds: although it is tempting to imagine that each animal is aware of the overall direction and purpose of the group as it moves through its medium, the observed coordination of the group depends solely on the sensorimotor activity of each animal as it responds to stimulus in its own immediate environment. Leading and flanking animals, for example, may respond to food or prey by changing their direction toward or away from the stimulus, while interior or tailing animals may simply react to minute changes in the spatial disposition of the animal in front of or beside them. As long as the members of the group continue to react appropriately (i.e., nothing occurs to compel each individual to follow other, more deeply necessitous behaviors) the school or flock remains organized as such. In essence, what is taken by an observer to be the astonishingly well-orchestrated behavior of the school or flock (the "group mind," according to an earlier interpretation) is not orchestrated at all: it is nothing more than the total effect of many small course corrections (structural changes) in compliance with a modest set of organizational rules. The larger point here—with respect to the proposed AI or the human brain—is that what we like to think of as mind, ego, self, subjectivity, etc., is simply our attribution of a governing core to a distributed, organizationally conservative process such as this, what Dennett calls a "Center of Narrative Gravity" (410). There is no seat of consciousness, a *cogito* in the Cartesian sense (or "Me" in the Emersonian one), but only many local sites where the brain responds to stimuli, the global outcome of which is the coordinated behavior we believe (wrongly) is being masterminded by a central processor.

Admittedly, the prospect of an imaginary mind seems to violate common sense. The self surely must be a thing apart from the physiochemical interactions that compose the brain and body, a hard kernel of ego that keeps us who we are across space and time. Even those who have given up on the soul find it hard to relinquish their minds, for how could there not be some sort of ghost in the machine, an entelechy that animates and gives focus to these three pounds of skull-bound meat? But common sense (as in the quotidian thoughts and feelings that shape our inner lives) is precisely what is at issue here, for in the enactive view, common sense now arises from the successful history of coupling between many sensorimotor structures and their specified environments, which together compose the ongoing project of individual growth (ontogeny) or species evolution (phylogeny). Common sense would then be defined as just this sort of embodied knowledge, knowledge that allows us to perceive, predict, create, and act effectively within our surround. The mind or self is perhaps no more than the sum total of this knowledge, a repertoire of habituated neural firings, flexible patterns of sensorimotor activity, and ready-to-hand experience. In other words, what we think of as the self may simply be the constant pulling together of a variety of neural operations, a self-generating program designed only by evolution, cultural history, and individual psychophysiology. Our perennial grasping after the certainty of ego-identity is thus a surface effect of a great many subsystems and microstructures working in tandem to preserve the brain's autopoiesis. [7]

The autopoietic view of mind as an answer rather than a question is not so very different from the Lacanian notion of the subject as a retroactively constructed entity that exists only as an explanation for various displacements in a field—in other words, an effect in search of a cause. The reason the subject so often feels alienated, ungrounded, at loose ends is because she really is: that is what it feels like to be a subject, this void at the center of a whirlpool. Likewise in deconstruction it is the rupture between signifier and signified that impels subjects to traverse endless chains of substitutions toward a ground, an identity, a transcendental signified, that never actually materializes. Such materialization, to paraphrase Derrida, could only be marked as the arrival of death or God, for in a manner of speaking the end of signification is either a pure absence or a pure plenitude—and for all intents and purposes the result would be the same: an end to the signifying process and therefore subjectivity itself. In both versions of poststructuralism, self-consciousness is finally just this desire for self, for the certitude of wholeness in the face of radical contingency and difference.

In systems parlance, a self-reflexive self—a mind that can consider its own existence—is the propitious issue of a highly differentiated, multilayered, closed form of neural organization, at the heart of which are a host of difference-producing operations and structures that permit the organization to exist at the price of its continual separation from an insuperable Other (its environment). According to this interpretation, we can dispense with the mind/body duality that has vexed philosophy for so long and conclude simply that mind and body are two parts of the same autopoietic process. Cognitive organization (mind) arises from a particular concatenation of bodily senses and neural networks that in turn continue to concatenate only so long as their coordinated organization can be maintained: mind equals body equals mind.

If it seems that I have only added yet another overlay of arcane technical language to an experience of self that most of us can safely take for granted, I think the epistemological lesson is perhaps a little more useful: If subjectivity is the self-description of a closed unity structurally open to the environment through a variety of sense organs and effectors, then subjects' feelings of both disconnection *and* contact with that environment come to be seen in a different light. Firstly, we now consider knowledge to be just another of the many adaptations we have evolved to allow us to cope (i.e., structurally couple) with environments; it is storable, transmittable, action in the world. [8] Secondly, because this knowledge of the world is embodied, not objective, there is no particular path the subject is forced to take in the realization of his autopoiesis; any path is permitted as long as it is viable, that is, it does not destroy his cognitive and/or bodily organization. Crudely speaking, if the subject decides to walk off a cliff, he will shortly discover the nonviability of this manner of structural coupling, not because his ability to properly represent the features of the world has let him down but because, despite the environmental cues that should have warned him away, he failed to secure the organization of his cognitive (not to mention physical) system.

Ultimately, then, we are simultaneously connected to this world through our sensorium yet disconnected to it, in that information selections can only contribute to the maintenance of our cognitive organization. The world is just the world we enact through living in it, and there is no ground but the ground we walk on. Thus our feelings of rootlessness are fully justified—but so too are our feelings of connection. The difference in affect may simply depend on the mental state we find ourselves in. When we engage in reflective, self-conscious thinking we feel disembodied, inasmuch as we are dealing with problems of organization (i.e., how we can adjust our minds to conform to what our senses are telling us or, said another way, how we can rationalize the world so as to preserve our cognitive integrity). But when we are not engaged in this problem-oriented manner of thinking, perhaps during well-rehearsed activities or autonomic functions, or simply when we allow our minds to wander, that is when we feel most embodied and grounded, most open to the *a-rational* possibilities of the world we have enacted through living.[9]

As Varela, Thompson, and Rosch have argued, this latter state can be cultivated. Drawing on the Eastern tradition of philosophy, they find a model for a state of heightened openness to the environment in "mindfulness/awareness meditation." They suggest that in our Cartesian heritage we have developed too much of a penchant for disembodied modes of reflection, those styles of thinking that abstract all experience down to the closed circuit of our consciousness and leave it under the impression the world is real only insofar as it can be represented confidently in the theater of our minds. In effect, the Cartesian tradition exacerbates the much-ballyhooed discontinuity between self and world, mind and body (and by extension, society and nature) by focusing, as it were, on the organizational closure of subjectivity at the expense of its structural openness. Varela, Thompson, and Rosch propose instead that once we learn to reflect on reflection itself as just another embodied experience, we can escape the closed loop of disembodied self-consciousness and regain that sense of connection we seem to long for so desperately. "When reflection is done that way," they claim, "it can cut the chain of habitual thought patterns and preconceptions such that it can be an open-ended reflection, open to possibilities other than those contained in one's current representations of the life-space" (27).

Practically, they suggest that a deeper understanding of the ego grasping that is a response to the apprehension of groundlessness has potential importance for the individual (who can learn to moderate such ego grasping and attain a greater degree of psychological comfort), as well as for society as a whole, the institutions of which (particularly those of science) are far too engaged in processes that separate, to our detriment, experience from facts. (This discussion, by the way, is not meant to introduce yet another "bad" dualism, that between reason and intuitive thinking, for *all* knowledge is finally *embodied* knowledge, dependent on a history of bodily action and response, and all thinking is a form of self-observation in which current states of mind are compared against previous ones, and projections of future states are either confirmed or denied. So what is meant here, rather, is that just as there are different sorts of ambulatory motion—walking, running, jumping—there are different ways of thinking, and that what I have called the disembodied style has been cultivated over the embodied one, even though both are finally examples of a common cognitive activity.)

As others have remarked, part of Thoreau's own intellectual achievement was to have aspired to a vision of nature, life, and literature in which the remoteness of the Cartesian subject is replaced by an observer who is very much a part of the world. Both as amateur scientist and as artist, Thoreau was committed to proving the facts of the world through his body before putting pen to ink; in this sense, embodiment appears similar to what Laura Walls calls his "epistemology of contact," by which she means

> a *scientia* that would be relational rather than objective. This "relational knowing" extended and applied the possibilities opened up by the disintegration of subject/object dualism, which encouraged the subject to "know" by seeing correspondence in the world's objects, as if they were the mirror of the self, or by "reading" the book of nature as if it were a text ready-made for decoding. By contrast, knowing as an active process in Thoreau's sense becomes no less than what H. Daniel Peck calls "worlding," the making of a world "by the interaction—the dance—of the creative self and the world."
> (147)

Quoting from the *Journal,* Walls supports her view that against the objective fallacy and the problems associated with representation, Thoreau proposes just such a relational stance: "The important fact is its [the object's] effect on me. . . . With regard to such objects, I find it is not they themselves (with which the men of science deal) that concern me; the point of interest is somewhere *between* me and them (*i.e.* the objects)" (10:164–65; quoted in Walls, 207). Walls tells us that in "Thoreau's alternative science authority comes from individual involvement and experience" and that "we are all similarly involved, implicated. As our designs tangle with those of willows and squirrels and oaks and beggar-ticks, we all become co-producers of Concord, and by extension, the 'environment' around us, wherever we are" (207). Walls's point is that Thoreau provides us with an example of how we too can move toward an epistemology of contact and away from our current model of knowledge (which can be called the epistemology of disembodiment). As neither a Hoonlike solipsist making the world in which he walks nor a detached objectivist recording "just the facts," Thoreau treads a middle way that brings the two perspectives into accord.

Sharon Cameron also finds in the *Journal* evidence for this dance between subjectivity and objectivity, whereby observation and reflection on nature constitute not merely steps toward an increase of knowledge but instead are methods to actually insert nature *into* the mind: "The internalization [of nature] is not the result of analogic correspondence conventionally understood . . . analogies cannot effect comparisons between nature and human nature (the two are incomparable); they must rather effect transfers, in the express sense of moving natural phenomena . . . into the mind and onto the page, where the mind can testify from close up to the fundamental difference between itself and what it contemplates" (15). Thus, Thoreau's practice in the *Journal* of attending to and describing the minute details of nature is understood by Cameron to mean that "to see nature—whether the flooded Sudbury meadows, or the swamp, or winter, or the mosquitos' humming—is to take it into the mind while all the time recognizing it is not of the mind" (153). His descriptions are therefore not sentimental representations, intended to evoke memories of favored natural objects by means of analogy or metaphor (although they do do that, in the weak sense that all writing is representative) but, as Cameron puts it, "they rather exist to enact displacements," (150)—or in my terms, they act as a kind of cognitive catalyst.

What exactly do they catalyze? Not a rapid search of a mental portrait gallery of nature scenes but rather the same state of neural activity that the described objects themselves originally excited. What seems like an image pulled out from an internal Rolodex of memories is instead a particular synaptic cascade that, once triggered, reproduces the mental conditions at the point of the original coupling. In terms of autopoietic cognition, writing nature would then be Thoreau's version of embodied knowledge: inscriptions of nature represent histories of couplings (visual, tactile, etc.) between his cognitive system and the world. It may seem like a small point—whether memories are pictures in the brain or neural ensembles that allow us to constantly recreate the pictures—but it means that, in a manner of speaking, the world is its *own* representation and that we keep bringing it forth again and again as we interact with it through coupling. The closed organization of the brain suggests that we do not mirror the contents of the world in our heads but instead at every moment use those contents as guides for coordinating our cognitive operations.[10] Without the ongoing history of structural coupling between the brain and an environment we would become autistic, for we need the world to act as the template on which the brain can anchor the overall coherence and disposition of its sensorimotor structures and processes, that is, its organization. Absent those structural regularities the organization would be stressed; and without the time to develop new structures (either through phylogenetic or individual change, depending on the speed and manner of environmental perturbation) the organization would eventually break down, as its structures found themselves in the grave situation of being unselective and unresponsive to the new environment.[11]

The balance between intimacy and otherness of nature both Walls and Cameron attribute to Thoreau in his inscription of nature is very much in accord with the cognitive stance proposed by Varela, Thompson, and Rosch in *The Embodied Mind,* their "middle way" by which to "get in touch" with self and world by "meta-reflecting" on our embodied interaction with it. Thoreau demonstrates the middle way as he oscillates between assembling the hard facts of nature so as to develop accurate, scientific representations of it and reflecting that such representations depend on the subjective experiences that color those facts in the first place. Nevertheless, my point is that the cognitive dislocation one expects to see produced in trying to straddle both styles of thinking—and which we do observe in Thoreau—is never the *consequence* of this balancing act but is in fact its *prerequisite:* cognitive dislocation comes first, as a result of the closed/open design of embodied cognition. So we must bear in mind that the reaffirmation of embodied knowing is not actually a solution to the Cartesian predilection for disembodied reflection: in the end both sorts of knowledge are always options for self-observing cognitive systems, whose fundamental mode of operation is drawing distinctions between one thing and something else. To be able to consider one's autonomy, to be able to reflect on one's reflections, to be able to consider the difference between what one takes to be one's self and what is taken to be the Other—all of these modes of thinking depend on the openness of structure and the closure of organization, that is, the idea that although we can sense an environment that is not the same as us, this *difference* cannot tell us how to organize our cognitive processes but only provide, by its continual reentry, the means to do so. The various dualisms we have come to know so well are therefore different ways of putting a name to the fundamental cognitive dissonance that comes about as conscious systems perceive the insuperable difference between themselves and their environments—and a fortiori the various attempts to eradicate those dualisms are fated only to produce new dualisms. In other words, the split—no longer understood as a subject/object, reason/intuition, or mind/body split but rather distilled down to the difference between the cognitive system and its environment—is not something we are ever likely to heal, expunge, or otherwise resolve, because it is the *very precondition of self-observation in the first place.*

Ironically, then, what Varela, Thompson, Rosch, Walls, Cameron, Peck, and presumably Thoreau himself hold up as an exemplary way of knowing ("relational knowing," "worlding," or "mindfulness/awareness") stands revealed as just such an attempt to enfold mind into environment, to give oneself over to the most "embodied" of all the embodied knowledges provided from the history of structural coupling, as if the contemplation of the bodily roots of thinking and perceiving could tell us how to think and act. But the most the attendance to such knowledge can really do is allow us to ignore, however briefly, the *wound* on which is built our subjectivity. If attention to structural "contact" gains any purchase at all—if, literally, we "forget the pain" of being ourselves for a moment—it can only mean that the fundamental rift between conscious system and environment is still in play, still presenting itself as a separation to be overcome. In other words, the system persists according to the principles of self-organization and autonomy, open structurally to the vagaries of its environment but creating its own information about how those environmental perturbations shall be taken. The environment cannot tell us what to think about it, how to relate to it, how to navigate through it; all it can do is cause us to try something else or continue to do what we have been doing successfully. So the final outcome of Thoreau's effort to hybridize distance with intimacy, objectivity with subjectivity is that it will fail to close the cognitive rift that allows the generation of those dualisms, will in fact only allow him to forget about them for a while—although clearly, as Varela, Thompson, and Rosch argue, that goal alone is certainly compelling. But once the observation of observation enters the evolutionary scene and offers a second-order, self-reflexive awareness of the difference between self (system) and Other (environment), the possibility of eradicating this rift has been closed off forever, for between death and God there exists only the autonomous consciousness constantly comparing itself against its previous states, never able to transcend the difference-generating operations that distinguish it not only from the environment but from itself from one moment to the next. To be an embodied conscious system means, at the most fundamental level, that cognitive displacement or dissonance will never cease.

I now return to the questions introduced at the beginning of this section: how does Latour's notion of hybridity differ from systems theory on the notion of subjectivity, and why does his "Middle Kingdom" finally fail to provide a useful framework within which to explain Thoreau's alternately connected/disconnected stance vis-à-vis nature? My initial answer to these questions was that while Latour's theory does provide a means to work through the blind spots of the modern constitution in its deployment of the tenacious nature/society distinction, it does not explain Thoreau's unease with those blind spots—his felt sense that something is amiss as he seeks purity *and* the middle ground, for there is a form of disconnect that follows him wherever he goes. What the autopoietic view of subjectivity and mind provide us is a framework within which that sense of detachment becomes the crux of all the ways a subject knows her environment, something that Latour's theory, in its delineation of subjective agency as infinitely mutable, hybridized, and nonautonomous, does not. In the autopoietic view, openness is predicated on closure, so that our capacity to respond or connect with our environment persists only as long as the cognitive closure of the brain can be maintained; without closure—and the resultant sense of disconnection—conscious systems could not exist as such, for they would be inundated and overwhelmed by environmental stimuli and, to state the obvious, rendered incapable of self-reflection. On the other hand, such that it can be said to explore the subject's response to environmental complexity, Latour's theory of hybridity conceives of the subject as a locus in a field of possibilities, weaving together lines of force and overcoming resistances as it mobilizes hybrids or intermediaries, with the "indisputable facts" of objective nature providing a check against the loosing of any "wild and uncontrollable" networks that a liberated subjectivity (and/or its society) might be tempted to produce (*We,* 14). As exhilarating as this model of subjectivity might be, it does not seem to apply to Thoreau. For despite his attempts to mitigate against the dualistic logic of the modern project (as demonstrated in Walls's and Cameron's work on his anti-Cartesianism) within which he is inevitably implicated (as I showed in the earlier sections of the chapter), Thoreau ultimately finds his selfhood bound up in *a desire to meld with his environment combined with a fear that he can never do so.* This disturbing combination of connection and groundlessness can be more usefully described, as I have suggested, as a feature, a condition, and a requirement of the autopoietic consciousness and the embodied nature of its knowledge.

What that means, practically speaking, is that no matter where he goes Thoreau does not leave behind his cognitive dissonance, for the plunge into new and startling environments cannot supply him, as he intermittently hopes, with a solution for what is at last a rift in his own subjectivity, not in the world. As Emerson says, "the ruin or the blank that we see when we look at nature, is in our own eye" (CW 1:43). The contact Thoreau seeks (and even at times fears), as well his sensation that his own body may be an alien substance, are both manifestations of this rift, a rift that means he is simultaneously bound ineluctably to a history of interactions with his environments even as he is left cognitively adrift in a self-generated thought-space of his species', his society's, and his own creation. He is an embodied being like all of us, determining as he wends his way in the world what counts as significant and how it hangs together; where he is exemplary is that he has given poignant voice to this irresolvable and often painful partitioning that makes awareness of self and world possible.

This autopoietic version of cognition can be summed up with the following chart, which presents the simultaneous, paradoxical *openness* and *closure* to the environment of the embodied cognitive system:

EMBODIED COGNITION

openness	*closure*
structural coupling	organization
sense of connection	sense of disconnection
relational knowing	Cartesian cogito
nature	society
body	mind
instinct	laws
wild	tame
freedom	constriction
good	bad

The essay "Walking," which by turns celebrates Thoreau's own sense of connection and by turns laments that others have none, amply illustrates these dual aspects of embodiment. The following discussion shows that the cognitive dissonance associated with autopoietic cognition manifests itself in Thoreau's separation of nature and society (variously figured as the wild versus town or the woods versus field). This separation—which Thoreau both wants to erode yet requires to be in place in order to make his claims in the first place—is finally asked to do too much work, so that in the end Thoreau comes to view his environments with the one distinction that seems to settle matters most decisively: the good/bad terms of the moral code. In other words, while Thoreau's attempt to navigate the paradoxical and often unsettling contours of what I am calling embodiment is a step in the right direction, the "border life" he constructs will finally look more like a repudiation of the social world on moral grounds than a true coming-to-terms with his ungroundedness. And that is why his protoenvironmentalism bears less fruit than meets the eye.

"Walking" without Grounds

"Walking" begins with this famous statement of intent: "I wish to speak a word for Nature, for absolute freedom and wildness, as contrasted with a freedom and culture merely civil,—to regard man as an inhabitant, or a part and parcel of Nature, rather than a member of society. I wish to make an extreme statement, if I may make an emphatic one, for there are enough champions of civilization: the minister and school committee and every one of you will take care of that" (NH 93). The passage is a powerful confirmation of the modern gulf between nature and society, and Thoreau lays out unequivocally on which side (of what for him will finally constitute a moral divide) he wishes to stand. He wants to think of man as a part of nature and not as a member of society; he claims (disingenuously, of course, as if he were taking up a proposition in a debating society) that because there are many who can speak for the social he will do the reverse. The immediate problem is that Thoreau cannot maintain the decisive distinction even in this initial gesture, because the "absolute freedom and wildness" he wants to present to man must always be embodied in man, and in fact is unrealizable without the cognizing process that domesticates or tames the very wildness he wishes to affirm. (He demands later in his typically paradoxical manner, "Give me for my friends and neighbors wild men, not tame ones," as if radical wildness could ever stomach sociality [NH 122].)

But the inevitability of that kind of embodiment is not a genuine obstacle to Thoreau's championing of nature because beneath his absolutism is the more modest goal of "Walking": to call for a better balance between wildness and culture, to present examples of and be spokesman for successful mediations. Thoreau does not want to throw society back into a state of savagery, for the sort of appreciation of nature he longs for actually depends on a relatively high degree of culture. (For example, he notes disapprovingly that "In their reaction to Nature men appear to me for the most part, notwithstanding their arts, lower than animals"—which is another paradoxical comparison, by the way, considering that nothing could be more wild, more natural, than a complete obliviousness to the aesthetics of nature [NH 130].) Instead, he seeks to improve society by first teasing out the elements of wildness in us that society has submerged, then proposing the superior mediations of wild and tame he wishes to inculcate.

From the second-order perspective of hybrid/nonhybrid any such mediations are, of course, where Thoreau starts out and where he remains, so that to the same extent he thinks he has propounded successful renegotiations of the natural/social divide he has also preserved that divide by imagining it requires negation in the first place. But we could also conclude that Thoreau's hybrid vision of humanity is an attempt to affirm wildness (understood as the undifferentiated and incognizable environment) as a kind of solution to the vagaries of embodiment. Let me explain what I mean this way: in the Latourian sense, Thoreau wants to generate hybrid intermediaries to bind or attenuate the wildness of a pure, unknown nature, which in its radical alterity is difficult to handle unless it is blended with more familiar, workable, and indeed, cultured materials; but in another sense, as intermediaries these hybrids are enlisted to help Thoreau invoke the *forgotten* or *latent* experience of joyful wildness that the "culture merely civil" has torn away or blocked. So when Thoreau speaks "a word for Nature" by writing about people, things, or activities that appear to blur the line between nature and society, he is in effect trying to reassert long-buried histories of structural coupling. In other words, he believes the "wildness" of "pure nature" is *inherent* in his "friends and neighbors" and everybody else, even if they now prefer to repress it. We are, he seems to say, always already "wild men" whether we acknowledge it or not, because the histories of our interactions with various environments are conserved in the structure of our bodies and minds (or more properly, as Varela, Thompson, and Rosch put it, in the combined "embodied mind").

Now, from my perspective it is important to remember that while our mind/body is indeed the product of such histories, this does not mean that there really could be a return to a point when we were somehow at "one with nature." There never has been nor will be such a point. Recognition of embodiment would not be, as with hybridization, a way to think the beyond (or the before) of the moderns' ontological distinction between something called nature and something called society; embodiment simply pertains to the epistemological consequences of social and conscious systems that use distinctions to preserve their organization against environmental complexity while yet remaining structurally open to stimuli. The embodied knowledge produced in these operations depends on the ongoing gradient of complexity between system and environment, for knowledge is in the last analysis rooted in the various ways that the system comes to know itself by means of drawing distinctions between itself and an environment. To be sure, Thoreau does not say anything like this. In his terms, rather, to be "wild men" simply means remembering that the connection between the natural and social worlds has never been broken, despite what society would have us believe, and that in reinvigorating the connection we will achieve a greater sense of harmony. But, again, under the paradigm I am advocating, connection and disconnection are two sides of the same coin. In my terms, a wild man could only be one who realizes that his autonomy—his wildness—precisely depends on his *closure* from a natural other, just as a tame man would be one who has forgotten that his civility is procured by remaining *open* to that same natural other. So although Thoreau's vision of wildness is prescient in that he focuses on the connection between human and environment, the crucial insight—that this connection comes about simultaneously with *disconnection*—is left out of Thoreau's romantic version of embodiment. And that is why his work remains conflicted: he maintains his belief that the feeling of disconnection can be replaced wholesale by a feeling of connection even as he repeatedly comes up against the fact that this former feeling always stays agonizingly in play. While Thoreau hopes his mediations can put in proper alignment the wild and tame features of the landscapes (both social and natural) he inhabits, observers should be aware that he will never overcome their ongoing separation. In short, where Thoreau imagines he is producing *metaphors of connection,* second-order observers see instead *metaphors of embodiment,* which always express both connection *and* disconnection.

From this angle, the paradoxical nature of embodiment is exemplified most dramatically in "Walking" by the figure of the walk itself, which Thoreau posits as a means of rejoining the domains of nature and society—even as he lets slip at times that nature stands as a kind of insuperable complexity that remains stubbornly out of reach. Walking fosters the intermingling of these opposing domains, so that a walker may step back and forth across the boundary between the wild side (the repressed, overlooked, or forgotten history of bodily interactions with the environment) and the tame side (the commonplace social and personal experiences that organize conscious experience). The antagonistic, uneasy relationship between the two modes is clear: "In my afternoon walk I would fain forget all my morning occupations and my obligations to society. But it sometimes happens that I cannot easily shake off the village. The thought of some work will run in my head and I am not where my body is,—I am out of my senses. In my walks I would fain return to my senses" (NH 99). The uncomfortable split he reports here and elsewhere is, I maintain, a result of the ungrounded nature of embodied knowledge, which means that the rift between system and environment—whether configured as a distinction between self and world, mind and body, society and nature—is never sutured, but can only be distributed, in the vain hope of resolution, across to other distinctions. What Thoreau seeks through walking, nevertheless, is precisely to defer the unease by making new sorts of distinctions, for he fears that he, like his society, is always in danger of becoming too self-absorbed, content to repeat to itself over and over the same story as to how identity hangs together: "We are now but faint-hearted crusaders, even the walkers, nowadays, who undertake no persevering, never-ending enterprises" (NH 94).

It is appropriate that one of the words Thoreau uses as a synonym for walking is "saunter," and that among its possible roots, as he points out, is the French term *sans terre,* meaning "without land or a home, which, therefore, in the good sense, will mean, having no particular home, but equally at home everywhere" (NH 93). As an embodied activity, walking reminds us that we are always without home (or ground)—even in those places where we feel most secure—if we separate ourselves from our bodily senses. But if we attend to those senses, then the notion of home could as sensibly apply to whatever place we find ourselves in: "He who sits still in a house all the time may be the greatest vagrant of all; but the saunterer, in the good sense, is no more vagrant than the meandering river, which is all the while sedulously seeking the shortest course to the sea" (NH 93–94). The idea that staying home can be vagrancy becomes an expression of Thoreau's apprehension that society and its members were increasingly wandering away from a potential source of novelty—nature—by becoming dangerously introverted, urbanized, and domestic. Walking will correct this vagrancy, literally and figuratively redirecting our attention toward new stimuli and shocking us out of our house-bound self-absorption. (Jane Bennett, incidentally, uses another of Thoreau's terms, *sojourner*, to make a similar claim: "Sojourners are on the road, moving through places, and those particular somewheres are essential to what they become. Sojourners are in search of a home but also value the sense of estrangement that propels them" [*Thoreau's Nature*, xxi].)

For Thoreau, then, the walk provides the distance to see that society spends far too much time focused on matters "in the house" and not enough on matters "out of doors" (NH 98). Walking addresses both society's ills and its cure: it symbolizes for Thoreau the critical perspective that must be acquired to observe his ailing, introverted society; and it provides an actual means by which that perspective might be cultivated. In a manner of speaking, society does not walk anymore—but it had best get back on its feet if it is to survive. The figure of walking becomes a way to express the wildness that the social system necessarily retains (despite its repression), and from the vantage of Thoreau himself as a conscious agent, the pedestrian nature of walking does what the more spectacular, epiphanic experience on Ktaadn could not—"grounds" wildness or unmediated environmental complexity, for walking knowledge is both *sans terre* and the grounded activity par excellence.

For second-order observers, Thoreau's favored mode of transport also expresses the dual nature of embodied knowledge: it is knowledge (whether cultural, psychological, somatic, genetic) that is both *grounded* in tangible histories of interaction between the body and the environment and *ungrounded* in that it corresponds to no pregiven route but instead remains prospective, a sauntering through a world that can at any time surprise us, and in which we will then find ourselves productively lost. Embodied knowledge—walking knowledge—is therefore free, wild, constructed, and flexible even as it is most assuredly tied to real histories and actual experiences or collisions between the body-brain and the world. It may be hardwired in the flesh or softwired in the fears, desires, or preferences that come to shape experience, but either way walking knowledge is never fixed beforehand—it only emerges as a function of the walk itself.

I now wish to refine this discussion of Thoreau's delineation of the coprocess of grounded/ungrounded walking, beginning with a consideration of the following passage:

I can easily walk ten, fifteen, twenty, any number of miles. . . . From many a hill I can see civilization and the abodes of man afar. The farmers and their works are scarcely more obvious than woodchucks and their burrows. Man and his affairs, church and state and school, trade and commerce, and manufactures and agriculture, even politics, the most alarming of them all,—I am pleased to see how little space they occupy in the landscape. Politics is but a narrow field, and that still narrower highway yonder leads to it. I sometimes direct the traveler thither. If you would go to the political world, follow the great road,—follow that market-man, keep his dust in your eyes, and it will lead you straight to it; for it, too, has its place merely, and does not occupy all space. I pass from it as from a bean-field into the forest, and it is forgotten. In one half-hour I can walk off to some portion of the earth's surface where a man does not stand from one year's end to another, and there, consequently, politics are not, for they are but as the cigar-smoke of a man. (NH 100–101)

Thoreau is plainly commenting on the relatively small space occupied by the physical plant of society. But at another level he is reflecting on the ephemerality and contingency of human affairs in contrast to the solidity of the natural world. The "political world," for example, has "its place" but "does not occupy all space" and appears narrow, artificial, and transitory compared to nature, just as a bean field is a monoculture compared to the wild diversity of the forest. The upshot is that the two domains of nature and society are distinct not only in terms of complexity but in the fact that the social world is evanescent—and easily shown to be so when we actually put ourselves physically into the many other places where society is not.

Yet even as Thoreau makes these implicitly unflattering comparisons, in which the social is made to look trivial alongside the natural, we discern that the figure of the walk will emerge for him as the connecting device, for although a walk takes you away from "the cigar-smoke" of politics, the "highway yonder leads to it" and, significantly, Thoreau "sometimes direct[s] the traveler thither." But, given that nature seems to be the place to be, why would he do that? Why not direct all traffic *away* from the back rooms and the market and into free and unencumbered nature? One possibility is that Thoreau is simply surrendering to the obvious, for all roads seem to lead back to town anyway, or rather from town to town, these narrow fields of "man and his affairs," which most people are obliged to till. "The village is the place to which the roads tend, a sort of expansion of the highway, as a lake of a river" (NH 101). Roads allow a kind of degenerated form of walk, a degeneracy the villagers themselves have come to embody, for "They are wayworn by the travel that goes by and over them, without traveling themselves." In general, says Thoreau, "Some do not walk at all; others walk in the highways; a few walk across lots. Roads are made for horses and men of business." Thoreau himself is "a good horse to travel, but not by choice a roadster" (NH 102). In effect, the road is difficult, if not impossible to avoid, just as in even the wildest woods it is difficult for Thoreau to shrug off the memory of the town—in other words, to give himself over completely to wildness.

Even so, there are some good roads, not surprisingly the ones most degenerated: "there are a few old roads that may be trodden with profit, as if they led somewhere now that they are nearly discontinued" (NH 102). The Old Marlborough Road is one such, a road southeast of Concord that by Thoreau's time had fallen into disuse and was therefore all the more useful to the walker: "What is it, what is it, / But a direction out there, / And the bare possibility / Of going somewhere?" (NH 103). Of the stone signposts along this road, which had eroded or pointed now only to long-defunct destinations, Thoreau writes, "I know one or two / Lines that would do, / Literature that might stand / All over the land, / Which a man could remember / Till next December, / And read again in the spring, / After the thawing" (NH 104). He seems here to hearken back to the sand images of the deep cut, to a kind of literature inscribed by nature itself. Or perhaps he means only to announce the final lines of the poem as a motto for the now blank stones: "If with fancy unfurled / You leave your abode, / You may go round the world / By the Old Marlborough Road" (NH 104). Strange to think that an abandoned road reclaimed by nature is the route to take to see the world. Because roads lead from town to town, from nexus of civilization to nexus of civilization, the walker must cut across these roads if he is to see anything worthwhile. In that case, leaving the road or at least taking the most overgrown path must be the true walker's first choice. From the vantage point of the wild, there appear to be no limits set to where we walk "through this actual world, which is perfectly symbolical of the path we love to travel in the interior and ideal world" (NH 105). To Thoreau the actual world is, like its ideal counterpart, inexhaustible, opening vistas so varied that "A single farmhouse which [he] had not seen before is sometimes as good as the dominions of the King of Dahomey" (NH 99).

Society, however, always attempts to diminish our perceptions in both worlds:

> At present, in this vicinity, the best part of the land is not private property; the landscape is not owned, and the walker enjoys comparative freedom. But possibly the day will come when it will be partitioned off into so-called pleasure-grounds, in which a few will take a narrow and exclusive pleasure only,—when fences shall be multiplied, and man-traps and other engines invented to confine men to the *public* road, and walking over the surface of God's earth shall be construed to mean trespassing on some gentleman's grounds. To enjoy a thing exclusively is commonly to exclude yourself from the true enjoyment of it. Let us improve our opportunities, then, before the evil days come. (NH 104)

What the social system seeks is to extend its "evil"—in other words, its particular principles of order in the form of property rights, political boundaries, etc.—into all parts of the natural world, thereby reducing natural complexity and our otherwise multiple opportunities for "true enjoyment." Not until we get off the road does that invasiveness become clearly observable, and the many overlooked possibilities of the aimless saunter begin to open before us.

At this point it might be tempting to surmise that Thoreau's angle of vision in this essay is once again simply a purifying gaze, and that in walking he wishes to align himself, as he claimed in his opening salvo, with nature and against a voracious society. But while that may be where he eventually winds up, his route to the position of moral purity is far more circuitous. As I have suggested, at this point the walk is better thought of as a connector of domains: notice that in the above passages Thoreau constantly asserts that walkers should not simply leave society behind for the natural world but must also bring wildness back to society by returning with the news of the journey after going "round the world." Thoreau says his own walks are shaped like a "parabola, or rather like one of those cometary orbits which have been thought to be non-returning curves, in this case westward, in which my house occupies the place of the sun" (NH 105). Interestingly, the essay itself has a parabolic shape in that after reaching a kind of central point of light—that of his most widely admired remark, "In wildness is the preservation of the world" (NH 112)—it ranges expansively before returning to where it began with the figure of "sauntering" toward the "Holy Land" (taken to mean nature itself) (NH 135). We recall from *Walden* and "Ktaadn" that broadly speaking Thoreau thought travel was unnecessary, for when it came to finding the "hard bottom" of reality he believed "the richest vein was somewhere hereabouts," that is to say, wherever one was prepared to "front the facts" (T 401). Walking thus seems to be a method of, to borrow the title of a poem by Wendell Berry, "traveling at home." As *returning* curves, then, Thoreau's journeys demonstrate that all trips into nature must of necessity come back to civilization. "Half the walk," writes Thoreau, "is but retracing our steps" (NH 94).

But what precisely does Thoreau hope to bring back home? What exactly is this wildness he perceives in the woods and meadows? The second half of the essay elaborates. Although elsewhere Thoreau says, "What we call wildness is a civilization other than our own" (quoted in Nash, *Rights,* 37), wildness is first and foremost for him a vital essence running directly counter to his insipid civilization. But civilization always has the potential to dilute this rich milk: "It was because the children of the Empire were not suckled by the wolf [like Romulus and Remus] that they were conquered and displaced by the children of the northern forests who were" (NH 113). Thoreau cites approvingly the "Hottentots," and "our northern Indians," whose eating habits prompt him to demand "a wildness whose glance no civilization can endure,—as if we lived on the marrow of koodoos devoured raw." Wildness is to be imbibed, like "an infusion of hemlock spruce or arbor vitae in our tea." Such natural foods are "probably better than stall-fed beef and slaughter-house pork to make a man of." Again following the digestive metaphor, Thoreau remarks: "When I would recreate myself, I would seek the darkest wood, the thickest and most interminable and, to the citizen, most dismal, swamp. I enter a swamp as a sacred place, a sanctum sanctorum. There is the strength, the marrow, of Nature. The wildwood covers the virgin mould, and the same soil is good for men and for trees. A man's health requires as many acres of meadow to his prospect as his farm does loads of muck. There are the strong meats on which he feeds" (NH 116–17). Wildness, so it would seem, is to be savored, eaten, taken in. These gastronomic images provide a serviceable insight into how Thoreau—once again with rhetoric that defies easy paraphrase—thinks of wildness: it is whatever cannot be digested by humankind, but in digesting it humankind is made better. "Life consists with wildness," writes Thoreau. "The most alive is the wildest. Not yet subdued by man, its presence refreshes him" (NH 114). In an image that reflects the paradoxical drive to enrich oneself by reducing wildness, Thoreau seems to suggest man must destroy nature in order to keep ahead of his own rapaciousness: "One who pressed forward incessantly and never rested from his labors, who grew fast and made infinite demands on life, would always find himself in a new country or wilderness, and surrounded by the raw material of life. He would be climbing over the prostrate stems of primitive forest-trees." The point here is that the attempt to be wild entails the diminution of wildness, a process that inevitably makes the world less wild. Although such destruction would not seem to be Thoreau's overt intent, it is an unavoidable part of his project, for to go into Walden Woods to live, or the Maine woods to climb, means, as we have seen, bringing your world along with you and pushing aside whatever existed before. "I think that the farmer displaces the Indian even because he redeems the meadow, and so makes himself stronger and in some respects more natural" (NH 118).

If these metaphors of the assimilation of wildness seem familiar it is because they, like walking, evoke an image of what I have been calling the process of embodiment. Indeed, Thoreau's ingestive tropology suggests how readers might want to visualize the manner in which a conscious system using perceptually guided action comes to think of its environment: as a source of stimuli for anchoring the system's operations. This idea is elegantly expressed by Bennett as follows:

> Wildness is the unexplored potential—of the outdoors or the self—always left over from even the most reflective or relentless exploration. It is the remainder or excess that always escapes Thoreau's taxonomies of flora and fauna or inventories of his

character or conscience; it is the difference of the woods that remains no matter how many times he walks them, the distance never bridged between two friends, no matter how familiar and intimate. The wildness of anything consists in its ability, on the one hand, to inspire fresh experience, startling metaphors, and unheralded associations, and, on the other hand, to challenge familiar experience, beautiful metaphors, and associational cascades. ("Primate," 254–55)

What Bennett describes as the "unexplored potential" that is wildness, Luhmann would conceive as the ever-retreating environment of a system. Walking into and ingesting wildness would then symbolize the manner in which this unexplored potential can be useful to a system: in prompting the production of new (or in the recollection of older) distinctions that add to the number of ways the system can know itself. Wild nature is a place where we are provoked to make such new distinctions. (But recall that this does not mean in distinguishing new items we are actually receiving new information about our environment. When a scientist or a poet observes something in her environment that no one has ever distinguished before, she only adds to the number of ways that humans can draw distinctions—and thus to the number of ways humans can describe themselves.)

Further illustrating his interest in assimilating the wildness through which he walks are a few more passages in which it is embodied knowledge—not a transcendent knowledge of nature—that Thoreau prizes, even if he does not fully realize it. For example, he notes that "In literature it is only the wild that attracts us. Dullness is but another name for tameness" (NH 119). The need for a "literature which gives expression to Nature" then seems to follow directly (NH 120): "He would be a poet who could impress the winds and streams into his service, to speak for him; who nailed words to their primitive senses, as farmers drive down stakes in the spring, which the frost has heaved; who derived his words as often as he used them,— transplanted them to his page with earth adhering to their roots; whose words were so true and fresh and natural that they would appear to expand like the buds at the approach of spring . . . in sympathy with surrounding Nature." The words "impress," "nailed," and "transplanted" are in one sense just a measure of Thoreau's enthusiasm for this wild literature. Yet such words are also a measure of the cultural force required to bend nature into literary service. Thoreau writes that "approached from this side, the best poetry is tame," but it is precisely a kind of taming Thoreau is proposing here, and as with the digestive imagery, the taming of wildness would seem to lead to a diminution of the very purity he wants to preserve. "You will perceive," Thoreau maintains, "that I demand something which no Augustan nor Elizabethan age, which no *culture,* in short, can give. Mythology comes nearer to it than anything." His demand may be satisfied only "when, in the course of ages, American liberty has become a fiction of the past,—as it is to some extent a fiction of the present,—[so that] the poets of the world will be inspired by American mythology" (NH 121). But once again, it seems that the wildness embodied in such a mythic literature is reliant upon the very cultural assimilation he rejects, for it is the "decay of other literature [that] makes the soil in which it thrives." In other words, the mythological work, in which a "pristine vigor is unabated," can only appear wild in contrast to a contemporary literature that will itself become the mythology of the future, indicating that the potential for wildness must already exist, however sublimated, within such literature even now.

So too is the desire for embodied knowledge encoded in Thoreau's discussion of animals:

> I love even to see the domestic animals reassert their native rights,—any evidence that they have not wholly lost their original wild habits and vigor; as when my neighbor's cow breaks out of her pasture early in the spring and boldly swims the river, a cold, gray tide, twenty-five or thirty rods wide, swollen by the melted snow. It is the buffalo crossing the Mississippi. This exploit confers some dignity on the herd in my eyes,— already dignified. The seeds of instinct are preserved under the thick hides of cattle and horses, like seeds in the bowels of the earth, an indefinite period. (NH 122)

This passage reiterates rather unambiguously his preference for the wild, yet what are we to make of the passage that follows it? "I rejoice that horses and steers have to be broken before they can be made the slaves of men, and that men themselves have some wild oats still left to sow before they become submissive members of society" (NH 123). The point seems to be not that domestication is strictly speaking unnatural, but simply that the social order ought to retain a bit of wildness for its own good. In this sense, Thoreau is again qualifying his espousal of nature conceived as a fully wild and complex zone of purity by imagining it as a desirable but finally junior partner in a history of biosocial interactions. A hint of wildness may be all that Thoreau requires in the end.

That view is given support when Thoreau reflects on his own connection to nature, which he wishes he could grasp ever more firmly. But the following intriguing passage reveals just how tenuous is that grasp:

> For my part, I feel that with regard to Nature I live a sort of border life on the confines of a world into which I make occasional and transient forays only, and my patriotism and allegiance to the state into whose territories I seem to retreat are those of a moss-trooper. Unto a life which I call natural I would gladly follow even a will-o'-the-wisp through bogs and sloughs unimaginable, but no moon nor firefly has shown me the causeway to it. Nature is a personality so vast and universal that we have never seen

one of her features. The walker in the familiar fields which stretch around my native town sometimes finds himself in another land than is described in their owners' deeds, as it were in some faraway field in the confines of the actual Concord, where her jurisdiction ceases, and the idea which the word Concord suggests ceases to be suggested. These farms which I have myself surveyed, these bounds which I have set up, appear dimly still as through a mist; but they have no chemistry to fix them; they fade from the surface of the glass, and the picture which the painter painted stands out dimly from beneath. The world with which we are commonly acquainted leaves no trace, and it will have no anniversary. (NH 130)

To paraphrase Emerson, it is the evanescence and lubricity of nature that moves Thoreau here, albeit with an emotion that seems to have little of Emerson's sadness or regret. The subtlety of nature, its "indirect stroke," does not for Thoreau signify a lack of contact but is instead a part of nature's dreamlike charm. Yet it is by no means clear from his delineation of nature and the surveyed human world imposed upon it which of the two is the more transient and ephemeral: while the boundaries of the farms quickly fade when we enter the actual territory, "Nature," "so vast and universal," has not itself emerged as a graspable domain. One wonders how we are supposed to "front the facts," and from where—nature or town—are we to take our bearings?

The impressionistic technique continues as Thoreau paints a picture of an imaginary family that *may* reside in the "stately pine wood" on Spaulding's Farm. He claims that

Nothing can equal the serenity of their lives. Their coat-of-arms is simply a lichen. I saw it painted on the pines and oaks. Their attics were in the tops of the trees. They are of no politics. There was no noise of labor. I did not perceive that they were weaving or spinning. Yet I did detect, when the wind lulled and hearing was done away, the finest imaginable sweet musical hum,—as of a distant hive in May,—which perchance was the sound of their thinking. They had no idle thoughts, and no one without could see their work, for their industry was not as in knots and excrescences embayed.

But I find it difficult to remember them. They fade irrevocably out of my mind even now while I speak, and endeavor to recall them and recollect myself. It is only after a long and serious effort to recollect my best thoughts that I become again aware of their cohabitancy. If it were not for such families as this, I think I should move out of Concord. (NH 131–32)

Here as in the previous passage Thoreau describes a vision of nature that is not radically at odds with the town but instead occupies along with it a kind of middle ground. Although he says of his imaginary family that "they are of no politics" and that they produce "no noise of labor," he also says the pine wood is a "noble hall" with its own "pleasure ground . . . in Spaulding's cranberry meadow," "gables," and even a coat-of-arms and attics—all furnishings and entailments most usually associated with baronial privilege (NH 132). Moreover, as Thoreau tells us, their "cohabitancy" with the other denizens of Concord, insubstantial as it may be, is what makes the town bearable. The point here is that far from being overwhelmingly natural, the ghostly family is decidedly linked with the social world. They are the wild friends and neighbors that make social life bearable.

I think what these last two passages confirm is that for Thoreau, fashioning the "border life" between wilderness and civilization was a compelling goal in almost everything he wrote, and that even his extreme statements of the priority of nature over culture were usually just the prelude to making the case for the border life. In my reading of the above passages, most significant is the blending of images of nature and images of town, the constant overlap and imbrication of the two orders Thoreau had identified at the beginning of "Walking" as radically disunited. Perhaps unsurprising, from Thoreau's initial withering look down on the narrow fields of the town from the wide vantage point of nature, he has chosen instead to bring nature into the town, and the town into nature, to juxtapose as closely as possible those two sorts of complexity. "I would not have every man nor every part of man cultivated, any more than I would have every acre of earth cultivated: part will be tillage, but the greater part will be meadow and forest" (NH 126). Keeping the wild (the complex environment) and the tame (the social system) side by side means that we could walk back and forth between the forest and the bean field. We could step from our house into the out-of-doors by bringing our "sills up to the very edge of the swamp" (NH 116). That Thoreau's attempt to speak a word for nature finally ends with him also speaking a word, however backhandedly, for a kind of cultured naturalism should not come as a surprise: to sustain the position of purity, as in the summit experience of Ktaadn or in the opening lines of "Walking" itself, is finally too fatiguing—and unattainable besides. Only by binding what he apprehends as valuable in nature to known, culturally familiar structures (a process I have described as the "walking," "digestive" knowledge that comes from histories of interactions between systems and environments) can his project remain viable and, ironically, permit the purity of an ever-retreating nature to be retained as a remote but tantalizing possibility. "Vast and universal" nature, whose "features" we have never seen, is unobservable and ungraspable without the attribution of meaning that comes by walking from the woods *back* to the town—from a fundamentally *meaningless* environment to the system in which meaning is made. Just as "Ktaadn" proved that hybrids underlay all his projects of purification, in "Walking" Thoreau's construction of an embodied version of knowledge is crucial for modulating the untenable position of purity laid out in the opening pages into the "border life" championed in the last. And I believe the direction—in my discussion of "Walking" and in this entire chapter—replicates that returning curve. For the desire to become "one with nature," to live the hybrid or border life, emerges out of a circular process, which starts when we suspect we have come loose from something more real than ourselves, and proceeds by working diligently to restore it—until the moment when once again we feel it slipping away. But because this process never ends, only by recognizing that circularity is where we begin *and* end (and this is the giant step that Thoreau along with his modern disciples never consciously take) will we ever gain the peace of knowing we had nothing to lose in the first place—to be alive means we will always feel lost and found at the same time, at once connected to and disconnected from the world we inhabit. As Emerson puts it, "to find the journey's end in every step of the road, to live the greatest number of good hours, is wisdom" (CW 3:35).

The American System of Nature

The Moral Code and the Blockage of Observation

In what must be one of the most memorable images in "Walking," Thoreau describes a discovery he makes in a tall white pine: "on the ends of the topmost branches only, a few minute and delicate red cone-like blossoms, the fertile flower of the white pine looking heavenward" (NH 133). Astounded and enchanted by this rare natural phenomenon, Thoreau "carried away straightway to the village the topmost spire, and showed it to stranger jurymen who walked the streets,—for it was a court week,—and to farmers and lumber dealers and hunters, and not one had ever seen the like before, but they wondered as at a star dropped down" (NH 133). What I think is particularly significant here—besides the prototypical Thoreauvian parabola that carries the news of wildness back into the town—is the selection of townsfolk Thoreau invokes: people involved in various activities peculiar to town, woods, and field, all different in outlook yet all now equally fascinated by the exquisite flower. Their reaction confirms something of Thoreau's basic optimism that the kind of wild culture he longs for is within reach because there remains in everyone, regardless of orientation, the hint of the undomesticated "seeds of instinct" he likes to see in farm animals, and thus the possibility that humans may yet be described as "nature looking into nature." But what is once again confirmed, too, is that the "narrow fields" of the town are not without their own element of wildness and that nature and culture are not so easily disentangled as Thoreau in his more passionate moments had imagined. In short, his invocation of nature and society was never the crucial way of dividing up the world he thought it was. This is not because this dualism is wrong per se, but simply that it only sees what it sees—and Thoreau's awkward straining to remain *within* while yet exceeding this code showed us some of its limitations. If embodiment means that our knowledge of the world is always partial yet bound to actual histories, open to change yet constrained by a reality that remains unknown, then we can and will produce oppositions that divide our world so as to help us observe and negotiate it; but perhaps with all its baggage, the nature/society dualism is a distinction that no longer serves us well.

Thus, while "Walking" marks a watershed moment when Thoreau's environmental flexibility shows through his penchant for absolutes, where he is less successful is with a notion that he tries to maintain even in the face of the inescapability of the embodied "border life": the fundamental moral difference between nature and culture. That moral coding is epitomized in "Walking" by his blanket statement that "all good things are wild and free," which means by implication that all things not wild and free are strictly speaking "bad" (NH 122). The moral binarism is a particularly disabling one, because it tends to sort, as deconstructionists have tirelessly shown, a great many other codes along its axis: beauty/ugliness, black/white, sane/insane, male/female, and so on. Like the economic code, the moral code can act like a powerful parasite that effectively blocks the nonmoralistic functions of the host systemic codes. Unlike the economic code, it has no function system of its own; it pervades the zone of culture, always available to anyone who wants to defend or damn another's distinction.

But why does the moral code always lurk at the edge of Thoreau's work? I think the obvious cause and the correct one is announced in the opening lines of the essay: "I wish to speak a word for nature, for absolute freedom and wildness, as contrasted with a freedom and culture merely civil" (NH 93). A central reason why Thoreau always wants to champion the border life is finally because he himself wants to stay at the borders of an increasingly complex and differentiated social system; his distaste for politics, the market, and the legal system—in short, his radical individualism and nostalgia for a more organic, sedimented order—is well documented. In his fine study of Thoreau's moral philosophy, Alfred Tauber notes that for Thoreau "morality has been extended into every part of experience" and thus "there is no neat separation between knowing the world (epistemologically) and valuing that knowledge (a moral judgment)" (6). "In the end," argues Tauber, "the two dimensions collapse into one, and . . . the world Thoreau sees and knows is the world he creates out of his moral attitude about that world and the ego which appreciates it." That ego, according to Tauber, belongs finally to a romantic hero, who is prepared to take on the universe in the name of his own imagination, creativity, and "the primacy of his independent personhood" (7). Always in danger of "crippling solipsism," Thoreau hovers at the edge of "normal life," one foot in town, one foot in the woods, casting his purifying gaze this way and that (7). In the terms I have been using, nature for Thoreau has to be coded as sublimely good because it serves in his politics as an open reproach to the ills of the society. It is the garden to society's devouring machine. Nature is right, society is wrong. The good/bad of moral judgment is Thoreau's code of choice. (And just as with the early Emerson, in the last analysis, Thoreau aligns and so buttresses his moral absolutism with the religious code of immanence/transcendence; but that is an argument I do not wish to trace here.) Yet in looking for the solutions to the problems of a functionally differentiated, complex modern society with a lamp of morality, Thoreau cannot finally bring us much closer to understanding the obstacles to environmental communication. This is because, as so often is the case, arguments rooted in the moral code leave out so much of the world as we know it that they are of little analytical use (although they often produce a great deal of Sturm und Drang, which is not always without value).

As I cautioned in my discussion of Emerson, Thoreau's attempt to grasp nature as an avoidance of society should not be reduced to the deep-rooted possessiveness of an imperial self. For despite his rabid individualism, it is safe to say Thoreau found the commodification of all things even more repugnant than did Emerson. Nor, taking an even broader view, should that avoidance be put down as just Thoreau's signature reaction to one of the sacred cows of the overarching ontotheological knowledge project of the West (i.e., the valorization of civilization itself). I would rather continue to suppose that, along with Emerson, Thoreau is embedded in a rapidly changing society pressured on every side with the problems of growing internal complexity and environmental variability. The differentiation of social systems requires that complexity be shared out among subsystems, codes, and programs that can better channel and coordinate internal and external environmental stimuli. Because systems see what they themselves determine to see, only if we foreground the necessity of blindness in *any* act of distinguishing will we be able to theorize the thread that connects the two American environmental traditions engendered by these two figures—which are, namely, from Thoreau the "deep ecological" moral tradition rooted in a notion of nature for nature's sake and from Emerson the "shallow ecological" perspective rooted in various notions of utilitarianism, resource conservation, and stewardship.

These distinct yet related traditions simply cannot be fully delineated by positing a different emphasis on, allegiance to, or abhorrence of, for example, capitalism, instrumental reason, or natural law. Rather, what distinguishes shallow and deep ecology is that though they both embody a theory of how social systems deal with environments, they posit different solutions. The former, in keeping with Emerson, more or less spreads the paradoxes of observation throughout the social system because it acknowledges the possibility of multiple points of reference and, by extension, multiple environments (including internal environments in addition to the natural world itself), which *cannot* be resolved into one; whereas the latter tradition, in keeping with Thoreau, attempts to devolve system and environment interactions onto what is finally a moral coding, and hence seeks to identify a stable and singular pattern of coupling between all of society and nature. But because the only way to deal with *environmental* complexity is to create more *system* complexity—and thus more pathways for intersystemic communications—it must be concluded that Emerson, even with all his experiential ambivalence (or perhaps because of it), provides a potentially more useful foundation for *environmental* perception than does the far more *nature*-attuned Thoreau. System hypercomplexity as the proper response to increasing environmental complexity—and in particular, the role of ecocriticism in theorizing those complexities—is the subject of this final chapter.

Coding Environments

On the ballot for the 1996 Sierra Club national election was a resolution that, if passed, would have required the club to call for a total ban on logging in all public forests, a policy which Sierrans, despite their long-standing opposition to reckless timber management, had up until then considered too inflexible. Supporters of the resolution wrote, "When John Muir was our Club's President, we advocated the 'immediate withdrawal of all public forest' from logging. We saved many forests with this message. . . . But as you read this, chainsaws rip through these same forests—urged on by a radical anti-environmental 'wise use' movement that pressured Congress and the President to suspend public forest protection laws." To rally public support, the supporters advised a return to "Muir's strong, simple message," suggesting that "recycling, alternative fiber, and waste reduction could save enough wood to end logging of public forests and still meet current timber needs without increasing logging on private lands. We can redirect the billions spent subsidizing public lands logging into economic support for workers." Furthermore, "Less than 5% of this nation's original forests remain. With so little left for wildlife and fish, ALL public forests are ecologically important. We must protect and restore recovering forests—in addition to protecting pristine areas—in large wildlands reserve." They concluded by combining these monetary and biodiversity arguments into one economic metaphor: "We're not so poor that we must log our public forests, nor so rich that we can afford to." The petition was signed by, among others, David Brower, a longtime Sierra Club director, founder of Earth Island Institute, and the so-called arch-druid of the environmental movement.

Those opposing the resolution conceded the power of Muir's "strong, simple message," but judged that the policy would actually undermine the environmental group's position in today's complicated political and economic terrain: "What forest activist hasn't dreamed of ending all commercial logging on our National Forests? But would such a position by the Sierra Club undermine the efforts to protect the most ecologically important forests—old-growth, roadless areas, endangered species habitat? Many experienced Club leaders think so." The opponents claimed that the strict language of the new provision would disable the ecological arguments now used to promote preservation, whether "the forest is public or privately-owned." By denying the possibility of land swaps or compromise plans for timber harvesting, the resolution actually "weakens our efforts to repeal destructive 'logging without laws' legislation and to defeat extreme congressional proposals to give away public lands." As an example, they cited a recent incident in New Mexico in which "impoverished Hispanic communities hung in effigy environmentalists responsible for a court injunction protecting Mexican spotted-owl habitat. We simply wanted the Forest Service to obey the law. But if the Club's position is, in fact, opposed to all commercial logging, then we have placed ourselves in a difficult strategic position with respect to local communities." They concluded by reaffirming the club's current approach, which "is flexible and allows groups to pick strategies best suited to local conditions." Those who backed the opposition to the resolution were headed, ironically, by Dave Foreman, then the newly elected Sierra Club director, self-labeled "eco-warrior" and deep ecologist, and the controversial founder of Earth First!, the radical environmentalist organization whose motto is No Compromise in Defense of Mother Earth.[1]

In the end, the "Zero Cut" policy was passed by Sierrans. But to place too much significance on this internal squabble over policy would perhaps be to overstate what was actually a fairly minor tactical difference as to how to achieve the same goal: to preserve and restore as much of America's forests and wild places as possible. Both groups understood that in a time of increasing economic insecurity environmental considerations were bound to be sacrificed on the altar of political expediency. The faction headed by Brower believed, apparently as Foreman once did, that when it came to saving the remnants of these forests, the best strategy was simply to adopt the extreme position and attempt to draw public sentiment in that direction. On the other side, Foreman, having seen the issues from both within the political system (he once worked for the Wilderness Society as a congressional lobbyist) and, more infamously, from without, decided that environmentalists must reserve the right to make concessions in the short term for long-term victories and to increase grassroots support among divergent interests.

Where this dispute becomes exemplary of a point I explore at some length in this chapter is in the way that it evades even as it invokes what I take to be the core issue of the proposed resolution. That core issue, it seems to me, is how shall the public forests—and, indeed, all the animals, plants, and spaces that we commonly gather together under the rubric "nature"—be coded. Brower's group was essentially asking that the Sierra Club agitate for the withdrawal of these forests from two specific function systems, to make them immune to economic and political considerations in the way that, say, the lands in the national park system are already supposed to be. He hoped that Americans would come to regard their national forests as sacrosanct repositories of natural wealth as opposed to merely natural resources. (The difficulty in articulating the former noneconomic notion of value outside the language provided by the economic system is a subtext in the final lines quoted above: "We're not so poor that we must log our public forests, nor so rich that we can afford to.") In Foreman's view, however, the fact that forests are understood even by some potential allies (such as the Hispanic community in New Mexico) as standing lumber should alert environmentalists to the fact that they cannot afford the luxury of remaining, as it were, second-order observers of the political and economic systems, deploying, as is their wont, only the "purer" codes of science, aesthetics, and spirituality to observe, describe, and champion the forests.

This way of framing the debate—that nature must either be made a full player in the economic and political systems or sheltered from them—is a constant source of friction in the environmental community and serves as a litmus test between the Emersonian reformers and the Thoreauvian radicals. Shall we, as some reformers have advised, put a dollar value on the environmental goods ("cost them out," in the language of accounting) so as to better reflect the financial and social price of destroying them? Or are we in that process tacitly surrendering to the function system that will always regard nature as nothing more than commodity? Reformers argue that inevitably the economic code is applied when it comes to national forests anyway; the challenge is to make the true economics of the forest sales known, since the political system tends to obscure the real costs of logging in order to appeal to specific constituencies. But once those external costs are included, logging actually becomes a huge net loss for government coffers, and so, in the age of deficit angst, becomes more difficult to countenance. In this vein, proenvironment, probusiness analysts like William Ashworth, Paul Hawken, and Martin Lewis, along with sympathetic politicians such as Al Gore, have explored various procedures by which to green economics.[2] Yet the call for a green capitalism must overcome a deep-seated antipathy and a well-earned mistrust on the part of many in the environmental community toward the profit motive, no matter how ecofriendly it may be made to appear. Much of the theoretical basis for modern environmentalism is imported from schools of thought—Marxism, anarchism, feminism, Luddism, libertarianism, and to some extent even liberalism itself—with long histories of resistance to the economic overdetermination of the world. The idea that mere market reform could solve the plethora of environmental crises seems implausible, given that the profit motive has contributed so mightily to such crises in the first place. Even steady-state economies, environmental indulgences (i.e., green taxes), and product life-cycle assessments cannot operate without the standard market incentives. When anything can be bought and sold, say skeptics, at some point everything will, and Thoreau's consoling observation—"Thank God they cannot fly and lay waste the sky as well as the earth" (NH 256)—seems a quaint and curious notion in this, the age of carbon sinks and tradable air pollution credits.

The dilemma for the engaged critic can be framed in the form of a question: Since even the *evasion* of the economic and political function systems is itself a form of interaction with them, how best to observe and critique that interaction? Does one champion a single, second-order perspective that can coordinate the economic and the political, not to mention the rest of the function systems, using the principles of an ecologically sound paradigm? Or is *coordination* precisely part of the antiquated language and rationality that social systems theory attempts to replace? Although it might appear I have already stacked the deck in favor of the latter response, it is by no means clear with what we shall replace the dream of coordination. My own inclination, as I noted in the introduction, is to throw up my hands. So this final chapter does not pretend to provide a way out of the dilemma, but merely a chance to rethink it through systems theory and within the context of two crucial topoi of American cultural politics, nature and pastoralism.

I begin by exploring the deep ecological approach to society/environment inter-actions, for deep ecology is probably the best articulated and most far-reaching—and certainly the most controversial—radical environmental critique we yet have. But I suggest that deep ecology is by no means as radical as it wants to be, and as a result cannot provide an adequate formulation of system/environment interactions. For as surely as does the shallow ecological, reformist response to environmental problems, deep ecology reproduces, in its construction of an ecocentric *self* in a milieu of intrinsic equality for all, the reductive coding of the economic function system as it manifests itself within the debilitating liberal programming of American politics. Deep ecology seems to find its roots—just as does mainstream, reformist environmentalism—in the attractive, nature-based logic of self-reliance and volun-tary simplicity advocated by both Thoreau and Emerson. Yet in doing so deep ecology ignores the other, more interesting implications for theory and practice the works of those two "friends of the earth" hold—implications that, as discussed in previous chapters, indicate that the concept of coordination of environmental response is problematic, just as Leo Marx's complex pastoralism marks only a partial and anachronistic response to the question of the relationship of literary texts to technocratic society and nature. By revealing the drawbacks of deep ecology, I can demonstrate how the systems paradigm offers a new way to think about how environmental problems must be addressed in a functionally differentiated society. With regard specifically to literary studies and the pastoral tradition of writing, I show what directions an ecocriticism informed by systems theory might take.

The Shallow and the Deep

Let us begin by considering the place of economic and political coding in environmental philosophy, whose poles are roughly marked out in the Sierra Club debate, or more generally by the so-called shallow and deep versions of ecology. While it is true that the field of ecosophy is far richer and more particularized than can safely be included in those positions, I do think it is possible to make a useful distinction based on what those two poles of American environmentalism represent: the nature of the relationship of humans and nonhumans. The deep ecologist stakes out a position in which humans and nonhumans are taken to be equal in the most important register: the moral one. As Aldo Leopold famously put it, "a land ethic changes the role of *Homo sapiens* from conqueror of the land community to plain member and citizen of it" (240). Shallow ecology, by contrast, cannot be said to engage in that kind of moral leveling, even if it does not exclude the possibility of making moral arguments on behalf of nonhumans. (For example, one shallow ecological position is that humans must condescend to be good stewards of the earth, following the model of Christian piety and noblesse oblige vis-à-vis nature that finds its roots far back in the Old Testament.) It may also seem that deep ecology is a radical denunciation of the economic and political codes from the second-order observational perspective of the moral code, while shallow ecology would be a reformist position that accepts the legitimacy of the economic and political function systems in the specification and resolution of environmental issues. However, once again shallow ecologists too may be highly critical of the capacity of economic and political systems to safeguard environments (e.g., green socialists).

The crucial division, then, may have simply to do with the degree to which deep ecologists are prepared to push the moral equivalence of nonhumans and repudiate sacrosanct concepts of instrumental reason, technocracy, economic growth, and so on—in other words, to a degree to which shallow ecologists presumably cannot go if they are to retain their allegiance to humanism. For example, *wealth* in deep ecological terms is deconstructed in a way one supposes reform ecologists would hesitate to endorse, for shallow environmentalism has staked much on the idea that there is no *inherent* contradiction between economic growth and environmental health that cannot be resolved through sounder management practices. But for deep ecologists, as Bill Devall points out in his aptly titled *Simple in Means, Rich in Ends,* "anti-consumerism as a general principle is consistent with practicing deep ecology. Yet we are told through advertising, by many economists and politicians, to 'consume more in order to keep the economy growing' " (83). Deep ecologists believe, rather, that "voluntary simplicity is often a necessary condition for maximum richness, intensity, and deepness of experience. Simplicity in lifestyle has been practiced by members of different secular and religious communities in different eras in North America, India, and Europe. In North America, tenets of simple living are found in communities of Amish and Hutterites, some Buddhist communities, and in the writings of many prominent authors, including Henry David Thoreau" (84). "Wealth" is no longer to be measured by GNP figures or personal income but in what can only be described as spiritual terms. Theodore Roszak says that deep ecologists have

> taken facts like this [the example of "simple" people] seriously enough to divide the environmental movement into two often heatedly contentious camps. They reject the premise that most of our ecological problems can be solved by a legislative agenda that settles for improved resource budgeting and better global management. Deep Ecology contends that our environmental crisis is more than a random catalogue of mistakes, miscalculations, and false starts that can easily be made good with a bit more expertise in the right places. Nothing less than an altered sensibility is needed, a radically new standard of sanity that undercuts scientific rationality and uproots the fundamental assumptions of industrial life. (232)

The key, then, to this "new standard of sanity" and spiritual reawakening is to abandon the shallow notion that environmentalism is simply about making sure the water is clean and the food free from pesticides before development proceeds apace. The deep/shallow difference can be more precisely characterized as the difference between an anthropocentric and a nonanthropocentric worldview. Anthropocentrism is, in its trivial sense, the idea that humans cannot help but observe the world *as* humans. But more important, anthropocentrism is a kind of *chauvinism*, manifested implicitly when human considerations and activities are placed at the vital center of things while the rest of the world's contents remain little more than props and stage dressing. Anthropocentrism would then be a feature, in varying degrees, of virtually all major religions and ideologies, and, indeed, of most human societies in general, past and present. The pervasiveness of anthropocentrism attests to its power and appeal; it seems to assume, however subtly drawn, an absolute onto-logical distinction between human and nonhuman. Directly addressing this issue, Warwick Fox claims that the crucial deep ecological insight that helps us overcome this profoundly entrenched anthropocentrism is that, in fact, "we can make no firm ontological divide in the field of existence: That there is no bifurcation in reality between the human and the non-human realms" (quoted in Devall and Sessions, 66). (Needless to say, what I argue is that while boundaries as such may not express an ontological difference, they can express a functional, epistemological one—and that to elide this difference is to pursue metaphysical holism at the price of blocking actual systemic change.)

The deep/shallow distinction is not completely without precedent, for one can return to the early part of the century and find it foreshadowed in the difference between John Muir's and Theodore Roosevelt's approach to nature. The latter's tenure as president was marked by a belated recognition that America's natural resources were finite and that its wilderness heritage was on the verge of disappearing altogether. This led Roosevelt to create national parks, national forests, and game reserves at a rate unmatched either before or since. But the guiding vision behind Roosevelt's conservation policy bore the seeds of the managerial/technocratic response to environmental issues that persists as the mainstream approach today. As Roderick Nash describes that philosophy, "utilitarianism and anthropocentrism marked the early movement. Time and again Pinchot, the first Chief of the U.S. Forest Service, pointed out that conservation did not mean protecting or preserving nature. On the contrary, it stood for wise and efficient *use* of natural resources. The idea was to control nature and serve the material interests of humankind but with an eye to long-term needs" (*Rights*, 9). In other words, conservation for Roosevelt and Pinchot was no more than prudent exploitation, to paraphrase Joseph Wood Krutch. Not surprising, this brand of conservation squared perfectly with a conservative economic policy in which deferred gratification today meant greater capital resources tomorrow. It also squared with the commonplace, utilitarian notion of what constituted a successful civil society: as Emerson had written in "Civilization," "the highest proof of civility is that the whole action of the State is directed on securing the greatest good for the greatest number" (w 7:34).

It is easy to see how the shallow version of conservation pioneered by Roosevelt and Pinchot (with much assistance, as I have argued, from Emerson) breeds not only today's mainstream resources management approach but its own strains of noxious environmentalism. More than a century after Frederick Turner's declaration that the frontier was closed, almost as long since Roosevelt left office, the so-called Wise Use movement continues to believe the only brake to expansion of mining, forestry, ranching, and wilderness recreational development is the limit of our imaginations. In an attempt to maintain and extend the resource extraction frontier, the raison d'être of the contemporary Wise Use movement (a congeries of ranchers, drillers, miners, developers, loggers, as well as a host of other wilderness "enthusiasts" and, of course, the various manufacturing and extractive interests that furnish them aid, comfort, and money) is to justify a similar American righteousness with regard to the remnants of their wilderness. The movement believes that scarcity is only a failure of will, that the diminishment of national expectations is a cynical tree-hugger plot, and that preservation of the remnants of public wilderness, strangely, violates God-given private property rights. Their alignment with the economic code is so deep-seated that even those organizations like the Sierra Club or the Wilderness Society that are actually trying to mediate between the economy and the other subsystems look to Wise Users as monovisioned as they themselves appear to be. According to two members of the movement's vanguard, Ron Arnold and Alan Gottlieb, "Environmentalism is a business. Like all businesses, part of the *modus operandi* of every environmental group is to put competitors out of business—but its competitors are more often the businesses that feed, clothe and shelter us all than they are other environmental groups. Environmentalists want your business. They'll do what's necessary to get it. Regardless of cost to the economy" (76).

Taking its cue from this vision but spinning it to straddle both the Emersonian and Thoreauvian sides of the environmental tradition (and the demands of an electorate growing increasingly suspicious of Wise Use–type rhetoric), the Republican party styled its environmental plank in the 2000 presidential campaign as "American Partners in Conservation and Preservation." Too superficial to even qualify as shallow, the key point throughout was the idea that "Economic prosperity and environmental protection must advance together. Prosperity gives our society the wherewithal to advance environmental protection, and a thriving natural environment enhances the quality of life that makes prosperity worthwhile." Note that while prosperity and protection are said to go hand in hand, it is clear that prosperity is first among equals. (To paraphrase Al Pacino in *Scarface*, "In this country, you gotta make the money first. Then when you get the money, you get the power. Then when you get the power, then you get nature.")

Thus, to maintain these positions of extreme piety, the Wise Use movement and the Republican party (along with much of the Democratic party) must give themselves over to the "prosperity, damn the costs!" side of the equation and paradoxically disassociate themselves from the very Judeo-Christian code of prudence and responsibility that Roosevelt's doctrine of stewardship was meant to defend in spirit if not always in practice. That code is clarified in Roosevelt's presidential address to a group of governors, entitled, aptly, "The Natural Resources—Their Wise Use or Their Waste." Here Roosevelt notes that "every step of mankind is marked by the discovery and use of natural resources previously unused. Without such progressive knowledge and utilization of natural resources population could not grow, nor industries multiply, nor the hidden wealth of the earth be developed for the benefit of mankind" (164). Although Roosevelt brackets the ethical and social dimensions of conservation as separate issues, even as he adumbrates the purely utilitarian argument the moral imperative is never far away:

The steadily increasing drain on these natural resources has promoted to an extraordinary degree the complexity of our industrial and social life. Moreover, this unexampled
development has had a determining effect upon the character and opinions of our
people. The demand for efficiency in the great task has given us vigor, effectiveness,
decision, and power, and a capacity for achievement which in its own lines has never
yet been matched. So great and so rapid has been our material growth that there
has been a tendency to lag behind in spiritual and moral growth; but that is not the
subject upon which I speak to you today. Disregarding for the moment the question
of moral purpose, it is safe to say that the prosperity of our people depends directly
on the energy and intelligence with which our natural resources are used. . . . We
have become great because of the lavish use of our resources and we have just reason
to be proud of our growth. . . . It is time for us now as a nation to exercise the same
reasonable foresight in dealing with our great natural resources that would be shown
by any prudent man in conserving and wisely using the property which contains the
assurance of well-being for himself and his children. (166)

Cynically, one might observe (as do deep ecologists) that in its appeal to the potential
for unlimited economic prosperity while tossing the bone of sustainable development, this passage embodies the approach still employed today by developers,
industrialists, and government planners to pacify a willing public as they set about
their task of reducing the world to a material storehouse. But in its invocation of the
responsibility of the present to the future, its argument that prosperity depends on
conservation and not vice versa, Roosevelt makes an argument that both deep and
shallow environmentalists could still rally around today.

We might also observe, however, that in its not so subtle reference to the notion
of wise use as a kind of therapy for moral decay, the above passage hearkens back
to Emerson's own expansionist exhortations in "The Young American": "The
continent we inhabit is to be physic and food for our mind, as well as our body. The
land, with its tranquillizing, sanative influences, is to repair the errors of a scholastic
and traditional education, and bring us into just relations with men and things" (cw
1:226). Ironically, that same Emersonian vision of nature also influenced the man who
is usually considered the paterfamilias of deep ecology, John Muir. Muir frequently
cites Emerson as his spiritual authority, but unlike Roosevelt, Muir has in mind the
ecstatic writer of *Nature,* not the "Yankee Sage." It is quite true that Muir was also
able to make anthropocentric arguments in the effort to preserve portions of the
wilderness: in his various campaigns to establish wilderness areas (like Yosemite),
he spoke of forest and watershed management, the recreational possibilities of large
natural areas, and like Roosevelt he was highly critical of the destructive penchant

of monopolies and the various "big money" interests. But in his books—and using a rhetoric that we recognize today as decidedly nonanthropocentric—he inveighed against the utilitarian "resourcism" shared by both Roosevelt and big money:

> Now, it never seems to occur to these far-seeing teachers that Nature's object in making animals and plants might possibly be first of all happiness of each one of them, not the creation of all for the happiness of one. Why should man value himself as more than a small part of the one great unit of creation? And what creature of all that the Lord has taken the pains to make is not essential to the completeness of that unit— the cosmos? The universe would be incomplete without man; but it would also be incomplete without the smallest transmicroscopic creature that dwells beyond our conceitful eyes and knowledge. (160–61)

The passage (from *A Thousand Mile Walk to the Gulf*) is typical of his at the time shocking attitude toward not just nature but humanity. Muir's centrifugal ethics is clearly prophetic of deep ecology's attempt to extend moral consideration beyond the human, and his decentered view of humanity is a cornerstone concept of most later attempts to build an environmental ethics.

Indeed, that commitment to a wide equivalence between humans and nonhumans in terms of intrinsic value is at the heart of the deep ecological program. The implications of the Deep Ecology Platform (DEP) worked out by Arne Naess and George Sessions can all be unpacked from two crucial principles, or ultimate norms—self-realization and biocentric equality—which reflect that equivalence. Self-realization, say Devall and Sessions, "goes beyond the modern Western *self* which is defined as an isolated ego striving primarily for hedonistic gratification or for a narrow sense of individual salvation in this life or the next. This socially programmed sense of the narrow self or social self dislocates us, and leaves us prey to whatever fad or fashion is prevalent in our society or social reference group" (66–67). Instead, true self-realization begins when we "identify with other humans from our family and friends to, eventually, our species. But the deep ecology sense of self requires a further maturity and growth, an identification which goes beyond humanity to include the natural world. We must see beyond our narrow contemporary cultural assumptions and values, and the conventional wisdom of our time and place, and this is best achieved by the meditative deep questioning process. Only in this way can we hope to attain full mature personhood and uniqueness" (67). In effect, self-realization begins when we fully appreciate Muir's protoecological point that "When we try to pick out anything by itself, we find it hitched to everything else in the universe" (248). The norm of biocentric equality, too, draws on that notion of interconnectedness: "all things in the biosphere have an equal right to live and blossom and to reach their own individual forms of unfolding and self-realization

within the larger Self-realization. This basic intuition is that all organisms and
entities in the ecosphere, as parts of an interrelated whole, are equal in intrinsic
worth" (Devall and Sessions, 67). Following from this norm is the crucial idea that
"we should live with minimum rather than maximum impact on other species and
on the Earth in general" (68).

Some critics see this reliance on intuition and intrinsic worth as evidence of
deep ecology's mysticism, its fundamental contempt for rationality. Critics as widely
divergent as futurist Alvin Toffler and philosopher Luc Ferry have launched scathing
attacks on deep ecology, citing the Nazi's environmental program—including the
Reichsnaturschutzgesetz and other laws for the protection of animals—as evidence
that radical ecology has an inherent affinity with totalitarianism.[3] But such attacks are
largely gratuitous, for they attribute to deep ecologists motives that perhaps betray
more about the attackers' own commitments to the project of reason as embodied in
liberal humanism than they uncover a sinister logic on the part of environmentalists.[4]
Given the extent to which rationality (as construed by the keepers of the humanist
flame) has failed to eliminate even the grossest inequalities within the human species,
the ambitious biocentric goals of deep ecologists seem by contrast highly laudable,
if at times pie-in-the sky, and the more objectionable statements of some of its
members ought not, as with any movement, be taken as indicative of the whole.

Nevertheless, there are objections to deep ecology that do have merit: from feminists, social ecologists, and others among the green movement who are attempting
to create with deep ecologists a broad-based critique of modern society and its
environment. In that spirit of cooperative but critical engagement, and from the
complex systems perspective I have delineated, deep ecologists' shortcomings as I
see them have more to do with their underestimation of the shape and scope of the
challenge at hand than in their quarrel with humanism and the logic of industrial
civilization. Because deep ecology is meant to be a profound inquiry into the ethics
of modernity, it relies on the paradoxical moral coding of the form good/bad to
observe the world, the goal being to determine precisely which human actions,
from an ecological perspective, are acceptable and which are reprehensible. In its
zeal, it seeks to coordinate the entire social system from the perspective of this
code; like other religions before it, deep ecology ultimately wants to discipline the
world through its moral coding, and while it does not promise transcendence per
se (rather, a form of immanence that ultimately is a kind of transcendence), it does
hold forth the dream of a harmonious society composed of self-realized individuals
rooted in an ecologically sane ground that underpins all other quotidian ways of
measuring the world. In a way, deep ecology seeks the ground zero of codes that
will coordinate all the others—a ne plus ultra second-order code. But in seeking
such depth, deep ecology mounts its critique on an outdated model of society: a

hierarchical model in which one totalizing perspective—derived from a plenipotent (if amorphous) concept of interconnectedness that has its origins in a combination of ecological science and the secular religiosity of, among others, Thoreau, Teilhard de Chardin, and Heidegger—can somehow observe the rest of society's systems, and, presumably by force of moral intensity, come to reorient all other perspectives.

The objections to such a model begin when we recall that there is nothing that can be said about the world except from within a system of communication. While this would perhaps stand as a truism even to deep ecologists, there are, as we have seen, consequences to the communicational closure of the functionally differentiated social system that serve to complicate natural contracts and any other declarations of the equivalence of all creation, humans and nonhumans. The first problem with this approach is simply that environments are always specified by individual systems. No system observes precisely what another system observes because, as we have seen, each has its own unique operational distinction, which by definition means that it specifies its environment independently of other systems, so that the contents of that environment are, quite literally, of a different nature. A religious system like deep ecology observes an environment in which a choice must be made as to whether a given communication, action, or event goes toward Self-realization or not, whereas, say, in the political system, the pregnant question is whether or not a communication goes toward getting and keeping power. The point here is that no matter the types of suasion used, deep ecology *simply cannot influence other systems to observe the same environment as deep ecology.* [5] In a manner of speaking, a rose is not a rose is not a rose in functionally differentiated societies. Thus, the idea *pace* deep ecology that all function systems could come to specify an identical environment, compelling and instructive in the same way, is a holdover from the time when it was believed that there was a single worldview or outlook that all of society shared or, as in the Marxist paradigm, a coherent material base that induced a coherent, if usually duplicitous, ideological superstructure. In a functionally differentiated society, however, the mechanisms of intersystem communication and resonance are too heterogeneous and ramified to be considered in this manner.

"Simplify, Simplify": Radical Ecology and Liberalism

Yet it may be unfair to understand deep ecology only through its most extreme formulations. After all, any comprehensive program of thought can be attacked on much the same grounds, that its reach must necessarily exceed its grasp. There is, however, a second drawback with deep ecology, one that is in fact far more mundane, and for this reason is actually the more troubling of the two.

Although I noted that deep ecology demands changes in economic and political behavior to make them consonant with the two ultimate norms, it is by no means clear that in its basic programming deep ecology is actually at odds with the economic system, nor in its political philosophy does it mark a significant departure from the American ideological mainstream. This is not simply a question of deep ecologists needing to unpack an as yet unarticulated radical agenda, for in a fundamental way the problem is precisely that deep ecological theory cannot engage with the economy and politics except on the most rudimentary level. And in that that lack of engagement the theory reconstitutes a conventional liberal disdain for the "deep" probing of politics and economy, as if there is nothing more to be said about traditional liberal virtues like democracy, individualism, property, and free markets—except perhaps that they too are, to borrow deep ecology's terminology, ultimate norms of intrinsic value. The classic short definition of liberalism says it consists of two freedoms: the negative freedom to be left alone by the state and the positive freedom to pursue personal autonomy. Liberalism guarantees the right to pursue private gain along with the right to expect minimal public interference when doing so, striking an always-uneasy balance between the individual and the claims of his society. Needless to say, the history of America has been replete with angry dialogues about how to reconcile equal freedom under democracy with the freedom to practice inequality in the economy. The two ultimate norms of the DEP replicate these twin pillars of liberalism by proposing a right to self-realization in a milieu of negatively defined biocentric equality (i.e., the freedom of each and every thing to pursue its self-realization according to its own lights without interference). As with liberalism, the former principle comes into immediate conflict with the latter when *my* freedom to self-realize intersects with *your* right to do the same; the liberal economy of the self makes life difficult in democratic politics because everybody is everybody else's environment. (This is not to say that democracy is untenable per se; it is to say along with Ernesto Laclau and Chantal Mouffe, that the essence of democracy is not its movement toward an omega point of happy and unconflicted consensus but rather its continuous and inescapable production of division and dissensus.) Deep ecologists, properly anticipating that self-realization will undermine biocentric equality, have added the caveat that the former project is understood to be limited only to the pursuit of vital needs. Yet that provision only reminds us of the inevitability of sociality in general, and politics in particular, for where else are things like vital needs to be determined? I may say unequivocally that it is among my vital needs to pollute, but you say that it is among your vital needs not to be poisoned. This example also reminds us that because the claim of vital need cannot be thought apart from variable notions as to what constitutes self-realization (and the plain fact that some entities have the resources to support stronger claims than do others), the economic sphere is also clearly in play.

Beyond this notion of vital needs, deep ecology simply attempts to lift the draw-bridge to the economic and political world so as to keep itself secure in a bastion of moral purity based on intrinsic worth and biocentric harmony. True, deep ecol-ogists rail against narrowly defined individualism, greed, corruption, and political expediency, but rather than challenging liberalism's attempt to reconcile the eco-nomic and political function systems, they tacitly accept its terms by synthesizing their ethical program (of positively defined, albeit decentered, individualism and negatively defined intrinsic equality) into a larger vision of the "self-in-Self," a kind of complete, interconnected, organic wholeness. "This process of the full unfolding of the self can also be summarized by the phrase, 'No one is saved until we are all saved,' where the phrase 'one' includes not only me, an individual human, but all humans, whales, grizzly bears, whole rainforest ecosystems, mountains and rivers, the tiniest microbes in the soil, and so on" (Devall and Sessions, 67). (The parallel distinction of "self" and "Self" and Heidegger's "being" and "Being" is not coin-cidental and has been explored by a number of writers.[6]) In effect, deep ecology imagines that the conflict between the vital needs of self and the biocentric equality of all selves (homologous to the central contradiction of liberal democracy) can be boiled down to a question of whether or not we come closer, through our various self-realizations, to this all-inclusive Self-realization, a kind of grand accord wherein all selves sacrifice as much or as little as biology and ecology have determined. Yet this movement toward an inclusive, holistic Self ultimately can only be undertaken as a leap of faith, "arrived at by the deep ecological questioning process [which] reveal[s] the importance of moving to the philosophical and religious level of wisdom. [It] cannot be validated, of course, by the methodology of modern science based on its usual mechanistic assumptions and its narrow definition of data" (66). Like liberal democracy itself, deep ecology defers the resolution of its inherent contradictions to a kind of postscarcity, postmillennial moment (always just around the corner) when the crucial antagonisms will vanish, a time when the meek shall inherit what is left of the earth. The harmonization of economics and politics, the private and the public, the self and Self finally can be imagined only by positing this kind of improbable transformation, so that both deep ecology and liberal ideology are in effect an attempt to yoke together two functionally distinct systems in an unholy alliance (and I use the language of religion here because the attempt to transcend the boundaries of two systems has very much a spiritual flavor, as deep ecologists—if not free-market liberals—frequently acknowledge).

The liberal programming of deep ecology calls to mind the paradox of all ob-serving systems, which, as a function of their first-order perspective, take their environments to be the world. The paradox of system coding is that codes are ulti-mately defined as x is not not-x, or not-x is not x. Observing codes are ways to make decisions about things, and programs are ways to determine the decision. In this case, the observing code of Self/not-Self (a variant of the immanence/transcendence code of religious systems) guarantees that deep ecology sees only what it can see. This is to be expected and is not in itself the problem. But in viewing society as a field in which there are only practices that go toward Self-realization and ones that inhibit it, deep ecology does not notice how profoundly its programming draws on the political and economic balancing act of liberalism. In effect, and as with liberal democracy itself, the antagonism between the intrinsic equality of all individuals and the freedom for a given individual to be unequal without limits is to be resolved by reference to the first principles (for deep ecology the ultimate norms and for liberal democracy the principles of liberalism itself). Yet those principles simply reaffirm that although we are all equal, we all have different interests, and depending on which part of the equation we are currently emphasizing, individual rights will be held up over public need, or the commonweal will be cited to temper possessive individualism.

The result of this conflation of two distinct functional domains is intimately familiar to us: our current society with all its particular blockages, including a propensity to view the natural environment as a resource for self-realization even when doing so undermines democratic, let alone biocentric, equality. The "tragedy of the commons," as Garret Hardin calls it, is one way of imagining how the programming tends to play out: anyone has an equal right to take from the common resource so as to pursue his own self-realization; at the same time, because costs are distributed equally means that there is no incentive for anyone to moderate his self-realization—in fact, there is every incentive to realize his own self before the resource is depleted. Possessive individualism trumps democratic equality every time, because the gains realized by the former are *individually* always worth the price of *commonly* jeopardizing the resource. Costs are collective while gains accrue individually. The point here is that there is a contradiction between processes of self-realization and processes of equality, a functional barrier between the two. To a large extent the ecological history of North America consists of a series of these tragedies of the commons: animal extinctions, overharvesting of forests, the pollution of water systems, the dust bowl, and so on.[7] (It should be added that by the twentieth century, of course, steps were taken to ensure that the commons was to some extent protected, though frequently the resource was not really secured *for* the public so much as secured *from* them, so that those individuals and entities with the economic and political power to draw from the resource could continue to do so with minimal interference: low-cost timber and mineral rights, grazing access, and now pollution credits all serve to shunt costs onto the public while returning to them only the mixed benefits of continued economic growth.)

To reiterate the point, whether you define self-possession as a narrow, private affair that produces a public good, or like deep ecologists as a broad, inclusive realization of self within a larger Self, a bottleneck occurs when you repeatedly come up against the fact that others' rights to self-realization inevitably conflict with your own—which the vital needs provision of the DEP clearly acknowledges. However sublimated that conflict can be made to seem, there is an opposition between individual interests and other interests, or self and Self. In systems terms, when individuals align themselves with the code of the economy, harmonizing themselves with its programming, they must develop their own autonomy, and the devil (environment) can take everyone else. But when they simultaneously align themselves with a political system whose program states that all individuals are to experience the same environment, a fundamental antagonism is put in play. The two sorts of systems involved are not congruent—their programs cannot be shoehorned together comfortably (except perhaps by the neoconservatives at *National Review*). But both liberals and deep ecologists in their own way propound an almost messianic belief that this antagonism will go away when everyone reaches the right state of heightened awareness, or at least when the apportionment of equality and inequality is arrived at equitably (although granted, for liberals, that belief must by now be a fairly cynical one).

As Harold Bloom has argued, the hopeful dream of melding individual self-interest with the common good *is* the American religion. In a like manner the program of deep ecology follows a trajectory that can be traced back at least to the visions of Thoreau and Emerson, which were in large measure attempts to configure the self-possessed Self-in-Nature as the linchpin of American democratic life. Deep ecology finds in Thoreau an explicit source for a self-abnegating view of vital needs. Thoreau's recurrent injunction to "simplify, simplify" evokes for deep ecologists precisely the sort of low-impact lifestyle they believe humans must now espouse. Less explicitly, that notion of simplification draws on Emersonian principles. In the Transcendentalist sense, a self-reliant state is not arrived at through the acquisition of material wealth (for the relinquishment of wealth can actually be a potent demonstration of the power of the self-possessed individual). The logic of the imperial self simply does not hinge on the ability to pay or not to pay under the economic system. Instead, there is a deeper principle of exchange disclosed, and the possession of an inalienable self—or rather, the continuing re-possession of a self always threatened by alienation—is what is at stake in a more generalized economy of loss and gain. Once you build "your own world," a "correspondent revolution in things will attend the influx of spirit," says Emerson, so that the world at large, with its rich and poor, grinding debt and enormous profit, is little more than the surface phenomenon of a more profound exercise in self-recovery (CW 1:40). In Lockean terms, the application of labor to nature mixes self with the world, and one thereby gains not simply material property but a firmer hold on one's own innate self. Yet once that equation is fully understood, in Emersonian terms the whole active labor process becomes superfluous, and one proceeds directly to self-possession by the exercise of *will* alone. In that nonmaterial sense of self-possession, deep ecology can certainly recognize something of its norm of self-realization.

How much of the deep ecological attitude of self-realization through voluntary simplicity is actually traceable to the Emersonian project? There are clearly some significant differences in the kind of individual imagined. Still, just as the deep ecologist's motive behind self-realization is to realize a broad identification with nonhuman nature, the Emersonian individual, say, of *Nature*, also seeks a heightened awareness of the larger world. From my perspective, then, the issue is not how far deep ecologists have gone in revising and correcting the excesses of the self-reliant self, but the fact that Emersonian individualism in fact preempts them: there is finally very little between Emerson and Thoreau on the vagaries of the self-in-the-world that does not anticipate what deep ecologists have to say on the subject of organic wholeness or self-in-Self. Quentin Anderson says of Emerson and Thoreau that "theirs was an effort, necessarily incomplete, to articulate a fresh set of ties between our individual existence and its complement, being in general, to see ourselves not in the light of the vexed history of the species but in that of the total conception of the scheme of things" (*Making*, 4). The figure of the transparent eyeball ("I am nothing; I see all") is very much in line with the deep ecological leitmotif of an individual suspended in a web of relations anchored at many more points than the quotidian dictates of body, ego, and social convention. One might be tempted to respond, a little too quickly I think, that Emerson's self is broad only so that it may be more narrow, whereas the deep ecological self is narrow only insofar as it must be to be broad. But what is far more significant—and this is where deep ecology does not go deep enough—is that the vulgar, narrow version of the self is always *latent* within this visionary self, a potent, self-seeking kernel straining to burst out, as indeed, Emerson's later writings are sometimes understood to confirm. The at times ugly politics of self-reliance is not to be understood as simply an aberration or regression from a finer, more evolved version of subjectivity; it is part and parcel of that subjectivity. What expands the self or narrows it is of a piece: a nucleus of something like desire (or perhaps, we might say, a difference between a system and an environment) that can never be elided, for it endures and produces effects, sometimes generous, sometimes mean. In this view, the self-realization promoted by deep ecology must always be recalled as *self*-realization, so that when deep ecologists make the self the lead item in their philosophical agenda yet deal so indifferently with its counterpotential for excess, they are charting a perilous course. What I think this double-edged capacity should tell deep ecologists is that despite the avowed deindividualized notion of the individual promoted by the DEP, self-realization cannot be—and ought not be—thought apart from the autopoietic principle it implies. This does not mean one cannot always try to temper self-realization—by, as we have seen, something like the vital needs qualifier, or by one of the various strategies Emerson and Thoreau used over the years to distinguish their notions of self-reliance from mere bourgeois self-aggrandizement. But more important I think it also means that we cannot expect what is finally an economically inflected production of self to solve the problems *it* generates through *its* operations for the *other* selves (or indeed the same self) aligned with *other* systems, using *other* distinctions and programs.[8] The Pandora's box that is self-reliance or self-realization will not be closed by the self *by itself,* or even by a self *in a Self.* Any such closure instead requires the development of a politics responsive to the existence of autonomous selves and autonomous systems, which are understood to be open to the autonomy of each other only as environment. This kind of politics recognizes first and foremost the futility of reconciling the deep goals of these distinct systems, for a merging of purposes would only undermine each system's unique autopoiesis. There is no true accommodation of individualism within democracy, nor self-realization with ecocentric equality. A systems politics takes their irreconcilability as a baseline assumption instead of an aberration that with fine-tuning could be set right. This politics' maximal goal may only consist of assuring that "all counties are heard from" so that each system is forced to respond to the irritability of its environment. And what *that* argues for, finally, is the necessity of critiques informed by second-order cybernetics and systems theory, whether the goal is to retrospectively understand the discourse of nature in the 1850s or to shape the environmental ethics of today.

Politics and the Neopastoral

If unabashedly ecocentric approaches such as deep ecology reproduce the typical blind spots of liberal essentialism, we are still left with the problem of actually articulating how a second-order approach could improve the view. What would such a critique look like? How might it modify current approaches to American literature and culture, particularly as they thematize the problem of nature? How might those modifications address the problem of praxis in a fully differentiated social system? I claimed at the outset of this book that I had no solutions, no particular hopes for what a systems perspective could do, only the sense that it might at least provide a cold shower to an ecocritical community that, while not needing to be reminded that theory is largely about finding new words with which to query the same old problems, does seem to need reminding that the answers theory produces come with no guarantee they will please. Sometimes, to borrow the old saw, you have to reach bottom before you can climb back up.

Still, I hope that previous chapters have provided some possible directions for further inquiry. Additionally—and recalling now that I began this book by considering the difficulties with American pastoralist approaches to texts—I want to consider how the systems approach might usefully update classic pastoral theory. To be sure, if deep ecologists can never let go of a certain sense of dejection stemming from humanity's primal sin against nature and subsequent fall, then pastoralists probably hold the converse but equally eschatological hope that someday we can be restored to the Garden. But the advantage of building upon the pastoral approach (as opposed to rehabilitating deep ecology or, in general, developing a political or cultural movement around the supposedly magnetic virtues of ecology or ecosystem, as if those concepts had some special hold on the human imagination, let alone on the human social system) is that pastoralism has always had as its central given the incontestable *entanglement* of humans and environment; so that unlike the more purely ecocentric theories described above, pastoral theory tends to focus most of its energies on the fact that people have to live in *this* world, contaminated and hybridized as it is, and not in the one imagined in posthumanist primitivism. The pastoral is indeed an anthropocentric concoction; but then, as I have maintained, anthropocentrism is not a matter of choice. So the point might be to make a virtue of necessity. Industrial neoteny, the reconstruction of the preindustrial in the midst of the industrial, may not be the best goal worth pursuing, but it may be the only one.[9]

Pastoralists hold out great hope that humans *can* create spaces in which people find balance with their surround. Refreshingly, they are convinced that the various interests that continue to compel people to pursue too-often antagonistic if not downright self-destructive directions *can* be mitigated. If the Emersonian and Thoreauvian traditions of ecological rationality and deep thinking are always practiced in a tragic frame, the pastoral is the comic corrective. Practitioners of literary pastoralism, for example, have written extensively about the kinds of places people seem best suited to live, survive, and thrive in; they draw on what experience has shown may be the most constructive, most sustainable ways for human beings to interact with their environments. Simply put, pastoralists have generally believed in the possibility of squaring the demands of humans with the iron laws of nature. At the very least, they believe we have no choice but to try.[10]

I do not want to come across as an unabashed proponent of pastoralism, however. The topoi of the pastoral is no less rived by competing interests than any of the other eigenvalues of North American culture. It has always served a variety of political masters, so much so that even the "iron laws of nature" often suspiciously validate the ideological predilection of those promulgating them. Still, the biological sciences have generated more or less reliable models about how ecosystems work, about their sensitivity to disruptions, about the rippling effect of such disruptions to the larger biotic community, and so on. More important, ecologists have learned how unpredictable such systems can be and why it is necessary to build in safeguards against our own inexpungible ignorance. Scientists cognizant of the limits of science help buttress the work of those interested in designing human spaces that do not begin with the demolition of the previous wild ecosystem and end in the impoverishment of the human residents themselves. For such theorists and thinkers the great challenge still remains: how do we make room for ourselves in this delicate and limited world while not in the process destroying it?

Granted, the answers to that question still get pursued only obliquely in the mainstream incarnation of the pastoral project, which has followed a trajectory that promotes neither altruism with regard to the environment nor humility for humans. Informed by the Rooseveltian notion of prudent stewardship, "actually existing pastoralism" is very much in lockstep with current market economics, and only tangentially is it in the service of those who would rehabilitate the world and the human role in it. Wendell Berry, who is probably the preeminent traditional pastoralist of our time, notes that "once the unknown geography [of North America] was mapped, the industrial marketplace became the new frontier, and we continued, with largely the same motives and with increasing haste and anxiety, to displace ourselves—no longer with unity of direction, like a migrant flock, but like refugees from a broken ant hill" (*Unsettling*, 3). If pastoralism once beckoned as a safe path through this hurly-burly, offering itself as a via media between the halcyon past and the hectic present, between a nostalgia for things lost and a frantic futurism that threatened to lose yet more—then the pastoral route no longer appears open today, at least not in any way that would be recognizable to Jefferson or acceptable to Berry.

But while the traditional pastoral ideal is foreclosed, a neopastoral appeal is beginning to sound, whereby the logic of the via media is, mutatis mutandis, translated across time and space into the terrain of contemporary America. This updated, highly compromised form of pastoralism forms a vital locus in the politics of culture, even as it departs from its traditional roots, for as profound new computer and communication technologies, new social arrangements, and new business and labor practices reshape the contours of our world at a dizzying pace, nostalgia and progress must be constantly reconjugated to spin the threatening forces into secure, acceptable American themes. For those who push for change as well as for those who have change pushed on them, the new pastoralism, despite its modifications, is still an extremely comfortable ideological domain—and rhetorical resource. The neopastoral appeal thus provides a feel-good method of nodding to both the liberal "party of hope" and the conservative "party of memory" (as Emerson would put it—although today it seems that the left has assumed the burdens of memory and the right the mantle of a remorseless brand of hope). No surprise here, however, for as I noted in chapter 1, pastoralism agrees with most shades on the political spectrum—from red to green to pin-striped blue.

The reorganization of the workplace exemplifies the way a neopastoral appeal can be mobilized in this, the postindustrial, postlabor phase of capitalism. Now that large numbers of mind-numbing, blue-collar factory jobs are in jeopardy or already eliminated, some look back with fondness upon if not the jobs themselves then the lifestyles they enabled, and unions fight to preserve what they can. But new technologies continue to spur the disappearance of whole sectors of the economy through the ephemeralization of processes of production and distribution, creating instability and hopelessness even in white-collar circles—along with, granted, a measure of greater freedom, leisure, and earning capacity for those fortunate enough to have the skills and experience the new global economy requires. The pastoral ideal in this era is morphed into the suburban, minivan- and Internet-linked home office, complete with its archetypal yeomanry: a "no-collar" pair of DIKs (double income with kids) toiling as independent information technologists. McLuhan's electronic cottage becomes the site of the new rural idyll, where time-honored American traditions of independence, hard work, and self-reliance mix with high technology to create a liminal space at once physically removed from the old centers of power and calculation in the city but virtually connected to them through worldwide webs of information. The electronic crofter comes to realize an information-age version of Marx's postcapitalist utopia: conducting e-commerce in the morning, gardening in the afternoon, and chatting in on-line salons in the evening.

Of course, this rural idyll (like those before it) is interrupted by a host of complications, not the least of which is its effective unavailability to the large majority of Americans who will never have the opportunity to actualize it—even assuming there was a demand in place for tens of millions of prospective infoentrepreneurs, whose hopes are in fact already being outsourced to IT sweatshops in the Third World. Just as with the pastoral of the nineteenth century, in the twenty-first the via media will evaporate upon closer inspection, remaining the pipe dream of Third Wave/Third Culture enthusiasts, technology boosters, free-market wowsers, and, in an odd juxtaposition, ecoromantics.

So while a market-based, neopastoralism for the masses is not really an option, one would be remiss in ignoring its power in the promotions of the corporate class, who organize entire marketing campaigns around the pastoral appeal because they know that in America it *sells*. The following copy from an advertisement that was distributed widely by the Saturn division of General Motors is exemplary of the way neopastoralism is used to pluck at the chords of consumer desire:

It's nice to know the environment also impacts the auto industry.

It's down Route 31, south about a mile and a half from the center of town, but pretty much hidden behind the land where the old Haynes mansion still stands. It's a very special place that we now call home. But it was special long before we got here. Over a hundred years ago, the fields around us saw Union and Confederate armies clash. In times more recent, these rolling green hills were home to several champion horses. One of which still holds the record as world's fastest pacer. Even today a little history is being made here by the fact that we're the only car plant we know of to employ a full-time farmer. Yep, we make it all, doors, fenders and alfalfa. Which makes our home a very special place indeed.

The accompanying photograph shows two children running around a pond in the middle of a vast green field, while another child is in the foreground mugging the camera. He sports a red straw hat pushed back off his head and a slight scrape on his nose. The picture invokes a kind of pre-Nintendo, prerevisionist epoch in American history, a time when children could play Cowboys and Indians in a safe and healthful environment, free from industrial pollutants, sexual predators, and the carping of the politically correct—the fifties, in other words. The caption reads: "The Saturn plant, as seen from just inside our white picket fence along Route 31 in Spring Hill, Tennessee." This is meant to be a joke, of course, for there is no factory in sight. The reason for this calculated dematerialization of the physical plant is explained in the ad's sidebar: "It's important that we look after the land around us. That's why, last year alone, we recycled, reused or reclaimed almost 59,503 tons of material. And when we built the plant, we did even more. We kept it from spoiling your view from Route 31 by excavating soil, building hills and transplanting trees already on the site. Heck, we even put birdhouses up all around." Like the factory—casually cropped from the picture yet foregrounded by its very omission— the pastoral appeal works by establishing a dialectic between a hypertechnology so good that it seems natural and unobtrusive and a nature so lovingly contrived that it verges on technological perfection. As the difference between what is real and what is simulation disappears à la Baudrillard, a sublime synthesis of human and environment is generated, with the Saturn plant folding itself seamlessly into the hills and into American history, tucked away behind the picket fence like grandmother's house (or, rather "mansion"), quietly producing cars and feeding off its own wastes, supplying habitat for birds and a playground for youngsters.

Only to an attentive reader is something else also notable for its absence: nowhere is there a sign of the workers themselves (with the exception, ironically, of the "full-time farmer"). Unsurprisingly, the fact that Saturn built its plant in rural Tennessee to avoid higher labor costs and environmental standards elsewhere is not part of this object lesson in greening the automotive industry. Instead, the neopastoral appeal works to ensure that an alternate view will take hold: that while other cars are made in big, overcrowded industrial centers, Saturns are made in the hallowed and verdant country; that while other cars are built by assembly-line workers in hard hats carrying lunch buckets (i.e., organized labor), Saturns are made by just plain folks who might as likely be found bird-watching or, heck, even cutting a field of alfalfa. [11] These dichotomies rely on a familiar, deeply entrenched mythic structure (city bad, country good), now retooled for the age of high technology. In contrast to Hawthorne's or Thoreau's travails with the local Concord railroads, no one who encounters the countrified Saturn plant should expect to be psychically wounded by it, so light is its presence on the land. Thus, there is simply no need for a "virtual resolution" of machine and garden *pace* Leo Marx. This is because no contradiction exists from the outset: from their inception, the machine (the Saturn plant) and the garden (the Tennessee hill country) are both equally fabrications—or, if one prefers, both are equally natural. Either way, a collision of nature and culture is not at issue, for these terms simply do not apply when "the plant" and "the plants" in Spring Hill both germinate in the same soil: the environmentally friendly, fertile minds of the engineers of the Saturn division, who are working diligently to ensure that it is no more onerous to toil in or shocking to coexist with the Saturn factory than it is, say, to tend Thoreau's bean field or dwell alongside Walden Pond. In Thoreau's terms, the engineers have indeed brought the factory's "sills up to the very edge of the swamp," with the signal difference here that not only are the sills man-made but so is the swamp. The Saturn plant and its surround become the high-tech version of the pastoral ideal, wherein the ephemeralization of the machine coincides with the constructedness of the garden to form a postnatural, postindustrial via media—the very poster-topography of Latourian hybridity.

What should we extract from such fables of postmodern pastoralism? The crucial lesson is that, as the advertisement itself acknowledges (and, indeed, uses as a selling point), no longer should we be under the illusion that we are dealing with anything other than an entirely self-conscious and self-authorizing pastoral mythology. The neopastoral cannot be construed as the preservation or reassertion of a previous harmony; it is instead the construction of harmony where none existed before. Just as the Saturn plant is situated in a highly landscaped, artificially enhanced rural site, in the age of environmental constructivism the pastoral itself exists as part of ground-up project of creation. In other words, the pastoral scene is a built thing—and, make no mistake, it is built very well. It is a site of *planned simplicity*, and like a well-tooled machine, form and functionality are in perfect balance, so that a user has merely to settle in and go. The neopastoralist who occupies this place is not required to mull over the vast (and potentially disturbing) knowledges that have gone into its construction, because the completely user-friendly interface renders the mechanisms silent, invisible, even elemental. Beyond preservation, beyond reconstruction, the contemporary neopastoral signifies the naturalization of technoculture: not better than nature, not a return to nature, but culture that simply *is* nature.

Leo Marx described three types of the American literary pastoral: the tragic, the romantic, and the vernacular, each with its own particular mythic structure and area of operation. The tumultuous collisions of machine and nature, of city and country are evaded—but not prevented—through the creation of imaginary spaces where the mind can roam. To these can now be added the techno- or neopastoral. Like the other three it offers a virtual resolution of the displacements and disruptions of modernity. But the particular strategies by which the neopastoral serves to decomplexify our hypertrophic machine age are virtual in the current, catachrestic sense of the word: in the sense by which advanced technology produces simulated spaces that abolish the priority of the real, blurring the difference between original and copy. Computer modeling, GIS, 3-D imaging, together with targeted ecosystem management and bioengineering—these are the tools with which the neopastoral space is constructed. Such tools allow extraordinary control over the boundaries between the virtual and actual space; the virtual space can be integrated into the real world with such precision that it seems of a piece with the previously existing topography. Virtuality, instead of marking the bounds of an exclusively imaginary realm, now floods over into reality. Take, for example, the controlled burning of Yellowstone Park and the reintroduction of wolves there: the effects of such interventions are modeled, predicted, monitored, and enforced; decisions about the life and death of animals and plants are made based on satellite telemetry fed into sophisticated algorithms that reveal carrying capacity, growth rates, or migratory patterns. That subsequent interventions (cullings, burnings, water release) are now more successful is not the most salient point, for interventions have always been made, whether actively or through benign neglect, whether with rifles and bounties or careless matches and Smokey Bear. The salient point is that the environments being created (or recreated) are now both real and virtual, for they exist as concrete existents and protean constructs at the same time. Yellowstone's perimeter is no longer simply the northwest corner of Wyoming; it extends into geosynchronous orbit, through the combined databases of the various arms of the Interior department, into the computers in travel offices and RV dealerships, and back into the park itself as millions of visitors plot their seasonal attack on its integrity by drawing on real-time analyses of the best sites to hear wolves howl.

The rise of neopastoralism will without doubt advance the notion that we now have the wisdom to design *with nature* the worlds we want and need not submit to the ones that have been forced upon us—whether by nature itself or by the blunders of our ancestors. That we can actually set things right may well seem like the latest form of the Enlightenment conceit. But it is a conceit that our increasing scientific and technological savvy seems to abet every day. As usual, and despite centuries of evidence to the contrary, many will assume that humans can even do nature one better. Unlike earlier forms of arrogance, this assumption of mastery does not emerge from an ignorance of the true extent of human ignorance, but rather from the discovery that ignorance itself can be quantified and factored into the equation. In other words, risk (as insurance sellers and poker players have always known) can be reasonably calculated. Perhaps our growing faith in the reliability of our ignorance has something to do with the fact that nature appears to organize itself spontaneously around a few fundamental rules, and that once we understand those rules there seems to be no reason why we cannot nudge the resulting organization in more useful directions—at least most of the time. This is, after all, exactly what the study of cybernetics was supposed to be about: to discover how to steer things. Principles of self-organization ensure that order manages to emerge out of even the biggest mess so that once we start the processes in motion, within acceptable latitudes of uncertainty results of a desired character ought to be obtainable. Why not deploy natural processes in the same way we deploy our own technologies? With a little tinkering in the now-navigable genome, we can even get nature to build things for us—bring nature along on a velvet leash instead of kicking and screaming. We do not have to know everything; indeed, we understand that we cannot have perfect knowledge in a noncausal universe. The capacity to self-correct is the real crux: we arrive at our destination by steering through a series of mistakes.

Sustainable development is one term that has emerged to describe the new optimism. Sustainable development suggests, for example, that we might practice sophisticated forest management regimes to produce lumber while leaving habitat for animals; we might design industrial processes that create zero discharge and cars that run off of the sun. If we can use the basic building blocks of DNA to invent better tomatoes and natural growth hormones to stimulate milk production, then the construction of entire environments well suited to our economic, social, and personal imperatives seems only a matter of scalability. Like the Saturn plant, a pastoral city (to borrow James Machor's term for the urban-rural synthesis) designed according to current best practices—complete with integrated wetland management and pest control, recycling programs and composting, community gardens and green spaces, ubiquitous public transport and local power generation—would provide habitat for birds, jobs for maintenance personnel, comfort and community for just plain folks and, relatively speaking, an improved relationship with the natural environment. Who would argue that such a community is more aberrant than the concrete waste-spaces produced under our present regime? This then is what neopastoral promises: the chance for a better, happier system of living based on a sophisticated fusion of the checkered results of the industrial age and the softer ideas and technologies of the age of bioengineering, cybernetics, and ecology.

I think it will have been clear that I am not suggesting neopastoralism is without its perils; indeed, as I have tried to demonstrate with the Saturn example, neopastoralism is nothing if not a product of the society within which it occurs. Moreover, I am not building a case for or against neopastoralism because, in fact, that sort of debate is already beside the point. Whatever we may think of the ethics, efficacy, and risks of this growing trend toward understanding environments as contingent, constructed, and labile, what the rise of neopastoralism alerts us to is that it is *control* over the shape of environments that is the vital issue of the day. Thus, it is no longer germane to agonize over whether or not nature is at an end, dead, or otherwise out of the picture. It is no longer germane to decry the fact that we have usurped the role of God or nature or both. Humans have already settled such issues, so to speak, with their feet and their pocketbooks. It *is* germane, however, to consider whether the environments we come to experience are determined by Saturn, Disney, and Dupont, whose stock and trade depends on a near-hegemonic angle of vision that is as powerful as it is limited, or determined by the hopes and dreams of citizens and by their compassion for the health and well-being of all living creatures. It *is* germane to consider whether the animals and plants that survive into the future are there because we value and celebrate their right to exist or because we value and celebrate their usefulness in medical research and genetic experimentation. In short, in the designation of certain environments by certain systems, what systems of social communication will be allowed to crowd out others and call the tune on the future of nature?

If there is any promise in neopastoralism as a way of "designing with nature in mind," it will come to nothing if it remains little more than a proxy for designing with business in mind. The clear and present danger is that the vision that asks us to look exclusively with the eyes of the market toward the world and its contents may succeed all too well and continue to obscure other modes of seeing, right up to the point that there is quite literally nothing left to see at all. As we have seen in our discussion of Thoreau, the central attraction of applying to the world a single code of observation was that, very simply, it made things simple. Single vision sweeps away the clutter of multiple—and *fundamentally* irreconcilable—modes of seeing. And there is no doubt that we still appreciate that sort of simplicity; indeed, we cultivate it. But the result of hewing too closely to a single code is clear: observation is blind to its own categories of seeing, and single-code observation is a recipe for singular blindness. Thus, in the collision of systems, as each tries to maintain autopoiesis without regard to one another, as each system loudly trumpets its own truth, the only way to foster a necessary balance is to prod systems through their environments, for any given system will not temper its own unique vision from the inside. Since the system's goal is to persist by processing communications along the pure pathways of its code, only if its environment impedes its operation when it attempts to do so will it steer its programming in a different direction—and then only in a way that allows it to preserve its organization. What all of this means is that there is no sense in which business will ever be green, for business aligns itself with the economy, which is fundamentally a system of exchanging anything for anything else for profit. Recall the fable of the scorpion that perversely stings the fox carrying it across the river: the agonizing, paradoxical feature of business vision is that it will take down itself and the world along with it unless it is held rigorously in check, for the simple reason that it cannot help itself.

Thus what the neopastoral *could* offer is a site and a metaphor for our willingness to resist the temptations of that kind of single-minded, single-code observation. Because neopastoralism draws on the old pastoral ideal of a harmonious middle ground, it becomes a locus for what we desperately require today: a rebalancing of all the multiple perspectives of our highly differentiated society. Neopastoralists acknowledge the pivotal role of the economy in the total social system—but strive to give more weight to science, law, religion, health, aesthetics, and politics. If we wish to live in a truly sustainable world, we must find ways to allow these other sources of social knowledge to make themselves heard over the din of the market. We require a new politics of systems, a chamber divided not by party but by perspective, because the parties as they stand now all speak, no matter what else they say to differentiate themselves, in a single, loud voice for the perspective of the economy. Only by balancing many partial visions can we begin to assemble environments even remotely adequate to both our democratic hopes and our biological limitations. The pastoral offers a rhetorical still point between the gravitational pulls of the numerous, competing functional perspectives of our highly differentiated society. All of their blind spots are concentrated in one place, exposed for all observers to see. I imagine the pastoral as a site where the cutting visions of different systems are brought to bear and, not resolving themselves into one harmonious vision, instead manage to *cancel* each other out: the economic sees the pastoral as the workplace; the political sees it as the voting booth (why else is Iowa a first stop in the American primary circuit?); the aesthetic sees it as the place of beauty; the scientific sees it as the ecologically sound; the medical sees it as the healthful. Amidst all these crisscrossing perspectives, the pastoral abides.

In this manner, the pastoral is not a common ground but an ungrounded rhetorical common, a place where irreconcilable, contingent distinctions may intersect and
have their say. Foucault terms such places "heterotopias," "which are something
like counter-sites, a kind of effectively enacted utopia in which the real sites, all the
other real sites that can be found within the culture, are simultaneously represented,
contested, and inverted. Places of this kind are outside of all places, even though it
may be possible to indicate their location in reality. . . . perhaps the oldest example
of these heterotopias that take the form of contradictory sites is the garden" (24–25).
In the garden, figured broadly as the pastoral, the joint realization of meaning that is
the essence of communication can begin, because no angle of vision does not belong
here. The strength of the pastoral is that, as a continuum of a great many possibles, it
can and does support all of those distinctions. This is because the pastoral has never
been characterized by purity; it has endured precisely because of its topical impurity,
its capacity to function as a mixed metaphor, a topos of hetero-origins. Unlike the
motif of the wilderness, which has not developed a comparable semantic flexibility,
the pastoral resists overdetermination by the economic because it galvanizes the
attention of so many other observational domains. Why is that? From its inception,
the pastoral has always promoted partial vision: between culture and nature, city and
wilderness, individual and collective, work and play. The pastoral is the via media
that invites paradoxical observations and exposes them. And the vectored sum of
these observations is a standoff—and perhaps the hoped-for systems pluralism that
would permit positive intersystem resonance.

Still, there may be other emergent green topoi, ones that, like the pastoral, would
permit the problem of the environment—which is really a problem of systems—to at
last become a topic of productive social communication rather than its blockage.[12]
The goal of a systems approach will be to find and study those communicational
resources that can help *neutralize* the economic system, which continues to purchase
its own autopoiesis at the expense of the other systems and the larger environment. If
we ever expect to find a sustainable home in this world, to produce an environmental
renaissance (a misnomer, I know, since we have never given birth to one before), we
must foster these other sources of social knowledge and let them be heard over the
market's blare. And perhaps the pastoral is what we are looking for. Indeed, there is
a growing trend among environmental communicators to repudiate purist notions
of environment based on wilderness in favor of a restorationist or reconstructivist
version of nature based on the pastoral. For a fact, wilderness as a battle cry has
rallied loudly; but so too only intermittently and never as steadily and widely as the
quietly rallying garden. Maybe that is because for so long the garden was located
literally at the edge of culture, while wilderness stood outside. The pastoral topos
represents a way to bring that outside into the system, where, very simply, we can

talk about it. And the discussion begins as it always does: in the struggle to find the words, the symbols, the themes, the languages that allow meaning to appear among us, and make improbable communication probable.

Toward Environmental Criticism

Of Emerson, Leo Marx writes that "No major writer had come closer to expressing the popular conception of man's relation to nature in nineteenth-century America" (230). I take it that this attribution is something of a compliment, if not to the conception itself then at least to Emerson's perspicacity in registering it. But for current-day environmental philosophers and deep ecologists Emerson's stock remains rather low. Thoreau's, on the other hand, is way up. It is hard not to see, for example, a fairly direct rejection of Marx's comment in Lawrence Buell's recent assessment of Thoreau: "no writer in the literary history of America's dominant subculture comes closer than he to standing for nature in both the scholarly and the popular mind" (*Environmental*, 2). Max Oelschlager, another Thoreauvian, sums up Emerson's contribution to the discourse of nature as follows: "For Emerson a wilderness odyssey was nothing more than occasion for mind to discover a reflection, first, of itself (nature as system of laws, concepts, and commodities), and then, finally, to confirm God's existence" (276). Scott Russell Sanders agrees: "Emerson was always a little too eager to hear the cultural mutterings of his own well-stocked mind, and thus his landscapes are less substantial than those drawn by many writers who followed his precepts—including, most famously, Thoreau" (188). Emerson, in other words, was interested in nature only inasmuch as it revealed something about humankind's position in the universe. Emerson may have enjoyed the woods and the swamps, but he could not write about them with the kind of passion for detail that Thoreau possessed. Emerson, self-described as "a very indifferent botanist" (w 12:150), is understood to have merely *used* those places to further another agenda, and certainly never argued *for* them except where they served to warrant those claims. What separates a true nature/environmental writer from one who simply wants to make nature a touchstone for other, more human-oriented projects is this attention to the environmental real and its complement, the ecocentric (read, decentered or nonanthropocentric) concept of self. Thus are we able to distinguish the impure from the pure, the shallow from the deep, the venal from the virtuous. Emerson is no good to us, Oelschlager seems to say, because he stood solely on the side of man; Thoreau on the other hand is virtuous because he wished to "speak a word for nature."

Yet what exactly does this mean, to conclude that Emerson was merely one of those "champions of civilization" Thoreau defined himself against? No doubt it is true that Thoreau was the better naturalist and walked the woods more than did Emerson; but beyond demonstrating the very obvious point that some writers are more engaged with the natural world than others, how does this segregation of the shallow from the deep on the basis of one's outdoorsy bona fides actually contribute to ecocriticism? Of course it is obvious that I am interested in challenging the value of this kind of partitioning in part because I find the deep/shallow distinction rooted in the reductive moral coding of the world. And although I think the effort to refocus on texts' instantiation of an environmental real is salutary, the idea that this real can be separated from the sociocultural conditions of its construction is, from the perspective of current critical theory, naive. Yet ecocriticism as it has developed in the last decade has staked much on the idea that critics must work assiduously to reassert the environmental real of the text, very often by showing how the author uses environmental descriptions to orchestrate a shift from an anthropocentric worldview to an ecocentric one. As with the deep ecologists, many ecocritics adhere to a more or less radical (but to my mind futile) impulse to sweep aside the cultural baggage that interferes with our apprehension of nature as it appears in literature, so as to reveal the dusty but still compelling environmental real buried under generations of anthropocentric criticism. Thus do Jonathan Bate and Karl Kroeber (in *Romantic Ecology* and *Ecological Literary Criticism,* respectively) resuscitate the Romantics' worshipful inscription of nature in poetry by recasting it into environmentalist terms—and then claim that in doing so they have generated an ecological criticism. Even Buell, whose monumental study of the environmental imagination in American literature and culture as filtered through Thoreau is thus far the principal text of the nascent ecocritical school, describes his book as a meditation on "the consequences for literary scholarship and indeed for humanistic thought in general of attempting to imagine a more 'ecocentric' way of being" (*Environmental,* 1).

I want to take up the theoretical drawbacks of this notion of "a more 'ecocentric' way of being" in a moment, but perhaps now is the time to acknowledge that Buell's ecocritical writings (and his pre-ecocritical work on Emerson and Thoreau, too, for that matter) cast a long shadow over this book, eclipsing it in advance as it were. I suspect they will do the same to every other attempt to reconfigure the ecocritical map. One cannot help but be awed by Buell's lucid, elegant style, his vast erudition and critical scope, his eye for details and ability to render them intelligible. Ecocriticism could have no better founding father. My reservations are not with his enormously helpful typologies and interpretations of the environmental imagination as manifested in literature, his interesting analyses of the big ideas he believes have contributed to ecological decline, but rather with the basic theory of cultural work presupposed by his sort of literary criticism, which in my reading takes as its sole political goal consciousness-raising. At least since Frank Lentricchia's

Criticism and Social Change, it has been understood that this goal is to be pursued in the context of pedagogy, with students and others in the community of inquiry the immediate beneficiaries of edification, and the wider community benefiting by extension. But should consciousness-raising, as the almost unspoken upshot of all that ecocritics do, be where their job ends? Should the result of the ecocritical endeavor—the communication of the critical reading itself to an engaged audience— mark a satisfactory conclusion to the process? Given that, as Luhmann has argued, the communication of environmental stimuli through the social system is entirely problematic, I think we need to attend much more carefully to the communication trail of the ecocritical result. We need to know, in other words, if there is *any* result that can be tracked beyond the literary system itself. Buell's challenge, then, is not simply to model an ecocriticism that will help shape an ecocritically charged pedagogy. (It is clear he has done that in spades.) His further challenge is to help us understand how doing ecocriticism makes a difference that actually makes a difference for the environment.

He writes that "it behooves us to look searchingly at the most searching works of environmental reflection that the world's biggest technological power has produced; for in these we may expect to find disclosed (not always with full self-consciousness, of course) both pathologies that bedevil society at large and some of the alternative paths it might consider" (*Environmental,* 2). According to his second major eco- critical intervention, he hopes "the reader will share [his] sense both of the power of environmental influences as a shaping force in works of creative imagination and of the power of those works, contending against the foreshortened vision that afflicts us all, to articulate what 'environment' is and might be" (*Writing,* 29). But are these not loose and inarguable targets? I find nowhere else in Buell's two books a more vigorous formulation of how he supposes ecocriticism shall mitigate those patholo- gies and afflictions, nor even a framework within which one could imagine how vision could be anything but foreshortened. In other words, the political/pragmatic dimension of Buell's work is undertheorized, with the synoptic attention to the va- garies of environmental imagining replacing a critical engagement with the obstacles to ecocritical praxis. What is ecocriticism for? Buell shows us only that ecocriticism can read (though, to be sure, in Buell's hands it can read very well).

In his earlier career as a literary historian of the American Renaissance and New England culture more generally, he was modest about the practical ends of criticism: provocation of other scholars and students through recontextualization and new interpretations based on meticulous research into periodization, canonicity, genre, and historical records. Buell's more recent criticism is undertaken with similar restraint. He is clear on the point that environmental facts can change the way we read literature; he is less clear about how reading literature might change an environmental fact. But with so much at stake, one wishes he would bring to bear his considerable acumen on the linkage between a literary articulation of the environment, its critical analysis, and the ongoing disarticulation of the environment by the social system. He comes closest to staking out a position in the special issue of *New Literary History* on ecocriticism:

> [E]cocritics have every right to believe that if they do their jobs right—not, of course to be taken for granted—they will not only be able to reveal to fellow literature department colleagues some hidden things about even the most familiar and classic works but also have a basis to consider themselves participants in a pandisciplinary inquiry of the first order of historical significance. From the multiple epicenters of this inquiry—through a mixture of collaboration, solitary concentration, and sheer luck—not just new regulatory codes, pharmaceuticals, engineering marvels and the like may ensue but new insights, new revaluations of the physical world and humanity's relation to it, that will make a difference in the way others live their lives. Admittedly nothing is more shocking for many humanists than to find their ideas taken seriously. But it might just happen in this case. That self-identified ecocritics tend to be folk who seriously entertain that possibility is one reason why the best ecocritical work is so strange, timely, and intriguing. (709–10)

This "pandisciplinary," multicentered inquiry is inherently appealing: it commends the emergence of a third culture that would move past C. P. Snow's two solitudes of humanities and sciences; it casts literary critics in important roles, coequal to the technologists and policy makers; it frames the overall project of inquiry in visionary terms. There is also a sense that the project's goals—no less than an overhaul of our relation to the world—require that systemic barriers to communication be overcome, that the disciplines must talk not just to one another, but to business too, along with government, the law, and so forth. It is worth noting, however, that this vision is entirely prospective; it is not something Buell claims is real, only that ecocritics will "have every right to believe" in its promise if they "do their jobs right." The whimsical quality of this passage is such that Buell closes by telling us that "it might just happen": I call this the glass half-full school of ecocriticism, and as I said at the beginning of this book I have no objection to it in principle. "For dialogue!" is always a fair response, a nod to the unfathomable ways in which talk might lead to action, and I agree that the best place to start the dialogue is at home. [13] But I believe to make those differences that might actually make a difference we must start, too, with far more pessimism about our chances of ever being taken seriously. As I have maintained, never has a school of criticism needed to think through more carefully the connection between its everyday practice and its worldly effect. But only when we come clean about the involuted, closed-shop character of the ecocritical dialogue will we be in a position to reflect on how it might be otherwise. That inwardness has nothing to do with the motives, intentions, and public stature of ecocritics, by the way; it has everything to do with the organization and programming of the systems of communication within which ecocritics operate. And even if we determine that that programming is impervious to ecocriticism (as I fear), well, then at least we would know what sort of conversation we were having. Recognizing that we are operating in an echo chamber might even elevate the dialogue—or radicalize it.

But to return now to the issue of the " 'ecocentric' way of being": does Buell mean that ecocritics should not be equally interested in why our literature has to date produced so little in the ecocentric way of being and so much in the antiecocentric way of being? The telling irony, then, that Buell here reveals about his books, and each of the other above-named ecocritical efforts, is that they are essentially calling for more ecocentrically charged approaches to what is the *already* ecocentrically charged tradition. In other words, what Bate, Kroeber, and Buell seem to envision is a kind of ecocriticism that knows in advance which authors are deep (or at least, protodeep) and then goes on to explain why. Authors who are *not* deep, quite frankly, are out of favor with those engaged in this sort of criticism. A brief perusal of recent, book-length ecocritical studies will confirm this pattern of attention to a familiar set of ecocentric writers: Thoreau, Burroughs, Muir, Austin, Leopold, Abbey, Carson, Dillard, and so on. The ecocentric bias extends to tastes in environmental theorists as well. For example, in Buell's reading of Luhmann on the inability of systems to match their environment point to point, he is surprised that "Luhmann himself seems to regard this prospect with complete equanimity" (*Writing,* 288). I agree with Buell that Luhmann's equanimity can be quite off-putting, like a grin on a corpse, but I suspect that what might be even more off-putting is Luhmann's outright dismissal of the moral approach, for morality, as we have seen, is at the heart of deep ecology and its ecocritical sympathizers. While I think Buell's work is too nuanced to be included unqualifiedly in that latter group, there is little doubt he tilts heavily toward Thoreau, the central presence in all his books, whose Romantic longing for "Contact!" takes us almost as far from a systems approach as deep ecology itself. And while Luhmann would say consciousness-raising is beside the point, Buell stakes his entire praxis on it. [14]

I do not mean to suggest, of course, that the work I have critiqued above is not valuable. Certainly it is, and for all of the reasons the writers of such studies adduce. But there are built-in imitations to the ecocentric approach. In a PMLA forum called "Literatures of the Environment," Simon Estok asks ecocritics a series of blunt questions: "How far can ecocriticism go from 'nature' and still be eco-criticism? What can discussions about texts that are silent on nature give us? Can someone such as Shakespeare fit into all this? How? How serious are we about making connections? . . . Are there revealing links between environmentally and socially oppressive systems, overlapping and interlocking structures that need to be examined? How far can we go with avoiding anthropocentrism?" (1096) He concludes his intervention with this rather stark challenge: "I have no interest in be-littling or criticizing the project of recouping professional dignity for what [Cheryll] Glotfelty called 'the undervalued genre of nature writing' . . . rather, I think it is important for all literary scholars to take the environment seriously, to see it as vital, to bother with the ways that we conceptualize and speak about (or are silent about) the natural environment. Otherwise, ecocriticism will be just one of those trends that temporarily guarantee an audience, publications, tenure, promotions, and so on. It won't change things." I could not agree more. I think if ecocriticism wishes to remain a rather inconsequential branch of literary criticism it can do no better than to continue buttressing the green canon and to shrink from a probing theoretical examination of what it thinks it is changing. If ecocriticism refuses to open up "environment" by defining it in a way that allows other literary scholars to find their way in, then ecocriticism will simply have chosen to harden up its own form of theoretical (and professional) bias, this time an ecocentric one.

In a discussion that takes Don DeLillo and Raymond Carver (among others) to task for their limited invocation of natural tropes, Scott Sanders sums up this "ecocentric-centrism": "However accurately it reflects the surface of our times, fiction that never looks beyond the human realm is profoundly false, and therefore pathological" (194). In effect, the sort of ecocriticism Sanders prefers works to elicit the overlooked or repressed environmental/ecological details of those particular texts (e.g., by Wordsworth or Thoreau) that are *manifestly* about nature anyway. But my point is that ecocriticism should be wary of this tendency to commit what I call the deep ecological fallacy: the idea that the job of ecocritics is, via the writers they approve of most, to champion, crudely speaking, the natural over cultural elements of the text under consideration, and so make their criticism uphold in a way that previous criticism did not the palpable and meaningful expression of selected texts' ecological unconscious. Perhaps ecocritics imagine that only in this way can they make good on their own environmental commitments in the world at large. But for ecocriticism to appear to those who do not practice it (but might) as more than simply a greening of the canon or the hagiography of favored authors (both activities, again I hasten to add, valuable in their own right, but hardly comprehensive), it seems to me that it must try to account for more than the particular attachments and predilections of individual writers. It must instead place their words in the contexts that extend well beyond the quotidian details of their ecosurround; it must do, in fact, exactly that which some in the ecocritical movement think ecocriticism should *not* do: talk about environment in terms that do not restrict it to questions of nature, landscape, or place. Rather than simply explaining through a green canon why ecocritics prize some environments over others or why other critics with different commitments have marginalized nature as setting, we must dare to do much, much more.

But what exactly? Where is one left as a literary or cultural critic still committed to making one's work a type of environmental activism? My own assumption has been that we require environmentally engaged critiques that *do not* hinge on the piling up of all the potentially ambiguous nature-related details of the texts in question. That road leads back, first, to a naive privileging of the realist text[15] and, second, to a naive rejection of literary theory in favor of analogies drawn from ecology. There is nothing stable enough in nature or even ecological science on which to build a critical social theory, let alone a literary theory. It is precisely because human social systems integrate so poorly with natural ecologies that we have environmental problems in the first place. We look to ecology for a stamp of approval on our cultural theories at our peril. What must be acknowledged, rather—and I have made this point many times before—is that the notion of environment cannot begin and end with nature, this entity that no serious person invokes without a disclaimer. Instead let us carry through on the premise that every text—not just the "most searching works of environmental reflection"—has a more broadly conceived environmental unconscious, that it creates for itself a systematized space of operation *inside* and an unsystematized *outside,* which it cannot by definition observe. Only second-order observers can do that. And what *that* means, I think, is that such observers ought to be less sanguine about carving out a distinct realm of ecocriticism (understood as a mode that distinguishes ecocentric textual practices from anthropocentric ones) and more focused on transforming criticism in general. If in *all* texts we understand ourselves to be faced with many different kinds of environments and environmental perspectives, *ecological* criticism might become part of a more broadly conceived *environmental* criticism.

Just to be clear, I am claiming that it is *not* the devotional texts of the green canon that need to be recuperated to an environmental agenda; they almost take care of themselves. Rather, it is every other text. What is needed are studies of antiecological and a-ecological writings, because those are the texts that constitute our true environmental heritage: the heritage of stupidity, destruction, greed, or, more sweepingly and accurately, the heritage of blindness that is associated with every parochial observation. Environmental criticism must look to the contexts that are unremarked, those that lie outside of what is distinguished; *environment* in systems terms is simply everything that the text does not speak about, or that is spoken about only to the extent that it may be safely contained, ignored, or overridden by other programs and distinctions the text finds more compelling. Environmental criticism is thus a criticism of ignorance.

Environmental criticism would explore the ramifications of perspectival and communicational differences in the creation of systems and environments—including but not confined to this polymorphous entity we have historically lumped under the term *nature*. Like the systems theoretical approach advocated by William Rasch and Cary Wolfe, this sort of environmental criticism, "by providing analyses that are not ontologically grounded along the lines of the traditional dichotomies governing thought which guide both idealism in its Kantian and Cartesian forms and materialism in its Marxist form (subject/object, human/nonhuman, culture/nature, organic/mechanical) . . . offers the possibility of a theory of knowledge that can account with greater range and power for what Latour has called the 'hybrid networks' of social, informational, and ecological systems in which we will find ourselves increasingly enmeshed in the coming years" (12). A criticism of systems and environment could thus take up the same concerns already explored under analyses of race, class, gender, nation, and so on. But make no mistake: this more broadly defined environmental criticism will still have much to say about environmental problems per se and nature traditionally understood, for what ecocriticism seeks to achieve by inculcating a more ecocentric way of being is, roughly speaking, the same sort of attention to local knowledges and multiple subject positions that a theory of autonomous systems also seeks. The crucial difference, however, is that whereas ecocritics hope to generate greater sensitivity to nature by teaching readers how to attend more carefully to the details of ecology and natural history that hitherto have been overlooked, the kind of systems savvy, environmental critic I am imagining will understand those details as distinctions made by observing systems, ones that could always have been otherwise. The way the observation was made, then, and not the observation itself is what is crucial—epistemology, in other words, over ontology. And while this latter critic may be every bit as concerned as the ecocritic for the fate of animals or ecosystems described and every bit as committed to promoting environmental awareness and a corresponding ethic of concern, this critic also understands that the question of consciousness-raising in individuals remains only one facet of a massively larger problem. (For a fact, being sensitive to or liking nature has never guaranteed preservation; people can like something but treat it inimically. Think, for example, of the animal lover who eats meat or the logger who lives only to be working in the woods.)

Environmental criticism therefore has a wider goal than unlocking the particular forms of nature awareness that it believes are expressed by writers, reside in texts, and can be revealed by attentive readers. Environmental criticism must also develop the frameworks within which those forms of awareness can be understood as social communications—social communications perhaps stimulated by environmental perturbations, it is true, but that nevertheless exist as communication and only as communication. Awareness, such as it is, can never be direct, transparent, and permanent with respect to environments, for these always remain fundamentally inscrutable from the perspective of a system. They are, very simply, that which does not communicate. We must bear in mind—no matter how easy it is to forget—that only by changing the system do we change its interactions with an environment. It matters little that one thousand, one million, or one hundred million Americans read *Walden* if there is no pathway by which to communicate its message from conscious minds to social systems. Why presume that because a few sensitive souls have found a way to think like a mountain that their fellow Americans will follow? Why presume that in the unlikely event they did follow, it would mean a jot to the global economy's appetites? The billions who have professed love for the peaceful doctrines of Jesus, Mohammed, and Gandhi only serve to make us wonder what the world would have been like if all along we had been following doctrines of hate; similarly, the doctrine of interspecies equity and ecocentric justice is no substitute for the hard work of actually figuring out how to make the system less risky. So, to put it in conventional terms, the problem is not to decipher what nature has to tell us (whether revealed in direct observation, through artistic and literary representation, or any other way, including, I suppose, an epiphany experienced while crossing a bare common or climbing a mountain in Maine) and then to broadcast this revelation to the world; it is rather to observe and theorize how systems establish environments in the process of communicating with and among themselves, and, to a lesser degree, how conscious systems interpenetrate them. (And I do not say "reprogram them" because, firstly, like all autopoietic entities, they program themselves; secondly, they are barely susceptible to all but the most extraordinary manipulations, with the results of such manipulations largely unpredictable; and thirdly, the sort of concentrated political power required to perform such manipulations might be more frightening than not taking the program in hand at all.) As critics—and this will be the stumbling block for many in the ecocritical community—we must be concerned with the observation of the observation, not the observation itself, and we should be interested in asking questions like "What would it take to square an economically inflected version of nature with an aesthetic one?" and not, as is too often the temptation, questions like "What does nature teach us?" Environmental critique, as an implicit social system critique, is thus about comprehending the notion of environment as a function of systems and about observing how such systems in turn function as environments for other systems. The goals are to theorize how systems interact; how new, more beneficial linkages between them might be formed; and, with respect to the literary system and its study, how a system with much to say but few to hear can be strengthened so as to resonate more robustly with other systems.

I give a brief example to illustrate the difference between an ecocritical and an environmental reading of a literary text. DeLillo's *White Noise* is the touchstone. It is a text that has already been used by others to test the reach of ecocriticism. In *Writing for an Endangered World*, for example, Buell notes that the central crisis of the story, the "airborne toxic event," is part of the broader "toxic discourse" of contemporary risk society, which, among other things, signals a cultural need for a "way of imagining physical environments that fuses social constructivist with environmental restorationist perspectives. Against the model often favored by ecocriticism hitherto, of an 'ecological holism' to which acts of imagination have the capacity to (re)connect us, toxic discourse holds that belief in the availability of such a holism by such means is chimerical and divisive" (45). At the same time, there is clear value in "both the rhetorical appeal and the benefit to human and planetary welfare of the ideal of a purified physical environment as an end in itself." Thus, toxic discourse performs double duty "to reinforce the deromanticization and to urge the expansion of 'nature' as an operative category." More precisely, Buell argues that *White Noise*'s toxic event, though invoked by DeLillo primarily to ironize the superficiality of middle-class suburbanite Jack Gladney's life and his scholarly obsession with Hitler, also has the effect of registering if not entirely comprehending America's anxiety about "toxic victimage" in the era of Love Canal and Superfund (52). While Sanders might read *White Noise* as a repression of toxic discourse and thus a turning away from nature toward the usual set of homocentric concerns, Buell refreshingly reads it as evidence of at least a "partial emergence" of awareness of toxicity from the environmental unconscious. But his concern is that by reading *White Noise* against the grain, he does a certain kind of violence to this nongreen text: "My metaphor [toxic discourse] elides, derealizes, somebody else's pain" (51). In other words, he worries about using Gladney's (and DeLillo's) toxic anxiety to score points for the environment at the expense of Holocaust memory, Gladney's trivialization of which the toxic event in the strong reading of the novel is clearly meant to underline. As Buell probes the effective range of ecocriticism,[16] he anticipates the point I want to make here a bit more strongly: that ecocriticism, as currently constituted, has no stake in reading texts that are not identifiably green because to do so makes the violence Buell describes inevitable. If you see as your rightful purview texts that explore human-nature dynamics then you must be wary of the vast bulk of American literature. By contrast, environmental criticism works equally well with texts that are problematic (as *White Noise* is) from an ecocentric perspective, or that are even anathema to such a perspective. That is because the critical interest lies not in the decisive moments of ecocentric awareness (or repression, suppression, or disavowal) but in any moments when texts are engaged in firming up distinctions that create environments that only second-order observers can see. Thus, it is irrelevant to environmental criticism whether DeLillo is commenting on toxicity and risk society or is simply using the toxic event to lay bare Gladney's shallowness. If the latter, DeLillo merely confirms that first-order observers are blind to the distinctions they use to observe, and that the environments created by those distinctions are relegated to communication's outside. If the former, DeLillo is a second-order observer of his own narratival distinction. Whatever the case (and one could summon textual or extratextual evidence to adjudicate if one is so inclined) the significant issue is this: it is not simply the "airborne toxic event" that makes this novel interesting to environmental criticism but potentially *all* its events, for there is nothing in this novel that does not imply an environment of one kind or another—Gladney's dysfunctional ménage, the college town, the television discourse, the Hitler studies program. All of these systems construct environments for themselves and are in turn constructed as environments by others. So to focus only on those incidents or settings that seem to register or fail to register ecotopoi is entirely reductive and leaves out the incontrovertible fact that anything in any novel is always registering an environment. Not every environment is going to be of interest to the critic, but the risk is that in ignoring some in favor of those most obviously concerned with the *oikos,* the critic will overlook that which may actually have the most to tell us about our human social system—how it got here, what costs are incurred to change it, what costs are incurred to keep it, what is excluded through its virtues, what is included through its vices, why it persists, why it is failing, why it is succeeding, and, centrally, why the problem of nature has to be understood not as a failure of the social system but as the very essence of its success. Though it cannot be in practice, in theory, environmental criticism is total criticism.

Robert Kern takes up this issue, helpfully I think, by noting that "ecocriticism becomes most interesting and useful . . . when it aims to recover the environmental character or orientation of works whose conscious or foregrounded interests lie elsewhere" (11). As he puts it, ecocriticism is "reductive when it simply targets the environmentally incorrect, or when it aims to evaluate texts solely on the basis of their adherence to ecologically-sanctioned standards of behavior" (11–12). What I am suggesting is very much in line with Kern's notion that ecocriticism is chiefly "a form of environmental advocacy" and not (or not only) literary criticism—though, to be sure, the advocacy cannot be effective if it appears as "literary or textual policing" (11). Ecocriticism would be "a critical and literary tool, a kind of reading designed to expose and facilitate analysis of a text's orientation both to the world it imagines and to the world in which it takes shape, along with the conditions and contexts that affect that orientation, whatever it might be. Texts, in this outlook, are environmental, but not necessarily environmental*ist*" (11). The danger of expanding ecocriticism to consider any text as potentially environmental (and thus blunting the specificity of the approach and sacrificing the text to the critical principle) is avoided by instead expanding the definition of *environmental* past a narrow preoccupation with nature to include any of a system's external unknowns. What is gained is a more generous, robust critical approach that moves us, ironically, away from the risks of a narrow ecocritical particularism toward an expansive engagement with the literary text as *literature,* the second-order observing device par excellence.

A woman is sitting on the deck of a cottage looking across a northern lake toward a newly constructed coal-fired generating plant on the far shore. Out on the lake, a canoeist paddles slowly by; a pair of loons dive, rise, and call; a V formation of geese honks overhead, wheeling to the west in search of a calm patch of water; an oily residue clings to a wave-washed, granite ledge. The woman ignores the foreground and continues to stare at the power plant. Presently she gets up and goes inside, perhaps to write yet another angry letter to her congressman. The question is this: is there anything about the foreground that could have prevented what has happened in the background? The lake provides contrast with the power plant, and in time the lake may even be destroyed by its effluents, but to comprehend the origin (and, perhaps, the end) of the power plant, one cannot dwell exclusively on nature. Said another way, to avoid toxic victimage one must sometimes ignore the beautiful view and contemplate the ugly one. But by keeping its gaze locked on nature, ecocriticism may never get off the porch. If this example is too cryptic, let me put it this way: ecocriticism wields a double-edged sword, in that what inspires it (nature) cannot be used against what it wishes to strike (the programming of the social system). There is no nature—and no nature problem—except from the perspective of a system. As Thoreau might have said, sometimes to see the woods you have to go into the town.

I anticipate the complaint that by defining the terms of the engagement as above I am simply bracketing out the very topos—nature—I (and ecocriticism) wanted to consider in the first place, and so now find myself, ineluctably, moving toward what would seem to be a highly anthropocentric position. Yet only if we imagine that a truly ecocentric criticism is possible in the first place can what I am suggesting be charged with anthropocentrism. Rather, I began this book by arguing that criticism is *always* system bound, and so, as we attend to environments from within our anthropic spaces, criticism too must be unavoidably anthropocentric. There is no reason to want it to be otherwise, for that would require the relinquishment of the self-reflective capacity that allows us to see why our anthropocentrism is so invidious in the first place. The best we can ever achieve is the cultivation of a more fully balanced and complexified set of observations of this otherness that we will no doubt continue to call, following a long and probably invulnerable tradition, nature. It is nature, and all that nature's degradation bodes for life (humankind included), that moves us; it is nature that supplies ecocritics with their passion and urgency. But it is not nature that provides the solution to the problem of nature. Nature is observed under systemic constraints, and so it is the character of those constraints and their modes of observation that require our scrutiny. Such observations may conform to any one of an array of systemic selections of environments that remain unknown, whose perturbations always and at any time can be glossed by individuals as evidence of the "Chaos and Old Night" that Thoreau perceived on top of Ktaadn, "the beautiful mother" of Emerson, or the "resources" of Roosevelt and Pinchot. The environmental critic wants to comprehend and remove the programmatically conditioned barriers *between* these various sorts of selections, to challenge those who speak in the name of systems to talk across their boundaries more considerately, in an attempt to ensure that what gets communicated about our environments will lead to less destructive, less counterproductive, and less cruel practices. This critic will make the attempt despite knowing full well that each of the various subsystems of the modern social system is seeking to foreground its own unique bias in the environmental unconscious of individuals.

The attempt thus begins in the context of its own ongoing failure. Ultimately, the only solutions to the nature problem—this great constellation of issues that extends from climate change to toxic food, from the commodification of animals to the warping of the genome itself—appear to lie in the direction of a greater differentiation of systemic positions rather than in their unification; an augmented network of interchanges between such positions rather than consensus; and an expansion of our measures of worth rather than, as Thoreau may have hoped, a simple and reliable economy of inherent, moral value. This is, admittedly, a tall order. But the perfectability of organisms or society once imagined by Enlightenment thinkers turns out to be, quite literally, a dead end. Maintaining and increasing the diversity of perspective, as with the diversity of genetic material, is the only survival strategy that appears to work across time and populations, as the fossils of hypertrophied species and overspecialized societies alike prove out. Ethical evolution—punctuated, fitful, and transitory as it often is—can continue only if we assure the many and varied ways of seeing the world are never occluded, the ways of voicing it never silenced. Some might still suppose that if only we can find a way to make certain the moral view of nature reigned supreme and universal, the rest will take care of itself. But from the systems perspective, just the opposite obtains: only by keeping in play all of the possible vectors of social communication can anything like balance between systems and environments ever be approached. In the same way that the structure of capitalism itself has yet to force capitalism's own demise, we cannot depend on nature to initiate changes in the social system any time soon, which is to say, not until a time when most of what we value about the nonhuman world has already been lost. Instead, the social system must tell itself how to listen to itself; in all likelihood what that entails is for each subsystem to differentiate itself ever more significantly from its peers, developing paradoxically both its capacity to run its own programs without regard to its environment *and* its capacity to select for and respond more congenially to stimuli in that environment. The latter capacity is not achieved out of good will; it is a direct result of the drive to achieve the former. This is not a formula for a balance of harmony but for a balance of terror: the model is mutually assured destruction. In this respect, since it is the economy that causes the most damage to the larger natural environment, one might reasonably wish for a day when the economy would be impotent to pollute and degrade the planet's ecosystemic services or draw down its unrenewable resources because to do so would instantly disturb and threaten the operations of the systems of health, science, law, and so on, which now would be as complexly single-minded as the economy. These other systems would consider any deployment of the old economic program (that is, processing all nature as externality or fodder) for what it always has been: a mortal threat to their own autopoiesis. Before the economy could do its dirty work these other subsystems would have sounded a klaxon that the political system could not ignore. To paraphrase Freud, the system must be a wolf to the system.

At the same time, I do not believe that taking the systems view is a recipe for an all-encompassing and hence flaccid moral/ethical pluralism. Rather, what social systems theory suggests is that pluralism is one response to environmental complexity: moral relativity and the incorporation of divergent viewpoints is the only option for complex systems that wish to remain viable. Relativism may create the impression that no viewpoint is better than another, but that is simply a price to be paid for assuring that the reduction of environmental complexity is not achieved at the cost of internal complexity. And, as I suggested in the introduction, ecocritical activity that flaunts a higher ethics is merely a sop that fills the gap where a viable green politics should go.

As David Mazel points out, we seem to have forgotten that an older usage of the noun *environment* privileged its active root, encapsulated in the now archaic verb form, *to environ* (*American,* 35–36). Environing is an activity that occurs whether we approve of it or not, for through autopoiesis organisms seek to control their boundaries within a larger field, an environment. By definition, each organism locates itself at the center of its *Umwelt* so that, if we wish to be rigorous in our usage, every living system must be understood as self-centric. In keeping with that usage, *Homo sapiens* has never been, despite frequent claims, a species that adapts well to its environments; it is, rather, an animal that preeminently seeks to environ itself in spaces (physical and conceptual) of its own making.[17] And what *that* means is that hand-wringing over our anthropocentrism (followed by well-intentioned but mostly vacuous calls to expunge it) will likely lead us nowhere. The "crowning irony" of that view, as Garret Keizer puts it, is that "to bring about a truly 'ecocentric' revolution, humankind would have to exercise a nobility of spirit that all but the most visionary humanists would have blushed to conceive" (44). The most pressing theoretical issues stemming from our current environing practices are no longer ones that can be charted on anthropocentric/ecocentric, natural/cultural, deep/shallow axes (not to mention a traditional left/right one). No, the most pressing issues have to do with learning how, why, and for whom do we insist on environing ourselves in spaces that conform overwhelmingly to the code of the economy. Environmental criticism, therefore, cannot be about trying to prod individuals to love, fear, or respect nature; that they will do for their own reasons and along a host of pathways that with few exceptions are outside the reach of criticism. Environmental criticism, as I imagine it, must instead be about an older *critical* task, a task that in its best moments steers at the stars, knowing full well it will never reach them. It is a task that in its American incarnations may yet be termed Emersonian: Where in our talking America do we find ourselves? Why have we drawn some things within our favored circles while sealing many other things out? How can we speak across our self-produced silences and enlarge our circles with dialogue beyond calculation, whose benefit overruns its merit? There is no doubt that nature—as the name for what appears sometimes within, sometimes without those circles—will continue to mark a crucial, if ill-defined, point of reference in their delineation. "Nature does not like to be observed," Emerson said (cw 3:29), but "nature will be reported" (cw 4:151). That we cannot see does not mean we will not speak. And so, as in the parable of the blind men and the elephant, we will do well to consider that nature may simply stand for that which passes in darkness and remind ourselves that no single vision can convey the environmental richness that we, in our dangerous but necessary blindness, occasionally sense is out there.

Coda

I conclude on a somewhat ambivalent note, which I think is more apropos the ethos of ecocriticism at present, and likely to remain so, necessarily, unless the portents change.

Faced with the daunting prospect of configuring a whole new range of concerns, ecocritics are understandably tentative in making any totalizing claims as to what ecocriticism can and should do. The systems approach I have outlined may seem to some readers to err too much in that direction. However, there is one totalizing claim few dare make but with which I suspect we all agree: namely, that there are no more pressing issues in contemporary theory—and that includes literary theory—than the ones ecocriticism wants to address. If even the most conservative projections are true, the twenty-first century appears to be shaping up as the epoch in which natural limits will reemerge with a vengeance. It is also likely—and this, significantly, may speak volumes about the root, autopoietic causes of the entire mess—that humans will find ways to adapt to the changing conditions. We are already taking to lathering on sunblock, drinking bottled water, weathering summer in winter, and forgetting what dawn once sounded like. But the fact that we can grimly put up with a thousand minor degradations in the name of economic necessity may be the least of our problems, for the biological impoverishment of the world, the reconfiguration of climates, and the toxification of the material bases for life will bring to the First World the kinds of human suffering and inequity now seen only in the Third—and with them a new world order Bushes Senior and Junior never imagined.

One of the best arguments for developing nonecocentric ecocritical perspectives, then, is that we need them to help prevent the erosion of gains that other critical schools have already made. Under the conditions I have just alluded to, other types of literary theoretical models currently more visible than ecocriticism may begin to lose some of their urgency, if none of their cogency. Critiques that have long pushed eloquently and forcefully for social justice, in effect, may take a backseat to the brutal logic of pure survival. People will not hear arguments on the fine points of sexism or the micropolitics of literary canon formation in a lifeboat; worse, no one may pause to note that "women and children first" smacks of the patriarchy or that the wealthy have taken the seats while the poor hang from the gunwales. I trust I will not be taken to say that those critiques could ever be irrelevant; I think I have already made it clear that environmental criticism as I imagine it cannot be understood apart from the whole panoply of issues raised by feminists, workers, intellectuals, aboriginals, animal rights activists, deconstructionists, Marxists, religionists, and, yes, liberal humanists. I am simply pointing out that in the same way that politicians now tell us environmental protection is possible only in a strong and expanding economy, in the dangerous decades ahead they may say that justice is a luxury we cannot afford, that broad social health in fact requires a more tough-minded approach to the society's and the planet's nonadaptive members.

While I would like to believe that the precious structures of civility and inclusiveness fought for and won by previous generations may yet be maintained in a climate of increasing environmental scarcity, I am reminded that my own generation has seen so much retrograde political, economic, and social movement that many of us have begun to question the whole notion of social progress in the first place. Perhaps democracy itself was only a brief interlude, to be replaced, as Andrew Ross suggests, by a "Chicago Gangster Theory of Life," wherein the social contract is exchanged for the corporate-backed feudal arrangement darkly forecasted by Christopher Lasch, Lewis Lapham, and Robert Kaplan, not to mention William Gibson and a slew of other prescient science fiction writers. Perhaps the functionally differentiated social system that Luhmann claims is unsurpassable (and which has indeed made untenable many of the hierarchies that blighted most of human history) could dedifferentiate given the right stimuli. A new sedimentation might then occur, a renaissance of a different kind, with roles, resources, possibilities, and programs for humans and others that would make our own time the halcyon days of the earth.

We all hope it never comes to that. The calamity awaiting our slow and inadequate responses to the signs of ecological collapse is a nightmare I do not wish to contemplate. Instead, I would rather pursue active and appropriate praxis in the quotidian spaces I inhabit. As a scholar of language and literature, I turn my attention to this question: what work can my field do to form part of the cure, if cure there is? Social systems can fail to acknowledge lethal perils, and nature never knows it faces them. Only human beings may observe their own demise.

Notes

Introduction: The Problem of Nature

1. While many systems theorists begin by claiming unequivocally "there are systems" and "do not advocate a 'purely analytical relevance' for systems theory [because] the concept of system refers to something that is in reality a system and thereby incurs the responsibility of testing its statements against reality" (Luhmann, ss, 12), others make the distinction between concrete systems ("nonrandom accumulation of matter-energy, in a region in physical space-time, which is organized into interacting or interrelated components") and abstracted systems ("relationships abstracted or selected by an observer in the light of his interests, theoretical viewpoint, or philosophical bias. *Some relationships may be empirically determinable by some operations carried out by the observer, but others are not, being only his concepts*") (Miller, 17–19; my emphasis).

2. The relationship between culture and society is a long-standing question mark in both the humanities (the collection of disciplines that tends to focus on cultural questions) and the social sciences (especially sociology, which of course takes society in toto as its problem field). The central question is: what is the connection between microcultural forms and activities and macrosocial, macroeconomic, and macropolitical mechanisms? Talcott Parsons, the most eminent American sociologist of the century, saw culture as one of the main subsystems in the functionally differentiated social system; Antonio Gramsci famously updated Marx's base-superstructure model to show that culture was the leading edge of potential shifts in the hegemonic power structures of society. There are a host of variations on these basic mechanistic and dialectical models, not to mention the widely held view that poststructuralism has pretty much driven a nail into the coffin of total social scientific description. Sociology itself has been taken to task not only by practitioners of cultural studies informed by poststructuralism but even by some sociologists who believe the search for social universals must be abandoned in favor of more local studies, i.e., exactly the sort of thing cultural studies has been doing since the days of Richard Hoggart and Raymond Williams. Needless to say, the assumption in this book is that culture and society are *not* the same thing, if only because we need a category for theories that aim to produce metacultural modeling. I would argue, in fact, that giving up on constrained macrosocial theories—ones cognizant of the challenges of the observer, situated knowledge, and local variability—is intellectually impossible. Macrosocial theory must be pursued if only on the basis of universalizing the problem of contingency and self-reference (e.g., Luhmann). We cannot *not* generalize. How,

for example, can we discuss globalization as it plays out at the level of a local culture if we do not have any way of theorizing globalization across cultures? In effect, you still need a social theory (or, better, a social systems theory) to talk about those things that while no longer understood to be universal *in* subjects are still universal in their capacity to *affect* subjects.

3. For a discussion of how ecological conditions may determine eating preferences, see Jared Diamond.

4. That ineffectuality, it seems to me, should not curtail ecocritical activity, though I will be at pains in this book to argue that ineffectuality must be confronted head-on. The pursuit of systemic inwardness is not restricted to the economy: in the university, a system in its own right, whole faculties of antienvironmentalism exist, in the sense that their knowledge projects have no bearing or bear negatively on the most pressing issue of our time. Ecocritics, to their credit and institutional peril, wish to steer their own disciplines in directions that at least confront, however elliptically given the insubstantial tools of their trade, the nature problem. The work of ecocriticism is to produce communications in the jargon of the university; accessibility beyond the ivory tower may be too much to ask for. Ecocritics undoubtedly help simply by thematizing the nature problem for others (colleagues, administrators, students, and staff) in their immediate system. The more ecocritics can reprogram the educational system to account for the nature problem the more this system will produce socially and environmentally beneficial output (i.e., graduates and expert communications). But the question remains: how much will a reprogrammed education system actually resonate productively with other systems? We clearly need more understanding of the limits of its reach—and how to extend its reach. (In chapter 5 I complicate this model somewhat, but I think the basic principle is sound from a systems point of view.)

5. My emphasis on the epistemological consequences of systems may surprise readers familiar with Luhmann, since Luhmann has written specifically on the environmental crisis in *Ecological Communication,* and so I might have been expected to filter my readings of Emerson and Thoreau through that book. Luhmann's warnings against anxiety and excessive moralizing do indeed inform my readings, but I do not share his (theoretically defensible to be sure) aloofness on the issue of whether there actually is or will be ecological catastrophe. For an excellent intellectual experiment that honors Luhmann's detachment more than I find myself able to, see Ingolfur Blühdorn's *Post-ecologist Politics.* Blühdorn, a political ecologist, takes Luhmann's thinking on environmental problems to its logical conclusion: that there really is no problem except a problem of perception, that the whole environmental movement has been in a sense the last (useless) gasp of the forces arrayed against modernization. Once the movement disappears, the problem of nature will also go away. Blühdorn brilliantly captures the sheer daring of Luhmann's achievement, which, if one steps back a bit, is to have made the social system appear to be the crown of creation, a kind of self-selecting superorganism that can deal with any problem it creates or encounters through self-generated solutions. Luhmann has, if one may put it this way, much confidence that what the social system needs, the social system will provide. Needless to say, my imagination puts it nearer to a borg, in that its capacity to assimilate all other species is to me no source of comfort. (For a

good sense of Luhmann's political quietism, see the interview in Rasch's *Niklas Luhmann's Modernity,* 195–221.)

6. Readers familiar with the recent critical efforts to detranscendentalize Emerson and Thoreau in favor of readings that emphasize their worldliness, their social writings, and their attention to science and natural history, may be somewhat disappointed by this book, in that it does not take up or add in any significant way to those debates. But I do think attention to Emerson's and Thoreau's transcendentalism as it links up to their epistemologies does in the end translate into material and social consequences—especially as those in turn relate to the environment. That, at least, is the argument of this book. But I readily admit I arrive there via a well-traveled route, which is to say, I take up some of the traditional, transcendentalist topoi of Emerson and Thoreau criticism (their ontotheologies or, as I see them, their environmental epistemologies) and pay little attention to their explicit writings on social and scientific matters.

As an aside, I think Emerson and Thoreau have much to say on the nature of belief, value, authority, selfhood, agency, observation, and so on, that still resonates. But their understanding of science, race, or economic theory is of little use to us today, for like others of their times they were woefully ignorant of many of the facts we now take for granted; we could learn more about physical laws, heredity, or market forces from the average high schooler. (As Thoreau says in *Walden,* "Practically, the old have no very important advice to give to the young" [T 329].) It is true, however, that sketching the contours of their ignorance (and occasionally prescient scientific insights—Thoreau has the most; see especially Laura Walls) can, in a general way, augment our understanding of nineteenth-century literary culture. There is much to learn here, and it is an academically rich vein, and currently heavily mined. It is also true, and also in a general way, that some of the ideas of Emerson and Thoreau that interest me most cannot be detached from their appropriations and revisions of the scientific and social theories of their time. Even so, I am not interested in tracing how they inscribed into their work the paradigms and breakthroughs of their time. My goal is, through the lens of systems theory, to reinterpret *how they understood what they were seeing,* because I think there, in those epistemologically charged pronouncements, emerge some of the most resonant and enduring motifs of their oeuvres. (See also chapter 3, note 15.)

7. To anticipate the objection that Emerson and Thoreau cannot support such readings because systems theory is a twentieth-century development, let me simply state that while the theory is new the systems are not. As Bruce Clarke says, "there is nothing new about the form systems must have in order to exist and to function—they must produce those forms of distinction that enable these operations of observation. Thus it may be assumed that premodern religions, philosophies, and literatures have registered insights into these matters, although under other vocabularies and figural regimes" ("Form," 1). In effect, Clarke reminds us that the retroapplication of theories is a bread-and-butter technique of literary and rhetorical criticism; the real onus on me then is not to show that we can apply systems theory to literary texts (of course we can) but that doing so is worth the effort.

8. The sources for these two meditations on berries have unusual provenances. The quotations attributed to "Resources" are from a report of a lecture published in the Boston

weekly the *Commonwealth* and were republished in 1932. The reports give some insight into Emerson's compositional method, in that local references (such as the one I cite at length here) were generally omitted from the print versions of his essays, including the two that the lecture eventually found its way into, "Resources" and "Inspiration" in *Letters and Social Aims*. (Anyone familiar with that volume knows something about the nonauthoritative nature of its redaction as well.) With the exception of the material in parentheses—which is the reporter's gloss on what Emerson said—according to the editor of the 1932 volume, Clarence Gohdes, the lecture is presented "substantially as Emerson delivered it, and it has not been, like most of his later essays, rearranged or cut by his biographer [James Cabot, also his literary executor and the assembler of the final version of 'Resources'] or his son [Edward Waldo Emerson]" (*Uncollected*, vii). Thus, despite its questionable textual authority today— or rather, precisely because its textual authority at the time was directly dependent on the public figure that was "Emerson"—the lecture reminds us that Emerson's work, for much of his life, was delivered to the public primarily through lecture appearances and that his influence on American culture must therefore have permeated only in its broadest strokes, because the subtleties did not travel well. By contrast, the material published under the title *Wild Fruits* had absolutely no authority in its time, not because Thoreau was little known (though that is certainly true), but because the text only saw the light of day 138 years after his death. If nothing else, the reception histories of these two works tell us something about the nature of the literary system (which I describe in chapter 3), which retains only that which can be made new for each succeeding moment in the system. Emerson's lecture is effectively dead because there is precious little in it of any use today, whereas the stillborn *Wild Fruits* is ideal for an age where its protoecological observations are eminently renewable.

Chapter One: Observing Nature

1. See Bookchin's many works, especially *The Ecology of Freedom* and *Remaking Society*, for discussions of ecoanarchism. See Sale's *Rebels against the Future* for a discussion of Luddism and neo-Luddism.

2. Nor was the Virgilian pastoral scene ever Virgilian, in that it too was always already set upon by outside forces, marked out for contamination at its inception:

> *Lycidas*: Moeris, why are you taking the path to town?
> *Moeris*: O Lycidas, we never thought that what
> Has happened to us was ever going to happen,
> And now we've lived to see it. A stranger came
> To take possession of our farm, and said:
> "I own this place; you have to leave this place."
> Heartbroken and beaten, since fortune will have it so,
> I have to carry these kids to town.
> I only hope bad luck for him goes with them.
> (*Eclogues* 9.1–9)

3. In a culture in which the story of Noah's ark is thought to have a happy ending (i.e., pairs of animals survive to repopulate the planet), it is easy to understand why, for example, many people believe that if we can save a few examples of each animal, we have preserved the whole species. They forget that genetic diversity is essential to maintaining viable populations, and this means that without large numbers, sufficient space, and a variety of habitats to foster genetic variability, species are as surely doomed as they would have been if the entire planet lay under three hundred feet of water.

4. It may be worth noting that in his biography, Pinchot cites Emerson as one of the "lovers of forests" but does not mention Thoreau at all (29).

5. Although I do not emphasize the work of Bourdieu, Giddens, Mouffe, and Laclau in this study, my readings of Luhmann, Varela, and Maturana are informed by their work; where appropriate I strive to make useful connections between systems theory, autopoiesis, and second-order cybernetics, and the perhaps more familiar critical concepts of the former group of thinkers.

Chapter Two: Systems Theory, Cybernetics, and Self-organization

1. Among the many general introductions I have encountered in my own reading, I recommend the following: *General and Social Systems,* by F. Kenneth Berrien; *The Web of Life,* by Fritjof Capra; *Complexity and Postmodernism,* by Paul Cilliers; *The Systems View of the World,* by Ervin Laszlo; *The Rise of Systems Theory,* by Robert Lilienfeld; and, of course, Ludwig von Bertalanffy's *General System Theory.*

2. Parsons's systems theory—which preceded by two or more decades the general systems approach of Bertalanffy et al.—is an instance of parallel theoretical innovation, and so does not fit easily into the trajectory under discussion here. However, Parsons's work is extremely important in relation to Luhmann's theory of differentiation, communication, and action: Luhmann was Parsons's student.

3. It is worth noting that in Miller's typology *society* is essentially another name for *nation.* Thus there is the Canadian society and the American society, and so on. "Supranational" systems would be those in which a "decider" function begins to extend across two or more societies, with other subsystems to follow. The United Nations is an obvious example of a supranational system's decider subsystem, but as yet it has no real ability to decide without the consent of many of its members. The European community, however, is beginning to "shred out" subsystems in the way Miller described, and so may be the best current fit for his model.

4. The full quotation is as follows: "Biology becomes identified with *the class of material realizations* of a certain kind of relational organization, and hence, to that extent divorced from the structural details of any particular kind of realization. It is thus not simply the study of whatever organisms happen to appear in the external world of the biologist; it could be, in fact is, much more than that. Biology becomes in fact a *creative* endeavor; to fabricate any realization of the essential relational organization (i.e., to fabricate a material system that possesses such a model) is to create a new organism. Seen in this light, we can see

the beginnings of a *technology* that comes along with theoretical biology, a technology of *fabrication*" (Rosen, 245).

Chapter Three: Emerson's Environments

1. As Katherine Hayles notes, the example of the toilet seems somewhat inapt, since in *The Tree of Knowledge* Maturana and Varela are less interested in machines than they are living systems, and for living organisms the key point is that material (i.e., protein) change is less important than "the way the material is organized" (*How We Became*, 152). As well—and I think this point may be even more germane—toilet organization seems to smack of an *allopoietic* system rather than an autopoietic one. Allopoietic systems can be compared to the cybernetic system described by Bateson, in which homeostasis is the goal, but homeostasis based on balancing inputs and inputs with the environment. The toilet is not immediately identifiable as consisting only in its water-regulating structures; there are other systems involved as well: connecting plumbing, flush handle, septic system. However, as Maturana and Varela suggest, even autopoietic systems can be part of larger autopoietic systems (e.g., cell organelles within cells, nervous systems within the body). Thus, the toilet example could be an autopoietic subsystem of a larger sewage system, and their point still valid.

2. We often forget that the sentiment revealed in these and other passages was in its time absolutely radical, and indeed verged on an apostasy that went beyond Emerson's break with the Second Boston Church and probed at the core of the Christian faith: the belief in Christ as redeemer. "[T]he way, the thought, the good, shall be wholly strange and new. . . . You take your way from man, not to man," Emerson writes in "Self-Reliance," "All persons that ever existed are its forgotten ministers" (CW 2:39)—and when we recall the Gospel of St. John, in which "Jesus saith unto him, I am the way, the truth, and the life: no man cometh unto the Father, but by me" (John 14:6), we get some sense of just how much Emerson was claiming in his devolution of spiritual authority to the autonomous self. (And while it can be argued that the ultimate ground of Emerson's scheme finally requires an external, transcendental reference, it is clear that that reference means nothing unless one is in full possession of one's "aboriginal Self.")

3. The contrast between an autopoietic view of systems and other paradigmatic ecological theories is well illustrated by comparing the work of Maturana and Varela to Edward Goldsmith's *The Way: An Ecological World-view*. In this ecosophical text, the former editor of the *Ecologist* suggests that "For natural systems to achieve their goal of maintaining their own and Gaian stability, they must be able to predict environmental changes to which they must adapt, as well as the environmental effects of such adaptations. There is every reason to suppose that they are well capable of doing so, providing such changes occur within their tolerance ranges" (153). Furthermore, "A living thing apprehends its environment by detecting data that appear relevant to its behavior pattern and interpreting them in light of its mental model of its relationship with it. This means that it seeks to establish their meaning and thereby to understand them" (158). Under autopoiesis there is an element of predictability

to systems' behavior, in that recurrent "successes" of a system in its environment may give it the appearance of correct adaptation to environmental factors. But this appearance is illusory. Autopoietic systems cannot predict or represent internally their environment, and they do not preview the effects on the environment of their own processes. Instead, they attempt to maintain their autonomy by modifying their internal structures to conserve their organization, regardless of what is happening in the environment: what looks to an observer like the system's responsiveness to environment is simply the system's specification of its own internal state. Goldsmith posits an open system, and as with the Batesonian cybernetic loop, it is optimized when the inputs and outputs between organism and environment have created the desired homeostasis (even to the point of a global, Gaian balance). With Maturana, and Varela, however, it is not a question of inputs and outputs, but of closure—and whether or not the system can maintain it in the face of environmental irritation.

4. Structural changes can be induced by the environment (e.g., an injury or a disease), but they are of a different order and clearly have nothing to do with the system's normal structural adjustments based on autopoietic factors.

5. For a complete discussion of these ideas, see *The Embodied Mind*, by Francisco Varela, Evan Thompson, and Eleanor Rosch.

6. The notion that an environment is always more complex than the systems it contains is easily proved simply by noting that while there is an infinite number of ways of distinguishing objects in an environment an observer has to choose a finite number of ways to do so. *Complexity* in general is an ambiguous term, and can mean the lack of information of a system in relation to its environment, or conversely the ability of the system to view the environment in a great number of ways. John Casti explains: "Suppose our system N is a stone on the street. To most of us, this is a pretty simple, almost primitive kind of system [or component of the environment] because we are capable of interacting with the stone in a very circumscribed number of ways. We can break it, throw it, kick it—and that's about it. Each of these modes of interaction represents a different (i.e., inequivalent) way to interact with the stone. But if we were geologists, then the number of different kinds of interactions available to us would greatly increase. In that case, we could perform various sorts of chemical analyses on the stone, use carbon-dating techniques on it, X-ray it, and so on. For the geologists, the stone becomes a much more complex object as a result of these additional—and inequivalent—modes of interaction. We see from this example that the complexity of the stone is a relative matter, dependent on the nature of the system with which the stone is interacting. And this idea is perfectly general, applying not just to stones on the street but to all systems" (276–77). We can also see in Casti's example that his view of complexity puts a premium on a system's "ways of knowing" objects rather than on its "ignorance"—the emphasis, I hope it is understood, that I prefer.

7. And for Luhmann "observation" is no longer meant in a visual sense alone but is consistent with any mode of "making a distinction" ("Theory," 12–13).

8. Luhmann puts it this way: "Raised to a penultimate concept, culture is everything that serves to resolve the paradoxes an observer encounters whenever he asks about the unity of the distinction that he uses, be it the distinction between system and environment,

or the distinction between knowing and ignorance, or the distinction between observer and observed. Resolving the paradox means a reintroduction of the identities that enable continued operations. This cannot occur logically, because paradoxes exist outside the boundaries of logic, which is itself a kind of culture, namely a kind of solution of paradoxes with the aim of setting up calculations. There are no clear distinctions either from being or thinking. The resolution of paradoxes can only occur in stages, that is, creatively (which does not mean arbitrarily). Culture seems to be the medium in which forms for resolving paradoxes can take on stable and, in their own time, plausible identities. Culture is the stock market where options for paradox resolution are traded" (*Observations*, 102).

9. Where the systems approach differs from—and I think improves upon—a straightfor-wardly materialistic critique (or the liberal humanist critique of Anderson, for that matter) of Emerson's supposed later conservatism is that by reading Emerson's epistemological difficulties as a response to complexity rather than as a reductive coding of nature into the terms provided by dialectical materialism, we can better evade the charge that the critique itself re-essentializes nature by assuming its commodified form as a falling away from some more real form of itself.

10. Gerhard Plumpe, in a discussion of Frederick Schlegel, suggests the code interest-ing/boring, which is somewhat closer to what I have in mind (see Müller). Niels Werber also suggests this code (see Holub). Luhmann's essay, "The Work of Art and the Self-reproduction of Art," proposes that a system of art includes literature, theater, plastic arts, and music, and differentiates "according to the special code *beautiful/ugly,* and . . . differences between the individual art forms are not immediately important" (ES 191). My discussion, on the other hand, is undertaken on the assumption that the differences are important.

It is also important to bear in mind that codes belong solely to systems. A system has autonomy when it can recognize what is proper to it and what is not; it is able to carry out operations on the communications it recognizes as its own and leave everything else to the other systems to deal with. But that does not mean its operations will be transparent to observers. In other words, the systems of art or literature may recognize art and literature when they see it, but that does not mean we do. This more nuanced understanding of the difficulty of giving a name to the media code of art I take to be one of the central issues of Luhmann's later work, *Art as a Social System.* In that book, Luhmann claims "it is not feasible to code the entire art system along the lines of dated/new, thus devalorizing the entire stock of existing artworks" (201). I cannot pretend to argue with Luhmann on this score, except to say that my analysis proceeds under the assumption (delusion?) that art is best understood as a series of linked subsystems rather than one combined system that uses the same code, whatever it may be, for texts, paintings, or music. That is to say, my strategy is to make literature into a third-order observing system, which can comment not only upon its own operations but the operations of other systems. Literature, for example, can speak much more fluidly about music than music can about literature. In this sense, literature may be a special case in the art system: a subsystem of a subsystem whose aim is to observe the observations of others. (If such is the case, we would at least be able to explain in systems terms why those who write literature and comment upon it feel so uniquely situated as to believe themselves obliged and competent to critique every other system of society.)

11. The work of the New Critics could be viewed from this perspective as an attempt to formally recognize the differentiation of an autonomous sphere of literary texts, texts that referred only to themselves and perhaps occasionally to one another. By postulating that poems were hermetically sealed, "well-wrought urns" *pace* Cleanth Brooks, the New Critics sought to control the flow of communication in and out of the literary system; but as subsequent generations of critics have demonstrated, the literary system is closed only so that it can remain open at the level of structure. It can, in other words, respond to the world beyond its borders (poems, for example, need not be only about their own autonomy and the autonomy of literary art), but it tries to do so on its own terms by marking some kind of aesthetic difference (i.e., there is difference between a poem about war and a newspaper report about the same topic). It can also transvalue texts from other systems into terms the literary system can operate on. Legal and political documents, scientific papers, and so on can become objects of literary study not just in order to study the process of communication, but as aesthetically inflected texts that contain the novel styles, language, or meanings that the literary system feeds on.

12. See especially the essay "Art and Oscillation" in Vattimo's *The Transparent Society*.

13. In many respects, Eliot's formulation of the literary tradition is isomorphic to this notion of an autopoietically generated literary system, particularly as regards the centrality of new works to the continuing self-organization of the tradition. Obviously, the introduction of new materials is necessary for any function system, in that according to Maturana and Varela's definition it is the regeneration of the system through continuous production of new components that allows the system to persist over time; but with the literary system, in both Eliot's conception of *tradition* and my own understanding of its coding, it is the relationship between the new communicational elements and old that is at the heart of the function of the function system itself. As Eliot puts it, "what happens when a new work of art is created is something that happens simultaneously to all the works of art which preceded it. The existing monuments form an ideal order among themselves, which is modified by the introduction of the new (the really new) work of art among them. The existing order is complete before the new work arrives; for the order to persist after the supervention of novelty, the *whole* existing order must be, if ever so slightly, altered; and so the relations, proportions, values of each work of art toward the whole are readjusted; and this is the conformity between the old and the new" (38–39). Eliot's "order" is narrower, a more restrictive system in terms of what it can observe than the closed/open organization and structures of autopoietic systems in Luhmann's theory, yet Eliot's new/old binarism here sounds very familiar: literary judgment, he writes, is "a comparison, in which two things are measured by each other. To conform merely would be for the new work not really to conform at all; it would not be new, and would therefore not be a work of art. And we do not quite say that the new is more valuable because it fits in; but its fitting in is a test of its value—a test, it is true, which can only be slowly and cautiously applied, for we are none of us infallible judges of conformity. We say;

it appears to conform, and is perhaps individual, or it appears individual, and may conform; but we are hardly likely to find that it is one and not the other" (39). What Eliot identifies is the paradox of the literary system, which finds literature new only so that it will have the chance to become old, and what is old is old only so that it can be used to decide what is new. The code allows the system to continually reflect the fact that it stays autonomous only so long as it can keep changing. If it cannot change it looses its coherence. Whence the taboo on plagiarism, dullness, and derivativeness, which is like a death sentence to literature.

14. It is difficult to understand now, for example, why the penetration of Marxist theory into the programming of literary assessment boded for some the eventual incoherence of the whole enterprise. The literary system instead came to be enriched by a variety of specifically Marxist-derived paradigms, which enabled literature to resonate more effectively with, in particular, the political and economic components of its environment. The communicational modalities to be opened up by the Internet, multimedia, and hypertext, not to mention perspectives drawn from ecocriticism, may also follow a similar trajectory, creating opportunities for the literary system to build up its potential to select, intercept, resist, or even anticipate and co-opt the positions, perspectives, and communications of other functions systems.

15. This is a long note that addresses recent issues in Emerson criticism that are somewhat tangential but nevertheless bear on the main argument.

Although I have chosen to explain the source of Emerson's orientation toward the new/old distinction in cognitive/psychological terms, there are certainly alternatives. Another intriguing rationale is provided by some of the recent analyses of Emerson and power. I am thinking here in particular of Michael Lopez's work on Emerson as a proto-Nietzschean in *Emerson and Power*, David Robinson on Emerson's pragmatics of moral vision in *Emerson and the Conduct of Life*, and Eduardo Cadava's analysis of Emerson's meteorological tropology as it tracks the social climate in *Emerson and the Climates of History*. In all three books, Emerson is refigured as a philosopher who, rather than (as Stephen Whicher argued) fell into a quiescent, post-"Experience" phase wherein he contented himself with submission to the transcendent forces that exceeded him, in fact deepened and extended his understanding of the material/social forces that had always confronted him in the here and now; he was—and always had been, even in the most ungrounded moments of *Nature*—a theorist of politics and power. Whereas the Emerson industry ever since the Matthiessen resuscitation saw the later period (from roughly 1860 on) as minor and to some extent even an outright failure, this new group of critics wants to read essays like "Fate," "Power," and "Illusions" as capstone achievements, works that solidify this long-suppressed or ignored focus of Emerson's thought—perhaps even his central topic all along. As Lopez puts it, "The deep animating intention, the recursive, agnostic pattern beneath his prose, seems to fall, ultimately, toward Nietzsche—toward the 'search after power,' toward what is usable and empowering, toward pragmatism, toward a philosophy that sees the world, the self, as something to be 'worked up,' toward a Nietzschean 'aesthetic ontology' and 'creative nihilism' " (*Emerson*, 10). The search after power was not Emerson's alone: as Lopez reminds us, the nineteenth century was obsessed with power's origins, means, and ends. So in this sense, as in others, Emerson was only a mind of climate. But if we agree with Lopez that power is the real story behind

Emerson's oeuvre (not, as the Whicherian tradition would have it, the rise and fall of transcendental idealism), then we have to face the fact that Emerson himself was wrong about what he thought he was doing. I do not think he believed power was his central topic—although that alone does not mean Lopez is wrong about its centrality. I would put it this way instead: power serves his central topic in the same way that environment serves the system, that is, as the Other that always gives the lie to any sense of systemic completeness. There is always more environment, more "outside" to deal with, and power—even "negative power"—is but one more concept Emerson deploys to register the desire to overcome, to remain open while yet being closed, to fill your environment with your system without losing yourself altogether. The fact that we do not bow to fate (read as "environment") without a struggle means we do indeed possess power. But it is the desire to remain closed to fate while yet being open to it that is to me the real thread that connects. My point, then, is that more so than other minds, his was preoccupied with sifting through the current "magazines" of power—wherever they were presumed to lie—so as to find the new ones, those still unexhausted by tradition and overuse. In this respect, I say that it is not the "search after power" itself that causes Emerson to want constantly to surpass himself but, as I have already suggested, a particular tic in Emerson's psychological makeup (a tic we all share but to different degrees of urgency) of which the search after power is but one manifestation. The existence of this tic does not make the search after power or its critical analysis any less real or important. Yes, Emerson sought to dissect power, along with many other things, but it was part and parcel of the search after the new, or what Robert Frost called (in "The Sound of Trees") "the reckless choice," a compulsion to "set forth somewhere" no matter how much age and wisdom bids one to stay (156). The impulse behind Emerson's work was finally a poetic one, with all the psychodynamics that lies back of that, and his written and spoken interventions into the causes and problems of the day were always filtered through that sensibility. Robert Richardson writes in his splendid biography of Emerson that "Poetry was for him never just a matter of writing, of expression, but always of connecting one's own small flame to the great central fires of life. Our days demand fire" (572). That demand was only in keeping with the movement with which he was so closely associated: as Lawrence Buell argues, "the spirit of the Transcendental movement is best understood by taking a literary approach to what the Transcendentalists have to say about the issues which preoccupied them, because their way of looking at those issues is markedly poetic rather than analytical and because they attached a great value to creativity and self-expression" (*Literary*, 9). Does laying everything off in the end to a poetic impulse belittle Emerson? I suppose that depends upon whether you think philosophy is a more weighty mode of examining life than poetry, or whether you think poetry might be a closet form of philosophy anyway.

Another concern raised here is the relation between power and systems theory itself. It is not an issue I take up directly in this book (though I do so implicitly throughout and especially in the final chapter), in part because Luhmann dismisses power as irrelevant to his systems approach, and in part because this book must concern itself first and foremost with the epistemological issues that underlie how power can even gain purchase in social systems in the first place: no power without differences, and differences emerge out of observations. But I do want to make one observation that is a little more gritty and perhaps has more to say about the worldly Emerson the critics of power want to produce: the functionalist reading of Emerson I offer in this book is on first blush quite consonant with the protopragmatist, pre-Nietzsche Nietzschean view of what philosophy's job is. That job is, as Marshall McLuhan might say (who was an Emersonian without knowing it), to develop "thought-probes" to bore into the layers of the complexity the world presents. The key Emersonian concepts—compensation, fate, truth, power, nature, and so on—all work precisely like this, and throughout the various stages of his career he uses them to drill into the deep strata of the natural and social worlds. That is the "on first-blush" consonance. But drilling is not a precise science, and the will to power has its flip side: Emerson must tinker with his bits, adjusting them to suit the changing times, and similarly are the yields of his probes changed by the times: "Once we thought positive power was all. Now we learn that negative power, or circumstance, is half" (w 6:15). Thus, Lopez's claim for Emerson's overall coherence—"that there exists, from his first book to his last, a fundamental, unchanging Emersonian psychology/philosophy" (*"Conduct,"* 247–48)—strikes me as an enormous burden that cannot be born by a method that owes at least as much to a recognition of the elusiveness of power as it does to a self-possessed search after power. What happens, in other words, when power cannot be appropriated, when we are impotent, time and again, before the world? To me Emerson's method is finally more descriptive than inductive, a registration of variable moods rather than a movement through or simply toward coherence: there is always the new fact arriving that throws off the paradigm. Emerson accretes layers to his project without resolution, without recourse to a final system of thought—or to a system for evaluating that thought. He was too open to the world's impress, the march of science and politics, the tumult of politics and law—the "new" in other words—to ever cap his wells and put away the drills. He was very much *in* the world, despite trying to operate above it. That is why his works, though magisterial on the surface and to the casual reading, often seem to admit doubt at some point, and make what had seemed to be the last word mere prelude. Those who read Emerson regularly are regularly surprised by him. You think you have him pegged and he pulls the pegs out. Should we submit to fate or take up arms against it?: one is never sure what Emerson thinks is the correct course, or even that there is a choice. Paralysis sets in. Again, I agree with Buell: "The ethical force of Emerson's later thought is always at risk of being recontained . . . by a cosmic bemusement that probably arose from the same irritation that provoked the ethical reaction in the first place: irritation at being confounded by the intractability of the problem at hand" ("Emerson's Fate," 24). What Emerson wanted was "a model not of perception but of 'right' perception" that would integrate epistemology and ethics (25). And that is precisely what systems theory says you cannot have.

To summarize: if power was Emerson's real topic, we do indeed have a way to recuperate and reintegrate his later writings into a revised, complex whole, and to avoid the Whicherian dismissal of those writings as evidence of his final descent into conservatism, of a retrenchment of the most reactionary elements of "Self-Reliance." I think avoiding the latter characterization is without question a good thing, since Whicher always radiates a certain condescension that casts Emerson as a bit of a rube—either a wide-eyed dreamer or a complacent old scholar. Nevertheless, I would argue that Whicher gets Emerson's personal trajectory pretty much right: not because I have fallen under the sway of New Criticism or seek to trivialize Emerson as a serious philosopher (see Lopez's "*Conduct,*" 245–46); not because of his alleged fall from idealism to acquiescence; and not because Lopez is wrong about power's continuous importance in Emerson's itinerary; but rather because in my systems reading the sheer complexity of things, power included, finally takes the wind out of Emerson's sails, just as it would with any thinker as intelligent, observant, and self-correcting as he was. In *Nature* the "spirit builds itself a house" (cw 1:44) and by "Fate" the "house confines the spirit" (w 6:9). The retrenchment is simply a recognition—conscious or subconscious; it matters to me little—of the futility of single vision. What Whicher reads chronologically as spring's enthusiasms replaced by autumn's resignations, and what Lopez reads synchronically as a lifetime of coherent attention to power, I read as a set of moods that sometimes owns up to the limits of observation and sometimes imagines there are none. If you trust Emerson as the most perspicacious of observers—whether he is looking inward or outward—and if you know that his society really was becoming impossible to gloss in any unified way using the theories of the time, then you know that the world did exceed his capacity to reduce it to fate, power, nature, self-culture, experience, and so on. And you know that he signals in various ways that he knew at some level this was so. But—and this is where I do take issue with Lopez's reading of a coherent Emerson who was a Nietzsche-before-the-letter and side instead with Whicher's more teleological reading—he kept angling for the right formula past the point when (it is clear to us now) no formula would be forthcoming; and this is why the recontainment phase of his career seems less significant and more orthodox than the earlier ecstatic phase. Though his understanding of the role of power in *The Conduct of Life* is more complex, he is less able to repudiate or gather up that power in new and interesting ways. In fact, if anything, he seems enamored and immobilized by power. Let us not forget it took the rest of the century after the Civil War to give us pragmatism, a philosophy that Emerson certainly influenced, the one that he seemed to be looking for, but which he was unable to produce himself. He could not give up on the "power-bringing words," as William James called them, the words that would open the gates of creation. Emerson knew he had never found the language for that task, but he would not allow himself to know that the task itself was futile. Now, if my reading here seems itself rather old-fashioned, consonant with the Modernist reading that relegated the later Emerson to cheery booster of the human heart and not plumber of its tortured depths, it is only because it contrasts with the views of those contemporary critics who feel the need to claim for Emerson an overall coherence that could balance a giving-up of the power-bringing words with a pulling-together of all his dangling threads. But I think it is a stretch to read Emerson as an archaeologist of power just as it would be a stretch to read him as a systems theorist. For me, it is enough to say that Emerson *registered* his time better than anyone else even if he did not *comprehend* it. (And all that really means is that we have a need to comprehend it differently than he did.)

16. It may seem a coincidence that the literary function system also discriminates among its communications on the basis of their novelty. Science looks for new facts while the literary world looks for new fictions. All of this is merely stating the obvious. But what proves interesting for the later Emerson is that as he begins to conflate the aesthetic code with the code of the economic sphere under the sign of the liberal self, the only function system with similar sweep and power to compete with the economic system head to head in terms of the obduracy of its code—science—fails to become a model site in which to locate Emerson's "One Man" of "the Divinity School Address." Recall, for example, that in *Representative Men*, no scientist is included. This is not to say that Emerson did not think highly of scientists. Of course he did. It is rather to say that the economic system becomes for Emerson the field where not just commodities but selves are market tested and hardened, where the most self-reliant, most original, and most powerful gain their rewards—and for "Man Thinking" (the scientist or scholar) only the first two superlatives generally obtain. Thus, the unity of society and man is best expressed not by king, president, pope, scientist, or poet but by the figure of the self-made entrepreneur observing the world from his profit/loss perspective. Foreshadowing Calvin Coolidge's aphoristic "The business of America is business" and Charles Wilson's unpremeditated disclosure that "What's good for the country is good for General Motors, and vice versa," Emerson concludes in "Experience" that "The true romance which the world exists to realize will be the transformation of genius into practical power" (CW 3:49). One can easily imagine how he would have felt about an Edison or a Henry Ford (or, for that matter, how they would have felt about him).

Chapter Four: Thoreau's Moral Vision

1. For a book-length study of this figure, as well as a comprehensive critical survey of the range of criticism that has focused on the passage, see Boudreau, *The Roots of Walden and the Tree of Life*.

2. In this vein, Jonathan Crary and Sanford Kwinter conclude in their preface to the volume of essays *Incorporations* the following: "One of the aims of this book, then, is to outline the ways in which overlapping 'biotechnic' arrangements have throughout the twentieth century brought about continuous transformations of a 'lifeworld.' Though the same relentless processes of modernization and rationalization continue today unabated, they have become increasingly and inseparably linked to the positive production of such generalized lifeworlds or ambient *milieus* as sites of invention and transformation. Neither human subjects nor the conceptual or material objects among which they live are any longer thinkable in their distinctiveness or separation from the dynamic, correlated, multipart systems within which they arise. Everything, and every individual emerges, evolves and passes away by incorporating and being incorporated into, other emerging, evolving or disintegrating structures that surround and suffuse it. Indeed, incorporation may well be the name of the new primary logic of creation and innovation in our late modern world" (15). What Crary and Kwinter have in mind here seems to be precisely the sort of "translationist" approach that Latour hopes to foster through the notion of the hybrid, which in its very

name reminds us of its multifarious, nonsimple origins. As Haraway has suggested, objects are boundary projects, far more complex and mediated than our current vocabularies allow them to be.

3. See especially McKibben's 1995 essay in the *Atlantic Monthly*.

4. See Kate Soper's three levels of nature in *What Is Nature?*

5. For example, it is a relatively well-established point in evolutionary biology that the colors of flowers and fruit have coevolved with the vision of the insects and animals that pollinate them and disperse their seeds. Both plants and animals benefit from the relationship (the plants increase their reproductive capacity and the animals get food) so that selective pressures favored striking colors and the color vision required to notice them. The larger question, of course, is "Did not colors exist before there were eyes to see them?" The answer is that the reflectance properties of elements and chemical compounds did exist but that without the evolution of vision to distinguish the different wavelengths of light our world would seem a drastically different place. Without color vision, would gold or precious gems have any value to us? More important, would these substances—now various shades of gray—actually be gold, red, green, etc.? The reality of colors is nothing more than a function of our ability to see them (as opposed to other possible wavelengths), or as Luhmann might say, the blind spot of particular distinguishing operations that select some realities at the exclusion of others.

6. The obvious connection to certain strains in phenomenology is encapsulated in a statement by Merleau-Ponty that Varela is fond of quoting: "When I begin to reflect, my reflection bears upon an unreflective experience, moreover my reflection cannot be unaware of itself as an event, and so it appears to itself in the light of a truly creative act, of a changed structure of consciousness, and yet it has to recognize, as having priority over its own operations, the world which is given to the subject because the subject is given to himself. . . . Perception is not a science of the world, it is not even an act, a deliberate taking up of a position; it is the background from which all acts stand out, and is presupposed by them: The world is not an object such that I have in my possession the law of its making; it is the natural setting of, and field for, all my thoughts and all my explicit perceptions" (*Phenomenology of Perception*, x–xi).

7. An interesting theory as to the origin of self-consciousness from a systems perspective is outlined by Eric Rosseel: "Self-observation occurs when the structural coupling of a human system to a specified ambience gets blocked by an environmental perturbation that is compensated by a 'breakdown' of the action of the system. As the system does not dispose of an adequate action that would have continued his drift in the ambience, 'mindless' automated action is interrupted and self-observation helps explore the plasticity of the systems and to develop a new 'creative' action that removes the blockage. . . . Only in those moments, we do see what we see, we look at the world and talk about the images we have formed. . . . In other words we act with Intelligence" (236). What I take this to mean is that self-consciousness emerges as a response by the neural system to problems that cannot be solved more economically by autonomic or instinctual operations. At moments when habitual actions and responses are inadequate, we find ourselves thrust into the creative, reflective, self-aware

states of mind we take for granted as the normal state of affairs; rather, according to this view, such states are, strictly speaking, the abnormal condition.

8. In his fascinating discussion of evolutionary epistemology, *Darwin Machines and the Nature of Knowledge,* Henry Plotkin argues that the term *knowledge* can be applied to any sort of adaptation, that, for example, "the fleshy water-conserving cactus stem constitutes a form of knowledge of the scarcity of water in the world of the cactus" (228). Adaptations are in effect "forms of 'incorporation' of the world into the structure and organization of living things" (xv). He contends that "knowledge is a complex set of relationships between genes and past selection pressures, between genetically guided developmental pathways and the conditions under which development occurs, and between a past of the consequent phenotypic organization and specific features of environmental order" (228). The more commonplace sense of the word *knowledge* can conversely be thought of as an epiphenomenal consequence of the more profound adaptive cognitive structures that gave an advantage to their possessors. A trivial piece of knowledge, such as the fact that "Germany won the World Cup, is really only the visible, or potentially visible, part of a complex multiple-layered and historically ordered hierarchical structure involving the genes which code for the brain structures that enable me to gain knowledge, development which led to the establishment of the required brain mechanisms, brain and cognitive states that are the present embodiment of that knowledge, and culture and its artefacts that allow me to learn rapidly and accurately what is occurring in a distant part of Europe" (229).

9. For a shorter, nontechnical discussion of these ideas, see Varela's *Ethical Know-How.*

10. The brain is not a mirror of nature, but neither is it a record needle that plays nature's tune; in effect it plays its own tune so long as nothing forces it to change the melody. Again Rorty is instructive: on the same subject his analogy between representation and world is to imagine mind as an encyclopedia, which "can get *changed* by things outside itself, but [which] can only be *checked* by having bits of itself compared to other bits. You cannot *check* a sentence against an object, although an object can *cause* you to stop asserting a sentence. You can only check a sentence against other sentences, sentences to which it is connected by various labyrinthine relationships" (100). In a sense, the brain is such a closed encyclopedia, which can reconjugate its contents in response to new facts so that it remains consistent and coherent across its organization. The relation between what the encyclopedia says and the contents of the world is relevant only in that the world can force the encyclopedia to reconjugate its contents: the world thus acts as stimulus, not as a point-to-point guarantee of truth, for truth only consists in the integrity of this organization, that is, there is no contradiction between the contents.

11. Note that this is not quite the same as Bateson's idea that, because our minds and environment are cybernetically linked, when we destroy the environment we automatically destroy the mind (see *Steps*). For, in fact, the mind is concerned only with maintaining its own organization, and organization may be preservable even though much in its environment is destroyed—as we know from bitter experience. It is the case, however, that one outcome might very well be the degradation of the cognitive organization, i.e., madness, assuming the right kind and degree of environmental perturbation.

Chapter Five: The American System of Nature

1. Dave Foreman's credentials as a deep ecologist were confirmed with the publication of his *Confessions of an Eco-warrior* in 1991, wherein he says, among other memorable things, "by using our guerrilla wits, we can use [the dying industrial empire's] own massed power against itself. Delay, resist, subvert using all available tools: File appeals and lawsuits, encourage legislation—not to reform the system but to thwart it. Demonstrate, engage in nonviolent civil disobedience, monkeywrench. Defend. Deflect the thrashing mailed fist of the dying storm trooper of industrialism as represented by the corporate honcho, federal bureaucrat, and tobacco-chewing Bubba. . . . Our self-defense is damage control until the machine plows into the brick wall and industrial civilization self-destructs as it must" (50). That sort of hyperbolic rhetoric is what has allowed the media to cite deep ecologists in the same breath as the Unabomber or the Earth Liberation Front. But it must be noted that Foreman has always been rather pragmatic in "defense of Mother Earth," writing in a shallow ecological vein that "we need professional lobbyists, scientists, attorneys, and accountants playing the game. But they need to up the ante and go on the offensive. We need competent administrators to manage multimillion-dollar-a-year budgets and large staffs. But they must be guided by the vision of Muir, Edge, Marshall, and Leopold—not by that of Harvard Business School" (212). It is precisely this blend of radical and reformist rhetoric that tips one off to the fact that deep ecology has strong roots in the *mainstream* tradition of American political thought, for what could be more prototypically liberal/progressive than to claim loudly we need to throw a wrench into the rusty gears of the system while at the same time standing ready in the wings with an oilcan to help it work more smoothly?

2. See Ashworth's *The Economy of Nature,* Hawken's *The Ecology of Commerce,* Lewis's *Green Delusions,* and Gore's *Earth in the Balance.*

3. See Toffler's *Powershift* and Ferry's *The New Ecological Order.*

4. For a critique of Ferry's book, see the review by Cary Wolfe in *Electronic Book Review.*

5. Critics of deep ecology are right in claiming that deep ecology is a pagan system of beliefs, if only in this respect: in order to create a social system based on the DEP, the functional differentiation of modern society would have to be undone, and a return to sedimented organization negotiated. (See, for example, Paul Shepard's *Madness and Civilization.*)

6. See especially Michael Zimmerman.

7. The alternative, briefly, to the liberal attempt to conjoin these two separate function systems would have to begin by clearly distinguishing the domain of the economic from the domain of the political, to encourage greater system differentiation instead of trying constantly to reconcile the demands of the market with the demands of equality. Ultimately, one would hope for an economy that was forced to discipline itself to the requirements of democracy, rather than the current situation in which democracy is increasingly a handmaiden to the worldwide project of unequal capital distribution.

This dichotomy between the functional and liberal view of economy-politics interrelations was clearly on display in a fascinating *Harper's* forum on the new economy between participants Edward Luttwak, a strategic analyst who gained popular fame during the Gulf

War; George Gilder, author of *Wealth and Poverty,* a Reagan-era, supply-side manifesto; and "Chainsaw Al" Dunlap, CEO of Scott Paper, notorious for laying off workers even during periods of high profit. The debate is exemplary of the difficulty Americans have in viewing the two domains separately, particularly when it is always in the interest of economic liberalizers to equate them.

> *Luttwak*: It's wrong to criticize CEOs as if they are, in fact, responsible for anything. They are not responsible. They're blind amoebas. Create a regulated, structured, stabilized environment for them, and they'll behave accordingly.
>
> *Gilder*: The idea that we have come from this stable, halcyon period of existence that is now being destroyed by runaway change is just preposterous. Change is inevitable. Change is good. The effort to stabilize is death. It's death for the economy, it's death for job creation, it's destructive to the society.
>
> *Dunlap*: What's happening, Ed, is that people in this country are starting to come to grips with the fact that the point of business is to make a profit. Profit, gentlemen, is not a dirty word. ("Does America Still Work?" 36–37)

What is significant about this exchange is that both Luttwak and Gilder appear to possess an autopoietic view of the economy: both understand the functional role of the environment in stimulating the system to produce structures in order to preserve autopoiesis. Luttwak argues that the solution to current crises of employment and social decay must begin by realizing that business will conform to whatever regulatory environment is imposed on it so as to maintain its profit-oriented organization; Gilder, however, argues that the system must be allowed to continue to think of its operations as the world and to ignore its environment just as it has always done. In other words, while Luttwak argues from the position of a second-order observer, Gilder argues for system autonomy from the first-order perspective of the system itself. The point is not that Gilder is wrong, only that his perspective is limited and finally self-defeating. The more he insists on the universality of his blindness, the more he makes the case for multiple observational perspectives. (Dunlap, even more aligned with the code of the economy than Gilder, simply tries, as is frequently the case of first-order observers, to make a moral virtue out of his own particular blind spot.)

8. And this is true whether we conceive of economy in straightforward terms as the self-serving actions of individual systems under scarcity or in Bataille's terms as general economy with systems operating under conditions of abundance. In either case, it is not the medium within which the system exists that is crucial (and whether or not materials are scarce or plentiful) but rather the basic functioning of the system's autopoiesis, whereby it looks to its own autonomy and perseverance first and foremost.

9. Timothy Sweet argues the georgic is a more useful category for the sort of neopastoral approach I outline here. I encountered his work on the georgic too late to incorporate it into my own, but I think the thrust of his claim is consonant with what I have in mind for a revised pastoral. He begins his book by meditating on Thoreau's bean field balance sheet and Emerson's well-known remark from *Nature* that "you cannot freely admire a noble

landscape, if laborers are digging in the field hard by" (CW 1:39). In effect, Sweet is concerned with the basic drawback of the pastoral: that it is a leisure-time scenario that tries to sweep labor and economy out of the picture. He sees Virgil's *Georgics* as providing the necessary remedy to our overestimation of the pastoral. He writes, "Georgic . . . treats those aspects of the pastoral, broadly construed, that concern not the retreat to nature or the separation of the country from the city, but our cultural engagement with the whole environment" (5). Sweet then approvingly quotes Lawrence Buell (in a passage Buell himself would do well to take more seriously, given his reluctance to engage fully with the thorny issue of ecocritical praxis): "the promise of pastoral aesthetics as a stimulus to ecocentrism can fulfill itself completely only when pastoral aesthetics overcomes its instinctive reluctance to face head-on the practical obstacles to the green utopia it seeks to realize. Only then can it mature as social critique" (5). My point in this section is exactly Buell's, and whether the critique draws on the pastoral or the georgic is not crucial; the crucial point is that the critique must draw on a systems approach to have the clarity to see that the key stumbling block to the green utopia is, as Sweet rightly points out, *Homo oeconomicus*—both as the species who lives by working nature and as the species who lives by ignoring it.

10. Among essays that explore neopastoralism or industrial neoteny, some of the best are collected by Baldwin, de Luce, and Pletsch in *Beyond Preservation: Restoring and Inventing Landscapes,* and by William Cronon in *Uncommon Ground.*

11. Saturn actually has produced another advertisement that does to some extent deal with the issue of labor, but in a way that cleverly elides almost a hundred years of automotive labor struggle by focusing, once again, on the idealized, mythic space of the rural community.

> Every so often, a group of Saturn retailers will come down to Spring Hill, Tennessee, and work the assembly line here at the Saturn plant. . . . And they do work side by side with the men and women who build Saturns for a living. It's more an exercise in team building than it is a lesson in automobile manufacturing. Although, to be perfectly honest, after a couple of hours, it can get pretty hard to tell a retailer from an autoworker. But then, at Saturn, that's sort of the point.

This vision of an expanded community of stakeholders is consonant with the pastoral ideal, wherein the toilers of the field all work together to get in the harvest, in a spirit of free association and cooperation. The sidebar is also interesting: under a UAW symbol, the copy reads: "Teamwork is not something we restrict to the Saturn plant. It extends out into the community, as well. UAW team members are helping raise money for Camp Fish Tales, a barrier-free camp for kids and adults with disabilities." And these country values do not stop at the Tennessee state line, for in a footnote we see Saturn's trademark neobucolism projected back into the very place where the automotive industry began: "In the same spirit, Saturn retailers across the country have begun building playgrounds to give inner-city kids a safe and fun place to play. Saturn owners have jumped in there too. In fact, not too long ago, they all got together and built twelve playgrounds in the New York area in just one weekend." How does this spirit of cooperation and urban renewal come about? The implicit message behind this happy merger of worker, consumer, and owner interest is that via their common passion for a high-quality, low-priced automobile, all classes may be transported back to an age of innocence, when all knew their place and role in the seamless web of pastoral life.

12. David Mazel makes a similar point, but does so by attributing to the environment itself the status of Foucault's *dispositif,* his term for an epistemological category capable of coordinating and supporting the research goals of otherwise agonistic fields. I think "environment" is too broad and historically unspecific to carry the freight he wants it to, but I very much like Mazel's formulation: "Out of an otherwise quite heterogeneous variety of disciplines, the 'environment' produces an appearance of order, relation, and presence. It is no more and no less than that particular abstraction that can be pondered not only by what we commonly think of as environmentalists, but also by the full panoply of artists who pronounce the environment beautiful, of scientists who discover it to be fragile and complex, of theologians who find it spiritually regenerating, of sociologists who recommend it as an antidote to the ills of urban society, and so on" ("American," 143).

13. See introduction, note 4.

14. Buell is not the only one to underappreciate Luhmann's pertinence. There has to date been very little use of Luhmann's work by English-speaking ecocritics. This is in part due to the unavailability of his work in English (although that has changed in recent years, especially with the spate of material coming out of Stanford and Michigan), and in part due to the sheer abstruseness of his theory. Environmental rhetoricians are among the very few to acknowledge him, but none—with the possible exception of Tarla Rai Peterson—have given him more than a passing glance. (See Peterson, Killingsworth and Palmer, and Coppola and Karis.)

15. If some ecocritics wish to advocate for the primacy of mimesis and aesthetic realism in environmental texts, well, more power to them. From my perspective that is clearly a ghettoizing move. The dangers of realism/representationalism have been well described by others. See for example Dana Phillips's "Ecocriticism, Literary Theory, and the Truth of Ecology." There Phillips takes a strip out of ecocritics, and Lawrence Buell in particular, for valorizing the referent overmuch.

16. I do acknowledge that in this second book, *Writing for an Endangered World,* Buell has attended more fully to other brown landscapes, such as the urban and industrial environments described by the likes of Dickens, Whitman, Joyce, and John Edgar Wideman. In so doing he continues the salutary work of pushing the boundaries of ecocriticism.

17. Timothy W. Luke discusses the concept of environing in the context of the Foucauldian notion of surveillance in "On Environmentality: Geo-Power and Eco-Knowledge in the Discourses of Contemporary Environmentalism," in the second special issue of *Cultural Critique* on the politics of systems and environments. Not surprising, Luke takes a relatively dim view of "environing," which he understands "engenders 'environmentality,' which embeds instrumental rationalities in the policing of ecological spaces" (65). The high-toned managerial impulses of the Worldwatch Institute and former Vice President Gore are for Luke exemplary of the way the systems theory approach will produce new and ever-more

insidious ways of disciplining the environment. My response is that he is quite right: the systems approach can and will be employed to manage environmentality along predictable lines (i.e., in the service of growth economics and continued First World hegemony). That is why the counterpotential for a systems theory *not* beholden to the status quo must be articulated. (Luke's *Ecocritique* collects several of his essays on this and other related topics.)

Works Cited

Adorno, Theodor. *The Adorno Reader.* Ed. Brian O'Connor. Oxford: Blackwell, 2000.

Anderson, Quentin. *The Imperial Self.* New York: Knopf, 1971.

———. *Making Americans.* New York: Harcourt, Brace, and Jovanovich, 1992.

Arnold, Ron, and Alan Gottlieb. *Trashing the Economy.* 2d ed. Bellevue, Wash.: Free Enterprise Press, 1994.

Ashworth, William. *The Economy of Nature.* Boston: Houghton Mifflin, 1995.

Baldwin, A. Dwight, Judith de Luce, and Carl Pletsch, eds. *Beyond Preservation: Restoring and Inventing Landscapes.* Minneapolis: University of Minnesota Press, 1994.

Bate, Jonathan. *Romantic Ecology.* London: Routledge, 1991.

Bates, Frederick. *Sociopolitical Ecology.* New York: Plenum, 1997.

Bateson, Gregory. *Mind and Nature.* New York: Dutton, 1979.

———. *Steps to an Ecology of Mind.* New York: Ballantine Books, 1972.

Baudrillard, Jean. *America.* Trans. Chris Turner. New York: Verso, 1989.

Beck, Ulrich. *Ecological Politics in the Age of Risk.* Trans. Amos Weisz. London: Blackwell, 1995.

Bennett, Jane. "Primate Visions and Alter-Tales." *In the Nature of Things.* Ed. Jane Bennett and William Chaloupka. Minneapolis: University of Minnesota Press, 1993. 250–65.

———. *Thoreau's Nature.* London: Sage, 1994.

Berrien, F. Kenneth. *General and Social Systems.* New Brunswick: Rutgers University Press, 1968.

Berry, Wendell. *Life is a Miracle.* Washington, D.C.: Counterpoint, 2000.

———. *The Unsettling of America.* San Francisco: Sierra Club Books, 1977.

Bertalanffy, Ludwig von. *General System Theory.* Rev. ed. New York: George Braziller, 1968.

Blühdorn, Ingolfur. *Post-ecologist Politics.* London: Routledge, 2000.

Bogdanov, A. *Essays in Tektology.* Trans. George Gorelik. Seaside, Calif.: Intersystems Publications, 1980.

Bookchin, Murray. *The Ecology of Freedom.* Palo Alto: Cheshire Books, 1982.

———. *Remaking Society.* Boston: South End Press, 1990.

Boudreau, Gordon V. *The Roots of Walden and the Tree of Life.* Nashville: Vanderbilt University Press, 1990.

Bourdieu, Pierre. *The Field of Cultural Production*. New York: Columbia University Press, 1993.

——. *Pascalian Meditations*. Palo Alto: Stanford University Press, 2000.

Buell, Lawrence. "The Ecocritical Insurgency." *New Literary History* 30, no. 3 (1999): 699–712.

——. "Emerson's Fate." *Emersonian Circles*. Ed. Wesley Mott and Robert Burkholder. Rochester: University of Rochester Press, 1997.

——. *The Environmental Imagination*. Cambridge, Mass.: Belknap Press, 1995.

——. *Literary Transcendentalism*. Ithaca: Cornell University Press, 1973.

——. *Writing for an Endangered World*. Cambridge, Mass.: Belknap Press, 2001.

Cadava, Eduardo. *Emerson and the Climates of History*. Stanford: Stanford University Press, 1997.

Callon, Michel, and John Law. "Agency and the Hybrid *Collectif*." *South Atlantic Quarterly* 94, no. 2 (1995): 481–508.

Cameron, Sharon. *Writing Nature*. Chicago: University of Chicago Press, 1989.

Capra, Fritjof. *The Web of Life*. New York: Doubleday, 1996.

Casti, John. *Complexification*. New York: Harper Collins, 1994.

Cavell, Stanley. *Conditions Handsome and Unhandsome*. Chicago: University of Chicago Press, 1990.

——. *Senses of Walden*. New York: Viking Press, 1972.

——. *This New Yet Unapproachable America*. Albuquerque: Living Batch Press, 1989.

Cilliers, Paul. *Complexity and Postmodernism*. London: Routledge, 1998.

Clarke, Bruce. "The Form of Metamorphosis: Systems Theory and *A Midsummer Night's Dream*." American Comparative Literature Association Conference, Boulder, Colo., April 2001.

——. "Science, Theory, and Systems." *ISLE* 8, no. 1 (2001): 149–65.

Coppola, Nancy, and Bill Karis, eds. *Technical Communication, Deliberative Rhetoric, and Environmental Discourse*. Stamford, Conn.: Ablex, 2000.

Crary, Jonathan, and Sanford Kwinter, eds. *Incorporations*. New York: Zone, 1992.

Cronon, William. *Changes in the Land*. New York: Hill and Lang, 1983.

——. *Nature's Metropolis*. New York: W. W. Norton, 1991.

——, ed. *Uncommon Ground*. New York: W. W. Norton, 1996.

Dennett, Daniel. *Consciousness Explained*. New York: Little, Brown, 1991.

Devall, Bill. *Simple in Means, Rich in Ends: Practicing Deep Ecology*. Salt Lake City: Gibbs Smith, 1988.

Devall, Bill, and George Sessions, eds. *Deep Ecology*. Salt Lake City: Gibbs M. Smith, 1985.

Diamond, Jared. *Guns, Germs, and Steel*. New York: W. W. Norton, 1997.

"Does America Still Work?" *Harper's*, May 1996, 35–47.

Ehrenfeld, David. *The Arrogance of Humanism*. New York: Oxford University Press, 1978.

Eliot, T. S. *Selected Prose of T. S. Eliot*. Ed. Frank Kermode. London: Faber and Faber, 1975.

Emerson, Ralph Waldo. *The Collected Works of Ralph Waldo Emerson*. Ed. Robert Spiller et al. 4 vols. Cambridge, Mass.: Harvard University Press, 1971–.

————. *The Complete Works of Ralph Waldo Emerson.* Ed. Edward Emerson. Centenary Edition. 12 vols. Boston: Houghton Mifflin, 1903–1904.

————. *Emerson in His Journals.* Ed. Joel Porte. Cambridge: Belknap Press, 1982.

————. *Uncollected Lectures.* New York: William Edwin Rudge, 1932.

Estok, Simon. Letter in the "Forum on Literatures of the Environment." *PMLA* 114, no. 5 (1999): 1095–96.

Ferry, Luc. *The New Ecological Order.* Chicago: University of Chicago Press, 1995.

Foerster, Heinz von. *Observing Systems.* Seaside, Calif.: Intersystems Publications, 1981.

Foreman, Dave. *Confessions of an Eco-warrior.* New York: Harmony Books, 1991.

Foucault, Michel. "Of Other Spaces." *Diacritics* 16 (1986): 22–27.

Freud, Sigmund. *Civilization and Its Discontents.* 1930. London: The Hogarth Press, 1982.

Frost, Robert. *The Poetry of Robert Frost.* Ed. Edward Lathem. New York: Henry Holt, 1979.

Gare, Arran E. *Postmodernism and the Environmental Crisis.* New York: Routledge, 1995.

Gilmore, Michael T. *American Romanticism and the Marketplace.* Chicago: University of Chicago Press, 1985.

Goldsmith, Edward. *The Way: An Ecological World-view.* Boston: Shambhala, 1993.

Gore, Al. *Earth in the Balance.* New York: Houghton Mifflin, 1992.

Gumbrecht, Hans Ulrich. "A Farewell to Interpretation." *Materialities of Communication.* Ed. Hans Ulrich Gumbrecht and K. Ludwig Pfeiffer. Stanford: Stanford University Press, 1994.

Haraway, Donna. *Simians, Cyborgs, and Women.* London: Routledge, 1991.

Hardin, Garret. "The Tragedy of the Commons." *Science* 162 (1968): 1243–48.

Hawken, Paul. *The Ecology of Commerce.* New York: Harper Collins, 1993.

Hayles, N. Katherine. *How We Became Posthuman.* Chicago: University of Chicago Press, 1999.

Hoag, Ronald Wesley. "The Mark on the Wilderness." *Texas Studies in Language and Literature* 24 (1982): 23–46.

Hohendahl, Peter Uwe, et al., eds. *New German Critique* 61 (1994): 3–202.

Holub, Robert. "Luhmann's Progeny: Systems Theory and Literary Studies in the Post-Wall Era." *New German Critique* 61 (1994): 143–59.

Horkheimer, Max, and Theodor Adorno. *The Dialectic of Enlightenment.* 1944. Reprint, New York: Continuum, 1989.

Howells, William Dean. *Literature and Life.* New York: Harper, 1902.

Jameson, Frederic. *Postmodernism, or The Cultural Logic of Late Capitalism.* Durham: Duke University Press, 1990.

Jehlen, Myra. *American Incarnation.* Cambridge: Harvard University Press, 1986

Keizer, Garret. "How the Devil Falls in Love." *Harper's,* August 2002, 43–51.

Kern, Robert. "Ecocriticism: What Is It Good For?" *ISLE* 7, no. 1 (2000): 9–34.

Killingsworth, Jimmie, and Jacqueline Palmer. "The Discourse of 'Environmentalist Hysteria.'" *Landmark Essays on Rhetoric and the Environment.* Ed. Craig Waddell. Mahwah, N.J.: Lawrence Erlbaum, 1998.

Kolodny, Annette. *The Land before Her.* Chapel Hill: University of North Carolina Press, 1984.

———. *The Lay of the Land.* Chapel Hill: University of North Carolina Press, 1975.

Kroeber, Karl. *Ecological Literary Criticism.* New York: Columbia University Press, 1994.

Krutch, Joseph Wood. Introduction to *Walden and Other Writings,* by Henry David Thoreau. New York: Bantam, 1962.

Laclau, Ernesto, and Chantal Mouffe. *Hegemony and Socialist Strategy.* London: Verso, 1985.

Laszlo, Ervin. *The Systems View of the World.* New York: George Braziller, 1972.

Latour, Bruno. "On Technical Mediation—Philosophy, Sociology, Geneology." *Common Knowledge* 3, no. 2 (1994): 29–64.

———. *The Pasteurization of France.* Trans. Alan Sheridan and John Law. Cambridge, Mass.: Harvard University Press, 1988.

———. *We Have Never Been Modern.* Trans. Catherine Porter. Cambridge, Mass.: Harvard University Press, 1993.

Lentricchia, Frank. *Criticism and Social Change.* Chicago: University of Chicago Press, 1983.

Leopold, Aldo. *A Sand County Almanac.* New York: Ballantine, 1966.

Levinson, Marjorie. "Pre- and Post-Dialectical Materialisms: Modeling Praxis without Subjects and Objects." *Cultural Critique* 31 (1995): 111–27.

Lewis, Martin. *Green Delusions.* Durham: Duke University Press, 1992.

Lewis, R. W. B. *The American Adam.* Chicago: University of Chicago Press, 1955.

Lewontin, Richard. *Biology as Ideology: The Doctrine of DNA.* Concord, Ontario: Anansi, 1991.

Lilienfeld, Robert. *The Rise of Systems Theory.* New York: John Wiley and Sons, 1978.

Lopez, Michael. "*The Conduct of Life:* Emerson's Anatomy of Power." *The Cambridge Companion to Ralph Waldo Emerson.* Ed. Joel Porte and Saundra Morris. Cambridge: Cambridge University Press, 1999. 243–66.

———. *Emerson and Power.* DeKalb: Northern Illinois University Press, 1996.

Luhmann, Niklas. *Art as a Social System.* Trans. Eva Knodt. Stanford: Stanford University Press, 2000.

———. "The Cognitive Program of Constructivism and a Reality that Remains Unknown." *Selforganization: Portrait of a Scientific Revolution.* Ed. Wolfgang Krohn et al. Dordrecht, Netherlands: Kluwer Academic Publishers, 1990. 64–85.

———. *Ecological Communication.* Trans. John Bednarz. Chicago: University of Chicago Press, 1989.

———. *Essays on Self-reference.* New York: Columbia University Press, 1990.

———. *Observations on Modernity.* Stanford: Stanford University Press, 1998.

———. "The Paradox of Observing Systems." *Cultural Critique* 31 (1995): 37–55.

———. *Social Systems.* Trans. John Bednarz with Dirk Baecker. Stanford: Stanford University Press, 1995.

————. "Theory of a Different Order: A Conversation with Katherine Hayles and Niklas Luhmann." *Cultural Critique* 31 (1995): 7–36.

Luke, Timothy W. *Ecocritique: Contesting the Politics of Nature, Economy, and Culture.* Minneapolis: University of Minnesota Press, 1997.

————. "On Environmentality: Geo-Power and Eco-Knowledge in the Discourses of Contemporary Environmentalism." *Cultural Critique* 31 (1995): 57–81.

Machor, James. *Pastoral Cities.* Madison: University of Wisconsin Press, 1987.

Marsh, George Perkins. *Man and Nature: Physical Geography as Modified by Human Action.* 1864. Reprint, ed. David Lowenthal, Cambridge: Belknap Press, 1965.

Marx, Leo. *The Machine in the Garden.* New York: Oxford University Press, 1964.

Matthiessen, F. O. *American Renaissance.* New York: Oxford University Press, 1941.

Maturana, Humberto, and Francisco Varela. *Autopoiesis and Cognition.* Dordrecht, Holland: D. Reidel, 1980.

————. *The Tree of Knowledge.* Rev. ed. Boston: Shambala, 1992.

Mazel, David. "American Literary Environmentalism." *The Ecocriticism Reader.* Ed. Cheryll Glotfelty and Harold Fromm. Athens: University of Georgia Press, 1996. 137–46.

————. *American Literary Environmentalism.* Athens: University of Georgia Press, 2000.

McIntosh, James. *Thoreau as Romantic Naturalist: His Shifting Stance toward Nature.* Ithaca: Cornell University Press, 1974.

McKibben, Bill. *The End of Nature.* New York: Anchor Books, 1990.

————. "An Explosion of Green." *Atlantic Monthly,* April 1995, 61–83.

Meeker, Joseph. *The Comedy of Survival.* 3rd ed. Tucson: University of Arizona Press, 1997.

Merchant, Carolyn. *The Death of Nature.* San Francisco: Harper and Row, 1980.

————. *Ecological Revolutions.* Chapel Hill: University of North Carolina Press, 1989.

Merleau-Ponty, Maurice. *Phenomenology of Perception.* London: Routledge and Paul, 1962.

Milder, Robert. "The Radical Emerson?" *The Cambridge Companion to Emerson.* Ed. Joel Porte and Saundra Morris. Cambridge: Cambridge University Press, 1999.

Miller, James Grier. *Living Systems.* New York: McGraw-Hill, 1978.

Mingers, John, *Self-producing Systems.* New York: Plenum, 1995.

Muir, John. *John Muir: The Eight Wilderness Discovery Books.* Seattle: Diadem Books, 1992.

Müller, Harro. "Luhmann's Systems Theory as a Theory of Modernity." *New German Critique* 61 (1994): 39–54.

Nash, Roderick. *The Rights of Nature.* Madison: University of Wisconsin Press, 1989.

————. *Wilderness and the American Mind.* 3rd ed. New Haven: Yale University Press, 1982.

Newfield, Christopher. *The Emerson Effect: Individualism and Submission in America.* Chicago: University of Chicago Press, 1996.

Oelschlager, Max. *The Idea of Wilderness.* New Haven: Yale University Press, 1991.

Parsons, Talcott. *The Social System.* New York: The Free Press, 1951.

Paul, Sherman. *The Shores of America: Thoreau's Inward Exploration.* Urbana: University of Illinois Press, 1958.

Peterson, Tarla Rai. *Sharing the Earth: The Rhetoric of Sustainable Development.* Columbia: University of South Carolina Press, 1997.

Phillips, Dana. "Ecocriticism, Literary Theory, and the Truth of Ecology." *New Literary History* 30, no. 3 (1999): 577–602.

Pinchot, Gifford. *Breaking New Ground.* 1947. Reprint, Washington: Island Press, 1987.

Plotkin, Henry. *Darwin Machines and the Nature of Knowledge.* London: Penguin, 1994.

Porter, Carolyn. *Seeing and Being.* Middletown, Conn.: Wesleyan University Press, 1981.

Rasch, William. *Niklas Luhmann's Modernity.* Stanford: Stanford University Press, 2000.

Rasch, William, and Eva Knodt. "Systems Theory and System of Theory." *New German Critique* 61 (1994): 3–7.

Rasch, William, and Cary Wolfe, eds. "Introduction: The Politics of Systems and Environments." *Cultural Critique* 30 (1995): 5–15.

Reising, Russell. *The Unusable Past: Theory and the Study of American Literature.* New York: Methuen, 1986.

Republican Platform 2000. Republican National Committee. 24 August 2002. <http://www.rnc.org/gopinfo/platform>.

Richardson, Robert D., Jr. *Emerson: The Mind on Fire.* Berkeley: University of California Press, 1995.

Rifkin, Jeremy. *Biosphere Politics.* New York: Crown, 1991.

Robinson, David. *Emerson and the Conduct of Life.* Cambridge: Cambridge University Press, 1993.

Rolston, Holmes, III. "Ralph Waldo Emerson." *Fifty Key Thinkers on the Environment.* Ed. Joy Palmer. New York: Routledge, 2001.

Roosevelt, Theodore. *The Roosevelt Treasury.* Ed. Hermann Hagedorn. New York: G. P. Putman's Sons, 1957.

Rorty, Richard. "The Pragmatist's Progess." *Interpretation and Overinterpretation.* Ed. Stefan Collini. New York: Cambridge University Press, 1992.

Rosen, Robert. *Life Itself.* New York: Columbia University Press, 1991.

Ross, Andrew. *The Chicago Gangster Theory of Life: Nature's Debt to Society.* London: Verso, 1994.

Rosseel, Eric. "Writers of the Lost." *New Perspectives on Cybernetics.* Ed. Gertrudis van de Vijver. Dordrecht, Netherlands: Kluwer Academic Publishers, 1992. 233–45.

Roszak, Theodore. *The Voice of the Earth.* New York: Simon and Schuster, 1992.

Sabin, Margery. "Literary Reading in Interdisciplinary Study." *Profession 95* (1995): 14–16.

Sale, Kirkpatrick. *Rebels against the Future: The Luddites and Their War on the Industrial Revolution: Lessons for the Computer Age.* Reading, Mass.: Addison-Wesley, 1995.

Sanders, Scott Russell. "Speaking a Word for Nature." *The Ecocriticism Reader.* Ed. Cheryll Glotfelty and Harold Fromm. Athens: University of Georgia Press, 1996. 182–95.

Santayana, George. "Ralph Waldo Emerson." *Critical Essays on Ralph Waldo Emerson.* Ed. Robert Burkholder and Joel Myerson. Boston: G. K. Hall, 1983.

Saturn Corporation. Advertisement. *Atlantic Monthly,* February 1997, 56–57.

Saturn Corporation. Advertisement. *Newsweek.* 19 May 1997, 1.

Serres, Michel. *Genesis.* Trans. Genevieve James and James Nielson. Ann Arbor: University of Michigan Press, 1995.

———. *The Natural Contract.* Ann Arbor: University of Michigan Press, 1995.

Shepard, Paul. *Nature and Madness.* San Francisco: Sierra Club, 1982.

Sierra Club. "Zero Cut Resolution." Sierra Club Board of Directors. 1996.

Slotkin, Richard. *The Fatal Environment.* New York: Atheneum, 1985.

———. *Regeneration through Violence.* Hanover: Wesleyan University Press, 1973.

Smith, Henry Nash. *Virgin Land.* Cambridge: Harvard University Press, 1950.

Snyder, Gary. *The Practice of the Wild.* San Francisco: North Point Press, 1990.

Soper, Kate. *What Is Nature?* London: Blackwell, 1995.

Stanton, Domna. "What Is Literature?—1994." *PMLA* 109, no. 3 (1994): 359–64.

Stevens, Wallace. *The Collected Poems of Wallace Stevens.* New York: Alfred A. Knopf, 1987.

Sweet, Timothy. *American Georgics.* Philadelphia: University of Pennsylvania Press, 2002.

Tauber, Alfred. *Henry David Thoreau and the Moral Agency of Knowing.* Berkeley: University of California Press, 2001.

Thoreau, Henry David. *Henry David Thoreau.* Ed. Robert Sayre. New York: The Library of America, 1985.

———. *Natural History Essays.* Salt Lake City: Peregrine Smith, 1980.

———. *Wild Fruits.* Ed. Bradley Dean. New York: W. W. Norton, 2000.

Toffler, Alvin. *Powershift: Knowledge, Wealth, and Violence at the Edge of the Twenty-first Century.* New York: Bantam, 1990.

Van Leer, David. *Emerson's Epistemology: The Argument of the Essays.* Cambridge: Cambridge University Press, 1986.

Varela, Francisco. *Ethical Know-How.* Stanford: Stanford University Press, 1999.

———. *Principles of Biological Autonomy.* New York: North Holland, 1979.

———. "The Reenchantment of the Concrete." *Incorporations.* Ed. Jonathan Crary and Sanford Kwinter. New York: Zone, 1992. 320–38.

———. "Whence Perceptual Meaning." *Understanding Origins: Contemporary Views on the Origin of Life, Mind, and Society.* Ed. Francisco J. Varela and Jean-Pierre Dupuy. Dordrecht, Netherlands: Kluwer Academic Publishers, 1992.

Varela, Francisco, Evan Thompson, and Eleanor Rosch. *The Embodied Mind: Cognitive Science and Human Experience.* Cambridge: M.I.T. Press, 1991.

Vattimo, Gianni. *The Transparent Society.* Trans. David Webb. Baltimore: Johns Hopkins University Press, 1992.

Virgil. *The Eclogues.* Trans. David Ferry. New York: Farrar, Straus and Giroux, 1999.

Walls, Laura. *Seeing New Worlds.* Madison: University of Wisconsin Press, 1995.

Whicher, Stephen. *Freedom and Fate.* Philadelphia: University of Pennsylvania Press, 1957.

Wiener, Norbert. *Cybernetics; or, Control and Communication in the Animal and the Machine.* 2d ed. Cambridge, Mass.: M.I.T. Press, 1961.

Williams, Raymond. *Keywords.* Rev. ed. New York: Oxford, 1983.

Wilson, Alexander. *The Culture of Nature.* Toronto: Between the Lines, 1991.

Wilson, E. O. *Consilience: The Unity of Knowledge.* New York: Knopf, 1998.

Wolfe, Cary. *Critical Environments*. Minneapolis: University of Minnesota Press, 1998.

———. "Old Orders for New." Review of *The New Ecological Order*, by Luc Ferry. *Electronic Book Review* 4 (1997). 27 August 2002. <http://www.electronicbookreview.com/ebr4/wolfe.htm>.

Worldwatch Institute. *State of the World 1993*. New York: W. W. Norton, 1993.

Ziff, Larzer. *Literary Democracy*. New York: Viking Press, 1981.

Zimmerman, Michael. *Contesting Earth's Future: Radical Ecology and Postmodernity*. Berkeley: University of California Press, 1994.

Index